Portable Postsocialisms

Border Hispanisms
*Alberto Moreiras, Gareth Williams, and Gabriela Méndez Cota,
series editors*

Robert McKee Irwin, ed., *Migrant Feelings, Migrant Knowledge:
    Building a Community Archive*
Juliana Martínez, *Haunting without Ghosts: Spectral Realism in
    Colombian Literature, Film, and Art*
Alberto Moreiras, *Against Abstraction: Notes from an Ex–Latin
    Americanist*
David E. Johnson, *Violence and Naming: On Mexico and the Promise
    of Literature*
R. Andrés Guzmán, *Universal Citizenship: Latina/o Studies at the
    Limits of Identity*
Eugenio Di Stefano, *The Vanishing Frame: Latin American Culture
    and Theory in the Postdictatorial Era*
Sergio Delgado Moya, *Delirious Consumption: Aesthetics and Consumer
    Capitalism in Mexico and Brazil*
Daniel Nemser, *Infrastructures of Race: Concentration and Biopolitics
    in Colonial Mexico*
Horacio Legrás, *Culture and Revolution: Violence, Memory, and the
    Making of Modern Mexico*
Samuel Steinberg, *Photopoetics at Tlatelolco: Afterimages of Mexico, 1968*
Charles Hatfield, *The Limits of Identity: Politics and Poetics in Latin
    America*

Portable Postsocialisms

New Cuban Mediascapes
after the End of History

Paloma Duong

University of Texas Press ❧ *Austin*

Copyright © 2024 by the University of Texas Press
All rights reserved
Printed in the United States of America
First edition, 2024

Requests for permission to reproduce material from this work should be sent to:
  Permissions
  University of Texas Press
  P.O. Box 7819
  Austin, TX 78713-7819
  utpress.utexas.edu

∞ The paper used in this book meets the minimum requirements of ANSI/NISO z39.48-1992 (R1997) (Permanence of Paper).

Library of Congress Cataloging-in-Publication Data

Names: Duong, Paloma, author.
Title: Portable postsocialisms : new Cuban mediascapes after the end of history / Paloma Duong.
Other titles: Border Hispanisms.
Description: First edition. | Austin : University of Texas Press, 2024. | Series: Border Hispanisms | Includes bibliographical references and index. | Summary: "A study of Cuban culture and media in the twenty-first century as both a global phenomenon and a local reality, at a time when the declared death of socialism coexists in tension with emerging anticapitalist movements worldwide"—Provided by publisher.
Identifiers:
  LCCN 2023015840
  ISBN 978-1-4773-2826-2 (cloth)
  ISBN 978-1-4773-2827-9 (pdf)
  ISBN 978-1-4773-2828-6 (epub)
Subjects: LCSH: Mass media—Political aspects—Cuba—History—21st century. | Socialism—Cuba—History—21st century. | Capitalism and mass media—Cuba—History—21st century. | Socialism—History—21st century. | Anti-globalization movement—History—21st century. | Social change—Cuba—History—21st century. | Cuba—Politics and government—In mass media—Political aspects. | Cuba—In mass media—History—21st century.
Classification: LCC HN210.Z9 M326 2024 | DDC 302.23097291—dc23/eng/20230712
LC record available at https://lccn.loc.gov/2023015840

doi:10.7560/328262

Contents

Acknowledgments   *vii*

INTRODUCTION   What Is the Postsocialist Condition?   *1*

CHAPTER 1   Cuban Travels: Hatuey in Ethiopia   *31*

CHAPTER 2   Portable *Pachanga*   *69*

CHAPTER 3   *Postsocialismos de Bolsillo*: Women and Fashion in Secondhand Time   *113*

CHAPTER 4   Cuban Screen Cultures   *141*

CONCLUSION   Cuban Mediascapes after the End of History   *197*

Notes   *223*
Bibliography   *241*
Index   *255*

Acknowledgments

The best parts of this book I owe to colleagues, mentors, friends, and family. I am grateful to have found many generous, brilliant people who lent an ear and urged me forward, answered profound and silly questions alike, read very, *very* rough drafts, invited me to awesome gatherings, and shared their erudition and feedback at different stages of this project: Andy Alfonso, Jerónimo Arellano, Vivek Bald, Odette Casamayor-Cisneros, Ian Condry, Sasha Costanza-Chock, Guillermina de Ferrari, Alejandro de la Fuente, Walfrido Dorta, Rubén Gallo, Shane Greene, María Gutiérrez, Ted Henken, Jackie Loss, Emily Maguire, Tom McEnaney, Paul North, Lisa Parks, Rachel Price, Eunice Rodríguez Ferguson, Paul Roquet, Mariano Siskind, David Tenorio, William Uricchio, Cristina Venegas, and Jing Wang. To all the MIT staff, colleagues, and students in Comparative Media Studies and Writing and Global Studies and Languages, thank you for so many stimulating conversations and for your decisive support. Carlos J. Alonso and Graciela Montaldo have been there from the start; I am forever indebted to their teachings. To Claudia Cadelo, Claudia González, and Daniel Preval—*les imprescindibles*—and to all my Cuban friends and contacts in Havana, Matanzas, Miami, Quito, New York, and beyond who shared materials and experiences and opinions and meals: I hope I have honored your trust. The arguments and interpretations contained in these pages are solely my own, as are any errors. The Postsocialist Horizons collective, the WWEW Lecture Club, the Hoyt Field crew, and the Latin American Media Studies group were precious spaces of reflection and companionship as I finished writing during the COVID-19 pandemic. To my *compinches* in thought and play, Katerina González-Seligmann, Heather Cleary, Valeria Luiselli, Hrvoje Tutek, Guido Herzovich, Rosario Hubert, Daniel Aguirre-Oteiza, Illiana

Cepero, Carolina Baffi, and Lara Tucker, thinking and dancing with y'all is always a privilege: thanks to your philosophical complicities, intuitions became form. To the fam, then and now—aba, abu, papi, mami, Xuan, Vadym, Sophia, and Oreo—my grounding stars.

Part of chapter 1 appeared as "Other Socialist Travels" in *Cuban Studies*; it is reprinted here with permission of the University of Pittsburgh Press. Sections of chapter 3 previously appeared as "Images of Ourselves: Cuban Mediascapes and the Postsocialist 'Woman of Fashion'" in *Cuba's Digital Revolution: Citizen Innovation and State Policy*, edited by Ted A. Henken and Sara Garcia Santamaria (Gainesville: University Press of Florida, 2021), 306–324; they are reprinted here with permission of the University Press of Florida. And last but not least: Alberto Moreiras, Kerry Webb, and the rest of the team at UT Press believed in this project and made it a reality with their wisdom, expertise, and graciousness.

Introduction
What Is the Postsocialist Condition?

The new cultural and media landscapes of Cuban postsocialism lay bare the depth of our political predicaments at the turn of the twenty-first century. While images of capitalist markets consume Cuba's national imagination, Cuban socialism continues to be a referent for anticapitalist politics worldwide. This illustrates the defining dilemma of our global postsocialist condition: the historical time in which declarations of the death of socialism coexist with the emergence of new anticapitalist desires. Standing at a crucial crossroads between these competing outlooks, Cuban cultural and media practices show how postsocialist critical theory can guide us in thinking about, and through, that condition.

Postsocialist thinking as a mode of critique developed in the late 1970s and early 1980s along with poststructuralist theories, postmodernity, and postcolonial studies. Any mention of "postsocialist" will likely conjure up theoretical hangovers from the heyday of *post*-isms in the 1980s, though the latest wave of *post-* terms in our midst—post-truth, post-neoliberal, postcapitalist—shows no sign of fatigue with the prefix. As Susan Buck-Morss points out, the prefixes *post-* and *neo-* (and I add *alt-*) still dominate our political lexicon at the start of the twenty-first century.[1] The *post-* in postsocialism signals a rupture, a change with respect to the word it modifies, while simultaneously acknowledging a continuity, a lingering effect, an unavoidable referent. As an analytic category and as a geopolitical referent, postsocialism has been sent away and welcomed back as a critical recourse against the ubiquitous legacies of Cold War epistemological frameworks.[2] Critical postsocialist thought is thus concerned with political imaginaries and vocabularies of social justice that are critical of the socialist past, critical of the capitalist present, and responsive to the recalcitrant demands for a future that hails us to do better.

Like kindred terms, "postsocialist" grapples with the promises of modernity and the failures of modernization as a collective emancipatory project organized via the nation-state and transnational capitalism. It is equally concerned with epistemological ruptures and the undoing of the universal subject, although only with the postcolonial can the postsocialist stake particular claims to geographical place. Sharad Chari and Katherine Verdery argue compellingly that postcolonial and postsocialist cannot be research paradigms indifferent to one another. Not only do they share concrete institutional and geopolitical histories; they also expose situated experiences of capitalist modernization. "Both labels signify the complex results of the abrupt changes forced on those who underwent them: that is, becoming something other than socialist or other than colonized."[3] In the postsocialist aftermath, the linkages between decolonization and socialism in what was the Third World impose a disproportionate toll on the regions that at one time trusted their futures to the expansion and radicalization of the Bandung project.[4]

Researching postsocialism has chiefly meant asking what it is and when it was. Less often are the places where postsocialism supposedly operates or the ways in which postsocialisms are unevenly experienced and called into question. Without any other qualifier, postsocialism recalls the ostensibly unique material quandaries of those living in the remainders of the grand socialist state projects of the twentieth century in Africa, Asia, America, and Europe. But postsocialism does not simply name whatever comes after socialism. Postsocialist contexts also include those where emergent and expanding markets coexist with a highly centralized political apparatus under single-party rule (such as China, Vietnam, and Cuba), where small and large privatization projects operate with the (nominally) socialist state as a commercial partner, and the communist parties lead political and economic planning in the last instance. Under such arrangements, economic growth and developmentalism become goals in and of themselves, while the values for which the socialist label once stood—egalitarian redistribution and socialization of wealth, the public guarantee of social goods and services, and above all democratization of political and economic instruments—vanish into abstractions. Here postsocialism signals the moment(s) of irreversible rupture between socialism as radical critique of the capitalist present, on the one hand, and political projects that usurp its name on the other. Postsocialism may therefore predate any official end of the socialist state under communist party rule. In this sense, *post* is not a placeholder for *past* but the marker of a special kind of historically and geopolitically specific consciousness.[5]

However, former socialist enclaves are not the only ones living in postsocialist times. The adjective "postsocialist" also describes a global subjectivity for which the end of twentieth-century socialisms had profound implications. Just as twentieth-century revolutions were worldwide events and constitutive parts of the imaginaries of shared mass utopias, their demise as laboratories of collective desire and radical change provides additional clues for critical reevaluations of what they were as opposed to what they called themselves.[6] This exercise can offer interpretative tools that speak to a common geopolitical present. That present conjuncture is one where there seems to be no alternative to capitalism, even while we confront the same historical conditions—flagrant inequality, violent dispossession, planetary destruction, political disenfranchisement, permanent war, forced displacement—that yield, now under a myriad of clashing ideological banners, a politics of insurgency left and right. Consequently, the end of the twentieth-century socialist projects defined by the revolutionary takeover of the state apparatus, and the stories we tell about that end, implicate us all both theoretically and experientially. All of us, everywhere, participate in the postsocialist condition; not all of us, however, live in postsocialist contexts.

The distinction between postsocialist context, as a geopolitical space linked to twentieth-century socialist projects, and postsocialist condition, as a shared global historical moment, is either unacknowledged or taken for granted without further problematization in most scholarly literature.[7] I insist on using this distinction to account for the dual character of the "postsocialist" as an adjective: on one hand, as a situated structure of feeling, as Raymond Williams theorized it, that is, an emergent expression of context-specific experiences, and on the other as the collective predicament of linked projects of modernity, as postsocialist critics such as Buck-Morss and Chari and Verdery have developed it. Context and condition are therefore mutually constituted, relational frameworks of analysis of the present conjuncture. As such, context and condition should not be understood as the new binary equivalent to East and West, communist and capitalist. Instead, we ought to ask how this global postsocialist condition operates and is made sense of in everyday life across different contexts. Popular postsocialist jokes speak to this issue:

> An émigré reports to her family back home: I have good news and bad news.
> The good news is that everything they told us about communism was a lie.
> The bad news, however, is that everything they told us about capitalism was true.

> Schoolteacher: "Pepito ¿what is capitalism?"
> Pepito: "¡A giant trashcan of cars, toys, and food!"
> Teacher: "Excellent Pepito! ¿What about communism?"
> Pepito: "¿The same trashcan, but empty?"
> (Pepito is the archetypal child protagonist of a popular joke series denouncing the absurdity of Cuban adult society.)

Whatever their situated critique of socialist official rhetoric, these two jokes raise the question of how constituents respond to, and experience, similarities and distinctions between "actually existing capitalisms" and "actually existing socialisms." To understand what the global postsocialist condition is, we must ask how it is experienced, and how it is made sense of, in its local contexts. Looking in tandem at the postsocialist condition and its contexts accounts for continuities and breaks, without retreating from the postsocialist's strong claim to the global or from anticapitalist critique. This also allows for a differentiation between exceptionality and particularity, that is, to describe the conceptual purchase of postsocialism as a particular articulation of global capitalism but not necessarily as an exceptional, geopolitically delimited historical phenomenon. This understanding of the postsocialist condition and the postsocialist context links two seemingly contradictory phenomena: Cuban socialism has been reactivated as an international object of political desire for the anticapitalist imagination in the twenty-first century, even while, simultaneously, the global market has become a national object of desire in postsocialist Cuba. A conceptual distinction between condition and context can address this apparent divergence between global postsocialist imaginaries and their Cuban counterparts.

In this book I chart the political imaginary of this postsocialist present as it is reproduced or contested in media and cultural artifacts and practices, in conversation with a critical corpus of the imaginary engaged with actually existing socialisms and the possibility of radical change.[8] A political imaginary is the set of symbolic referents (the enemy, the people, the common good, the shared past, the desired future) that can legitimize as much as contest a given organization of power in a particular social formation; that ideologically anchors the collective identities, practices, values, and meanings (victory, freedom, security, equality, etc.) organized around those referents; and that consequently shapes hegemonic and counterhegemonic processes of domination and resistance within which concrete, historically specific citizen needs and demands (self-determination, well-being, belonging, and so on) are pursued and managed. This notion of the political imaginary relies on post-Marxist elaborations of Gramsci's theory of hegemony and recontextualizes it as a specific intervention in the postsocialist mediascape. If political dominance is achieved not only by coercion but also by the consent of the governed, that consent results from the ideological operations and concrete institutional practices by which various particular interests and social actors come to see their values represented in a centripetal relation within the dominant imaginaries. That hegemonic relation is, however, always incomplete, contingent, and rearrangeable. The cultural and media spheres are not the only terrains where political imaginaries are in play. But they are key spaces where these imaginaries, and the loyalties and values they command, are built, communicated, internalized, contested, or reorganized through the (re)production of social meanings.[9] This approach to the political imaginary attunes us to its discursive, cultural, technological, and aesthetic dimensions; that is, to the political work of culture and to the cultural work of politics.

These imaginaries also incorporate and influence distant reception contexts and constituencies. As I will contend in chapter 1, traveling images of Cuban socialism contribute to the tendency to exclude Cuba from postsocialist critical thought. This does not mean, however, that these secondary audiences are straightforwardly deceived or that these values and meanings do not have real, everyday effects wherever they arrive. For example, an Argentinian colleague tells me the story of his parents: communist militants who looked toward Cuba and the socialist bloc as beacons of hope in the grim experience of right-wing military dictatorships and whose ideas about those worlds, and the one they were justifiably longing for, were shaped by the cultural and media materials—music, magazines, news—they received from Cuba. Such modes and contexts of dissemination muddy the gap between the socialist values communicated by those symbolic goods and the socialist character—or absence thereof—of the society that produced them. There are those who benefited directly from this transnational reach, too. Another colleague, for example, brings up the immense gratitude of the Haitian people for the help of Cuban doctors after the 2010 earthquake. This is their direct experience of the Cuban

Revolution as a self-advertised sponsor of internationalist solidarity in the Global South. It is as real as that of the Cubans who have experienced political persecution and severe scarcity at home, or of the doctors who participate in these same programs, torn between the opportunity to earn hard currency abroad and the exploitative conditions under which they do so. In the following chapters I take on some of the cultural and media forms of circulation of, and reactions to, this double identity and examine the political imaginaries they buttress at home and abroad.

I contend in this book that engaging the global postsocialist condition from the perspective of the Cuban context must attend to the explosion of images, narratives, and new media practices chronicling change and continuity in everyday life at the turn of the twenty-first century. I will ask how, by whom, and under which conditions they are generated and how they differ from top-down images of postsocialist Cuba, whether they are of national or foreign origins. I will consider how popular, mass, digital, and lettered cultures without distinction register the internal transformations of Cuban postsocialism, as much as how they converse with global phenomena, like the rise and fall of self-styled left-wing governments in Latin America and the rekindling of an anticapitalist ethos in the post-2008 world. Cultural and media takes on these changes will show how postsocialist Cuban culture and its underlying material conditions follow regional patterns in twenty-first-century Latin America, refute persistent images of exceptionalism that still inform scholarly and popular discourses about Cuba, and shape political imaginaries within and beyond its national boundaries.

The Cuban Postsocialist Mediascape: Periodizing Continuity and Change

Key questions about Cuba—whether it is postsocialist and whether it is exceptional—are tied to issues of periodization and are shaped by the response of Cuban cultural and political narratives to the postsocialist condition as defined by the crisis and collapse of twentieth-century socialisms elsewhere. Straddling symbolic and material dimensions and, simultaneously, local and global events, it is neither possible nor helpful to pinpoint a year when postsocialism began. But as a national context and a symbolic framework responsive to (1) a local set of social and material transformations and (2) the double crisis of credibility of twentieth-century state socialist and neoliberal capitalisms, we can say that Cuban postsocialism takes definite form around the turn of the twenty-first century. In this book I focus primarily on the first two decades of the twenty-first century to account for cultural and media responses to specific transformations in the Cuban context: the domestic expansion of transnational capital; the massification of digital technologies; the reorganization of state and informal economic and cultural spheres; and shifting patterns in the transnational exchange of people and things. Yet during this transformative period global images of Cuba as a place of zero change were on the rise. One of my tasks here is to examine the implications of these narratives of continuity and change and to review the impact they have in the ways we all—Cubans and non-Cubans, citizens and scholars—think about Cuba, capitalist imperialism, and progressive politics in Latin America.

A few points about periodization might be in order. The events of 1989–1991 were enormously significant, but for Cubans they did not translate into perceptions of clear political change, as they did for citizens of Latin America, Asia, and Eastern and Central Europe facing the political and market transitions of the 1980s and '90s. In Soviet and post-Soviet literature about perestroika and its aftermath, the sense of anticipation and the evidence of change are palpable. These might have proved misguided from a later perspective, but in the early 1990s the popular imaginary soared with images and expectations of freedom and consumption as markers of the end of socialism. As Svetlana Alexievich puts it: "It was 1991.... What an incredibly happy time! We believed that tomorrow, the very next day, would usher in freedom. That it would materialize out of nowhere, from the sheer force of our wishing."[10] One of the key differences in postsocialist Cuba is the absence of a similarly well defined, dramatic arc of illusion and shock, of before and after. Quite a lot of things have changed since the 1990s in the economic, social, and cultural spheres. But because the political apparatus remains largely intact, there is a widespread perception that nothing has substantively changed. The decade of the Special Period in Times of Peace (1990 to circa 2000) did, however, expose the cultural and political mediation strategies through which Cuban society domesticated, administered, or willfully erased its encounter with the Soviet Union.[11] A national narrative of survival emerged instead, amid the worst economic crisis since the 1930s: Cuba seemed to avoid the script of socialist collapse unfolding elsewhere and was asked to offer inspiration to an international political left imaginary marked by defeat and disorientation. This sense of survival and exceptionality set Cuba apart from its counterparts and allowed it to play an important role—similar to the one it fulfilled in the 1960s—in the short-lived buzz generated by the possibility of a "twenty-first-century socialism" bolstering the wave of electoral victories by Latin American political parties self-identified with the left.

The harsh 1990s paved this apparent but misleading continuity of Cuban socialism with the legalization of self-employment; the dollarization of the economy; controlled participation in the global market; increased family remittances; constitutional changes; heavy state investment in tourism, biopharmaceuticals, and medical services as untapped sources of national revenue; the strategic commercialization of national culture; and a key advising and trading role in Venezuela's Revolución Bolivariana that secured access to fuel. In fact, Hugo Chávez's election in Venezuela in 1998 and his death in March 2013 may be as important to Cuba's postsocialist periodization as the fall of the Berlin Wall in 1989, the diplomatic rapprochement with the United States in 2014, or the death of Fidel Castro in 2016. Secret negotiations between the US government and the Cuban government, conducted mostly through the Vatican, began the month following Chávez's death. These talks partially reestablished the diplomatic, and thus the economic, relationship between the two countries, at least until 2017, when they were interrupted again.

The Elián Affair (1999–2000) launched the next redefining phase of Cuban socialism on the world stage: "The Battle of Ideas," an ideological platform and political strategy that doubled down on the rhetoric of state- and party-led national revolutionary survival while recognizing the threat of a new media ecology to their narrative monopoly. The creation in 2003 of the digital platform *Cubadebate* (Cubadebate.cu), "against media terrorism" to counter "disinformation campaigns about Cuba," the University of Information Science, a computer technology university and research center created in 2002, and the Cuban Wikipedia *Ecured* started in 2010 are examples of this official digital strategy, which also expanded the Joven Club de Computación y Electrónica (Youth Computing Club) founded in 1987 to promote mass digital literacy. Mobile telephony and digital media and internet access have grown steadily every year with the unrestricted commercialization of cell-phone service to all citizens since 2008, the expansion of wider public access to the web from 2015 onward, and the rollout of home internet access and 3G/4G mobile data between 2016 and 2018. Up until then restricted access was granted only to the Cuban intranet, via job-related accounts, or through hotels with hard-currency privileges. Meanwhile, a thriving microcosm of alternative and informal media objects, uses, and networks—from account-sharing, software-tinkering, and hybrid offline/online circuits to networks fueled by peer-to-peer exchange and digital storage devices—kept Cubans connected and updated, albeit unevenly. In addition to the comparatively low growth of internet connectivity at the start of the century, several other factors contribute to the frequent portrayal of Cuba as a digital detox destination or as the next layover for techno-solutionist democratic exports: the continuing state monopoly over mass media, and its overt political censorship and repression, are compounded by inequities, discontent, and internalized perceptions of isolation and underdevelopment, which in turn are window-dressed with tourist-oriented, self-exoticizing marketing narratives about Cuba's lo-fi authenticity. As chapters 1 through 4 show, these views reproduce misleading assumptions about the relationship between media technologies, everyday citizens, the state, and markets in Cuba.

At the start of the century a gradual economic recovery breathed air into the national debate on reform and renewal. Starting in January 2013, Cuban citizens no longer needed an exit visa to leave the country. This change in restrictions on travel and return, in place since the late 1960s, contributed to the reorganization of the diasporic economy of remittances and to shifts in Cuban patterns of migration. In addition to permanent emigration toward historical exile destinations like Miami and Madrid, more Cubans come and go as temporary migrant workers, or as gray- and black-market mules, to a wider range of destinations, from Panama to Moscow. Digital technologies and more flexible travel policies have reshaped the circuits of production and dissemination of material and cultural goods as a result.

The transferences of power from Fidel to Raúl Castro between 2006 and 2008 and from Raúl Castro to Miguel Díaz-Canel between 2018 and 2021, and the flurry of congresses of the Cuban Communist Party (PCC) in 2011, 2016, and 2021, confirmed the military's and the party's control over the economic and political spheres while preparing the terrain for more substantial economic transformations and for the first generational transfer of power since 1959. Seemingly under the same rubric of the 1959 Cuban Revolution, the single-party state remains the main capitalist actor as both owner and regulatory enforcer in the new postsocialist economy and as the sole commercial partner of foreign capital, with direct control over the most profitable industries: medicine, tourism, and mining. Since the mid-1990s, the domestic economy has primarily relied on remittances, on sole traders and small family-based businesses (*cuentapropistas*), and on informal and black-market practices. In this sense, the state has selectively retreated from some spheres without abandoning its commitment to centralized power, as Cuba's erratic rapprochements with foreign capital investments and with the internal market economy continue to expand or contract depending on US policy, domestic pressures, and the perceived needs of political stability, although without transforming major structural obstacles to the development of a domestic nonstate economic sector (e.g., access to import/export supply chains, stable regulatory environments, and credits). These measures could be read as uneven and perpetually insufficient gestures toward economic reform, but they could just as well be interpreted as a further de facto precarization of labor and social welfare in a context of increased corporatist statecraft and regulatory instability. These *raulista* market reforms kicked into high gear in 2011. They were later expanded in response to the deterioration of the national economy beginning in 2019, to the COVID-19 pandemic, and to the unprecedent demonstrations of popular discontent that took place on July 11, 2021 (11J) in several provinces, which were met with heavy police repression, a new round of emergency economic measures, a three-day internet and social media blackout, lengthy jail sentences for protestors, and an updated censorship law (Ley 35 2021) for the digital age.

The rhetoric accompanying these transformations is as crucial as their content. In February 2018, an internal electoral party process designated Díaz-Canel as Cuba's first civilian president since 1976 (and arguably since 1959). Díaz-Canel's digital footprint, which can be traced to October 10, 2018, when he joined Twitter, revolves around two main themes/hashtags: the insistence on a unified national identity and culture (#SomosCuba), and the continuation of the Cuban revolutionary socialist project into the twenty-first century (#SomosContinuidad). Both are heavily promoted by the PCC and state media. Meanwhile, the online version of *Granma*, the main newspaper of the PCC, published a comprehensive guide for international investment in Cuba.[12] The digital guide explained the legal frameworks of the free trade zone inaugurated in the port of Mariel in several of the languages of Cuba's most important trade partners in the twenty-first century: Italian, Vietnamese, Portuguese, Russian, and Chinese. In short, at the same time that the government aggressively courted international investments, its domestic policies scrambled to update the Cuban economic model without disturbing the political status quo, extoling the virtues of socialist morality against foreign influence and unbridled consumerism even while witnessing popular discontent and economic inequality deepen significantly.

The rhetoric and policies that have shaped Cuban postsocialism and its legacy in Latin America place it in an explicit dialogue with what Verónica Gago has called "the return of the state," an alliance between state developmentalist interventionism and the restructured interests of transnational capital in the region. This pact presents itself under the guise of progressive forces because its political representatives declare themselves the enemies of the same neoliberal logic that they are successfully deploying.[13] While Cuba tends to be singled out as a regional exception in almost every single approach to the country and to Latin America, it has followed the same path from ideological collapse to the language of state-led recovery, parallel cycles of crisis, and selective abundance—in short, a course in no small measure interdependent of the region as a whole, that is, "from the misery, scarcity, and unemployment of the early twenty-first century (and the forms of struggle and resistance that emerged then) to certain forms of abundance found in new forms of consumption, work, entrepreneurship, territorial organization, and money."[14] The combined effects of a new Latin American geopolitical landscape—with electoral regrouping of professed left-wing populisms and popular insurgency against neoliberal legacies—including the economic reforms spearheaded by Raúl Castro, the changing cultural and media landscapes, and the continued affective investment on Cuba as a symbol of global progressive politics in the wake of the Pink Tide, call for a comprehensive reexamination of contemporary Cuban culture and society and of the political purchase of Cuban socialism in postsocialist times.

The crisis of hegemony of the Cuban socialist project, however, has opened only tenuous possibilities for reaggregating counterhegemonic demands from the different and overlapping social actors and identities that critically engage it (entrepreneurs, youth, women, Afro-descendants, artists, professionals, peasants, nonstate workers, intellectuals, LGTBQ+ activists, and so on). In addition to effective and systematic policing of any dissenting voices and assemblages, government opposition has long been overcodified as conservative and opportunistic; by the same token, despite the revolutionary government's incapacity to carry out urgently needed social and economic justice, any radical imaginary that would cut across different sectors to produce horizontal alliances has long been tainted by association to the discursive and institutional revolutionary monopoly on social and economic justice. The economic, sociopolitical, and media conditions of the Cuban postsocialist moment, however, allow for both discursive and practical spaces of alternative visions of the future that call into question the symbolic legacies of those established political landscapes. Therefore, the postsocialist conjuncture demands that we reorient our own gaze away from seemingly established political positions of the postsocialist script—dissident intellectuals, melancholic revolutionaries, bureaucratic loudspeakers—and toward the disaggregated, competing narratives emerging in this context. Such narratives include discourses and practices that may or may not be politically explicit and may or may not seek hegemonic articulation but find legible elaboration in cultural and media spheres and actualize more nuanced representations of political change and revolutionary continuity. Simultaneously, the postsocialist context demands that we submit to greater theoretical scrutiny the many faces of state and capital domination, demonstrating that materialist critiques are not exhausted by class reductionism and economic determinism; they are not mutually exclusive of, and in fact must ground, the questions of representation and identity that studies of cultural mediation tend to foreground.

This is where the research agendas of Latin American cultural and media studies find common points of dialogue with postsocialist thinking regarding the reconfigured relationship between markets and the state and the challenges that digital and social media cultures present for rethinking economic consumption and development, cultural representation, and political participation in the region. The notion of mediascape for Latin American cultural and media studies has been taken up more recently by Jossianna Arroyo, Jerónimo Arellano, and Ana López. "Mediascapes," a term coined by Arjun Appadurai, are the new landscapes where the everyday social experience of meaning, values, and worldviews is created and disseminated in a multimedia, multiagent context.[15] In the case of Cuba's postsocialist mediascape, we are dealing with two specific problems within this general methodological approach: the concurrent rise of global anticapitalist movements and of declarations of the death of socialism, and the transformation of the cultural and media landscapes in which those political imaginaries are produced and disseminated. The study of the Cuban postsocialist mediascape from this interdisciplinary perspective can give us tools to think beyond the binary of change and continuity and through the heterogeneity of the postsocialist condition and its contexts.

The Cuban postsocialist mediascape accommodates competing visions of a present in which nation-state and transnational markets, the PCC and global finance, intersect with informal and hybrid economies mediated by local digital cultures. This mediascape is "postsocialist" in several ways: despite the country remaining nominally socialist and governed by a communist party, Cuba's economy, culture, and society engage a range of mixed models caught between the old bureaucratic command economy and the new domestic and international market investments, between the former horizons of egalitarianism and the new differentiated demands for recognition. All the while, socioeconomic inequality continues to grow. Access to the public sphere remains contested, but the state's monopoly over traditional mass media technologies must contend with the persistent challenges of digital connectivity and with new patterns of travel and migration. The four key transformations of Cuban postsocialism—expansion of transnational capital, proliferation of digital media, and reorganization of increasingly decentralized economic and cultural sectors—shape this mediascape, in which mass consumerism is a novelty and socialism, as a political project and collective memory, "passes, but it does not pass away."[16]

The Cuban postsocialist mediascape reinforces Appadurai's argument that the nation-state can be theorized not only as a counterhegemonic force vis-à-vis the global financial markets but also as an instrument of elite power that seeks to impose and maintain its own hegemony over other domestic agents, foremost among them its own constituencies. As such, this mediascape is a mosaic of competing narratives about the postsocialist moment that engage with persistent, top-down views produced about that reality, such as the official narratives of the government or the exoticizing foreign gazes that render Cuban socialism an international object of desire. Such a multiperspective reflection on Cuban postsocialism might help contextualize not only its own artifacts and the gazes that mediate their symbolic circulation abroad but also the global signs that travel through Cuba's symbolic and material networks. For instance, even as the records of the Latin American Pink Tide governments in the first decades of the twenty-first century on extractivism, feminism, grassroots democracy, and indigenous protection yield new theoretical and empirical debates on the limits of traditional left populisms, a persistent narrative of Cuban exceptionalism and the concomitant fetishization of its 1959 revolution as a viable socialist alternative, even at the turn of the twenty-first century, have prevented it from being more closely analyzed both from a postsocialist critical perspective and as part and parcel of those regional dynamics. As I will show, one way to redress that oversight is to trace the cultural and political imaginaries in which Cuba participates as a social reality and as a contested symbolic space simultaneously and to investigate the conditions in which those images and narratives of Cuban postsocialism are (re)produced.

As an analytic framework, the notion of mediascape encompasses the more narrowly politicized focus that has been the dominant concern in media studies of "actually existing socialism" as simply a confrontation between civil society and the state. But it also incorporates popular, everyday cultural and media practices that may not be overtly antagonistic. In other words, the proliferation of civic media and the study thereof—the objects, platforms, and practices that agents, communities, and institutions engaged in social change deploy deliberately and purposefully—have transformed the mechanisms as much as our understanding of the politics of civil society. However, an overly narrow focus on civil society defined as consciously self-organized agents working toward social and political change independent of, but in dialogue with, the state apparatus—might not capture the multiple terrains of struggle, material and symbolic, involved in the dynamic, nonlinear processes of social transformation and its attendant political imaginaries. How, then, might forms of noncivic media, or media practices that might not be primarily considered as consciously designed tools of social change, be understood to embody, inform, and transform the social text? And how might they, as objects of research, help us better understand both the abstract and the concrete dimensions of the collective demands, agencies, and desires of the new constituents of the media?

For example, as I elaborate in chapter 4, the framing wars around the 11J protests underscored the contest between the remnants and revivals of Cold War binaries and the emergent and alternative forms of political understanding and media participation. As Emilio Santiago Muiño put it: "Showing solidarity with the Cuban people and their just demands for urgent needs and for democracy too without playing to the regressive global right is complex."[17] Interventionists and free-marketeers quickly moved to discursively co-opt the citizen protests and reframe their sympathies as part of a broader right-wing offensive, particularly in the United States, while others came out in support of the Cuban government and its narrative that the protests were unfounded, astroturfed disinformation campaigns organized by the US Central Intelligence Agency. What was lost in much of the immediate, global mainstream media reports about the protests were the individual voices of protestors and Cubans themselves—who were making and sharing memes criticizing conversations about them in real time—as well as efforts to source reports back to serious, on-the-ground coverage by independent media outlets such as *elTOQUE*, *El Estornudo*, and *Periodismo de Barrio*.

This pattern follows the relatively narrow selection of the loudest voices and agents that prevails in English-language media and cultural scholarship about Cuba, which tends to exclude subjects uncomfortable to or outside of preexisting frameworks of analysis of Cuban (post)socialism. Cultural studies about Cuba that address the expansion of consumerist imaginaries and identity politics from the 1990s onward, for instance, seldom relate such phenomena with the role of Cuba's party-led state as a domestic commercial actor. They do not approach the spheres of consumption and counterhegemonic politics in relation to the state's own hegemonic investments and to its developmentalist extractivism and market alliances before 1989. This is apparent in the treatment of what we can call "virtuous postsocialist subjects" such as the writer Leonardo Padura and Cuban hip-hop, to give two examples. Certainly, valuable insights emerge in critical engagement with their works—in the case of hip-hop, this would be the class and race intersectional demands of culturally and economically disenfranchised youth. But the disproportionate scholarly attention focused on these topics and the comparative neglect with which other voices are met (Ena Lucía Portela and reggaeton come to mind here as the foils of Padura and hip-hop) reproduce Anglo-American research agendas and privilege voices that can be reduced, whether fairly or not, to discourses of revolutionary disenchantment and performative anticommercialism. Virtuous postsocialist subjects fit a neat narrative of a Cuban socialist legacy that, despite its political errors and repressive record, needs to be saved from the inroads of transnational capital.

One way to see this is as the effect of cultural studies' disciplinary origins and its unresolved relationship to "actually existing socialisms." As a discipline that rethought the traditional categories of Marxist cultural theory in the twin crucibles of de-Stalinization and decolonization, cultural studies has dealt with the experience of historical communism qua political and philosophical project. But it has not been able to translate equally well its critical tools—more adroit at engaging the culture industries of capitalist societies—to give accounts of (post)socialist cultural industries and the socialist state's own experiments with mass and digital media. The field of postsocialist cultural studies in Eastern Europe, Yugoslavia, and Asia has nonetheless grown considerably. Yet Cuba's supposed exceptionalism, and the fact that its revolution was perceived to be part of the same New Left milieu from which cultural studies as a discipline was born, have shielded more theoretically rigorous analyses of its culture from those perspectives, something that I explore in chapter 1. Therefore, I build on the research agenda of cultural studies (a concern with popular and mass cultures, the struggles for social recognition and meaning, media representation practices, and counterhegemonic identities) by bringing postsocialist thought as radical critique of both the communist past and the neoliberal present to bear on the discipline's foundational political stakes as a critical practice only obliquely engaged with actually existing socialisms.[18] Cuban culture, then, is ordinary: in the common sense of that word, that is, unexceptional, and in the sense of being seen as Williams described the study of culture as a whole way of life.[19] At the same time, participatory mediascapes invite us to rethink the role its presumed exceptionalism plays, both domestically and abroad, and how this exceptionalism is construed and reproduced as a traveling cultural media object.

In this sense, Jesús Martín Barbero's influential development of a research agenda around production, mediation, and interpretation in mass media consumption practices in Latin America—continuing the work on Gramscian hegemony developed by the Birmingham school of cultural studies and Stuart Hall in particular—remains an open line of inquiry. At the same time, we must attend to media spaces and cultural agencies beyond the models of identity and hybridity developed by Barbero and Néstor Canclini as definitive cultural theories of a distinct Latin American modernity from which a regional set of emancipatory policy goals can then be derived.[20]

Cutting across genre-specific boundaries, postsocialist cultural and media studies offer interdisciplinary tools to map a social text that is as attentive to the proliferation of capitalist practices in postsocialist times as it is cognizant of the productivist and consumerist imaginaries that remained at the center of socialist life throughout. By looking at Cuban postsocialism, we can better understand what contemporary postsocialism *is* and what state socialism *was*: not the absence of capitalism but the presence of a differently organized kind of capital. Focusing on these continuities, and on the different ways in which the social text engages with them, places the Cuban present in conversation with scholarly approaches that highlight "the similar historical trajectories of state-interventionist capitalism and 'actually existing socialism' as two quite different variations of a common phase of the global development of capital."[21] The postsocialist injunction to rethink statization and privatization as apparent opposites underscores how materialist critiques cannot be limited to vulgar economisms, and how they must necessarily engage context-specific questions of representation, identity, and intersectionality.

The theoretical implications and the political stakes of continued engagement with twentieth-century socialisms from Marxian and post-Marxist perspectives cannot be higher: postcapitalist thought must engage seriously with the legacy of historical communisms if it is to dispel the myth that there is no alternative to the organization of life by capital or that resistance to it must necessarily pass through the strong statist model.²² In the twenty-first century, after all, the interests of the single-party state and of transnational capital are increasingly indistinguishable from each other, but they are organized against the interests of everyday citizens. This meeting point, between postsocialist critical thought and Latin American cultural and media studies, shares critical concerns with comparative approaches to the legacies of capitalist/colonial domination addressing the conditions of possibility for "technosocial spaces beyond the profit-motivated model of Silicon Valley and the control-motivated model of the Chinese Communist Party."²³

My primary objective in this study is analyzing the social text that emerges at the intersection of culture, media, and politics as reconstructed and read through cultural artifacts and media practices (literature, music, art, sneakernets, memes), political events, and fragments of everyday life. I juxtapose cultural objects and media practices that are not usually interpreted together to focus on the production of a social text and its uneven mediatizations, as formulated by Henri Lefebvre: "Each of us is constantly—everyday—faced with a social text. We move through it, we read it. Through this text, and through reading it, we communicate with others, with the wider [*globale*] society on the one hand and with nature on the other. At the same time, we are all part of a social text. Not only do we read. We are also read, deciphered, made plain (or not). We are all both subject and object."²⁴ In *Rhythmanalysis* (2007 [1992]), his last book, Lefebvre charts an approach akin to Appadurai's mediascape ("the mediatized everyday"), although focusing on what he calls "rhythmanalysis." *Rhythmanalysis* poses questions Lefebvre previously raised in *The Production of Space*: Does socialism produce its own space, and how might that inquiry help us probe the nature of "actually existing socialism"?²⁵ Socialisms, Lefebvre writes in *Rhythmanalysis*, "have not yet gained in prestige or in clarity."²⁶ Lefebvre's unorthodox Marxism belongs to a tradition of critical engagement with the historical experience of state socialism that this book puts in conversation with Cuba as a case study and that ultimately searches for ways in which anticapitalist political imaginaries—confronting the communist past and the capitalist present simultaneously—can gain in prestige and clarity through critical engagement.

This interpretative practice encourages a renewed pursuit of prestige and clarity for the double denunciation of inherited frameworks of interpretation regarding the communist past and the capitalist present. To be sure, cultural and media practices are only one way to map how the market operates as a national object of desire and how the reorganization strategies of the revolutionary state in the postsocialist economy make themselves (in)visible to its different constituents. But one possible outcome is that Cuba could no longer stand as a privileged epistemic place or ideal laboratory, as a passive subject/object always on the verge of change and awakening (as it has been previously). A single focus on either continuity or change would be equally untenable. The better question would be how the continuities and breaks between "actually existing socialisms" and "actually existing capitalisms" can be rethought for a critique of the present and for the reconfiguration of future politics as we travel between, read, and are read by those spaces.[27]

Portable Postsocialisms in Context

In the postsocialist mediascape, "change" and "continuity" operate as the ultimate floating signifiers in the political imaginary. Floating signifiers are linguistic or nonlinguistic signs whose unstable meanings assign them a special cultural relevance to the social bond: a word, a phrase, an image, a symbol, a color. On account of that indeterminacy and signifiers' representational power, the field of meaning in which they operate is politically consequential and relationally defined. Divergent, and at times conflicting, meanings of change and continuity are wielded by the different constituents of Cuban postsocialism. My interest in floating signifiers links the political sphere to its discursive and technological (re)productions in the cultural realm, that is, to the aesthetic and media dimensions of the political signifiers of Cuban postsocialism.[28]

Take, for instance, all the possible responses to this exhortation: "Faced with the capitalist world crisis, we have no other choice but to unite in order to confront it," reads a billboard from August 2009 on one of the façades of the Habana Libre Hotel, at 23 y L, a major urban intersection (fig. 0.1). What the Cuban landscape lacks in grossly oversized publicity it makes up for in monumental political adverts, both old and new. As in the first joke quoted above, Raúl Castro's statement can be read at face value as a correct diagnosis of the post-2008 global financial crisis; but for those well versed in the idiolect of the PCC, it is just another iteration of the government's long tradition of self-aggrandizing anti-imperialist, anticapitalist rhetoric. It is a type of rhetoric that casts Cuba's brand of socialism as the singular and necessary agent of anticapitalist opposition and that positions Raúl Castro's economic reforms as the only

Figure 0.1. Havana, L y 23, August 2009. Author's photo.

available political avenue to survive and overcome the latest crisis. Its preferred keywords are commitment, resolve, endurance, continuity, solidarity, courage, unity, and so on. The phrase on the billboard comes from a speech delivered in April 2009 to the Bolivarian Alliance for the Peoples of Our America (ALBA) just as Raúl Castro's program for domestic economic reforms was taking off. ALBA's name invokes José Martí and Simón Bolívar as icons of a teleological discourse in which Bolivarian governments claim to continue the project of nineteenth-century Latin American independence. ALBA was founded in 2004 by Cuba and Venezuela on a platform of social justice and advocated for the economic and political integration of Latin American countries as an alternative to Pan-American free trade agreements and organizations that include, and are structurally advantageous to, the United States.

The proprietary signs of Cuban's historical socialism (heroism, sacrifice, resilience, and monolithic unity in the fight against US imperial capitalism) were deployed in this case by Fidel's brother (who had just officially assumed the country's leadership) and by the PCC's mass communication organs to re-present themselves as the people's champions against the 2008 crisis of world capital. But who (else) does official state iconography address? From any other point of view, it can be read as a credible critique of a world system amid a catastrophic crisis, a welcome contrast to the lack of accountability of its architects and to the corporate bailouts that characterized institutional responses to the 2008 economic disaster in advanced industrial centers. Locally, it is little more than discredited government propaganda that is ignored on the street and mocked online, in contrast to its earlier revolutionary clout and spontaneous mobilization capabilities. It is also a constant reminder of the PCC's continued hold on public space and political power, a space where Cuban socialism and its signs even today perform as signifiers but do so in permanent hegemonic crisis.[29]

This split gaze has a long history. A form of truth-telling about the world order that disguises the party/state's own local hegemonic operations, this message repeats the counterhegemonic identity of Cuban socialism with respect to neoliberal globalization. Conversely, during Perú's 2021 electoral campaign, billboards featuring slogans such as "Think of your future, [say] no to communism," "Making more for my effort is freedom," and "Socialism leads us to communism" popped up throughout the country, presumably against Pedro Castillo, a candidate identified with a traditional left platform. As living legacies of the Cold War media contests, red-washing and red-baiting are complimentary semantic operations that conceal kinships between competing forms of extractivism and domination.

One of Alen Lauzán's comic strips from a series on the 2014 diplomatic thaw between Cuba and the United States, also set in the landmark Habana Libre Hotel, addresses such maneuvers of (in)visibility of transnational capital in postsocialist Cuba (fig. 0.2). Lauzán, a cartoonist based in Chile, worked for the Cuban state newspaper *Juventud Rebelde* and its humor supplement *Dedeté* from 1995 to 2000. In 2008, Lauzán created the digital humor supplement *Guamá* (the name of a historical Cuban indigenous chief but also a play on the name of *Granma*, the PCC's official newspaper), parodying the Cuban official news in style and substance; it circulated in Cuba through alternative networks and social media. He has become one of the most prolific and recognizable graphic humorists of postsocialist Cuban culture abroad. Lauzán depicts a chronology of the building's renaming: "Habana Hilton" before 1959; then the "Habana Libre," adopted after revolutionary takeover; and a mock "China Hilton," in a projected but not so implausible near future. This triptych signals a coming change that is not a return to an Americanized prerevolutionary Havana but a leap to an American/Chinese–led transformation in which the words "Habana" (a stand-in for local constituents) and "Libre"/"free" (a signifier of political or social values) are altogether absent: "The time, the implacable one, that passed," reads the caption. The Habana Libre Hotel is not only an important hotel at

Figure 0.2. "El tiempo, el implacable, el que pasó." Image courtesy of Alen Lauzán.

a major urban intersection; it is also an iconic political landmark. During the 1959 Cuban Revolution, it became the provisional headquarters for the rebel army leadership upon their arrival in the city; and along with the Hotel Nacional, it was one of the state-provided lodgings for foreign dignitaries and guests of the revolutionary government. The Habana Libre Hotel is also where the first antenna for satellite cable TV was installed and is one of the most popular wi-fi hotspots in the capital.

The Chinese and American media conglomerates Huawei and Google both vied for a presence in the rapidly expanding Cuban media market: Google with limited runs of free internet pilot programs and local servers, Huawei as the preferred government contractor for the development of all wireless and cable infrastructure for ETECSA, the Cuban state communications company. China's large investments in Cuba have less to do with any ideological affinity than with its One Belt, One Road initiative (BRI), a program that includes strategic investments in resource extraction and infrastructure development throughout Latin America and other parts of the world.[30] In fact, similar to the 1987 Soviet law on joint ventures with foreign capital (and despite the restrictions of the US embargo), Italy, Canada, Spain, Germany, Vietnam, Mexico, and Brazil have all invested in the Cuban postsocialist economy since the early 1990s. For example, Nestlé, one of the most reviled and powerful economic actors in developing regions, entered the ice-cream and bottled water and beverages markets in 1996 and 1999, respectively. In 1999, Nestlé acquired San Peregrino, which had been a foreign partner in Cuba's bottled water and beverages company, Ciego Montero; and in 2017 it announced plans to expand local production with an investment of 54 million Swiss francs in the Mariel Special Development Zone.

Severe water shortages, droughts, and contamination of tap water are everyday realities for Cubans. This same scarcity ensures profits for the monopoly controlling bottled water, which is sold to visitors with hard currency; reinvestment of those profits into infrastructure and ecological preservation is altogether absent from public discussion and exempt from independent regulatory oversight. Moa's cobalt and nickel open-air extraction mines, among the most environmentally opaque operations in Cuba, are run jointly with the Canadian mining company Sherrit International Corp., which supplies manufacturers around the world.[31]

Between 1990 and 1991, Fidel Castro expressed the dilemma that, in order for Cuban socialism to survive, it had to use capitalism to subsidize it.[32] But this official rhetoric of survival collapsed the distinction between two very different things: the survival of whatever could be saved of Cuba's revolutionary investment in social and economic justice, and the political continuity of the ruling elite. After Soviet economic support was withdrawn, only the second element—the political elite and party-state apparatus—remained unchanged. Before 1990, beneficial credit and trade accords for Cuban sugar allowed the government to maintain an unprecedented if unsustainable track record of investments in education, urbanization, health care, and culture. These policies buoyed popular support for many decades and functioned as a credible trade-off for the revolution's less attractive features. After the Special Period, official discourse finally abandoned the definition of socialism as a transitional period toward a fundamentally different mode of production. Through all those changes, before and after 1989, what has remained firmly in place is the government's reliance on an export-oriented, extractivist economy. This ranges from sugar and revolution in the past, to tourism and solidarity-as-commodity in the present, most notably through international trade agreements accommodating the rental of Cuban doctors and other service personnel.[33]

By the late 1980s, with perestroika news from abroad, the desire for the (full) arrival of the market was a general expectation that was only partly frustrated in turn-of-the-twentieth-century Cuba, though its arrival was obscured by the permanence of the political apparatus. The market did arrive, only under a different guise. In the aftermath of the 6th PCC Congress in 2011, the Cuban state pushed measures of fiscal austerity, efficiency, and discipline (very much in line with global neoliberal trends). But it did so without breaking apart the for-profit monopolies that make its military a de facto governing corporation, addressing the regulatory obstacles to popular economic participation and production growth, or reforming a state policing apparatus that abrogates its most basic protective mandates. This process, led by the party through joint ventures with foreign capital, has been doubly reframed: as a state-led recovery and as an economic opening blazing the paths of Cuba's twenty-first-century socialism.

A closer look at Cuba's cultural and economic landscapes therefore demonstrates how increasingly vital it is that we do not reduce the undemocratic and dispossessive operations of transnational capitalisms to the presence of McDonald's, Starbucks, and fast wi-fi or to the absence of single-party rule. Moreover, party-led economic planning around an export-oriented, extractivist economy is not a post-Soviet phenomenon: a sugar-based export economy, and the aggressive politics of labor extraction and control, preceded the development of the tourism industry and the large-scale export of medical personnel that support the Cuban postsocialist economy. This aspect of "actually existing socialism" presents a special challenge to critical theory:

> Critical theories of capitalism that deal only with overcoming the bourgeois mode of distribution cannot fully grasp this dimension of capitalism and, worse, can veil the fact that overcoming class society entails overcoming the foundation of the mode of production. Thus, one variant of traditional Marxism became an ideology of legitimation for those social forms—the "actually existing socialist" countries—in which the liberal bourgeois mode of distribution was abolished but the capital-determined mode of production was not, and the abolition of the former served ideologically to veil the existence of the latter.[34]

To stop treating Cuba as an exception, especially with respect to other experiences with actually existing socialism, has important implications not only to critical theory but also to Cuban and Latin American studies. It means, for example, that we should certainly include Cuba in critiques of extractivist developmental policies shared by both right-wing and progressive Latin American political projects, despite the large-scale, involuntary greening effects of its sudden economic collapse in the early 1990s.[35]

Consider how a traveling act such as Argentine artist Dolores Cáceres's neon signs announcing "*No vendo nada*" (I don't sell anything) intervenes in this ideologically dense and economically opaque postsocialist context (fig. 0.3). Exhibited in Argentina, Uruguay, and Cuba, these neon signs are a running commentary on the global continuity of capitalism against the ubiquity of advertising in public space; they are also a reflection on the artist's place in these circuits as a producer of commodities for an international market. But the various meanings Cáceres's signs acquire upon arrival call attention to the local articulations of the (art) market in turn. The Havana Art Biennial opened in 1984 as a showcase for art from the Global South; that is, primarily from circuits other than Western Europe and North America. Yet its claim as an alternative forum for artistic projects invested in postcolonial and capitalist critique has been

Figure 0.3. Dolores Cáceres, "No vendo nada." O'Reilly Street, Havana, 2015. Author's photo.

complicated by frequent allegations of government censorship and also by its growing profile as yet another layover in the transnational itinerary of art buyers after 1989. Cáceres's brightly and strikingly colored "I don't sell anything" signs recall, incidentally, the explicit rejection of commercial art that gave rise to the Havana Biennial as a utopian space for tricontinental art originally. Simultaneously, the signs also point to the ironic saleability of the anticommercial stance, the commercialization of new Cuban art after 1989, and the state investments on tourism and doctor exchange programs that rely on the Cuban Revolution as a marketable commodity, selling precisely that which is seemingly "not for sale." This includes the myth of its socialist survival against all odds, the illusion of its once signature but now defanged social programs, and its anachronistic ideological performance at home and abroad repackaged as a commodity for political tourists. Cáceres's signs not only intervened in the space in which they were exhibited; they were resignified by it as well. In this iteration, placed in O'Reilly Street in Old Havana, the neon sign was not turned on. The 2015 Havana Art Biennial was plagued by electricity blackouts.

The installation worked as a fortuitous historiographical commentary on the politics of public space and advertising in postsocialist Cuba. Old Havana, the colonial quarter, is the main site of a tourism-oriented reconstruction and preservation project administered by the Office of the City Historian. One of the first financially autonomous state institutions, this office was a model for the fiscal autonomy of other state enterprises. In photos of Havana predating 1968 (when private enterprise was finally eliminated), the street is peppered with advertisements for businesses and foreign companies. Five decades after the disappearance of commercial advertising from public spaces, Cáceres's sign for the XII Havana Biennial shared space with the publicity footprint of the mixed economy. But this space is not exactly a return to a prerevolutionary scene where domestic businesses shared space above all with major US brands: informal trades, sole traders and small family-run businesses, state-foreign joint ventures, and timeworn socialist iconography interpellate the passersby now (fig. 0.4).

The study of the Cuban postsocialist mediascape can illuminate these continuities and ruptures between "actually existing socialisms" and "actually existing capitalisms" in everyday contexts. The way that Cuban socialism circulates as an international object of desire because of its apparently exceptional status (a humanist socialism, a survivor of postsocialist transitions "frozen in time") speaks to the postsocialist condition understood as a crisis of the political imaginary that pits a discredited

Figure 0.4. Aguacate between Obispo and Obrapía, next to O'Reilly Street, Havana, 2017. Image courtesy of Claudia González.

vocabulary of political action against the systemic failures that demand radical change. Insufficient attention paid to that disjuncture may better account for why Cuba still operates as a doubly exotic space of exception, i.e., a Caribbean communism; why its brand remains a compelling if misleading story about capital accumulation and anticapitalist sentiment in postsocialist times; and why, in turn, it still effectively fans red-washing rhetoric and red-baiting panics.[36]

In chapter 1, I analyze the reactivation of Cuba as an international object of desire at the turn of the twenty-first century with the expansion of its tourist economy. "I want to go to Cuba before it changes," a sentiment that circulates widely, provides the point of departure to rethink both "the new trip to Cuba" and "the old trip to Cuba" through the lens of the trip to socialism as a twentieth-century genre. Recovering a current of left dissent, the first chapter analyzes the construction of Cuban exceptionalism in New Left thought; and the permanence of those images, despite the shift from a Cuban socialism seen as exportable in the 1960s, to one perceived in the present as portable: consumable but contained.

The subsequent chapters survey Cuba's postsocialist media and culture and their attendant political imaginaries through forms of portable postsocialism: music (chapter 2), fashion (chapter 3), screens (chapter 4), and fictions of the end of history (conclusion). Each of these categories construes the portability of Cuban postsocialism differently: as a place constituted by new forms of travel to and from socialism, as an experience narrated anew and made sense of in and through digital media, and as a composite political imaginary that is remediated, transported, and translated through cultural processes of world-building and identity formation. These chapters explore how, in tandem with the theoretical decomposition of the Marxist universal subject of history, the Cuban crisis of revolutionary hegemony put situated pressures on the state's homogenizing cultural models of ideologically appropriate political subjectivity. A plurality of identities emerged in its place: remnants of statist egalitarianisms, intersectional visions of social and economic justice, consumerist approaches to empowerment along racialized and gendered axes, and traditional conservatisms all seek political representation and public recognition, though in uneven material and symbolic conditions and in a new media environment. These irruptions questioned the degree to which state cultural initiatives harbored actually existing practices of invisibility, discrimination, and professional typecasting along racial and gender lines even when they uplifted and promoted folk traditions or increased general access to high culture.

Through the examples of reggaeton and punk as marginalized sounds, for example, chapter 2 shows that the sonic dimension of the postsocialist experience cannot be understood solely in terms of a competition between global music markets and local musicians or from the perspective of a confrontation between state censorship versus individual freedom. Rather, the notion of *pachanga*, or "national festive spirit," opens up an analysis of revolutionary productivist masculinity as a racialized trope historically mobilized by the state sonic industry and challenged by contemporary soundscapes. Chapter 3, on women's fashion, and chapter 4, on what I call "screen cultures," in turn detail how much the context-specific uses of technologies shape the aesthetics of local advertising and the audiences of political projects as these practices contend with their infrastructural as well as sociopolitical conditions of production and circulation. These perspectives favor an approach to participatory media and cultural practices not only as sites where broadly conceived emancipatory struggles or their suppression are decided but also as constantly renegotiated spaces where everyday survival and immanent community architectures are at stake.

Finally, in the conclusion I return to Cuba's widely accepted exceptional status as the last standing survivor of twentieth-century state socialist projects to connect narratives about "the end of history" with end-of-the-world tropes. I illuminate how the state is brought into question in apocalyptic and postapocalyptic tropes in Cuban postsocialist cultural and media practices. Cuban postsocialist "fictions of the end" link the fate of the idea of "the end of history" as a political fiction with the figure of the state, establishing critical continuities between the eschatological imaginaries of "actually existing socialisms" and of "actually existing capitalisms." As such, postsocialist fictions rework a political unconscious casting modern nation-state projects as dysfunctional disaster managers and, all too often, as disaster catalysts themselves while they simultaneously betray a desire and a need for other forms of effective collective action.

Cuban postsocialism is portable in myriad ways. The end of exit permits, repatriation and investment programs for former émigrés, debt renegotiations and economic trade agreements with Latin American, Eastern European, and Asian countries, and large-scale programs for state-mediated employment of Cuban professionals in foreign missions have all transformed earlier patterns of permanent immigration into complex constellations of migrant and flexible labor, multiplying routes of cultural and material exchanges between Cuba and the world. Miami businesses advertise in Cuba's underground digital networks to secure potential customers, to influence family and friend circles distributed across the Florida Strait, or to create name recognition in a future Cuban market. Local advertisers and influencers take to Instagram, Facebook, Telegram, and WhatsApp as these platforms gain ground among the growing number of Cubans with regular access to internet on their phones. The possible import of Asian postsocialisms for some, and of Central and Eastern European postsocialisms for others, has grasped popular domestic imaginaries of change and critique as well. The digital remediation of samizdat literature and the increase of curated, partial news from other postsocialisms widened the transnational reading networks brought on by portable USB devices initially and by greater social media and internet access later. These imaginaries and programs for capitalist transition had already crossed the Atlantic once en route to Eastern and Central Europe, first rehearsed in the Latin American experiments with neoliberal privatization from the 1960s to the 1990s whereby the toppling of socialist and progressive governments gave way to repressive dictatorships.

To speak of portable postsocialisms is to speak then of pocket postsocialisms, or *postsocialismos de bolsillo*. The pocket here is a double metaphor. First, it is a figure of cultural democratization (as in pocketbooks, or *libros de bolsillo*), placing participatory digital media in a longer critical conversation about the emancipatory illusions of market-mediated practices of mass culture. Second, it is a site indexing the material dimensions of these media and cultural practices, where both global and local postsocialist imaginaries involve algorithmically customized attention economies, precariously self-financed investments in the promises of digitally brokered upward mobility, and both top-down and bottom-up structures of misinformation, amplification, surveillance, and monetization of individual digital engagement, all within the reach of our pockets. The Cuban postsocialist mediascape confronts us, specifically, with popular imaginaries of change and with everyday desires for nonstate economies that are, however, not synonymous with neoliberal politics or capitalist desires. This does not mean the nonstate and informal cultural and media sectors in which those imaginaries emerge exist apart from the exploitative dynamics of the media ecosystems in which they, and we, are all embedded. But it does invite us to read beyond the essentialist romanticizing of disconnected authenticity, beyond the democratic promises of equal access to the digital and informational economy, against techno-solutionist and postideological visions of political change, and against the grain of dominant "deficit models" of media critique that normatively measure the practices, agencies, and aspirations of users against assumed standards naturalizing the very inequalities they aim to critique.[37] This emphasis on Cuban postsocialist portability also signals a need to look beyond, though not away from, identitarian representation and its interpretative frameworks toward portability's scaffolding structures: remediated power dynamics and digital communication infrastructures in dialogue with what Andreas Wittel called the microsociologies of "networked sociality."[38]

Underscoring the *portability* of Cuban (post)socialism therefore calls attention to a participatory mediascape in which cultural and media artifacts and imaginaries circulate unevenly and are decontextualized and recontextualized again and again. To insist on this aspect of the portability of postsocialisms links the new routes of exchange and travel that organize material and symbolic flows between Cuba and the rest of the world with the reorganization of the social imaginary during a profoundly transformative period, highlighting their links to contemporary media practices. It opens up the possibility of seeing postsocialist context and condition as a continuous totality that is differently experienced, locally articulated, and unevenly mediated by political power, access to media technologies, and cultural exchange. This attention to portability, producibility, and consumption underscores what we all contribute to these flows of exchange as participating media agents and spectators of the Cuban context, understood as both a particular social reality and a contested symbolic space.

The study of cultural artifacts and practices across a range of media, and by diverse agents, delivers a complex picture of how Cuban and non-Cuban constituents of the revolutionary legacy accept, reject, or transform narratives of political continuity and social change. These stories impugn the official, single-party state's monopoly on the history and definition of Cuban socialism, as well as foreign exoticizing perspectives on Cuba, both of which are detrimental to debates about progressive political and cultural values in Cuba outside of a narrow revolutionary statist framework or an equally narrow anticommunist opposition. This combination of romanticism and commodification has been equally counterproductive to debates about what viable alternatives to capitalism and conservatism look like in Latin America. Inasmuch as Cuba's impact as a traveling media object scrutinizes the promises and pitfalls of the modern nation-state, traditional party politics and ideological identities, and the global market beyond its borders, I contend that the postsocialist mediascape implicates us all in the critical task of understanding the political possibilities and foreclosures that media technologies and cultural representations sustain.

As Offlaga Disco Pax sing on their album *Socialismo Tascabile* (Pocket-sized socialism), "nel 1975 Il socialism era come l'universo: in espansione" (In 1975, socialism was like the universe: in a state of expansion). We no longer inhabit that moment, but its legacy haunts the present. In this common present—in the postsocialist condition, in the informational age—the ways in which culture, media, and politics intersect to engender diverse cultural strategies and competing political imaginaries must be considered both comparatively and in their own contexts. After all, extractivist capitalism, state repression, corporate intrigue, organized media piracy, participatory cultures and vernacular media literacies, and the emergence of new tech elites complicit in the external and internal digital segregation of users are neither unique to Cuba nor alien to Latin America's recent history. The challenge remains of how to recognize systemic global patterns in their particular expressions and how to scale critiques accordingly.

CHAPTER 1

Cuban Travels
Hatuey in Ethiopia

For a Cuban, meeting strangers in the United States (outside of Miami) always involved an entirely predictable script. As soon as that staple of social intercourse "Where are you from?" was uttered, the response "from Cuba" invariably elicited some version of "How did you get here?" and "What was it like living under communism?"[1] "What do you think will happen when Fidel is gone?" was another favorite until 2008, when the Cuban leader smoothly exited the public eye for a relatively quiet retirement until his death in 2016. However, the immediate reaction to the mention of Cuba has become eerily repetitive: "I want to go before it changes!" Once the conversation gets going, some version of "I hope Cuba does not become [Haiti, Puerto Rico, Miami]" usually finds its way into the dialogue. This shift became more pronounced after December 17, 2014, when the US and Cuban presidents at the time, Barack Obama and Raúl Castro, announced the first change in diplomatic relations between the two countries in over fifty years. Secretly negotiated in Canada and at the Vatican, the new accord partially relaxed one of the last remnants of the Cold War era: the US economic embargo on Cuba, a set of executive and legislative statutes severely restricting trade and travel between the neighboring countries in place since 1962. Cuba was suddenly everywhere, and the world was on the lookout for what such an announcement could mean.[2]

Writing the contemporary is inescapably risky and inevitably (auto-) ethnographic. As far as drive-by ethnographies go I, too, have a taxi story. My ride with an Ethiopian-born cab driver en route to the 2015 American Comparative Literature Association meeting in Seattle was memorable for two reasons. First, it was a notoriously anomalous interaction with respect to what had been happening during the previous months since December 2014. Second, it suggested that those other customary, dreaded queries that always followed "Where are you from" and "What do you research?" could be seen otherwise. Having learned that I was from Havana, the taxi driver asked me excitedly if I remembered the name of an indigenous chief who, about to burn at the stake for sedition, had rejected the priest's last entreaty to accept the Christian god of the Spanish conquistadors and thus be saved from eternal damnation. "Hatuey!" I blurted, and he asked me to write down the name and to recount the anecdote. How had news of Hatuey reached Ethiopia? The driver—with a rural background, in his midfifties, driving in Washington State for over ten years, a veteran in the trenches of the postindustrial service economy, I learned—was told the story about "the first rebel of the Americas" by Cuban teachers as part of their civilian and peacekeeping missions after the Ogaden War (1977–1978), an experience he recalled with admiration and gratitude. Cuba's military deployment to the Horn of Africa and the war in Angola were the stuff of international legend and not an insignificant source of domestic discontent and public taboo, a double legacy of secrecy and success capped by Nelson Mandela's visit in 1991 after his release from jail and by the televised death-penalty trial in 1989 of Cuba's top-ranking general, Arnaldo Ochoa.[3] This encounter invited a more serious reflection about the global constituencies of the 1959 Cuban Revolution, how they saw themselves implicated in its unfolding dénouement, and how their passions engaged a dichotomy at the core of its foreign and domestic policies, images, and subjects still in place today.

In the 1960s the world flocked to Cuba to see the birth of a socialist revolution. In the first decades of the twenty-first century, the world hurried to witness the remnants of that socialist project and its predicted imminent demise. The discredited grand narratives of socialist and capitalist modernities, which deepened after 1989 and 2008, respectively, have defined a current global crisis of legitimation of politics as usual. No wonder the Cuban postsocialist moment has generated a whirlwind of visits, interpretations, media images, and affects anticipating the end of the last socialist project in the Western Hemisphere simultaneously as a world event and as a symbolic closure for bygone utopias. Contemporary accounts of these trips constantly reproduce the image of Cuba as an exceptional space at the same time that they produce it as an unexceptionably fashionable place.

Looking at the syntax of the phrase "*I* want to go before *it* changes," it would be easy to dismiss the relationship between the speaking subject

"I" and the recipient object of curiosity and desire "it" as yet another expression of naïve political tourism. In its most perverse formulas, this operation relies on a differential intercourse between those who enjoy the luxury of travel to politically and climatically exotic locations (and all that this might entail: disposable income, free movement across borders, a detached provisional sympathy for the wretched of the earth, the environmental violence of mass tourism) and those expected to perform accordingly and to surprise pleasantly, conforming to commodifying, culturally reproduced, and internalized exoticizing tropes. The effects of these interactions are ironized astutely by the Cuban writer Ena Lucía Portela through the character of a Cuban writer debuting in a literary market driven by layer upon layer of neocolonial sensibility and political voyeurism:

> Because many people, even knowledgeable and educated people, think that if you, as Cuban, don't make at least a joke a day, even a bad joke, a despicable gag, it may happen that your countrymen will accuse you of being a square and a foreigner, for clowning is one of the main dogmas of national identity. Then one finds out that the right-wing tourists come to smoke [a] Cohíba, drink rum, and hook up with a *mulata*—or anything else—and to dance rumba until 5 am without a care in the world [*muertos de la risa*], while the lefty tourists come to learn and offer their solidarity and support to "the country of the *cronopios*," also without a care in the world. One cannot get mad and complain and demand less simplification and more respect saying that there are also tragic and boring and dense and operatic and half-suicidal people living in Cuba because we and only we are responsible for all that confusion.[4]

To prospective travelers, it would be easier still to point out how much Cuba has already changed (and ask, in turn, what is meant by "change"). With respect to what measures and when would Cuba have changed: In 1968, the year of the Revolutionary Offensive, when all independent economic activity was abolished and agriculture was fully state-centralized? In 1976, when a new constitution institutionalized the heterogenous processes unfolding since the 1959 revolution? In 1986, with the announcement of the "Rectification of errors and negative tendencies," a program designed to maximize economic productivity, and battle not only waste, corruption, and inefficiency but also economic decentralization and political liberalization, in order to rein in any desires for a tropical perestroika? After 1990, when the Soviet subsidies stopped, the Cuban economy collapsed and the country opened to the dollar, to international markets, and to small family businesses and sole traders? After 1998–2000, when Venezuelan oil trade agreements kept the command economy afloat long enough to redesign its market strategies? In 2014, with the 118 Law of Foreign Investment updating the previous laws from 1995 and 2004, which offered better guarantees and investment incentives for foreign capital? Suppose we consider the desire to witness the last throes of a historical communism no longer reproducible anywhere as a symptom of a more intractable condition; such an approach would call for an investigation into the political imaginaries and cultural referents informing the idea of going before Cuba changes as both a historiographical premise and a geopolitical promise. It is therefore necessary, but not sufficient, to point out the inadequacies of these romanticized images of imminent change and stationary time. The postsocialist condition demands a serious inquiry into the imaginaries behind wanting to go to Cuba before it changes.

As a country that did not follow the timelines of other historical communisms after the Cold War, whose experimental thaws and restructurings did not fit the narrative of earlier communisms or of other 1990s transitions, "frozen in time" has become synonymous with Cuba's identity as a new global destination. The popularization of this image—a country standing still in time—was reinforced in the 1990s by a deep economic depression as much as by the apocalyptic discourses about inventive survival and aestheticized poverty that emerged around it. It was then endlessly recycled and effectively commodified in much of the Cuban literature, film, and arts in and about the afterlives of the 1959 revolution over the previous three decades. These are tales of sensual poverty and neurotically uncertain futures. They chronicle the tribulations, successes, and identitarian minefields of a subsistence economy, thematizing ruin and decay as everyday experiences and as an allegory of a national history whose promises of a radiant future were suddenly upended.

Nonetheless, the resilience and particularities of the Cuban socialist experience remained a more viable and agreeable model of socialist politics for many onlookers, as it had been in previous decades. For multiple reasons—not the least because the Cuban Revolution of 1959 coincided with the rise of the New Left and participated in the sensibility of the socialist humanisms of the 1960s—the Cuban socialist experience has always been approached, and has advertised itself, as a more sympathetic and at least partially successful alternative to the Soviet and Chinese models of modernization and communist party rule. Cuba leveraged this symbolic capital again when it turned to international tourism as one of the main sources of hard currency in the absence of Soviet subsidies.

Like the trip to Paris, to the Soviet Union, or to China, the trip to revolutionary Cuba is a twentieth-century genre. By "genre" I mean that travel to these historical, geopolitical coordinates is generally framed by well-established tropes, characters, and plots. Prevailing images of revolution and rumba, of a land frozen in time, rest on several faulty premises. But these assumptions are rooted in a curated selection of images, sounds, and expectations built over years, constituting a media archive that can bolster expedient arguments about continuity and change depending on the occasion and the speaker. Their source is a vast and intricate literary and audiovisual corpus of motley travelogues.

Both the old and the new trips to Cuba partake in several travel narratives at once: oscillating between pilgrimage and discovery, they combine the sedimented histories of travel to the erotically charged premodern new world, to the alternative modernities of socialism—once a trip to the *future today*, now a trip to the *future past*—and to the feral landscapes seemingly far removed from the nine-to-five grind that cater to postmodern mass tourism.[5] Some, like Portela's character above, resent the casual violence that a tourist gaze as gleeful spectator of another's history exerts on the performative tenor of social intercourse. Others, like the poet and essayist Hans Magnus Enzensberger in his memoir/travelogue about the 1960s, find themselves as helpless characters in the hangover of a shared history: "I just can't say why I've found it so difficult to free myself from that little, insignificant, crazy island."[6]

The atypical travelogues of René Dumont and Enzensberger present an opportunity to reevaluate the conditions that produced the trip to Cuban socialism as a genre, that is, to scrutinize those New Left images of travels to Cuban socialism that have prevailed in contemporary global media, as well as the modes of critique that they have enabled or hindered since. Challenging standard periodizations, their texts predate the famous break between foreign sympathizers and the Cuban leaders in 1971 on issues of political freedom, a discussion that did not engage theoretical or economic issues and that therefore left untouched the question of Cuban socialism's apparent historical exceptionality. As far as socialist transitions are concerned, Dumont and Enzensberger put Cuba directly in contact with the left critique of "actually existing socialism," a current of thought undertheorized in most intellectual histories and polemics that deal with the 1959 revolution and its aftermath. This tradition of left dissidence and materialist critique has remained largely invisible within Cuba. Thinking about the new trip to Cuba through the lens of the old one speaks to the cultural assumptions and political expectations that give meaning to its contemporary forms as a genre. This juxtaposition renders a seemingly worn-out genre, "the trip to socialism," as something other than a nostalgic, consumerist, or voyeuristic exercise.

The Old Trip and the New Left

In the 1960s the trip to Cuba was usually undertaken by those curious about, and sympathetic to, the revolutionary process underway; most were officially invited by the new government. A casualty of Cold War sensibilities, travelogues to actually existing socialisms became the target of habitual reactionaries and penitent apostates. They were read as tangential (literary) oddities or else were quickly put behind and forgotten as products of their time, as youthful indiscretions, by their own authors. Criticism of such politically motivated travels was never far behind. Scathing indictments of commitment at a distance, neocolonial condescension, willful hyperopia, blind sectarianism, and wanton exoticism have been de rigueur in commentaries about these "fellow travelers" and "political pilgrims."[7] Directed in particular at those traveling from North America and Western Europe to Asia, Latin America, and Africa, these critiques constitute a subgenre of their own. Clustered around a series of stereotypes—the caviar left, champagne socialists—these critiques became fashionable from the 1980s onward, when the prestige and credibility of revolutionary socialisms began to wane and the neoliberal offensive took off around the talking points of Reaganism and Thatcherism.

While there is a substantial bibliography on this relationship between foreigners and the 1959 Cuban Revolution, the frameworks through which those exchanges have been analyzed, and the resulting interpretive outcomes, have only begun to be reexamined more seriously. Growing scholarly attention has finally been paid to different approaches explaining how Third World engagement provided critical tools to intellectuals and to oppressed minorities and classes in advanced industrialized countries to rethink, and even organize against, their own domestic issues. But even more sympathetic or nuanced approximations to the corpus of Cuban travelogues and the phenomenon of political pilgrims end up revisiting the usual suspects—Sontag, Sartre, C. Wright Mills, Cortázar, García Márquez, Leroi Jones—and more or less contain the same plot: they take for granted the divide between local constituents and external visitors and continue to rely on commonplace framings such as "they saw what they most wanted to see" or "they instrumentalized it strategically: it was productive for their respective domestic struggles."[8] These are interpretative operations reliant on corpus-building, narrative analyses, and implicit historiographical premises that favor only some aspects of the trip to socialism. However, they help little to understand the processes of recovery, witnessing, and belonging that sustain the new trip to Cuba and the desire to go before it changes.

Meanwhile, a parallel and complementary travel archive tracing the movement of peoples and goods within the Second World circuits remains largely unexplored. This is also true of the corpus of critique of the non-communist left, that is, those who criticized the standard assumptions of the New Left and Third Worldism from more radical or skeptic socialist positions in their own time: Raya Dunayevskaya, C. L. R. James, José Revueltas, Cornelius Castoriadis, K. S. Karol, René Dumont, and Enzensberger, to name a few. The political position and the tenor of these lesser-known texts are quite different from the stock intellectual responses to the transformations of the Cuban revolutionary process throughout the 1960s: strident disillusionment (Mario Vargas Llosa), cautious criticism but principled commitment (Julio Cortázar), and unconditional public defense (Gabriel García Márquez), to give three classic examples from the Latin American canon.

In Latin America, the 1959 Cuban Revolution unleashed and arrested reactionary and progressive forces in equal measures. Right-wing military dictatorships—and the US economic interests backing them—wielded it as the ultimate boogeyman. At the same time, Cuba was a refugee haven and a source of material and symbolic support for much of Latin America's discontented, disenfranchised masses and for the armed guerrillas who sought to take over state power in their names. Modern revolutions have always been global events no matter where they take place. As symbolic events they change what is possible in the realm of political action, and as vectors of a world-system organization they have concrete material effects on other world events in direct and indirect ways.[9] Thus, the transnational constituencies of the 1959 Cuban Revolution contributed significantly to its status as everybody's revolution, nurturing the affective investments it has subsequently marshaled and that underpin its global image to no small degree.

Just as the international left recovered from de-Stalinization philosophically and politically, Cuba's 1959 revolution was the second stage—after Mao's China—of a revamped revolutionary socialism that came to define the political stages of a 1960s New Left. Anti-imperialist movements for decolonization and revolutionary socialism in the Latin American, African, and Asian 1960s further expanded the category of the revolutionary subject beyond the urban proletariats of the industrial centers of capital. Latin American dependency theory rendered visible a planetary division of labor, meting out a materialist critique of the political economy of colonial imperialism and its historical reproduction in postindependence modern nation-states that rejected the postponement of socialist revolutions in favor of anti-imperialist pacts with the national bourgeoisie, as Moscow dictated.[10] Simultaneously, labor, land, and rights conflicts confronted the alliances of militaristic states and transnational corporations that perpetuated them in Guatemala, Brazil, Argentina, Bolivia, and Cuba. Motley and incommensurable strands of communist and noncommunist lefts demanded that previously excluded identities of the social were accounted for both practically and theoretically, and so they were all part of this moment of redefinition and reckoning. The surge of socialist humanisms in formerly colonial, mostly agrarian societies was also part of the theoretical and political overhaul of Marxisms, as were the Althusserian school (antihumanist, structural/scientific), the attention to working-class culture and other forms of the popular, and the discovery of culture as an effectual terrain of political and ideological struggle in its own right.[11] All kinds of revolutions, whenever and wherever possible, were demanded in multiple sites at once. They were consequently grouped under the umbrella of this New Left; so, too, was the Cuban Revolution of 1959.

Marcuse's widely reprinted 1968 lecture "On the New Left," for instance, joins Cuba and the alternative in the same framework of socialist revindication: "The second great problem for our strategy—we are constantly faced with the demands, 'What is the alternative? What can you offer us that is better than what we have?' ... We will say, it is perhaps, it is probably going to be built up in Cuba. It is perhaps being built up in China. It is certainly fighting in Vietnam [against] the supermonster."[12] The revolution was perceived as actualizing a socialist alternative modernity in more ways than one and for more than one constituency. In the trip to Cuban socialism, older tropes—the legacy of Caribbean exoticism and the privilege of the round-trip escape—are not entirely absent from its narrative framings, but they are entangled with the perceived *historical superiority of the revolutionary other* as prototype. The success and reproducibility of the Cuban experience elsewhere became the most pressing question. The implications for the global revolutionary and decolonial movements of the mid-twentieth century were theoretical and practical.[13]

While the best-known travel accounts to the Cuban Revolution, by C. Wright Mills, Susan Sontag, and Jean-Paul Sartre, for example, emphasize these senses of a different kind of *other*, for many visitors the revolution in Cuba unfolded as a necessarily common experience, wherein success necessitated an unprecedented level of horizontal commitment to that collectivity. For many travelers, for example, the question was not one of political posturing or distanced curiosity, as it might have been for the more notorious visitors from the Global North; it was one of survival. Writing in 1972 from his exile in Havana, the Brazilian film director and principal figure of the Latin American Third Cinema movement Glauber Rocha finds himself not only at ease but living the change in everyday life, which he describes as a

> permanent dream in front of this blue sea in this land of myths, *a crioulada* [black Cubans] calls me "Seven-headed Lion," the *pais-de-santo* [santería priests, *babalaos*] enjoy *Barravento* and *Ganga Zumba*; our films every week on the screen, our music all day on the radio, I'm very happy [as if?] in Recife, I'm very happy in Bahía, and every road leads to the sea. I don't use money, forgot that burden, I go around by bus and by foot, I exercise, treat the gastritis which has retreated into ulcer, read anthropology and the *babados* [leaflets/writings] of crazy Germans that people there should read more to stop talking revisionist nonsense. I am happy and I am homesick.[14]

The last sentence appears originally in Portuñol, though he is writing to a Portuguese speaker: "Soy feliz y tengo saudades." Here Rocha favors a portrait of everyday minutiae to reflect on revolutionary change over any descriptive theorizing, reminiscent of Walter Benjamin's refusal to theorize revolutionary change prematurely in his Moscow diaries of 1926–1927.

Yet the conclusions drawn from the Cuban experience were not always free from the problems that had also plagued the old left vis-à-vis Soviet communism and Stalinism. Raya Dunayevskaya's break with Marcuse on this point is poignantly illustrated in her correspondence with Marcuse and Erich Fromm and in her articles for the "Two Worlds" column of her *News & Letters* magazine. Dunayevskaya was a Ukrainian-born, US-based translator, Hegelian scholar, and union activist. She had been Trotsky's secretary in Mexico and the founder, with C. L. R. James, of the Johnson–Forest Tendency, a post-Trotskyist current of American socialism. Dunayevskaya temporarily broke off a prolific correspondence with Marcuse in 1961, for disagreements over, inter alia, Marcuse's take on the ideologically appropriate position for New Left Marxists with respect to China and Cuba: unquestioned enthusiastic support. While the 1959 Cuban Revolution and the 1917 Russian Revolution were not the same, Dunayevskaya conceded, she considered the theoretical and political position of Marxist intellectuals vis-à-vis the takeover of the state apparatus by a vanguard communist party to be following a similar, and similarly dangerous, historical pattern. She read this as both a theoretical and a personal failure by the very intellectual community invested in revising Stalinist and other orthodoxies, a failure motivated by a zealously partisan "organic communist mentality," by a lack of engagement with Marxist theory as a whole (Dunayevskaya was the first English translator of Marx's early manuscripts of 1844), and by a refusal to carry out a rigorous materialist (i.e., Marxist) critique of those self-styled socialist societies that were, from the perspective she had developed, not socialist societies but bureaucratic state capitalisms instead.[15]

Neither Dunayevskaya nor Marcuse ever went to Cuba. But similar tensions will appear in the original reception and subsequent neglect of the Cuban travelogues of the French agronomist René Dumont and the German poet and essayist Hans Magnus Enzensberger. Providing some of the lesser-known but more insightful accounts of the Cuban revolutionary transformations in the 1960s by outside observers and from a critical left perspective, Enzensberger and Dumont had been invited as foreign technicians rather than as touring visitors. Because a large sector of the high- and upper-middle-class managers, technicians, and other professionals had left as anticommunist panic set in, a country undergoing a massive reorganization of its economy was in urgent need of these. Enzensberger and Dumont's substantial works on the Cuban Revolution were criticized, dismissed, or largely ignored by both sides of the ideological battle in their own time and in most subsequent scholarship. But these texts demonstrate how the open-then-betrayed-revolution and from-enthusiasm-to-disillusionment tropes flatten out a heterogeneous historical process with multiple constituencies. They show how the standard descriptions of foreign sympathizers as selectively blind, self-serving strategists, or simply as swept up in the spirit of the decade, do not include the full range of positions and attitudes about the process or consider the complexity of those interpersonal exchanges.

Dumont and Enzensberger: Change, Continuity, and Materialist Critique

Never published in Cuba, Dumont's commissioned reports on the agrarian reforms of the 1960s and his subsequent meetings with Che Guevara and Fidel Castro are unique documents of the problems of information and management at the heart of the command economy as it was implemented as early as 1959. His two books, *Cuba: Socialism and Development* (1970 [1964]) and *Is Cuba Socialist?* (1974 [1970]), detail how the unwillingness of the Cuban revolutionary leadership to incorporate local expertise and foreign advice, and the degree to which they knowingly ignored internal and external factors in agricultural planning, contributed to the deterioration of the Cuban economy in the first decade of the revolution. Dumont covers a lot of ground, from optimal soil drainage conditions for banana trees to the stages and types of large-scale agricultural and industrial reorganization and diversification needed to stabilize food security while balancing socialization with international market prices and foreign policy constraints.

Dumont belonged to a group of foreign technicians who, whatever their day-to-day disagreements with the Cuban revolutionary government, did not see a revolution with which their relationship had to be acknowledged as one of cultural difference—as was the case for Sontag, Sartre, and others. This was a revolution that wholly implicated them, to whose leadership they had all the right to speak. Their work was not simply, or even primarily, about solidarity, sympathy, or adventure. It was an expression of their commitment to a world-historical process: the first book is dedicated to the Algerians. Against a tradition that automatically suspects every foreigner's opinion of performing a colonial gesture—as a Cuban colleague suggested to be the case when we discussed Dumont—he can hardly be read, and dismissed, as another neocolonial voice. Dumont does not give unsolicited advice; he is an invited collaborator, not a self-appointed public intellectual. (Frantz Fanon thought of the work of foreign technicians as forms of reparations in rapidly decolonizing contexts.) When he offers technical and political criticisms, he does not wield his knowledge simply against those of all Cubans but against the small cadre of inexperienced and dogmatic managers and always by invoking the trove of local peasant and technical knowledge that he recognizes as the source of his own knowledge about the specific conditions of Cuban agriculture. Moreover, Dumont harshly criticizes Sartre and other panegyrists of the revolution for misrepresenting the Cuban reality and for legitimizing its worst tendencies.[16] Likewise, he castigates the national and international presses, and the revolutionary leadership, for heeding those accounts alone: "[Fidel] receives more foreign friends than experts. It is not a question of the 'direct democracy' evoked by Sartre, for in the last analysis he [Fidel] reaches the big decisions alone, after having discussed them. And he turns the other decisions over only to the men on his team, the men he trusts."[17]

Against the twin backgrounds of de-Stalinization and the Sino-Soviet split, Dumont recognizes the "irreplaceable" ideological contribution of Cuban socialism to the international left: its historically needed and politically effective "romanticism."[18] At the same time, he points out how that romanticism translates into a ruling mindset of quasi-religious messianism, a fervor that relies on the manifest misrepresentation of achievements, on unrealistic and subsequently always broken promises, and on a tight-knit brotherhood of former *guerrilleros* to keep the official narrative at all costs.

These foreign technicians and advisers, travelers of a different sort, saw Cuba as a collective laboratory of international socialism, a unique political opportunity to test and develop new economic and political practices of global relevance that did not repeat the Soviet debacles. This is why Dumont insists on the continued importance of the revolution while at the same time criticizing its leaders for a lack of understanding of socialist theory and of the temporalities of change. The problems detailed in these works boil down to a series of interrelated categories: excessive centralization; rushed and scaled-up experiments; a combination of improvisation, triumphalism, ignorance, dogmatism, and cronyism at the leadership level; various forms of dispossession of the workers by the state; militarization of political and economic spheres; and general disregard for core socialist principles, local knowledge, and past experience.[19]

A revolution that was neither in an advanced industrial country nor undergoing decolonization, one without large natural and human resources at hand, presented a singular challenge. Notwithstanding that legacy, which was compounded by the enormous external pressure exerted on Cuba—especially by the United States' aggressive economic and political stances—Dumont concludes that the policy failures of the Cuban revolutionaries were the direct result of their own incompetence and dogmatism. By 1969, Dumont's early warnings had become a matter of fact, as highlighted in this representative passage:

I am inclined to think that dogmatism, with its corollary of unlimited personal power (which obscures judgement), is the principal cause of Cuba's present difficulties. It was a priori decided to eliminate all forms of cooperatives in agricultural production as well as in the crafts and in distribution. (Lenin acknowledged the socialist character of cooperatives; only Stalin placed above them state property, incorrectly seen as belonging to "all the people.") The elimination of market relations inhibits and even prevents serious economic analyses. The revolutionary has been preferred to the expert, when an attempt should have been made to retain all Cubans with something to contribute to the revolution, even non-conformists. By giving abusive privileges to those who are (or call themselves, for it's easy to do) revolutionaries, there is a strong risk of corrupting them, of making them incapable of correcting the situation. Private activity was eliminated and the peasantry definitely disposed before this was economically or politically justifiable. All this has led to a hyper-stratified structure, proudly referred to as being "the most socialized in the world" (but alas neither the most efficient nor the most democratic), of giant production units too difficult to organize, given the present skills of the technicians. And the waiting lines lengthen. The people have deserved better.[20]

If statization and socialization were demonstrably two distinct, or even contrary, processes, it would mean that any revolutionary takeover of the state would not automatically lead to the construction of socialism or necessarily move a given society any closer to it. Dumont—and other contemporaries like Paul Sweezy and Charles Bettelheim—laid the groundwork for later reassessments of Marxian theory positing that the elimination of markets and private property alone, or their mechanistic subsumption to a centralized state authority, would not necessarily result in the equitable distribution of wealth or in the abolition of alienated labor as such: "We have reproached it [the Cuban revolutionary leadership] for sometimes preferring, out of dogmatism, the relatively easy, but soon paralyzing, step of a State takeover to the difficult construction of a socialist regime with a cooperative base."[21]

The revolutionary leaders, however, were not the only ones conflating capitalist market practices with basic accounting, legitimate needs and demands with fanciful bourgeois desires, and capitalist private property with other forms of ownership. This is, after all, an error that has plagued traditional currents of Marxist economic planning of different schools, though it is not textually supported by Marx and Engels's writings, as Samuel Farber asserts in the context of the Cuban Revolutionary Offensive of 1968: a paradigmatic example of the conflation between "private property in general and capitalist private property in particular."[22] Whatever the true political motivations of the revolutionary leadership to pursue these measures, another question altogether is why these equivocations were also reproduced, and papered over in later years, by the failure of many New Left socialist theorists to respond accordingly to these concrete experiences. Other contemporaries of Dumont shared his concerns in whole or in part, but they had different methodological or political approaches: K. S. Karol zeroed in on the more sensationalist and nefarious aspects of the internal power struggles in the revolutionary leadership, surveying the consolidation of its authoritarian/bureaucratic tendencies; meanwhile, unlike Dumont, economists like Sweezy, Michel Gutelman, Bettelheim, and Mandel clashed with specific Cuban policy decisions but did not openly question either the socialist character of the transformations underway or the good faith of the Cuban cadres.

Dumont's observations offer an unlikely case study for later reassessments of Marxism arguing that the elimination of markets and private property alone, or their mechanistic subsumption to a centralized state authority, not only does not result in the equitable redistribution of wealth or in the abolition of alienated labor but also negates them. Postone's groundbreaking study of Marx's mature social and economic theories comprehensively revises the emphasis on the market and on private property of certain traditional Marxisms, that is, their understanding of capitalism only from the perspective of distribution. This traditional focus is derived from a definition of the law of value that overlooks Marx's fundamental arguments about value and labor in capitalism, namely, that capitalist value is not only a historically specific form of distribution of wealth but also a historically specific form of its production, one that is realized by the "historically determinate character of labor in capitalism as constituting that society."[23] Yet many a Marxist economist treats labor as a transhistorical category of social production, opposing an inalienable social character to the way labor appears, distorted, as a private form of wealth production only when mediated by market categories in capitalism. As Postone stresses, Marx's critique is not of private labor from the standpoint of social labor. Instead, the key difference between Marx and classical political economists like David Ricardo and John Locke is that the dual character of labor as private and social is itself the defining feature of the capitalist mode of production—"the specificity of commodity-producing labor"—that generates social wealth at the expense of individuals. Consequently, such traditional (mis)readings have posited that "overcoming capitalism would involve the supersession of a mediated form of social relations by a direct unmediated form."[24] And because the law of value and the mediated social character of labor are understood to be only categories of market distribution, these theorists pit market (as capitalist) against plan (as socialist) without considering the mode of production common to both and the always already mediated character of social relations. These assumptions are in Sweezy and Mandel. But most significantly they lead to the *guevarista* exaltation of full economic centralization and of sacrificial, disinterested labor for the nation as a form of political schooling, with the party/state as the exclusive organizer of the social (and now presumed unmediated) labor.

The immediate pragmatic consequences were that grandiose planning from offices far away from the ground realities, based on unrealistic or improvised production goals and managed through a centralized budget that kept little track on the return on investment of public expenditures, translated into a fatal combination of rigid and uninformed decision-making at the top and, at the same time, of chaos and abuse at the bottom. Dumont's studies stacked further details showing that the state monopolies over design, production, distribution, and management had not made better use of the limited number of knowledgeable personnel available. Neither had they facilitated a more effective administration of the machinery that was in short supply. Both were additional arguments made by Guevara as the rationale for total centralization, becoming points that were accepted at face value even by foreign economic technicians, such as Mandel, wary of excessive bureaucratic centralization. In this sense, the New Left's image of Guevara as a challenger of Soviet Union orthodoxy and as a beacon of a new kind of Leninism is itself a persistent misconception. Among other things, it conflates his economic critiques of the Soviet Union before and after collectivization with a departure from Stalin-era foreign policy conservatism that ignored Moscow's directives against international armed insurrection that had been followed by Latin American communist parties hitherto. As in the case with Mao's critique of Soviet revisionism, it matters which Soviet Union Guevara was criticizing. Although in political terms his arguments for sparking socialist revolutions contradicted certain aspects of the established Communist Party policy to ally with the national bourgeoisies, in economic terms he dismisses only Lenin's recourse to the New Economic Policy in the

1920s and denounces the modest market and production reforms that began in the early 1940s in the Soviet Union and kicked into high gear later in the 1960s. As such, Guevara's critique of the Soviet Union's market revisionism was hardly a theoretically novel decolonial radicalization of its tenets, or a return to a more textual, humanist Marxism, despite his own self-assessments on this point.

In fact, Guevara's economic and social theories were simply a continuation of a certain orthodoxy in Marxist theorizing shared with interlocutors like Mandel and Sweezy, but its implementation was to be complemented by a moralist mass reeducation program on the meaning of socialist labor, closer in spirit to Leninist party vanguardism. An abridged exposition of these views appears in Guevara's commonly cited 1965 letter to Fidel on the subject of socialist transitions. Addressing criticisms about the lack of worker participation in labor management and economic planning, Guevara insists once more on the immediate suppression of market categories as a Marxist prerequisite of socialist planning; misrepresents the content of Marx's *Critique of the Gotha Programme*; defends the notion that only a technical cadre and not a workers' assembly can make "rational" decisions in socialist planning; and opposes any arrangement in which the workers could politically antagonize "the great unity of the state" on behalf of their own interests.[25] As Postone demonstrates, these views followed a commonplace but inaccurate interpretation of Marx's law of value, much like other socialist economists of his milieu. But in Guevara's case they combined with a view of party/state governance that was, contradictorily, both narrowly materialistic—relying on the elimination of material incentives to develop revolutionary consciousness and exalting the intensification of labor demands by the state as a tool of social transformation—and broadly anti-economistic—positing that a political elite could generate a socialist mass consciousness from the top down without having achieved corresponding material and political conditions (meaning independent from the form of the social relation established by the dominant mode of production).

This brings us to another key point of identification between Cuban socialism and the New Left culturalist approaches to revolutionary change of the 1960s, although it is one that has not been consistently analyzed in relation to these economic matters.[26] Combined with the revolutionary state's heterogeneous, ambiguous, and all-too-often politically arbitrary and theoretically incoherent approaches to cultural policy, and obscured by the specific image of *"Revolución y pachanga"* that became one of Cuba's cultural mobilization calls at home and abroad, this *guevarista* rhetoric around consciousness-building and the rejection of material incentives helped deflect more serious analysis of the accumulative, productivist logic underlying the statization of the economy and simultaneously complemented the New Left interest in converging forms of "cultural revolution" divorced from mechanistic materialisms.[27] In turn, the New Left's rejection of the kind of narrow economic determinism and the base-superstructure model, which characterized more rudimentary Marxisms, all too often resulted in the failure to consider economic and material arguments altogether. As Stuart Hall put it:

> What has resulted from the abandonment of this deterministic economism has been, not alternative ways of thinking questions about the economic relations and their effects, as the "conditions of existence" of other practices, inserting them in a "decentred" or dislocated way into our explanatory paradigms, but instead a massive, gigantic and eloquent disavowal. As if, since the economic in its broadest sense, definitely does not as it was once supposed to do, "determine" the real movement of history "in the last instance," it does not exist at all![28]

The significance of Dumont's critique therefore extends beyond the granular issues of agrarian development and the economic history of socialist transitions. While the expansion of transnational markets from the 1990s onward has made possible analyses of the Cuban state's capitalist ventures in recent years, and a narrow language of state capitalism was reintroduced by Fidel in the 1990s and was later fully embraced in the *raulista* reforms, the critique of its political economy in previous decades has not caught up with other (post-)Marxian approaches to "actually existing socialisms" as systems defined not by opposition to capitalism but by a differently organized mode of capitalist production.

Before the 1971 arrest of the poet Heberto Padilla (the Padilla Affair) became the cause célèbre of the great divide regarding the changing sympathies of foreign intellectuals for the Cuban Revolution, it was the discussion about the speed and methods of the economic transition to communism that first set off deep disagreements with the socialist economists who had been invited to Cuba in the mid-1960s as foreign technicians: Mandel, Dumont, Bettelheim, Sweezy. It could be argued that the Great Economic Debate (1963–1964) was the most important, defining moment of the Cuban revolutionary transformation, and certainly it was the most relevant process to any historical balance of the socialist experience with revolutionary state takeovers in the twentieth century. Yet the prominence of the Padilla Affair, and the many more books that have been written about it, is symptomatic of certain historiographical tendencies that view the 1959 Cuban Revolution simply as a succession of victories and betrayals or that continue to organize history around the stories of notable individuals. Meanwhile, the circulation of one image of these economic debates and transformations—as a fight against material incentives—over other characterizations like Dumont's—as a process of statist dispossession—is tied to the uneven travels of some accounts over others.

For all the contemporary neglect that surrounds his work on Cuba today, Dumont was the protagonist of his own cause célèbre in the early months of 1971 and was accused of being a CIA asset, though this was eclipsed by the more publicized arrest of Padilla for counterrevolutionary sympathies on March 20, 1971. An article published in *Le Monde* (March 4, 1971) reproduces a press note by the French version of the Cuban PCC periodical *Granma* from February 21 alleging the Cuban agronomist Raúl Alonso Olivé had been arrested earlier that year for providing the CIA with information about Cuban agriculture and for passing on this and other data to Dumont, thereby establishing Dumont's direct link to a Cuban CIA asset.[29] According to Dumont, however, he had met Alonso Olivé—a Cuban expert in pangola grass, black beans, papayas, and other crops—at the suggestion of the revolutionary government's own agency for agriculture and land reform during his first trip to Cuba. The CIA's declassified report on these events sheds further light on the specific contribution and threat that a critique like the one asserted by Dumont posed to Cuban leaders. Declassified in 2006, a special weekly report titled "Castro and His Critics" (July 16, 1971) details how the CIA analysts interpreted Fidel's reactions to Dumont and Karol. As depicted in this report and in others, Dumont and Karol continue to be considered "pro-Castro" and pro-Revolution critics by the CIA: the anonymized analysts give credence to their specific observations, but as can be expected they do not dwell on socialist theoretical subtleties and differentiation.[30] In fact, the content of Dumont's and Karol's analysis seems to be far less interesting to the CIA analysts compared to Fidel's reaction to their criticism, namely, his inability to accept expert criticism and implement change.

This reaction, and the CIA analyst's interpretation of it, are particularly relevant in light of one of Fidel's most effective and commonly repeated arguments against breaking ranks to dissent with, or criticize any aspect of, the revolutionary leadership's decision-making, even from a place of commitment and support: doing so would give weapons to the enemy. But this enemy had vast intelligence resources of its own and little need for such ammunition.[31] Conversely, the repression of dissent from the left was an effective tool of power consolidation, eliminating internal reform mechanisms and consequently preventing the success of alternative socialist models. The automatic dismissal of any other outsider's opinion as just another form of subtle colonialism became an official narrative precisely at this time. Directed explicitly toward many of the same personalities he had once welcomed as foreign technicians and international ambassadors, Fidel's famous response to the foreign critics of the Padilla Affair in his closing speech at the First Congress of Education and Culture in 1971 accused them of projecting liberal bourgeois notions onto Cuban socialism when they condemned lack of press freedom or the censorship of artists and intellectuals—an "intellectual gossiping" that was very far from everyday people's needs and desires. This tactical displacement of any critique of the revolution onto the sphere of bourgeois notions of freedoms is part of what makes Dumont's interventions, as much as their poor reception, all the more relevant both to a materialist analysis of Cuban socialism and to a theoretical and historical reassessment of its relationship with the global New Left.

Dumont's definitive expulsion from Cuba becomes a comic episode in Enzensberger's memoir/travelogue. The final straw came when (allegedly) the French agronomist voiced his dislike of Fidel's camembert experiment just when the leader's calamitous adventures with the dairy industry were taking off. In contrast to the matter-of-fact, data-rich style of Dumont's reports, the emphasis in Enzensberger's literary treatment of these same events, from a similar perspective, is on the power of narratives to shape collective perceptions of history and revolution and on the power of literature to investigate and demystify them.

The 2014 publication of Enzensberger's memoir/travelogue from the 1960s, *Tumult*, provides yet another opportunity to review the ways in which accounts of the trip to socialism have been explained away by reductively psychologizing the figure of the New Left intellectual or by focusing on a narrow corpus that fits those characterizations. Critical reception of Enzensberger's Cuban works, and of his magnum opus, *The Sinking of the Titanic* (1980 [1977]), in particular, highlights how the Cuban Revolution served as raw matter, as a formally clever and politically expedient device to address the impasses of a German left caught between the FGR and GDR as two equally undesirable models. In such a reading, the sinking of the *Titanic* is but a natural metaphor for a misplaced emotional investment, another story about the disillusion with and failures of twentieth-century socialism understood as the armed takeover of state power.[32]

But *Tumult* cannot be categorized as yet another testament to that narrative of melancholic disappointment. And neither can *The Sinking of the Titanic*, for that matter. Indeed, Enzensberger's voice as a contemporary narrator of a past life is estranged from, but does not renounce, his younger self. The narrator refuses to draw conclusions from the exercise of the memoir: "It is with reluctance that I leaf through the memoirs of my contemporaries. I don't trust them one inch. . . . The transitions between a deliberate lie and tacit improvement, between a simple mistake and subtle self-presentation are difficult to determine."[33] The significance of these travels, based on diary entries and annotated clippings, is reconstructed in the act of a double contextualization, and respective cross-examination, of past and present convictions. The aged author ("85, more or less") interviews his younger self, "a stranger to me . . . a younger brother I hadn't thought of for a long time," with postscripts and poems interspersed throughout.[34] The text unpacks many of the themes contained in Enzensberger's earlier essays and poems as the literal unpacking of the writer's forgotten personal archive of two trips to Russia and of his time living in Cuba when he stumbles upon them in a basement (or so we are told). The formal treatment of the first-person narrator, the cross-examination of memory, the descriptive punches thrown at other famous personalities of the decade, and its characteristically unforgiving skepticism toward all parties, including the author himself, make *Tumult* a metacritical work of socialist travelogues.

Surveying revolutionary changes, whether positive or ill-advised, *Tumult* highlights the continuity of the legacies of colonial history, chauvinism, racism, petty corruption, and "the everyday deal by which loyalty is exchanged for pay and obedience for toleration."[35] The year 1969 finds him in Havana studying the 1959 issue of *Bohemia*, Cuba's leading magazine, the first issue following the victory of the guerrillas. Enzensberger is amused to find in the same issue a condemnation of the Soviet intervention in Hungary (considering how Cuba's strategic support of the Soviets' 1968 Czechoslovakian invasion is fresh in 1969) and Fidel's early speech reassuring that the revolution would not be a communist one: "These old newspapers give a snapshot of a time. The revolution is in the balance, at its most dangerous moment. The mixture of mutiny and marketing—Guevara on the left and Brilliantine on the right—that was normal at the time but is disturbing today."[36] "Today" here means the scarcity of the late 1960s, which was nonetheless framed and accepted largely as a necessary sacrifice, the combined result of a very real US economic war and, as it was still possible to be read then, the government's trials and errors with an unprecedented process.

The travelogue examines the poet's memories of 1968 and 1969 after the Revolutionary Offensive, experiencing the outcomes of the Great Economic Debate. The parallels between then and now—the unpredictable repetitions of scarcity and precarity, of change and continuity, and of the always-present parallel, informal markets—mean that Enzensberger could have written the following passage about 2022 instead of about 1968: "In the summer of 1968, there was a flourishing black market. . . . Workers sold shoes they'd made from old car upholstery and strips of leather they'd stolen from their shoe factory. . . . The Cubans, who had lived in one of the most fertile countries in the world, had too little to eat."[37] Similar to Dumont, who confronted these same continuities of revolutionary mismanagement, Enzensberger mulls over more conscientious, informed approaches to change and the negative impact of the flattery and self-deception contained in the travel accounts of foreign intellectuals like Sartre. The economic and structural focus of Dumont's and Enzensberger's works also set them apart from other better-known and occasionally critical travelogues, like Andrew Salkey's *Havana Journal* and Ernesto Cardenal's *En Cuba*, which record problems they encounter but whose observations remain at the level of personal and implementation errors.

The anecdotes in *Tumult* will not be altogether surprising to those familiar with Enzensberger's "On Leaving America," *Havana Inquiry, The Sinking of the Titanic*, "Tourists of the Revolution," "Portrait of a Party," "Constituents of a Theory of Media," and poems such as "Lachesis Lapponica" and "Old Revolution." All these works deal directly or indirectly with his Cuban sojourn or with Cuba as an object of international revolutionary desire. *Tumult* parallels the main historiographical investigations of *The Sinking of the Titanic* only now in autobiographical key, that is, the place of enunciation of the poet as artist and as human vis-à-vis history and the questioning of historical memory as a construct between event and process, experience and representation. This is not to say that Enzensberger's poems are reducible to or explained away by his prose works or that *Tumult* finally establishes the author's real intent. I argue that they must be read together because the conversation between the two illuminates the philosophical projects of these texts—as critical meditations on the experience of revolution—as much as it underscores the political implications of the interpretations and dismissals they have elicited.

What is perhaps his best-known Cuban poem, *The Sinking of the Titanic*, demystifies epic visions of history by retelling it as a shared story of believing in and becoming ushers of a different world, deconstructing the exceptionalities of Cuban socialism as a chronotope in the process. In the twenty-ninth canto, for example, this historiographical problem of framing revolutions in terms of endings and beginnings, of conceiving them as visions of total change, fully comes to the fore:

> What were we talking about? Ah yes, the end!
> There was a time when we still believed in it
> (What do you mean by "we"?), as if anything
> ever were to founder for good, to vanish
> without a shadow,
> to be abolished once and for all,
> without leaving the usual traces,
> the famous Relics from the Past—
>
> a curious kind of confidence!
> We believed in some sort of end then
> (What do you mean by "then"? 1912? 1917? '45? '68?)
> and hence in some sort of beginning.
> By now we have come to realize
> That the dinner is going on.

Faith in the one revolution to finish them all ("there was a time we still believed") and in a single collective subject of historical change ("What do you mean by 'we'?") gives way quickly to the realization that putative ends and beginnings—the very discursive logic of postrevolutionary triumphalism—cannot do away with the present pasts.[38] The temporalities of revolution and of social change do not march in step ("the dinner is going on"). Jennifer Hosek rightly reads the poem as staging "a commonly fated, interconnected world of constrained actors," yet it is far from clear whether that also means that through this emphasis on continuities and grievances the text "simultaneously forecloses the possibility for fundamental improvement. Through subjectivity and multiplicity, the poem suggests reform rather than radical change."[39] Contrary to this reformist interpretation, elsewhere in the poem, and in other texts about Cuba, Enzensberger's questions revolve around whether the revolution failed because it did not go far enough, because it did not go where it should have gone (e.g., to the working masses), or because it could not do so given specific political and theoretical constraints:

> I didn't want to admit to myself
> that the tropical party was all over.
> (What do you mean by party? It was need,
> you bloody fool, need and necessity.)[40]

The phrase inside the parentheses parodies precisely the discourse of former revolutionaries, voiced in the preceding lines, who, disappointed by history, might embrace the realpolitik of reform. The self-interrogating, multitudinous voices that follow it recognize the historical necessity of, and the popular demands for, the revolutionary event itself while denying the messianic utopianism of its uncritical supporters as a form of understanding history (or of doing politics, for that matter): a phrase like "need and necessity" speaks to those two dimensions of the revolution.[41]

This ill-fated party theme returns in a dinner scene, a recurring formal device in the poem, where guests and menu change but the dinner goes on, like history. Accordingly, the revolutionary dinner between foreign fellow travelers in the Hotel Nacional, throwing each other pieces of bread and quotes from Marx and Engels, takes place "where the gangsters used to dine long ago." In an international media context that wants to publicize and exalt only positive revolutionary changes—the improved situation from the prerevolutionary past, the possibilities of the future—Enzensberger uses the dinner metaphor to highlight continuities instead, comparing the prerevolutionary alliance between the American mafia and the Cuban ruling elites with the one between the foreign observers and the new guerrillas in power.

Like *Tumult*, Enzensberger's *Titanic* is a critique of a revolutionary theory that presents socialism as a fait accompli after a state takeover, but it is not an indictment of the demand for radical change. If anything, it is the tragic staging of the possibility of its survival, embodied in the lone survivor of the wreck who swims and cries. The poem hardly pits reform against revolution. The poem's apparent political undecidability, its ironic self-distancing, and its polyphony of selves are hardly expressions of reformist regret but rather deliberately deployed aesthetic devices that invite readers and comrades to a politically uncomfortable philosophy of history, cognizant of contingency and indeterminacy, in which the pattern should be visible by now: "What I wish you, as I wish myself and us all, is a little more clarity about our own confusion, a little less fear of our own fear, and a little more attention, respect and modesty in the face of the unknown."[42] In this sense, Enzensberger's poem embraces a post-Marxist understanding of revolutionary politics, giving poetic voice to the dialectical play between the internal logical contradictions and the powerful social effects of all discourses of radical emancipation, from Christianity to communism.[43] Above all, the poem reflects on the significance of the stories we tell ourselves about history. The *Titanic* may have sunk, but we are still haunted by its demise.[44]

As in "Tourists of," Enzensberger writes in *Tumult* about foreigners as if he were not one, and about Cubans as a foreigner who knows all too well what he is, while questioning the presuppositions that condition that gaze. In "Tourists of, " that self-aware distance outlines the limitations of a literature written by politically inspired travelers to ideologically exotic locations. The text examines the production of these texts in the context of propaganda wars between actually existing capitalist and communist political apparatuses, not the travelers' personal commitments or motivations. The larger epistemological issue, asserts Enzensberger, is that these modes of travel and their narratives hinge on individual—and highly individualized, when they took place as part of official guided tours—experiences that were read in rarified informational contexts.

Whatever their aesthetic value and political purpose, these narratives could hardly be asked to inform accurately, much less to offer the kind of comprehensive scholarship that could not be produced, yet was urgently needed, about the different historical experiences with revolutionary state socialism. He criticizes in particular those who stayed discussing Lukàcs in the lobby of the hotel while ignoring the water shortages of the working classes outside. For any renovation of the trip to Cuba, the concluding prescription of Enzensberger's "Tourists of " might be as good advice as it was then: "Now that traveling is ceasing to be an individual privilege, it should then be possible to launch a massive attack on this overdue task that no one has performed as yet: the analysis of socialist societies or those that go by that name. Individual messengers cannot undertake such an investigation."[45] Significantly, this text is not simply a critique of fellow travelers. It is a critique of the travel-to-socialism genre, of the conditions in which it was carried out and written about. Above all, it encourages analyses of Cuban socialism from a materialist, empirical perspective instead of those that make the facts fit the theory, in which the anecdote matches the expectation. Continuity and change framed the inherently editorialized narratives of revolution and, as such must be subjected, now as much as then, to historiographical scrutiny. Stumbling upon the fragmented archive of his travels to socialism in *Tumult*, the back-and-forth between the present/narrator and the past/youth puts this reminder in circulation once more.

With the exception of short essays published while he was still living in Cuba (e.g., *Las Casas y Trujillo* [1969]), Enzensberger's Cuban works were published on the island only in the samizdat cultural journal *Diáspora(s)* in 1997; it was a very short selection. The addition of *Tumult* to his Cuban works sets up a parallel between his 1960s sojourn and the present, as it highlights the relevance of his prescient concerns with partisan conceits and with continuity and change as problematic frameworks for the Cuban revolutionary experience. Another important clue to contextualize Enzensberger's Cuban works is his concurrent interest in, and historiographical treatment of, the confrontations between communists and anarcho-syndicalists during the Second Spanish Republic and the Spanish Civil War in *Der kurze Sommer der Anarchie: Buenaventura Durrutis Leben und Tod* (published in 1972, three years after his return from Cuba).

As a formally astute and politically atypical account, Enzensberger's *Tumult* is a vantage point from which to retrace the history of change and continuity as the built-in framework of these travel narratives: the measuring of the distance between theory and practice, the sounding of the depth of the revolutionary ruptures with what came before. A less common practice is to distinguish, as Enzensberger and Dumont do in these works, socialist change—sustainable change that targets economic and social injustices—from change for change's sake, or change for the benefit of outside observers and of the new ruling elites. While Dumont and Enzensberger are seldom read with the better-known corpus of travel accounts to the Cuban Revolution, they deviate from the standard narratives of disappointment with socialism, historical betrayal, and youthful or politically naïve enthusiasm voiced by estranged positions of solidarity at a distance. Their everyday observations and the theoretical conclusions they draw from the process, speaking as political constituents rather than as mere visitors, demonstrate the range of critical positions from the left at the very onset of revolutionary transformations.

New Itineraries for an Old Revolution

Old travelers wanted to see it because it had changed, they were told; new travelers want to see it because it hasn't, they are told.

Immediately after Obama's and Raúl's simultaneous announcements of 2014, as narrated by Carlos Manuel Álvarez in "Cuba post Castro, una aproximación," "Havana begins to be flooded by tourists. The hipsters of the world hurry to book their plane tickets. Everyone wants to see the last retro corner of the West before it disappears. With '50s cars, no WhatsApp, no Smartphones, with people not on their way to work their heads sunk in their touch screens, but elbowing each other to climb first on an overcrowded bus."[46] This is an excerpt from the opening text of a series of *crónicas* about what's new and old in twenty-first-century Cuba, *La tribu: Retratos de Cuba*, a collection of essays first published in emerging digital platforms like *OnCuba* and *El Estornudo* and other international media outlets. The texts polemicize with the image of Cuba as a doubly exotic space of exception in postsocialist times—a Caribbean communism—and counter flat narratives of the contemporary by offering a wide array of characters and experiences: new Cuban images in the form of prose "portraits" (*retratos*) of the "tribe" (*tribu*) aimed at an equally eclectic audience. Álvarez engages with those tropes from the consciously assumed perspective of a millennial *cronista*: with the sensibility of a compulsive selfie-taker, he captures the effects of the decentralization of the state at the same time that the socialist signs of the Cuban Revolution remain ubiquitous in the twenty-first century.

A similar sense of distance between Cuban reality and the new alliances resulting from high-level talks between the two governments inspired a popular (shared, liked) comic by the political cartoonist and well-known satirist of Communist Party media outlets Alen Lauzán: "The bad thing about the thaw is that we keep on being penguins," reads the caption in a city of penguins with the Cuban capitol building in the background now flying the US and Cuban national flags together. Released around Obama's visit to Cuba in March 2016, the reggaeton singer Yulién Oviedo's song "Cuba Is Fashionable" echoes instead those who celebrated the normalization as the beginning of a mutually beneficial affair in which Cuba's most important offer to the world was its congenital, easygoing hedonism rather than its revolutionary fervor of yesteryear: "Whoever doesn't come here is crazy, because the bridge has been built. . . . The party never stops / we begin at night and don't stop 'til the morning," etc. An open-air Chanel fashion show on the sumptuous colonial walkway of the old city in May 2016 certainly answered that invitation.[47]

With Cuba imagined as a unique cocktail of revolution and rumba, as a land frozen in time, as a digital detox destination, and as the last bastion of socialism in the Western Hemisphere, at the heart of the new trip to the island nation are two narratives folded into one: this new trip builds on the assumptions and expectations of the old trip to Cuba, but the new travelers' relationship to Cuba is quite different from the relationship between the fellow travelers of the 1960s and Cuban socialism as a project still under construction back then. If the significance of the 1959 Cuban Revolution, to progressive and conservative forces alike, was once its symbolic and practical *exportability* (as witnessed by Che Guevara's *foco* theory and by Cuba's central role in transnational left networks and nonaligned struggles during the Cold War discussed above), it could be argued that it is the *portability* of the accounts of its postsocialist survival—instantly and seamlessly communicable and consumable but politically, historically, and geographically contained—that challenges and inspires alike its global constituents in the twenty-first century to embark on a new trip to Cuban socialism, long after the idea of a revolutionary takeover of the state apparatus has lost political and theoretical viability.

Political personalities and the global culture industry—celebrities, films, TV episodes—rushed to capitalize on the moment. A corpus of new Cuban images proliferated, superimposed on the established postcards of vintage nostalgia and allegorical ruin, of poor but happy people, of sexually assertive mixed-race dancers in a tropical playground of utopian wills elsewhere foreclosed. Beyoncé and Jay-Z, Katy Perry, Mick Jagger, Laura Pausini, the Kardashians, the leaders of the Armed Forces of Colombia, *Fast & Furious 8*, *Transformers: The Last Knight*, *Mozart in the Jungle*, Patriarch Kirill, Pope John Paul II and Pope Francis, the late chef Anthony Bourdain, *Top Gear*, Netflix, Airbnb, Google, Putin, and a continuously expanding cast have partaken in the new trip to Cuba over the past two-plus decades, featuring in various media as part of some momentous if vaguely defined historical happening. The opening scenes of *Transformers* reenact Cuba's exceptionality: "Transformers are declared illegal on earth. The world has set up a new paramilitary force, the TRF. Except in Cuba, Castro lets them sun on his beaches."[48] Despite significant transformations since the 1990s, this industry of (dis)enchantment is still based on images of "a land preserved in time," as the ad for the 2019 screening of Peter Chang's *Cuba: Journey to the Heart of the Caribbean* at the Boston Museum of Science puts it, publicizing the latest in a string of audiovisual high-end productions purporting to capture a glimpse of the island's vanishing singularity.

However, the present appeal of a vintage Cuban socialism is hardly an unqualified nostalgia for the past, a run-of-the-mill Ruinenlust. The deep political crises in the United States during the 1960s—the Vietnam War in particular—drove fellow travelers like Enzensberger, who at the time was in residence at Wesleyan University, to stay in Cuba for a time.[49]

How many of today's political crises tempt the contemporary traveler to see the island firsthand? How many of today's democratic failures have inspired a look back through the archives? The public image of the trip to Cuba continues to be shaped by the accounts of celebrity travelers (as Enzensberger had warned against). Yet Cuba hardly functions anymore as a direct vehicle to question inequalities and oppression elsewhere: its revolutionary model is no longer reproducible on the global stage. But how are we to understand, if we take it seriously as a symptom, a verse such as Jay-Z's "I'm like Che Guevara with bling on, I'm complex" from "Public Service Announcement (Interlude)," one of the most iconic songs of the rapper at a turning point of a revamped hip-hop industry?[50] Beyoncé and Jay-Z's 2013 much-publicized trip to Cuba had something in common with Simone de Beauvoir and Jean-Paul Sartre's 1960 visit, namely, a search for an alternative, even if the alternatives were only superficially the same: from "socialism with swing" to socialism with bling.[51]

The desire to go before "it" changes is the desire to witness, whatever its failures and achievements, historical evidence that radical political change was, at some point, a real possibility. Cuba is not just a theme park of the Cold War, a place where tourists go to confirm the failure of socialism.[52] Fairly or not, it is also a pilgrimage site for unfulfilled political desires in a present searching the past for new vocabularies of social justice. Simultaneously, Cuba's function as political museum shields that desire from its expression into any concrete political gesture, staging its continued commodification instead: Cuban exceptionality is an alibi against structural critique, the neutralization of utopian thought in the present. Just as Cuba was in the 1960s a constitutive part of the Third World as a space of transnational alliances and structuralist critique for the New Left, the trip to Cuba today is the space of mutual (mis)recognition in which historical disillusionment with one's own political context meets collective *hauntologies*—the persistent desire for another future against all odds, the refusal to give in to "capitalist realism," that is, the impossibility to imagine an alternative.[53]

The spatial politics of these political desires predates the 1959 Cuban Revolution. Cuba's emergence as a tourist destination for US citizens was cemented as a direct consequence of the 1920 alcohol prohibition laws, when the number of Cuba-bound US tourists also doubled. As we can see from the Bacardí advertising campaign posters and postcards of the period, the expansion of the Cuban rum company in this decade—Hatuey beer was launched in 1927—dovetailed with Cuba's growing reputation as a conveniently close place for carefree fun, relaxed restrictions, a delightful climate, and charming people. In fact, one of the stated aims of the revolutionary movement after 1959 was to end Cuba's status as a dissolute playground of Mafia-managed entertainment. The forbidden product being consumed in later trips to Cuba may have been different—first alcohol, then socialism—but what remained was the idea of Cuba as a provider of transgressive desires not available to travelers in their homelands: alcohol in the 1920s, radical politics from 1959 onward. The difference is that while travelers did find what they were looking for in the island in the first half of the twentieth-century—unadulterated liquor and licentious adventures—they could not find a legitimate socialist project in Cuba—not in the early 1960s, when it could have been seen at least as a still unrealized possibility, and much less sixty-plus years after that. Dominant discourses about Cuba continue to traffic in different versions of this (dis)enchantment with the Cuban Revolution. Cycles of economic adjustment and official reports from within respond with images of continuity, refurbished heroism, and calls for investments and solidarity at once. In some narratives, therefore, Cuban socialism remains or is reactivated as an international object of political desire; in others it is the global market that emerges as a national object of desire instead, a localized desire that is codified and managed differently within and beyond Cuban borders by different constituencies and stakeholders.

The new trip to Cuba is therefore a contradictory operation, but it is not a politically hollow one: it is reliant on the supposed exceptionalism of Cuba, but at the same time it renders it as just another chic destination of the Global South, thereby proving, even accelerating, its nonexceptionality. (The plot in *Fast & Furious 8* moves seamlessly among Havana, New York, and Berlin.) The local economy has felt the paradoxical effects of these operations: in the 1990s, state-managed infrastructures for international tourism had been presented as the solution to continue to subsidize social programs after the loss of Soviet support, but while some sectors of the new private economy have benefited greatly—as the state tourist facilities compete with an emerging and increasingly sophisticated private sector catering to tourists—food scarcity and prices have rocketed whenever already strained resources have been redirected to satisfy this sudden rise in demand. The reopening of Varadero beach resorts to jump-start international tourism during the COVID-19 pandemic led to a public health crisis in Matanzas Province that contributed to the street protests of July 11, 2021.[54]

Under the surface of History (with the capital *H*), there have been social, cultural, and economic changes bubbling up against these odds since the 1990s. Yet simultaneously Cuba continues to be presented as being on the brink of an imminent transformation forever postponed: from the exiled salsa star Willy Chirino's 1991 classic hit "Nuestro día ya viene llegando" (Our day is coming) to the latest reports in the *New York Times* stating "no one can predict what will happen to Cuba in the coming years, which is why you must rush there now. As in, right now."[55] This version of the end of the Cuban Revolution has been, above all, a projection stemming from the dissolution of Eastern European communisms between 1989 and 1991. The day of reckoning, like all apocalyptic prophecies, keeps getting recalculated and postponed by its prophets. This does not mean that old travels are not remediated, too: the state-sponsored Coloquio Internacional Patria invited young, foreign digital media influencers who support the revolution and identify as left-wing. In the historic Casa de las Américas on March 15, 2022, they debated anti-imperialist and anticapitalist digital and social media strategies and promoted Cuban socialism as a viable destination once again—as a place to go to, as a model to aspire to.

Sensationalized accounts of the trip to a new Cuba as a narrative genre—those that continue to represent it as an exotic land frozen in time or as a heroic monolith of socialist survival for better or worse—also tend to eclipse the other trips of Cuban postsocialisms today, different from the one-way mass exoduses of the 1960s, *El Mariel* in 1980, and the raft phenomenon of the 1990s. Many Cubans now come and go—as rented workers, as mules, as flexible migrants—and make up an emergent formal and informal network importing cultural and material commodities and creating new routes of remittances. Like most of us, twenty-first-century Cubans—or at least an increasing number of them—have the ability to generate, access, and share images of themselves in dialogue with those from abroad and those of mainstream and official media. They show not only how Cubans see themselves but also how they want to be seen and how they imagine and construct the world(s) they inhabit—where they see change, where they see none—and how these accounts travel in a new mediascape. It is not even required to talk to people; now that it is less dangerous as Enzensberger points out above—they are actively involved in the production of their own images: the images are talking back.

A brief comparison between Fidel Castro's trip to New York City in April 1959 and the responses to Obama's visit to Havana in March 2016 can further illustrate the composite political imaginaries of the global postsocialist condition and the myriad contexts through which postsocialism travels as it is lived, represented, and critically interrogated across narratives of continuity and change in this new Cuban mediascape.

Google searches about Cuba spiked in March 2016 during Obama's visit to the island, much as they had in December 2014, when the rapprochement between the two governments was first announced. The unprecedented visit of a sitting US president in almost a century, and the well-documented and thoroughly studied love/hate affair of Cubans and Americans since at least the 1895–1898 Spanish–American War, could have predicted a reasonably warm reception. But all accounts report the veritable skipping of a national heartbeat. Here was the ultimate "new trip" to Cuba.

If Obama's 2008 victory as the first US Black president was a historical watershed, during his 2016 visit its symbolic weight was rekindled by many Cubans and appropriated as their own, much like New Yorkers falling in love with Fidel during his visit in April 1959. Now available on YouTube, an archival newsreel commentary by Peter Roberts of "News of the Day" highlights just how many Americans looked up to Fidel and Cuba's 1959 revolution as their own hero too: "New York's Pennsylvania Station rarely has seen anything like it. Only the magnetism of a Castro could produce it. For this is a spontaneous (inaudible) for sure unrehearsed enthusiasm greeting the Cuban premier, bearded Fidel Castro."[56] Half a century later, the rest of the world saw the significance of Obama's visit to Havana as the first of a US president to the country since 1928 and as the definitive crack in a Cold War–era iceberg with similar excitement.

For Cubans on the island there were far more remarkable aspects about Obama's personal rapprochement with Cuba. The palpable emotion is captured as he strolls with his family under the rain, in the videos recorded with phones and shared on YouTube and Facebook, where people scream, whistle, clap, cry, and cheer from their balconies and windows. Word on the street focused on their (seemingly) unaffected and unassuming demeanors, on their visit to a family-owned private restaurant (San Cristóbal, the same *paladar* made famous by Beyoncé and Jay-Z in 2013), and, above all, on their race. In this sense, the racial dimensions of Obama's 2016 Cuban trip must be juxtaposed with Fidel's visit to New York the following year in 1960—when he met with Malcolm X, stayed in the Hotel Theresa in Harlem, and cemented the ideological affinities and tactical alliances between the Cuban Revolution and the US civil rights movement.

Obama was visiting Cuba at a time when the historical record of the 1959 Cuban Revolution on race was being more openly and polemically questioned. This same historical record—a mix of successes, failures, and silences—was predicated on the achievements of the 1959 revolution in comparison with the abysmal, entrenched, and catastrophic racism of the United States, immortalized in Santiago Álvarez's classic photomontage *Now* and reaffirmed in Cuba's continued protection of Assata Shakur as a symbol of its historical solidarity with the US Black left. This bond, further secured in particular by Cuba's foreign policy record of solidarity and military support against South Africa's apartheid regime, has been rekindled and maintained through research missions and people-to-people travel as well. In the aftermath of one such trip in 1997, Manning Marable insisted on the indelible meaning of Cuban socialism to the Black American community: "For black America, Cuba remains part of the imagined community of the black world, a contradictory yet hopeful site of where race might be transformed, if not entirely dismantled, as a social force."[57] Such reflections open the volume of collected travel accounts of a delegation of African American scholars and writers, a trip to Cuba organized by the Institute for Research in African-American Studies at Columbia University and hosted by the now-dissolved Center for the Study of the Americas in Havana, published in the journal *Souls*. They highlight the multiple and legitimate forms of belonging that the 1959 revolution as a symbolic event and its aftermath as a particular reality continue to elicit around the world.

The polemics around the Cuban revolutionary politics of race exploded and intensified during the Special Period of the 1990s. The Obamas arrived at a time when Cuban and Cuban Afro-descendant scholars, artists, and activists were questioning the revolutionary myth of its socialist racial democracy: "The current and historical realities demonstrate the scant presence of black Cubans in the wealthiest and most influential sectors of society; while we represent the majority in the disempowered and poorer strati, and in prisons, of course."[58] These critiques pushed back against a long nation-building tradition of incorporating and supporting the participation of Cubans of African descent and the celebration Afro-Cuban culture as part of a seamless narrative of transculturation and where Black Cubans were celebrated primarily as "raceless Cubans" as part of a public reaffirmation of the narrative that racism belonged to the prerevolutionary past. The Obamas' visit, and the president's speech at the Gran Teatro de La Habana on March 22, 2016, underscored that contrast: "The visit brought visibility to something that wasn't non-existent in Cuba, but has been traditionally denied or misrepresented through history: black agency."[59]

A polemic about an article highly critical of Obama's visit published in the official press with a racist headline ("Negro, ¿tú eres sueco?" by Elías Argudín Sánchez in *Tribuna de la Habana* on March 24, 2016)—bringing attention to the subtle and not so subtle ways racism was alive and well in revolutionary Cuba—and Obama's own remarks during his Havana speech extolling the virtues of US-style democracy that had led him to the highest office of the country, show, when put in juxtaposition, the blind spots of both US and Cuban exceptionalism when confronting each other's official narratives:

> When I first started school, we were still struggling to desegregate schools across the American South. But people organized; they protested; they debated these issues; they challenged government officials. And because of those protests, and because of those debates, and because of popular mobilization, I'm able to stand here today as an African-American and as President of the United States. That was because of the freedoms that were afforded in the United States that we were able to bring about change.[60]

As head of state, however, Obama could not recognize the civil rights gains that he benefited from and simultaneously denounce the fact that he was an exception and not a representative example of the widespread institutional racism that had seen the Black Live Matters movement begin in 2013 to converge around this hashtag. And despite talks of thaws, mutual aid, understanding, and looking forward to the future, Obama also did not explicitly recognize how the US foreign policy toward Cuba in the 1990s contributed directly to the collective misery of the Special Period, to the popularization of the sentiment that Obama quoted (and mispronounced) in his speech: "No es fácil" ([Life] It's not easy). There were no self-critical attempts on behalf of the US government to recognize that the economic embargo that began under President John F. Kennedy—and that would remain in place after Obama because its abolition requires congressional action—had been a historical and a political mistake at the height of the Cold War.

For many Cubans, that critical horizon mattered little at the time of Obama's visit, when the Cubans' fervor for Obama reached its apogee. The prospects of participating in the American markets and benefiting from new investments opening to Cuba offered those on the island a glimpse of an immediate material improvement to their everyday lives that went beyond matters of ideological purity or nuance. "If Obama ran for election in Cuba now," I heard in conversation, "he'd win by a landslide." The Cuban humor duo Teatropello's YouTube skit "Obamanía" registers particularly well these racial and economic imaginaries mobilized by Barack Obama's visit to Cuba. In the skit, the sudden "sainthood" of Obama as a savior in the syncretic pantheon of Afro-Cuban religions sets up the pleas for the promised change that never arrived, while Obamanía itself becomes the subject of parody. The rise and fall of Obamanía in Cuba followed, though much more quickly, the same patterns of mania for Obama in the United States and elsewhere, synthesized in the narrative arc of the "Thanks, Obama" meme—from ambiguous sarcasm to wishful disappointment. When Obama announced the following year, in January 2017, that the "wet foot, dry foot" policy of automatically admitting Cubans who managed to arrive on land in US territory would end, the backlash was swift. A dramatic rise in border crossings followed thereafter, anticipating the elimination of the remaining provisions that offer political asylum and adjustment of migratory status to Cubans in the United States. These benefits set them apart from all other Latin American migrants, making Cuban Americans a disproportionally powerful, privileged political group in the United States.

Of the many viral memes that Obama's trip to Cuba generated, one encapsulates like few others the popular reception he received on arrival: it photoshops Obama's silhouette onto the façade of the Cuban Ministry of Interior, substituting Enrique Ávila's sculpted semblance of Che Guevara based on Alberto Korda's famous print "Guerrillero Heroico," which towers 36 meters over the Plaza de la Revolución (fig. 1.1). The digital mockup of what we could call an "Obama Heroico"—several versions of this meme went around social networks—summarized the range of attitudes on both sides of the Florida Strait, prompted by the March 2016 visit and its aftermath: adoration, curiosity, skepticism, gratitude, grievance, and irony (several other memes focused on Nicolás Maduro as a scorned lover in an impossible love/hate triangle between the United States, Venezuela, and Cuba). The "Obama Heroico" is an anonymous, user-generated (or at least user-circulated) image. Unlike an anecdote or a travelogue, it is a collectively made artifact: every share and like move it around and re-create it, no matter who created it first.

The "Obama Heroico" meme switches Che's quote "Hasta la victoria siempre" (Ever onward to victory!) for "No es fácil." This is one of the Cuban phrases that Obama's speechwriters chose for the US president to say in Spanish during his initial announcement of the change in relations on December 17, 2014: "Cubans have a saying about daily life, 'No

Figure 1.1. Obama Heroico. Cuban meme circa 2016.

es fácil.' It's not easy. Today the United States wants to be a partner in making the lives of ordinary Cubans a little bit easier, more free, more prosperous." A common catchphrase that connotes exasperation and hopelessness in response to a frustrating situation or person, it was popularized by a 1988 Van Van song:

> No es fácil, que no que no, no es fácil
> Mi mujer con sus peleas
> el agua que no llegó
> hay un juego de pelota
> y se rompió el televisor.

So while the saying is used to underscore quotidian hardships, it is used specifically to express exhaustion and impotence with an intractable situation. Recontextualized in the digital mockup, the optimistic promise in Obama's use of the phrase answers back in turn with a wary gaze, invoking the possibility of a new meaning: an Obama frustrated with what he finds in Cuba, and a Cuba frustrated with Obama's promises.

Before Obamania there was Gorbymania: this same narrative of hope and disillusion was rehearsed nationally before. A similar mood of anticipation and excitement preceded the historic visit of Mikhail Gorbachev in April 1989, a time when the Cuban government was juggling the need for continued Soviet support and the official rejection of Gorbachev's reform program as a model for Cubans to follow. The joke form of this expectation was a pun on the phonetic similarity of perestroika with "stoic waiting" in Spanish: "In the Soviet Union they have perestroika, in Cuba we have *la espera estoica* [the stoic waiting]." In many ways, the situation in 2014–2016 was a similar one: with the death of Hugo Chávez and the clear need to diversify further from its Venezuelan dependency, the Cuban government was looking for improved relations with the United States to jump-start economic growth, while vigorously resisting any political concessions to the regime-change components of America's Cuba policy. The key difference between then and now, however, is that Obama and Che—as stand-ins for capitalist and socialist promises, for global markets and national interests—seem fully interchangeable, equally subject to dismissal as would-be saviors. The "Obama Heroico" meme makes legible the apparent illegibility of their kinship. They appear pragmatically indistinguishable as far as everyday strategies that channel desires for cultural recognition and economic survival are concerned.

The meme is a paradigmatic example of what Hito Steyerl has called "a poor image," building on the Cuban film theorist Jorge García Espinosa's *Imperfect Cinema* to read the legacy of Third Cinema theory in the logic of circulation of the postmodern digital image:

> Poor images are the contemporary Wretched of the Screen. . . . They testify to the violent dislocation, transferals, and displacement of images—their acceleration and circulation within the vicious cycles of audiovisual capitalism. Poor images are dragged around the globe as commodities or their effigies, as gifts or as bounty. They spread pleasure or death threats, conspiracy theories or bootlegs, resistance or stultification. Poor images show the rare, the obvious, and the unbelievable—that is, if we can still manage to decipher it.[61]

All of these "poor images"—and not just visual images but texts, sounds, artifacts, practices—construe Cuban postsocialism differently. But all of them circulate sometimes parallel to, and at other times become embedded in, the media networks and interpretative communities where dominant narratives of Cuban postsocialism travel, too.

In this mediascape not all narratives are equally portable; neither are they allocated the same value. Here is where cultural critique and media analysis can elucidate where postsocialism as state capitalism makes itself visible—or not—in our own contemporary mediascape as much as in the past. As Enzensberger reminds us in *Tumult*, revolutionary travelogues— and now many of the portable accounts of Cuban postsocialism—are works of self-emplotment, the product of a subject who is self-consciously inserting and writing herself into what is perceived to be a historically and politically defining experience. As media that are put again and again into circulation, they constitute an archive of narratives upon which the trip to (post)socialism as a genre is built and endlessly reproduced. But if old trips to Cuba can still be found, and read anew, then perhaps new trips, and therefore modes of thinking beyond the postsocialist impasse when it comes to Cuba—being critical of the communist past, being critical of the neoliberal present—can be possible, too, though *no es fácil*.

CHAPTER 2

Portable *Pachanga*

What does postsocialism sound like? And why does it matter? If there is a sphere where the everyday narratives and rhythms of change and continuity in postsocialist Cuba take center stage, remediated, it is the sphere of music. Popular dance music has long been a representative vault of chronicles of everyday life, accompanying leisurely activities, political acts, religious ceremonies, and everything in between. Already in 1853, the Colombian Nicolás Tanco Armero—who would initiate the human trafficking of indentured Chinese workers, or coolies, from Macau to Cuba—noted that "everybody dances in Havana without regard for age, class, or standing.... All day one hears the dances being played, be it in private houses, or by the organs that roam the streets, to whose sounds the passerby usually dances."[1] From the 1920s onward, Cuban dance rhythms have been one of its most recognizable exports: rumba, mambo, *son*, cha-cha-chá. Simultaneously, popular music and dance have remained an important cultural site of contested negotiations over national identity. A vast scholarship deals with this two-sided dimension, addressing specialized questions from the perspectives of sound studies, ethnomusicology, and cultural anthropology, for example. Here I am interested in both more abstract and more specific questions than those generally addressed in those pursuits: To what extent do the sounds of Cuban socialism remain activated, and where have they been superseded by others? How do these continuities and changes shape the postsocialist soundscape, and what kinds of political narratives and imaginaries do they make (in)audible?[2]

Consider three contrasting yet representative points of entry into contemporary Cuban music (though there are many more):

Track #1: "I climbed onto the bus and it was surreal: my song was playing on the stereo! I paid 1 CUC for 2 weeks of promotion in *El Paquete*. But that one didn't stick." When I meet him in a dance floor, LOWE is twenty-two, a university student, theater actor, and aspiring trapton singer. He tells me how hard it is to hit that elusive triad of success: making a good song, securing recording and promotion financing, and resonating with the audience. Production with a good deejay and strategic placement in the popular sneakernet *El Paquete Semanal* (The Weekly Package, shortened to "*El Paquete*" herein) may translate into airplay but not always into popularity. LOWE plays me one of his trapton songs on a Huawei cell phone: a moody, beat-driven reflection on the commercialism, frivolity, and posturing of mainstream trapton and reggaeton artists, where money and social networking are more important than flow.[3]

In Cuba much like everywhere else, digital technologies for the production and dissemination of music outside of expensive professional studios, major labels, and financed airplay and promotion—from sneakernets to Spotify—have opened avenues of access to new voices, new sounds, and new topics and to the reissue of local catalogues for global audiences. Additionally, they have affected the state-owned recording studios, official musician associations, and mass media outlets. The postsocialist music scene has been impacted by the emergence of home music studios and alternative networks of music production and dissemination in particular. Foreign labels like Planet Records and Sony have also tapped into this emerging market and its new talent pools, generating a structure where local, underground popularity translates into international circulation and economic success after signing.

The cultural apparatus of the state has reorganized, too, to confront both the digital turn and its own entrance into the global market, tapping new commercial avenues for Cuban music and licensing its back catalogue. For example, the state recording label EGREM partnered with Sony in 2015 for the distribution of its collections, and in 2006 the National Council of Scenic Arts absorbed the originally underground urban music promoters P.M.M. (Por un Mundo Mejor [For a better world]). These cultural institutions of the bureaucracy seek to diversify their messages and offerings in the face of increasing competition while also maintaining a monopoly on traditional mass media and a grip on policing practices and styles that might erode the "Cuban music" brand or challenge their monopoly and policing power. Inasmuch as they partly overlapped with *reparto* subcultures, first *timba* and later reggaeton presented challenges to those interests; these styles remained crucial to the nightlife entertainment economy that was reborn with the state-managed tourism industry. This generated a contradiction between what the cultural critic Iván de la Nuez characterizes as the government's economic model, on the one hand, and its moral model on the other.[4]

Track #2: These changes intersect with the leftovers of a distinct revolutionary soundscape. The persistence of an explicitly politicized, collective aural memory is acutely present in discussions about and within Cuban music. At an impromptu postconference jam session in February 2015, Emily Maguire, a Cuban studies colleague, remarked that one could not help but notice that all the Cubans who grew up with the 1959 revolution knew by heart all the same songs, regardless of personal tastes and ideological commitments, and that every gathering ended with someone playing a guitar and everybody else singing along.[5] Similarly, in one of his posts, the literary critic Gilberto Padilla Cárdenas invites everybody to write in the article's comment section their own soundtrack of Cuban socialism, to join him in documenting "the hit parade of communism," that is, the songs that reinforced the revolutionary state's official narrative and amplified and made memorable its messages: "Don't political systems generate their own sonority—songs reduced to slogans—their own fanfare? The Cuban state is like that unbearable singer who instead of focusing on himself and the sound of his own voice observes the faces of his listeners in a bar, controlling everything."[6] Padilla Cárdenas's note is aimed at that same sonic community noted above by my colleague and highlights that the conditions—political, mediatic, generational—under which such a collective, self-reflective investigation of the sonic experience of Cuban socialist mass culture can be carried out are finally in place. In this sense, Cuba's contemporary soundscape is not only an opportunity to analyze how the meeting of digital media, international and domestic markets, music, and the state showcase contested narratives of the postsocialist present. It also invites a reflection on the afterlives of the performative homogeneity of socialist mass culture, which, just like capitalist mass culture, was neither as homogeneous nor always as narrowly ideological as its official soundtracks seem to suggest at first listening. Consequently, mapping this soundscape also attends to the lesser-heard forms of incomplete participation in, or outright subversion of, the sonic investments of the revolutionary party/state on the production of a national imaginary in its own image.

Track #3: The reach of this official soundtrack was not limited to Cuba or to Cubans abroad. If there was ever a soundtrack of the revolution, *nueva trova* (new ballad), and Cuba's foremost singer-songwriter of the movement, Silvio Rodríguez, would feature in it prominently. The digital afterlives of Silvio Rodríguez's 1992 song "El necio" (The fool) on YouTube—included in Padilla Cárdenas's list above—are another way to map both the historical importance and the postsocialist contexts of reception of the sonic imaginary of Cuban socialism beyond its national borders. The *nueva trova* emerged specifically under revolutionary conditions, and the genre became an international cultural ambassador of Cuba's socialist project. A socially conscious song movement, with a high dose of conversational lyricism and political commentary, and a purposeful demystification of musical spectacle and of the musician star-system, *nueva trova* overcame an initial suspicion from the authorities to gain full state support starting in 1967, with the Primer Encuentro Internacional de la Canción de Protesta in Varadero, Cuba, becoming part of a broader phenomenon with counterparts elsewhere in Latin America and North America. At a time when the right-wing repression of progressive cultural movements was on the rise in the Americas, this music served as a form of alternative sociability and political identification for the distinct forms of youth culture and student activism that emerged in the long 1960s.

I single out the song "El necio" because it reckons explicitly with the untimeliness of socialist revolutionary ideals after the disintegration of the socialist bloc in Eastern and Central Europe between 1989 and 1991. At a time when the old state anthems had nothing much new to offer as a way to rehabilitate the credibility of a state ideology facing an unprecedented existential crisis, "El necio" became a personal anthem to many "sincere believers," to borrow Slavoj Žižek's expression. With more than 20 million combined views on YouTube as of July 2020, the song is among the three most popular of Rodríguez's songs online, along with classics like "Mi unicornio azul" and "Ojalá," which became hits in earlier decades when Rodríguez was at the height his fame in Latin America. In "El necio," the poetic voice vows to hold fast to the ideological certainties of the past, to the old revolutionary ideals, keenly aware of their impertinent obsolescence but unwavering in the face of violent threats of political revenge and historical revisionism. He knows himself "a fool" for refusing to follow the changing tide of politics. From the perspective of its local context, the song parallels the official narrative of the old revolutionary guard who, unable to stir the country out of yet another collective trauma and self-inflicted crisis, doubles down on their position: "yo me muero como viví" (I [will] die as I lived), repeats the refrain. Driven by the guitar's down strums, the song's melancholic but defiant lyrics can be read from a domestic perspective as romanticizing the ruling bureaucracy's obstinate, dogmatic conservatism, rendering it instead as the righteous, incorruptible choice of an individual—a valiant fool—who resists an invitation to change his convictions even in the face of historical defeat:

> They invite me to repent
> They invite me to not lose
> they invite me to un-define myself
> they invite me to so much shit.

However, from a continental, digitally streamed perspective, listening to the song signals a rejection of the TINA (there is no alternative) myth, making it an anthem against its neoliberal legacy in Latin America.[7] The summer of 2019 witnessed a surge of massive street protests in Latin America against social and economic inequalities, against political instability and corruption, against state repression and police brutality, and against precarity and privatization—in short, against the active legacies of the aggressive neoliberal transformations ushered in by the US-backed right-wing military dictatorships of the second half of the twentieth century. Since the protests began, the YouTube comment sections for the different copies of Rodríguez's song resurfaced fiery debates about the 1959 Cuban Revolution and its mixed legacy for Latin American today. As protestors demanding social and economic justice took to the streets in Chile, Colombia, Argentina, Bolivia, Ecuador, Venezuela, as the people protested aggressively neoliberal austerity measures, foreign intervention in politics, and militarized statist repression and paramilitary violence, the heated commentary on Silvio Rodríguez's song ranged from denouncing the hypocrisy of Cuban leaders and the failures of its single-party state model to celebrating the inspirational value of the Cuban leaders' resolve against the insurmountable odds of antagonizing American imperialism.

Rodríguez's music remains a symbol of left-wing politics in the Spanish-speaking world and a key referent in the sentimental and political education of several generations. His interview in *Otra vuelta de tuerka*, the TV program of the Spanish vice president and leader of the Podemos political party Pablo Iglesias, and the comments on the YouTube video, highlight the role this music had in cementing the affective investments of an entire generation in the Cuban revolutionary project as a master signifier of the very notion of a Latin American socialist alternative. In the 2021 regional elections for the presidency of Madrid, the candidate of the neofascist party Vox, Rosario Monasterio, touted her heritage as the daughter of Cuban exiles who therefore knew how to combat the "cultural hegemony of the left" and the left's "totalitarisms," embodied (allegedly) in Iglesias's competing candidacy.[8] Surely there are no practical political affinities between Iglesias—the Podemos candidate who was also spokesperson for one of the most compelling progressive proposals to come out in the wake of the *indignados* movement—and the Cuban revolutionary guerrillas who substituted the Batista dictatorship they toppled with another one. But it is the space of symbolic legacies that allows for that ambiguous play between red-washing and red-baiting, which in turn fuels the mobilization of nationalist right-wing rhetoric around the political panic of Cuban socialism and its (ex)portability. With over 1.6 million monthly listeners on Spotify, Rodríguez music still proves compelling.[9] Cuban socialism as the site of actualization of the song's message is an image that continues to travel digitally across geographies and generations.

The recovery of an untimely political foolishness was not the only postsocialist remediation of the protest song genre taking place in the Cuban soundscape at large. As I traveled through Quito, Ecuador, in the summer of 2010, graffiti in the skatepark of the Carolina Park stopped me in my tracks: "Porno para Ricardo" (Porn for Richard). Written in large blue letters across a wall and without any explanation, it called on unsuspecting passersby to look up what that enigmatic and potentially naughty title was. Porno Para Ricardo was the name of a Cuban anticommunist punk band of short-lived notoriety, a group I had been hanging out with and writing about at the time. Tens of thousands of Cubans arrived in Ecuador between 2008 and 2015, the only country during this period for which Cubans needed no entry visa. Some headed to Quito to stay in the Andes; others pursued a long and perilous journey to the US border. When I returned to the park a week later—camera in hand to document my finding—the graffiti had already been painted over. However an ephemeral trace, the graffiti showed that other postsocialist narratives were traveling across generations and geographies: many Ecuadoreans were torn between, on the one hand, the urgent need for the reforms proposed by Rafael Correa's administration (Correa had been one of the electoral victories of the Pink Tide) and, on the other, warnings that he could follow in the footsteps of Cuban revolutionary leaders. The latter's corruption and authoritarianism—confirmed (as some Ecuadorians saw it) by the sudden mass arrival of these Cubans—had unleashed upon Ecuador a sudden flood of migrants from the island.

Finally, comments on the YouTube streams of Rodríguez's songs often compare the lost art of these classic protest songs to the aesthetic simplicity and the lack of political commitment of newer genres, like reggaeton, that make up the bulk of the playlists of today's Latin American youth culture. Never mind that the protest song has been revived in the feminist movements sweeping Latin America (though the movements' relationship with the traditional left parties in the region remains tense at best).[10] Such criticisms of reggaeton touch not only on generational shifts, ideological differences, and stylistic preferences but also on aesthetic value judgments steeped in class and race prejudices that marked the reception of popular music in the past and of reggaeton in the present. This contrast made the reggaeton version of "El necio," released in 2018 online by one of the most polemical representatives of Cuba's underground reggaeton style, Chocolate MC, a doubly subversive, and certainly scandalous, act. *Nueva trova* was the popular soundtrack of Cuban socialism, but there is no doubt that reggaeton reigns supreme in the postsocialist soundscape. And while the moral panic of reggaeton in Cuba shares some features with the negative reception that the unstoppably popular reggaeton has received in other Latin American contexts, it also shows features that speak directly to the symbolic and hegemonic functions of Cuban socialist sounds and the extent to which the postsocialist soundscape brings them into question.

A sequel to his influential work on urban space and the category of the everyday, Henri Lefebvre's last book, *Rhythmanalysis* (2004 [1992]), invites us to think about city spaces from the perspective of sound, specifically rhythm. One can reframe other questions Lefebvre raises in that work and his previous ones addressing socialist space: whether socialism produced its own space, and how that inquiry might help us probe into the nature of what actually existing socialism was, instead of what it was said, "so confusedly," to be.[11] Suppose, then, that we tuned into the sonic life of postsocialism as part of this inquiry: Was there a (Cuban) socialist sound? What does (Cuban) postsocialism sound like today? And what kind of rhythmic patterns of power, capital, and life would a rhythmanalysis of the (post)socialist city play up? Even a minimal nod to Lefebvrian rhythmanalysis, for instance, could challenge ruinology as the dominant approach to Cuban culture. From the 1990s onward, Cuba has been widely advertised, and has advertised itself, as "frozen in time." As a result, Cuba's démodé artifacts—its deteriorated physical appearance, the sweet cadence of the congas and flutes of the traditional *son*, the apparent survival of its revolutionary state—routinely double as outpost signages in the story of the passing of twentieth-century socialism everywhere else, or as vintage collectibles, ready-made scenes of a commercial(izable) desire, a desire that consumes a present desperately searching for political reinvention in the shared experience of a once radical past.

Ana Dopico has shown how the visual language of the photography of Cuban transportation, through the foreign lens especially, performs an imperial, consuming gaze, reinforcing peripheral notions of anachronism and ahistoricity.[12] As if no time has passed at all, when I arrive at the Boston Museum of Science on August 19, 2019, to watch Peter Chang's *Cuba: Journey to the Heart of the Caribbean*, a traditional-sounding but electronically mixed Cuban *son* greets me in the lobby, playing across the ticketing area as a mood-setting prelude for this film essay on contemporary Cuba. Except in twenty-first-century Cuba, the music blasting from *almendrones* (as Cubans call their 1950s American cars) is no longer that of the *son*, still widely used to signal that we are in the presence of "Cubanness." In her landmark study of the media history of surfaces, Giuliana Bruno remarks in her passing through Havana that the city invites the intimate, projective, and reflective modes of the first person, of the travel diary, highlighting the beguiling sensuality of its museological charm: "Havana impressed me with its intense, and intensely ruinous, urban atmosphere. The layers of history that are deposited here are frozen in the surface of its fantastic architecture. In this city, history is written in stone and melancholically arrested in midair."[13] But are Havana's surfaces (still) readable only in their historical depth, as living ruins of a foreclosed collective dream? For example, why not listen to, rather than look at, that ultimate figure of Cuban vintage that is the refurbished 1950s American car, the *almendrón*, appearing in all those infinitely reproduced postcards of vintage Havana? As it happens, the vicissitudes of urban transportation are linked to the scandal of portable media; the postsocialist city can be heard at the intersection of popular music, digital media, and the informal economy. Tuning to an entirely new soundscape will take us further away from photogenic poverty and residual charm, from those static visions of Cuba as a place outside of the rhythms of the worldly contemporary that merchants of ruinology tend to fuel.

International images of Cuban socialism and national desires for global markets converge and confront each other in the realm of popular music. Novel, portable forms of listening and being listened to address the postsocialist cultural investments of both the state and the market in Cuba in a transformed media context. Two linked notions of the portable are at work here. One is a new sense of portability, that of digital media: made possible by its miniaturization (which makes content and devices available at home or easy to carry); by its increased affordability; by its sharing and streaming capabilities (expanding circulation and access, though often in unequal ways); by its customizability as personal accessory (making it part of new processes of identity formation and display); and above all by its additional productive—and not just reproductive—capabilities for the generation and circulation of cultural content by consumers and amateur artists (multiplying emergent voices and their audience reach). The other is a much older, sensorial mode of portability, that of music and lyric in the song form: the portability of the chorus/refrain as aestheticized speech that is easily memorized, that lingers and enters the popular lexicon as a ready-made semantic unit but whose semiotic possibilities are never fully closed, whether as text or as sound.

The meeting point of these two senses of portability—where old slogans and songs are remembered, remixed, or substituted—is where the polemics around the postsocialist remediation of Cuban music play out and where the battles over who gets to listen, be listened to, and preserve or redefine its brand are most ardently fought. In the section below, I discuss *pachanga* as a key concept that can guide us in tuning in to the heterogeneous sounds and tracks of Cuban postsocialist culture. I then consider how the production, circulation, and reception of punk and reggaeton in a new media context interrupt *pachanga* as the meeting space of state cultural policy and competing music markets, taking on issues of nationalism, class, and race in postsocialist Cuba.

Postsocialismo y Pachanga: from *P.M.* to P.M.M.

One of the unofficial slogans of the early revolutionary soundscape was "Revolution and *pachanga*," a descriptor of the Cuban revolutionary mood at the start of the 1960s. A type of dance music popularized in the late 1950s, just as the insurgence movement that led to the revolution was taking off, *pachanga* became a synonym for "fun party." Sometimes attributed to Ernesto "Che" Guevara, sometimes to Raúl Roa, the different senses in which the phrase *"Revolución y pachanga"* have been invoked are even more important than its origin: it has meant both a socialism accompanied by a festive, fun-loving spirit and a socialism a bit too informal and relaxed and therefore in need of corrective discipline. *Pachanga* thus functioned as a consensus-building tool as much as the calling card of Cuban socialism at home and abroad. This aesthetic of joy was a welcome contrast for a post-Stalinist left recovering from a crisis of credibility, but it also threatened the reorganization of labor and the transformation of social consciousness proposed by a revolutionary vanguard reared in guerrilla discipline, heir to a Catholic, white creole, bourgeois cultural sensibility. Thus *pachanga* stood for a fun conga session at a political rally, but it was also tied to popular imaginaries of leisure and working-class entertainment that had to be either harnessed or eliminated with the revolution, along with all other perceived vices of the prerevolutionary nightlife: gambling, prostitution, and conspicuous consumption of American commodities. Both senses of *pachanga*—the liberating and the disciplinary—influenced early international and domestic images of the Cuban revolutionary process and simultaneously informed cultural policy and its different receptions at home and abroad. This split reflected the same duality at the heart of Cuban socialism that we discussed in chapter 1.

One need not go further than Agnes Varda's classic *Salut les Cubains*, a photomontage that combines off-screen narration and Cuban music to capture the synthesis of socialism and cha-cha-chá. Throughout the piece, Varda's voiceovers remark upon the great contrast between the material poverty and the cultural wealth of the Cubans. Shown again in 2015–2016 along with archive photographs at the Pompidou, the thirty-minute film incorporates Cuban rhythms and dance as formal audiovisual devices in the making of a documentary about revolutionary change. Varda uses music as a way to organize the filmic experience around a different kind of moving image, calling attention to the moment of photography as a pause in a sequence of extra-photographic movements carrying on at the vertiginous rhythm of political transformations. Varda also puts popular dance music at the center of a quasi-anthropological gaze from which to understand a local kind of radical left political imaginary that appears inseparable from its fun-loving cultural traditions. Cristoph Kalter describes Cuba and Algeria this way: "The first two stations in the invocation of the Third World were attractive primarily because—as drivers, as models, as inspiration, or at least as a symbol—they stood for the radical break with the familiar the radical Left was after, but for which it found hardly any points of reference or connection in France, or in the First and Second Worlds overall."[14] For the global 1960s, *"Revolución y pachanga"* was a powerful image on two accounts. First, it combined the possibility of rejecting the Soviet monopoly on actually existing socialism, with its connotations of steely orthodoxy. Second, it tapped into the preexisting seductions of colonial tropical stereotypes that lived on the consumption of its melodies and rhythms: rebel masculinity, beautiful women, sexually charged festivity, racial and cultural remixing, and an inviting climate.

This image—plus the sounds that accompanied it, disseminated it abroad, and lingered in the imagination—is also at the core of another influential French account of the trip to socialist Cuba as a genre: Ania Francos's *La fête cubaine*. Songs and slogans appear alongside each other to shape a continuous experience of dance and revolution: "Les miliciens remontent dans leurs camions. '*Muchacha si los yankees vienen, quedan!*' Je veux bien le croire! Les camions démarrent et j'entends sur un air de chachacha: '*Que vengan (bis) pero-que-pongan-los-pies-que-vamos-a-darles-mimtrailletta-de-la-cabeza-a-los-pies*' [sic]." (The militias return to their trucks. *Girl if the Yankees come, they'll die.* I want to believe them! The trucks start and I hear them over a cha-cha-chá tune: *Let them come, but they put their feet here we are going to gun them up and down*.) Francos is attentive to, but powerless to resist, the sensory seduction of the political spectacle—mass parades, labor mobilizations, conversations with other international visitors and Cuban revolutionaries. Rifles and maracas become indistinguishable revolutionary instruments in this "great *pachanga*." The travelogue is a document of the ubiquity of a media campaign that construed the revolution as a street party with a new vanguard political party as master of ceremonies, promoting a very particular sonority to go along with it: "Radio-Rebelde qui diffuse en permanence les discours de Fidel, des consignes révolutionnaires et des chachacha" (Rebel Radio constantly broadcasts Fidel's speeches, revolutionary slogans, and cha-cha-chá).[15]

Like its images, its ambassadors, and its texts, the sounds of Cuban socialism—of its choruses and its slogans—traveled far beyond local listeners, expanding its symbolic status as the exemplary pioneer of the Third World emancipation struggles of 1960s and as a new type of socialist experience altogether with respect to its Eurasian counterparts. These distant listeners were largely spared the embodied routines, the labor and leisure rhythms, punctuated by that soundtrack but were no less of an intended, and attentive, audience. Thus at the core of the debate of what Cuban socialism was—and, for my purposes here, what Cuban postsocialism is—stands the 1959 revolution's dual status as an abstract and as a concrete event, as a symbolic referent, and as an everyday experience. The link between its soundscape and this double ontological reality is crucial to unpack the inconsistencies—and incommensurable legitimacies—between what Cuban socialism was and what it was said to be by its different constituents. The objective is not to establish a historical truth but rather to acknowledge the significance and heterogeneity of these perspectives, to examine the cultural and media artifacts through which they were shaped and consolidated, and to weigh their conceptual purchase and influences in the present.

Take, for instance, Cuba's resonance in certain Marxist thinking and how much of it was articulated in terms of those sonic aftereffects: "Since, today, capitalism defines and structures the totality of human civilization, every 'Communist' territory was and is—again, despite its horrors and failures—a kind of 'liberated territory,' as Fredric Jameson put it apropos of Cuba."[16] Let us put aside Žižek's argument about the symbolic function of "actually existing socialism" as a whole for a moment and focus on the language that, via Jameson, illustrates it. "Cuba, primer territorio libre de América" (Cuba, first liberated territory of the Americas) was another recognizable slogan of the 1959 revolution. The original phrase originated in the clandestine radio station of the armed insurrection wing of anti-Batista opposition in the 1950s that would eventually topple the dictator: "Here Rebel Radio. Broadcasting from Sierra Maestra: liberated territory in Cuba." After 1959, the phrase was modified to include the whole nation, not just the mountain complex where the rebels first set up headquarters. This signaled toward the continental exportability of its model for social and political change, in which Cuba would be the first of many other national revolutionary liberations. Common in political acts of the 1960s and reproduced in other media—posters from OSPAAL, Marxist tracts by Eduardo Galeano, Regis Debray, and Che Guevara—it became a common slogan of Radio Habana Cuba as well, a short-wave station broadcasted for an international audience in multiple languages. Its signal could be heard throughout the Americas. Radio amateurs and fellow travelers tuned in to it, and so traveled its signature tagline.

Žižek's source for the previously cited Jameson quotation is not clear (is it hearsay?), but a passage in *The Political Unconscious* provides some clues. Writing about the key Cuba scene in *The Godfather Part II*, Jameson points out that the moment of fraternal betrayal within the Mafia family coincides with the interruption of Michael Corleone's Cuba trip following news that the Cuban rebels have successfully ousted the dictator Batista, whose administration favored Mafia business investments on the island: "The climactic end moment of the historical development is then reached (in the film, but also in real history) when American business, and with it American imperialism, meet that supreme ultimate obstacle to their internal dynamism and structurally necessary expansion which is the Cuban Revolution."[17] However, Jameson's perceptive psychoanalytic reading nonetheless conflates the temporality within the film—the scene that depicts the arrival of the rebels in January 1959 that spoils the Mafia's ambitions—with the temporality of the political changes that led to the US embargo on Cuba, in a way perpetuating an official retroactive narrative that the events of 1959 were always already the beginning of an anti-American, anticapitalist, socialist revolution. The other key distinction to be made here, absent in Žižek's argument and only implicit in Jameson's reading, is that of a revolutionary event that promised and delivered liberation not from capitalism per se but from American imperialism specifically. Žižek's and Jameson's overinvestment in the symbolic importance of a space liberated from direct American domination for the anticapitalist imaginary, however suggestive, misses the kind of critical, materialist reading that earlier critiques from non-communist leftists and later post-Marxist scholars have been better poised to do vis-à-vis other forms of capitalist and imperialist domination operative in actually existing socialisms.

The other important context of this slogan is Fidel Castro's speech of September 2, 1960. "The First Declaration of Havana" convened the masses to Revolution Square as a response to the Declaration of Costa Rica of August 1960, in which the Kennedy government presented arguments to isolate Cuba politically and economically at the meeting of the Organization of American States. Based on the vociferous support of the large crowd of people on the plaza—though still a small fraction of the total population—this was a "general assembly of the people of Cuba" whose authority supposedly emanated from the expression of popular sovereignty present there. As such, these voices, answering the call-and-response structure of the speech, are part of the official transcript.

In the speech Fidel lays out the legitimate grievances of the country against the United States' history of economic, military, and political intervention and outlines the new policy directions—domestic and foreign—that the country will now be able to pursue as a sovereign nation, based on the legitimacy of the revolutionary government as an expression of popular will. The First Havana Declaration condemns racism, the exploitation of women, and all other forms of social and economic inequality and discrimination; stipulates its commitment to agrarian reform and to the nationalization of natural resources and its condemnation of oligarchy and monopoly; rejects the Monroe Doctrine and its afterlives; and proposes the reestablishment of diplomatic relations with the Soviet Union and the People's Republic of China. To each of these proposals, the people screamed in favor. Most significant, the speech addressed all Latin Americans, offering a road map to political independence, to the protection of natural resources, and to the pursuit of social and economic justice in the entire continent, to which Cuba pledged itself as only the first in a continentwide movement of liberation. A few months afterward, in the wake of the Bay of Pigs invasion in April 1961, Radio Habana Cuba would be officially launched to spread the word as an important piece of the Cold War propaganda race. The United States, in turn, had already been deploying very effectively radio propaganda in the Americas and would continue to do so: Operation Sherwood in support of the 1954 CIA-backed coup in Guatemala, and Radio Swan in the wake of the Bay of Pigs invasion.[18]

These rhetorical frameworks of exceptionalism, liberation, nationalization, and statization associated with Cuba served to reject and denounce the real, predatory footprint of American imperialist capital. But they also worked to obscure the revolutionary state's own operations to extract surplus value from labor, to define political participation as acquiescence, and to organize all social life exclusively around its own productivist, militarized, disciplinary designs. The question of a territory liberated from what exactly should follow. To return to Žižek's argument, and to the idea of Cuba as a liberated territory it invokes, the notion that actually existing socialism "seemed to pose an effective threat to the global rule of capitalism" must be rewritten with an emphasis on "seemed."[19] Effectively, "actually existing socialisms" continued and expanded the global rule of the capitalist mode of production, introducing other competitors to American and European capital and disrupting, but not interrupting, the colonial and neocolonial supply chains established up until then. Ironically, it was precisely the sonic legacy that began in the 1920s, the decade when Cuba became a party destination for Americans escaping Prohibition and when Mafia investments took off, that built the bridge between *Revolución* and *Pachanga* (and rum and tropical sensuality) for international audiences, as witnessed by songs such as Red Norvo and Mildred Bailey's "The Weekend of a Private Secretary" and Bing Crosby and the Andrew Sisters' "South America Take It Away," which continued to publicize those images well into the 1940s.

On the national front, the place of popular dance traditions in revolutionary times was much less straightforward. Insofar as they were assumed (by foreigners and Cubans alike) to be the expression of a quintessential national character—a constitutive inclination for *pachanga* above all—the question was whether that character could be harnessed as transformative energy.

The year 1968 saw the escalation of a political offensive to implement *guevarista* economic guidelines, including the dramatic shrinking of material incentives for workers (in the form of lower or stagnant wages, elimination of bonuses and overtime, and decreasing consumer commodities); public campaigns emphasizing the moral value of labor for the nation and for the transformation of social consciousness on the road to communism; the need for an expansion of working hours including unpaid "volunteer" work; and the tightening parameters of censorship. Responding to some of these transformations, and by then aware of the reeducation labor camps of the mid-1960s for homosexuals, religious persons, and other perceived misfits (UMAP), Susan Sontag ponders the relationship between the two senses of *pachanga*—the festive and the unruly—in telling fashion:

> The way the Cubans have of making work seem like fun (lots of talking, joking, high noise level, lack of punctuality, irregular hours, absence of hierarchy and deference, and plenty of inefficiency) reassures American radicals who have dreaded discovering anything like the regimentation and bureaucratic lifelessness which make a mockery of the pretensions to revolutionary socialism in most countries belonging to "the socialist camp." On this score, the American visitors are right to be reassured. After ten years of revolution—think of what happened in Russia in a similar period—the Cuban revolution is astonishingly free of repression and bureaucratization.

Sontag's essay is doing two things simultaneously. First, it is trying to parse the continuities and ruptures between the Cuban Revolution and the American New Left at a time when the Cuban leaders were actively cracking down on youth culture and individual rights. Their problem was not only the unruly tendencies of the national masses but also the continued penetration of Anglo-American artifacts, whether or not they were countercultural. Cuban revolutionary leaders rejected and persecuted the core symbols of the same New Left that so admired them: rock, free love, drugs, long hair for males, freedom of expression, homosexuality, and pacifism. "Marxism and marihuana," as Roger Bartra described that initial honeymoon between the cultural revolution of the 1960s and the Cuban Revolution in the Americas, were no longer revolutionary bedfellows; the hair politics of *barbudos* (bearded revolutionaries) and hippies could not be reconciled in the end despite having a supposed common enemy in the "short-haired robots."[20] To bridge such dissensus while remaining political allies, Sontag contends, the individual imaginary of liberation of the American New Left had never been, and could not be, the goal of the revolutionary Cubans; that is because they were not focused on individual values (as Americans were) but on public ones: community, solidarity, and consciousness. Second, her argument continues, not only are those measures needed to build a public revolutionary consciousness by the Cuban government misunderstood by foreigners as repressive measures; in addition, Sontag implies, that fun-loving, relaxed Cuban character might have benefited from a little corrective discipline during a time when all efforts to build socialism required utmost discipline even while such a national character acted as a natural check on the excesses of Soviet-style dogmatism.

In this context, Sontag's key reference is Che Guevara as the political source and personal model of that transformative consciousness. In his words, "This will be translated concretely into the reconquering of one's true nature through liberated labor, and the expression of one's own human condition through culture and art."[21] Commercial capitalist culture and Soviet socialist realism were both rejected by Guevara, but what is meant by "culture" and "art" remains Arnoldian in its content and statist in its form. The masses of *pachanga*-loving Cubans needed to be taught how to be proper revolutionaries: "How to make each worker feel the vital necessity of supporting their revolution and at the same time that work is a pleasure, feel what all of us feel *up here*?"[22] With a few notable exceptions and until the rise of British cultural studies, Marxism as a whole had a contradictory and tense relationship with mass, popular, and working-class cultures, relegating these practices to the realm of alienated subjectivity and false consciousness or treating them as remnants of regressive and premodern values. A key moment of Fanon's *The Wretched of the Earth*, which Che Guevara was reading in the 1963 Spanish translation and that heavily inspired his seminal "Socialism and Man in Cuba," lays out precisely a vision in which popular and folk-dance traditions run counter to authentic liberation: "Another aspect of the colonized's affectivity can be seen when it is drained of energy by the ecstasy of dance."[23]

In the time subsequent to the revolution, those emancipatory energies were seen as a distraction to productive labor, best put under the guidance of those above who knew better. Then again, Che Guevara reportedly was a notoriously bad dancer.

Sontag's analysis, like those of her contemporaries, started from the assumption that Cuban revolutionaries were socialist and explained away all their decisions based on that nominal definition, effectively ignoring core socialist values in the process and thereby redefining socialism to fit the facts, much as had been done before in the Soviet case with the old left. This is not the place to explore at length the coloniality of Sontag's or Francos's gazes, the absence of a socialist framework of analysis—despite their declared sympathies—or the historical inaccuracies of these otherwise fascinating documents. The main concern here is how enduring this gaze has been and how this second sense of *pachanga*—as a domestic problem and as a national asset—was entangled with the politicizing of popular culture and of labor discipline in ways that obscured the nonsocialist character of economic statization. The problem with this approach was not that New Left intellectuals were deceived or ignorant about the negative aspects of "actually existing socialism," but that they were unable to see and to say that whatever was happening in Cuba at the time was not socialism at all. This reluctance to critically engage with Cuban socialism would remain at the core of what Claudia Gilman has called "the politics of the sayable" (*lo decible*) among Latin American left intellectuals and is linked to a phenomenon that Raya Dunayevskaya forcefully dubbed "the conspiracy of silence" among her New Left colleagues on the North American intellectual scene.

On the domestic front in the 1960s, the idea of revolutionary *pachanga* as the collective unleashing of libidinal and ludic energies hitherto oppressed—in few texts more memorably and idiosyncratically narrated than in Reinaldo Arenas's *Before Night Falls*—competed with other instrumental, disciplinary approaches to *pachanga* beyond the realm of labor productivity. The fun-street-party aesthetic was an early effective mobilization tool in the creation of a revolutionary identity fully identified with the state. Moreover, the incorporation of *pachanga* to the identity of the 1959 revolution had a distinctly racialized and working-class component. *Pachanga* was another expression of the social significance of music, dance, and popular rituals and underscored the contribution of African culture to the national culture. But as Walterio Carbonell contended in 1961 (something for which he was subsequently punished), this was not always openly recognized in the white, aristocratic notions of national culture that prevailed among many self-identified revolutionaries and Marxist intellectuals in Cuba.[24]

Lillian Guerra has identified an early strategic use of *pachanga* by the revolutionary state as part of a wider campaign to align party loyalty and political participation with the desires of hitherto marginalized subjects—women, youth, Black Cubans, and the working, unemployed, or underemployed classes—to gain recognition and social standing.[25] The performance of racial integration by combining mass rallies and dance music continued a long prerevolutionary tradition of using popular music at political events, the most notable of which was perhaps the "Chambelona" uprising of 1917, named after the eponymous conga. Now, however, music and dance were no longer ornaments of the illusion of prerevolutionary democracy but instead were placed discursively at the center of the formation of a revolutionary state promising true democratization. According to Guerra, *pachanga*-style revolution as a calculated strategy of mobilization declined after 1961, as certain leisure practices became potentially subversive to the goals of homeland defense readiness and the idea of a homogenous revolutionary subject.[26] The climax was reached with the well-known case of censorship of the documentary film *P.M.*. Unlike Jorge García Espinosa's ideologically appropriate film of the same year, *Cuba Baila*, *P.M.* featured the unscripted, unvarnished, drunken dancing of a predominantly Black working class after dark. Here was *pachanga* without socialism in its full, sensuous glory at a time when the revolution was under siege from both real and perceived enemies. An emergent official culture of sacrificial commitment and discipline made any such display of frivolous enjoyment, however harmless, untimely at best and subversive at worst. But *pachanga* also came to be seen increasingly in that decade as counterproductive to the bookish, Europhile concepts of national and universal culture that informed the early programs of socialist enlightenment, on the one hand, and to the demands on increased labor power imposed by the new politics of developmentalist statization on the other. The political and cultural legacies of "*Revolución y pachanga*," however, did not end there.

Revolutionary cultural policy on this front was constantly forced to reckon with the preexisting social commitments of popular music and dance, but that policy was neither systematic nor uniform through the years. Moreover, Cuban policy did not follow any single, coherent cultural theory or political dogma, Marxist-inspired or not. Rather, it was an amalgam of calculated interests, inevitable compromises, and persistent preconceptions.[27] Responding to several needs—competing for the

Cuban music brand with the rise of salsa in New York, fulfilling the entertainment needs of its citizens, and maintaining hegemony and the role of the state as provider and benefactor in the popular cultural sphere—official cultural and media institutions followed the logic of import-substitution to promote a modern, national revolutionary identity that reaccommodated imaginaries of leisure and consumption with state-produced mass cultural commodities. Outside the US market, select Cuban bands had continued to travel on tour, and the TV programs "Para Bailar" (1978–1983) and "Para que tú lo bailes" (late 1980s) created national amateur competitions with a high dose of pedagogic content, promoting specific ways for the mass public to participate in wholesome, family-friendly formats in national culture as administered and defined by the state. "Para Bailar" required couples to demonstrate abilities in traditional and folkloric genres (mambo, rumba), modern national styles (*son*/casino), and select international styles (like pop and rock). The winners of these competitions sometimes went on to become important TV stars. Rebeca Martínez, a TV aerobics instructor, fashion icon, and '80s sex symbol, conducted "Gimnasia musical aerobia" dressed like *Flashdance*'s Alex Owens. Such programs continue today, though they are more closely fashioned after the American-style reality TV formats; these include *Bailando en Cuba* and the Cuban version of *American Idol*, *Sonando en Cuba*, which began in 2015 and whose second season included interactive voting via text message. An important change is that these programs are now produced by RTV, a commercial wing of the state's Instituto Cubano de Radio y Televisión. RTV was created in 1994, but its offerings did not expand in earnest until 2007 with the adoption of digital TV technology. It produces original content, liaises with foreign productions, licenses national TV content abroad, and imports equipment.

These entertainment-oriented investments did not mean that the political-parade-as-street-party principle, the aestheticization of state-organized productivism through music, and the more direct forms of political instrumentalization of music and dance programming and instruction toward the mass formation of a revolutionary subject ceased. These parallel investments would continue in the marches and the songs that were sung during volunteer and school-in-the-country work, the job- and school-based amateur culture programs, and the very name of the most influential of Cuba's popular dance music bands of the twentieth century, Los Van Van, based on the slogan of productivity of the failed 1970 Ten Million Sugar Harvest, "Los diez millones van, y de que van van." Moreover, when performed at massive political gatherings, slogans and songs together—along with other compositional elements like the parade, the hymns, the colors, the energy of bodies sounding in unison—materialized into a single voice the aggregated screams of the anonymous mass of individuals, thereby effectively anthropomorphizing, embodying, and reenacting the abstract concept of the people.

Propagandistic elements characteristic of these political events have to be considered not only (not even primarily) for their ideological content; in addition to their disciplinary effects, they should be read for their performative value, that is, as vital components of the aesthetic and emotional experience of the spectacularization of the political: "If we dismiss the very personal aesthetic effect of communist parades, we will miss something that was at the core of this type of assembly."[28] These other forms of state-sponsored *pachanga* reflect two key points. First, the combination of propagandistic, hegemonic, and commercial needs was there from the first decade of the revolution; and second, the official move to orient and commercialize popular entertainment and leisure time did not suddenly begin after the 1990s with the rise of the tourist industry and with the expansion of transnational capital in Cuban territory. This second aspect was integral to the revolutionary government's hegemonic investments as provider and organizer of the standardized programming of popular culture with a strong national identity component.

If *socialismo y pachanga* defined the sonically enduring and politically effective combination of these elements, then *postsocialismo y pachanga* is defined by two moments: the return of an outward-facing, tourist-oriented *Revolución y pachanga* in the 1990s—with *timba* as soundtrack but under the aegis of what Antonio José Ponte called "*la fiesta vigilada*" (a party under surveillance)—and the late 2000s, with the rise of reggaeton, digital media, and transnational markets in Cuba. "Reencarnación," the artist Lázaro Saavedra's video montage of *P.M.* to a tune by Elvis Manuel, an early precursor of underground *reparto reggaeton*, draws a parallel between the early efforts of the revolutionary state to harness *pachanga* and its current efforts to rein its most subversive afterlives. But only if one looks at these efforts through the classic confrontation of revolutionary state and individual artistic freedom, or exclusively through the lens of a persistent anti-Black, anti-popular, and anti–working class aesthetic, can one-to-one parallels be drawn. The state's approach to cultural policy in the twenty-first century incorporates greater economic interests, protection of a more clearly defined brand, and the need to retain control of social discontent narratives and of media infrastructures in the age of digital connectivity and increasing exchanges with the United States and the Cuban diasporas.

The map of these exchanges and interests becomes even more nebulous in the case of P.M.M. (Por un Mundo Mejor), a party and event company that began with DJ Hectico (Hector Díaz Yáñez) in 2005 and was institutionalized in 2006. Using the slogan "Those who move Havana" and a sleek marketing campaign (digital and analog), P.M.M. came to dominate a thriving and lucrative nightlife entertainment industry in Cuba, where state performance venues and independent businesses (bars and restaurants that double as dance clubs) compete for clientele. P.M.M. is the other face of La tribuna anti-imperialista (an open-air venue located across from the US diplomatic mission headquarters), where massive concerts under classic socialist banners take place, the latest installment of the political-parade-as-street-party gesture. But both are key sites of a revamped, state-sponsored strategy of *postsocialismo y pachanga*. With the growth of tourism and the modest economic recovery of the first two decades of the twenty-first century, P.M.M. became the preferred agent for the organization of the more glamorous and expensive parties and concerts around the country. It maintains cutting-edge equipment, large and professional crews, and a range of performances on offer, from LED screens to professional dance troupes, catering to foreign tourists and Cubans with access to hard currency.

The rise of P.M.M. is directly tied to the commercialization of culture by the state institutions to which it ultimately responds as part of the National Council of Scenic Arts and to the development of these government agencies as middlemen in contracts, payments, and the promotion of Cuban artists and musicians abroad. A Miami office of P.M.M. Production Events USA exists, and online they advertise as being able to promote artists and organize shows both in the United States and in Cuba. It is far from clear what the relationship between the two is, if there is any. According to public business filings with Florida's secretary of state, P.M.M.'s Miami office belongs to an entertainment limited liability company and began to operate in 2011.[29]

The battles over the postsocialist soundscape and over the new subversive forms of *pachanga* can be told through a tale of two songs: Osmani García's "Chupi Chupi" (Sucky Sucky) and Porno Para Ricardo's "No comas tanta pinga comandante" (Don't be such a cocksucker, Commander). Both songs allude to oral sex (one being an imperative to do it, the other being an imperative not to). Both engage in the lyric and sonic subversion of militant revolutionary masculinity, of disinterested productivism, of wholesome working-class entertainment, and of the accepted norms of popular national music as a brand. The modes of these potentially subversive forms of postsocialist *pachanga* are ubiquity (the ubiquity of consumer culture and viral "bad music" versus the old ubiquity of the state sonic machine), vulgarity (as an aesthetic value and as a political stance), and autonomy (as way to map the changing relationship of audiences and artists to market and state forces). At the same time, these two examples are symptomatic of some of the limits of those subversions, whose explicit articulation seems to be possible only on the basis of phallic emulations and other forms of wounded hypermasculinity. Nonetheless, these songs show a far more complex, multifront battle over the content, ownership, and authorship of Cuban music between the leftovers of the revolutionary soundscape, the Cuban state as both commercial investor and ideological policeman, and a host of new actors seeking social and cultural recognition as much as personal economic gains in a transformed media and market context.

Almendrón Playlists: Vulgarity, Ubiquity, and the Semiotics of the Urban

Moral panics over reggaeton have brought into relief historical tensions within Cuban culture regarding the visibility and incorporation of its Afro-Cuban elements, much in the same way *son* and rumba did in the early twentieth century and *timba* and hip-hop did in the 1990s and early 2000s. The national debate over reggaeton focused predictably on reggaeton's lack of social and aesthetic propriety: on its obscenity (in dance and speech), on its foreign origins, on its consumerist imaginaries, on its repetitiveness and simplicity, and on its sexual objectification of women. But it also highlighted the continuity of issues of class and consumerism in revolutionary discourse and the tacit rules regarding who could stake a claim to wealth accumulation and who could not in postsocialist Cuba. After all, charges of vulgarity against popular culture have long codified profane enjoyments in the service of "legitimizing social differences," especially those of race and class.[30] In these aspects, the Cuban reggaeton debate shares features with similar controversies in other Latin American countries, though the particularities of the postsocialist political and media contexts set it apart in others.[31] The reggaeton polemic has played out in the official and the independent presses, in the comments sections of YouTube videos and social media, on the street, and finally in the regulatory language of Decreto Ley (Decree Law) 349 (2018), which extended state cultural policy to the emergent nonstate cultural sectors.

Complaints about the vulgarity of reggaeton in Cuba were almost always tied to its ubiquity: "One cannot avoid it, it is playing everywhere, even the children are listening and singing along!" The song "Chupi Chupi" marked a before and an after in the story of Cuban reggaeton. The polemic over this song also coincided with the split between commercial and underground reggaeton becoming more nuanced, although the labels "commercial" and "underground" can be somewhat misleading. The state was confronted with the need for an explicit policy, and the networks of informal distribution expanded exponentially. Before the moral panic over reggaeton moved on to other public enemies (e.g., to Chocolate MC and his groundbreaking "Bajanda"), "Chupi Chupi" was the song most often picked as an example of everything that was wrong with the genre in Cuba, though García recorded his first album (*El Malcriao* [2011]) with the state label EGREM, a rare incursion into urban music for the label. *La transparencia del tiempo* (The transparency of time [2018]) by Leonardo Padura, whose bestselling detective novels have turned the journalist and novelist into a postsocialist phenomenon in his own right, provides a useful example of the function that this song in particular, and reggaeton in general, acquired in the social text. The novel documents and exploits the cultural politics of remediation I am sketching here.

Reggaeton is heard diegetically throughout the novel as a marker of urban squalor and criminality. In one scene of the novel, the recurring protagonist of Padura's crime series, the former cop turned private eye Mario Conde (alias "the Count"), muses about postsocialist Havana's demographic and spatial peculiarities, prompted by the salacious soundtrack of his *almendrón* ride:

> The beats of a reggaeton began to play at a deafening volume (was it the same as the one from the tenement, or was all reggaeton alike and hence why he could not differentiate between songs?); the irruption of the song caused the other nine passengers of the taxi, including the driver and excluding "the Count," to answer with an almost coordinated movement of hips and shoulders, followed by the sing-along of a tune whose lyrics everybody (with the shameful exception of "the Count") knew, growl by growl.[32]

Prone to social ruinology, Padura's aging, melancholic protagonist ponders the cultural gap between him and his fellow, younger, less-cultured passengers, serving to highlight the unexpected sonic overlap between the tenement and the rest of the city stitched together by the *almendrón* as a medium: the same song playing everywhere. Padura's character is both a Kantian and a revolutionary listener, someone whose sensibility has been cultivated in the dynamics of the socialist enlightenment described above, someone who in many ways is a "fool" in the sense of Rodríguez's postsocialist anthem "El necio." Padura has written essays on the topic of "good music," and Conde, a thinly disguised alter ego of Padura himself, constantly marks his distance with the revolutionary state of the past, but only by moderately expressing the kinds of self-criticism that official rhetoric has already performed or authorized: regrets for his former homophobic views and a personal disillusion with the supposed flawlessness of the socialist system he once believed in. At the same time, the defining psychological traits of the character across all novels, and the source of melodramatic tension in the plots, build on his boasting of an old-school integrity, on his reluctant capitulation to participating in the hybrid economy, on the sacred male bonds of friendship, and on his superior aesthetic sensibility: this former cop turned private eye has literary ambitions. In many ways, the success of Conde as a character is modeled on the same discourse of the Cuban state brand, that is, as an imperfect but exotic survivor of a supposedly untimely political and cultural project.[33]

The setting of that scene inside an *almendrón* is crucial. Since the early 2000s, these cars have worked increasingly as fixed-route pool taxis—comparable to *combis* or *micros* in other Latin American cities—or as high-end luxury rentals for tourists and special events. This classic car has become the ubiquitous marker of Cuban visual identity and seemingly incontrovertible proof that the country is indeed stranded in time. The *almendrón* derives its iconicity from being able to synthesize other key narratives of Cuban postsocialism as well. For example, as the paradigmatic example of native ingenuity it reinforces a self-image that Ariana Hernández-Reguant traces back to the mythical figure of a socialist amateur inventor and that the artist Ernesto Oroza calls the "technological disobedience" of postsocialist survivalism.[34] But the *almendrón* was above all a practical response to the hybrid economy following the economic crash of the 1990s. Under their hoods, 1950s-era Chevys, Cadillacs, and Fords are retrofitted with motors and parts from Toyotas, Hyundais, and Geelys, vehicles that began arriving with the reopening of international trade. Additionally, a renewed proliferation of working *almendrones* was driven by the 2010 expansion of self-employment licenses in the transportation sector. The modest availability of fuel that the trade accords with Venezuela have made possible since 2000 made the return of these vehicles to the streets a tenuous sign of being on a road to recovery.

Cubatón (Cuban reggaeton), *almendrones*, and *El Paquete* (the package)—the most famous of Cuba's informal distribution and advertising networks for digital media—thrived together during the second half of the 2000s. All three began in the informal hybrid economy and are local variants of global phenomena: reggaeton, informal transportation, and peer-to-peer networks.³⁵ Bypassing traditional media and official airwaves, the production and circulation of reggaeton in Cuba was initially a homemade phenomenon. Reggaeton's widespread popularity and the promotional work of home studios and informal digital distribution networks led to the eventual professionalization and international success of select *cubatón* household names. *El Paquete* and similar sneakernets facilitated offline alternatives to streaming, delivering music directly from local musicians and home studios to listening devices (though in the context of uneven, and often scarce, web connectivity). In turn, taxi drivers played the latest hits on their car stereos. The *almendrón* was a test market for local musicians, the daytime mover of Havana's new nightlife sounds. As a testament to this, Cuba's first taxi-hailing app is named *Bajanda*, the same as Chocolate MC's hit.

The love became mutual: the economic crisis of the 1990s intensified the enduring obsession of Cubans with everything transportation-related, and *cubatón* was no exception. There is even a low-budget independent film starring Osmani García of "Chupi Chupi" fame, *Buquenque*, which tells the story of an aspiring reggaeton singer who works as an assistant to an *almendrón* driver. One could map the international success of the best-known *cubatón* group, Gente de Zona, by looking at the kind of vehicle featured in their video clips through the years: from bicycles in "Somos Cuba" with Isaac Delgado in 2011 to retro-chic *almendrones* in the superhit "La gozadera" and BMWs and yachts in "Traidora," both with Marc Anthony in 2016. But what kinds of urban spaces do the *almendrones* and all the other vehicles that play urban music, like bicitaxis and even public buses, produce by their reggaetonic whirring through the city? And why has this sound become a polemical marker of the postsocialist city?

If you are of a Kantian persuasion and find yourself in a Havana *almendrón* reluctantly tapping your feet to the bass beat after a futile attempt to resist, you are not alone. Music, Kant said, is like perfume. It invades the freedom of others because it exceeds the range of its intended recipients by its very nature: we can close our eyes but not our ears. The philosopher gives as an example someone's train of thought (his own?) being interrupted by religious hymns sung by inconsiderate neighbors. But Kant is doubly relevant for his turn of phrase: music depends on a certain lack of urbanity (Urbanität). Urbanity in this context means two things: it refers both to being measured, well-mannered, and proper and also to a cognitive response that starts with a determinate idea and only afterward gives rise to a sensation such as aesthetic pleasure. For Kant, the visual arts promote "the urbanity of the higher powers of cognition" in contrast with music, which moves from the provocation of an immediate sensation to the evocation of a general idea instead.[36] Kant's system of aesthetic categories places music highest among the arts that play with sensations (Empfindungen) but lowest with respect to the kind of cognitive faculties that his definition of aesthetic judgment is meant to cultivate. By saying that music lacks urbanity because it primarily activates the passions and because it physically exceeds the circle of its intended listeners, Kant restores to this sense of cool rationality, self-restraint, and politeness ("urbanity") the spatial dimension of its etymological origins: the idea of the *urbs* as an organized, enclosed space, whose walls stave off the fear of unwanted contacts and unseemly sights but wherein proximity and mingling with strangers require clear categories of exclusion, inclusion, and acceptable behavior.

Modern urban space, connected by transit, multiplies the unpredictability of encounters among classes, races, and genders, chance meetings that can be as attractive as they can be threatening. This gave rise to a distinct literary tradition at the end of the nineteenth century concerned with the modernization of public transit, the attendant moral panics of city life, and the new roles of literature in such a world.[37] In many ways, Padura's novel marshals a twenty-first-century version of this trope, with the *almendrón* as the moving medium of reggaeton and as the metaphoric vehicle for all the social and aesthetic decay that the unchecked circulation of such music stands for.

Urban transportation and portable entertainment are very old partners, from paperbacks and boomboxes to headphones and pocket devices. Whereas Muzak, a company that once offered custom-design soundtracks for consumer spaces, referred to its program editors as "audio architects," digital media invites us to be our own audio architects or at least sonic landscapers. Here the availability of software tools for musical production by amateurs, and the ubiquity of digital streaming and sharing, have played crucial roles in the global success and local adaptability of reggaeton and other "plebeian musics," as George Yúdice has described them.

This remediated hearability carries these sounds outside their primordial zones—favelas, *llegaypons*, *chabolas*, *villas*, *arrabales*, shantytowns—places beyond the now metaphorical city walls (*extramuros*).

The undisciplined circuits of informal digital media, on the one hand, and of the *almendrón* routes on the other, blur the polite limits between *solares* and *repartos* (tenements and suburbs) and the curated, tourist-friendly images of the city proper, between unsanctioned speech and the gatekeepers of good taste and public decorum.

This is especially the case for reggaeton *reparto* (also *morfa*, *ragamorfa*, *rastamemba*), or "the reggaeton of the poor," as Jesús Jank Curbelo dubs it. *Reparto* is a world apart from the more polished, sanitized reggaeton of romance, money, and clubs. It differs from mainstream reggaeton in its sonority and song structure and in its explicit references to sex, drugs, and the unglamorous bustling and hustling of everyday life. Its video clips and songs are ripe with references to the woes of riding public buses (*guaguas*), the cheaper and less reliable alternative to the relatively more expensive *almendrones*. This reggaeton style is part of *reparterismo*, a Cuban subculture associated to poor, working-class, and predominantly Black neighborhoods, whose first soundtrack was the *timba* in the 1990s and that included shout-out lyrics to these less visible subjects: "Los sitios is a working neighborhood, sensible to Cubanness, where my lover is."[38] *Reparterismo* takes its name from *repartos*, or neighborhoods, but it literally means "distributions."[39] Like reggaeton, *timba* was viewed with official suspicion as being vulgar, low-class, and all too real yet contagiously festive and commercially successful enough to discipline, invest in, and channel lyrically away from the everyday chronicles of the predominantly Black working classes and toward themes of heartbreak and sexual conquest.[40]

The label "Urban Latin," widely in use in the music industry, brings together these and other unruly irruptions and represents them in a more neighborly, more agreeable, and more profitable face, blending under a single trademark both mainstream and far-out sounds. The moniker was born in the 1970s in New York City. Popularized by the WBLS-FM deejay Frankie Crocker, it described radio playlists that encompassed genres bourgeoning in predominantly African American and Latino communities like rhythm and blues, rap, and soul. But the ascendency of the "urban" as a commercially strategic racial and ethnic marker accompanied the displacement of predominantly poor and Black communities in major US cities to make way for new urban development, especially freeways. What was called "urban renewal" was, as James Baldwin memorably put it in a 1963 interview, nothing but a euphemism for "negro removal." (Moments before speaking about gentrification and the tearing down of African American neighborhoods to make way for federally subsidized development projects, Baldwin refers explicitly to the Cuban Revolution to illustrate the problem of recruiting young Black Americans to fight for the supposed liberation of others on behalf of a government that does not treat them as constituents with fully guaranteed citizen and human rights.) As a label used in commercial music, "urban" conceals the structural violence of its spatial origins with a euphemism, acquiescing to demands that its sound attains a measure of Kantian Urbanität: that it be well-mannered, at least in name.[41]

These umbrella tactics to commercialize both the mainstream and the less lyrically innocuous tunes are less effective for state cultural institutions and other regulatory government bodies juggling their own commercial interests (in the form of tax revenues, performing and entrance fees in clubs and shows, and as representative agents), a public-facing rhetoric in opposition to vulgarity and commercialism, and an interest in keeping media and cultural production strictly regulated and under the state's sole purview. Describing a situation identical to the one cited above in Padura's novel—sitting in an *almendrón*, listening to the same racy tune as Mario Conde, "Chupi Chupi"—the prominent independent blogger and journalist Yoani Sánchez contends that this all-or-nothing approach is a catch-22: the state is faced with either providing airplay for popular songs whatever their content or being seen as a censor, as with the ongoing "Chupi Chupi" polemics. In this role, authorities cannot fulfill any basic regulatory mandates; neither can they satisfy the legitimate demands of the dancing public if they do not allocate spaces to other musical tastes and social identities. Moreover, faced with the persistent challenges of digital connectivity, the state's heavy-handed control over the media charges any unofficial and informal content with an intrinsic and attractive subversiveness. Without many alternatives, all unsanctioned content is indiscriminately pushed to unofficial networks of distribution and accessed together, where it exceeds the circle of those who seek profane enjoyments ubiquitously and continuously.

The added charge of ubiquity to the standard accusation of vulgarity underscores the ongoing fragmentation of the former revolutionary project of a socialist soundscape (in which music has been a historically political, and highly politicized, forcefield) and the specificity of the media context in which Cuban reggaeton circulates. The government's continued monopoly on traditional mass media, given its track record, blurs the line between any necessary regulation of the public sphere, on the one hand, and politically motivated censorship and discriminatory prescriptive moralisms on the other. As the Cuban legal scholar Julio César Guanche argues, apropos of Decreto Ley 349, prescriptive cultural moralisms do not fight against inequality and social differences. At best such discourse conceals them; at worse it reinforces them. Moreover, these unresolved issues are all the more problematic for a revolutionary state that loudly declared it had eliminated racial discrimination in the 1960s and that, for decades, considered any public discussion of the enduring and pervasive anti-Black racism in revolutionary Cuba a taboo subject.

Through these regulatory overreaches, the Cuban government insists on its traditional role as the main provider of entertainment and information, as the organizer of leisure practices, and as the primary arbiter of good taste, ideological propriety, and aesthetic value. The ideological and commercial administration of national culture as both commodity and hegemonic tool, as much as the regulation of profits and personnel allowed to represent those investments at home and abroad, are at stake. Decreto Ley 349 is addressed to those new voices, like reggaeton, and also to the growing host of independent artists and dissident activists who "under the guise of art" (*intrusismo profesional*) act "in detriment to the image of our creators and of art in general."[42] Any opposition to official state cultural policy and to the vague directives of socialist virtue, aesthetic integrity, and traditional morality ("*contaminación del clima sonoro*," "*jerarquías artísticas*," and "*buenas costumbres*" illustrate the linguistic register of the law's sponsors) is preclassified as mercenary, foreign, kitsch, vulgar, and illegitimate. The problem, of course, is that the state cultural institutions not only have a history of arbitrarily applying these types of regulation to cases of political censorship and moral policing; they also commercialize and market quite successfully national culture.

The long practice of regulation and cooptation of *pachanga* by the revolutionary state demonstrates again how vulgarity—or what is perceived as vulgar—has been both a threat and a leverage point for official cultural politics. The reliance of these pronouncements on preexisting moral panics around reggaeton and consumerism mobilizes well-established racial and class-based notions of national culture as the raison d'état, even while they rein in a highly profitable and massively popular phenomenon whose success has been tied in no small degree to the networks of distribution and promotion for local music associated to *El Paquete*.[43] No state has the capacity to assume all the demands for entertainment, information, and cultural expression of the population at large. Because it insists on ascribing itself such roles, it underperforms as a provider and is overstretched as a watchdog, which engenders a mix of apathy, mockery, distrust, and antagonism. In turn, this drives the very proliferation of underground, informal, and/or parallel cultural and communication networks it seeks to discipline.

Put simply, the moral panics of reggaeton are not that far away from the usual anxieties of the modern city and mass and popular culture, especially those that the genre elicits for its sexually explicit lyrics, its unreserved celebration of consumer culture, and ultimately for its racial, gender, and class markers. But the unstoppable explosion of reggaeton in the Cuban musical scene revived a history of struggles over the contested vault of "Cuban music," conceived of by different stakeholders as a nation-building identity, as cultural patrimony, as a disciplinary mechanism, as a lucrative brand, or as a real-time pulse of social life.[44] The polemic also accentuated the clash between Cuba's strong tradition of nationalist essentialism and its transnational, multiethnic, multiracial Caribbean identity.[45] Reggaeton initially traveled westward to Havana from cities closer to the radio waves of the Dominican Republic and Puerto Rico. Despite such Caribbean bona fides, the popularity of reggaeton in Cuba raised concerns among the restless commissars of national purity about foreign elements corrupting the Cuban musical identity. This reception also displayed an overwhelmingly reductive, Havana-centric image of the national image at the expense of Cuba's other regions because it betrayed city dwellers' unease with patterns of internal migration: over several decades, the wave of migration to Havana from these provinces has been the source of another consistent urban preoccupation in the capital.

Like *almendrones*, reggaeton will no doubt pass eventually, at least as an architect of Havana's soundscape. In the meantime, the *almendrón* playlists and their critical reception provide an alternative remix of everyday rhythms, what Lefebvre calls "the mediatized everyday" of public, fictional, private, dominating, and dominated rhythms of the city, a more complex record of the desires, aspirations, and fears of its inhabitants.[46] They invite us listen to, not just to hear, the rhythms of life bubbling under, in sync with, or thriving against the uneven and combined predations of state and capital.

What appears is a new cultural map of postsocialism, one in which the aggressive visibility of foreign capital, of consumer desires and mass culture, and of more pronounced social and economic inequalities are not new phenomena with respect to revolutionary Cuba but rearrangements and intensifications of preexisting dynamics. This shift in focus problematizes two dominant narratives: the official, party/state's monopoly on the history and definition of Cuban socialism; and the foreign exoticizing gazes where Cuba—and with it the consumption of Cuban culture, including its old revolution and old cars—remains, and is reduced to, an object of political desire and curiosity. Cuban reggaeton plays in syncopation with respect to the marketable downbeats of revolutionary (dis)enchantment: the aestheticized silence of the ruin as allegory (as opposed to the very real and fatal building collapses in neglected urban structures); the reactionary nostalgia for a developmentalist, prerevolutionary modernism; the competitive forces of accelerated capital accumulation and extraction; the bureaucratic investment in the political survival of the revolutionary state and its songs, its slogans, and its echoes; and the ideological nostalgia for alternative forms of wholesome, committed *pachanga* and uplifting cultural programs of socialist enlightenment.

Postsocialist Punk and the Limits of Cock-rioting: Autonomy as Style

Few bands have taken on those sonic state investments as ruthlessly as Porno Para Ricardo did. In 2006, one of PPR's songs addressed Fidel directly: "Commander, don't be such a cocksucker." At first sight, the chorus of "El Comandante" may appear as only a trivial vulgarity. But with that gesture, the band shook the acceptable canons of political songwriting in Cuba and redefined *pachanga* as a hedonistic, antiestablishment pleasure in obscene irreverence. Their demand for pornography—expressed in the name "Porn for Richard" and in various songs—codified a deliberate aesthetics of social indiscipline aimed at desacralizing government officials as much as polite protocols of political critique.

The band formed in 1998 and secured a couple of shows in local rock venues. Rock is a genre historically marginalized and informally played and listened to in Cuba, but through the 1980s and 1990s it gradually became more accepted, though rarely was it still part of the mainstream musical scene. PPR released a homemade EP (*Pol' tu culpa*) in 2002, recorded their first album (*Rock para las masas . . . (cárnicas)*) and, like Osmani García, were nominated for the national video-clip competition (the Lucas Prize) for their rendition of the soundtrack of the blockbuster Soviet cartoon *Bremenskie Muzykanty*. However, PPR's status underwent a dramatic change when a combination of incidents contributed to radicalize the lyrics and focus of the band. In April 2003, PPR's front man, Gorki Ávila, was arrested during the annual rock festival Pinar del Río, and after a controversial legal case he was condemned to four years in prison for drug possession. (Ávila's arrest coincided with the imprisonment of seventy-five dissidents in March 2003 and thus was widely perceived as politicized.) Meanwhile, Ciro Díaz, the band's lead guitarist and songwriter (and a mathematics instructor at Havana University at the time), was fired. Gorki's arrest in 2003 began an international campaign of support for his freedom that offered the group its first exposure to a wider public, launched partly by the alternative blogosphere. Subsequently their lyrics became more explicitly antagonistic, especially with the recording of a double album in 2006: *Soy porno soy popular*, a play on words with the slogan of the national brand of cigarettes, and *A mí no me gusta la política pero yo le gusto a ella, compañeros*. Three more albums would follow, *Álbum Rojo Desteñido* in 2009, in 2013, *Maleconazo ahora*—named after the little-known, violently repressed uprising along Havana's famous Malecón that took place in 1994—and *Ataque sónico*, named after the mysterious "sonic attacks" suffered by foreign diplomats in Havana, in 2016.

Each local reiteration of the punk ethos and aesthetic engages the specific forms of political and cultural hegemony of their context, as Shane Greene has asserted with respect to the Latin American scene in general and the Peruvian case in particular.[47] Punk revival acts are not rare well into the twenty-first century, and postsocialist punk has found its iconic sound in Russia's Pussy Riot. But only at the surface level can parallels be drawn between the feminist, anticapitalist, and antiauthoritarian punk act Pussy Riot in Russia (2011–present) and PPR's own antigovernmental cock-riot. In PPR the appropriation of punk has a more limited political range with deeply misogynistic undertones, performing singularly focused critiques of the government ruling party, revolutionary sonic memory, and local rock scene.[48] In the summer of 2009, "El Comandante" was still played by guitar aficionados—including the guitar player of the band—and accompanied by the enthusiastic voices of disgruntled urban youths who gathered in the park "G y 23," a countercultural space that became increasingly policed and eventually neutralized. As of 2023 it is unclear if the band is dissolved, as only the front man remains in Cuba. Nonetheless, and however briefly, they repositioned in the public eye a political subject who, via the bad word as aesthetic procedure, exploited the parallels between the slogan and the song chorus, dispensed of the double entendres that sugarcoat and dissimulate politically charged lyrics to avoid censorship, and challenged the new state policy aiming to absorb and discipline the previously marginalized rock and rap scenes with the creation of the Rap Agency and the Rock Agency.

Spoken interludes made the self-produced albums into metonymic artifacts of everyday sound bites: songs are organized around intermissions that parody national mass media—radio, television, and newspapers. The graphics mimic symbols of official ideology, using images of ration cards, the color red, heroes, made-up acronyms, and mock slogans. "Comunicado manifiesto" recycles the political lexicon of state propaganda to substitute militarized productivism and party loyalty with leisurely pleasure and individualist concern. It deploys these values in a parody of the call and response that radically refuses the demand for total participation characteristic of the slogan culture and the forms of subject interpellation typical of the revolution:

Choir: We!
Gorki: Members of the Porn for Richard collective want to ratify our unwavering oath to fight for whatever cause we want.
. . . .
Choir: We swear!
Ciro: To not be loyal to any party except our own, the individual, we are not left or right or middle, we don't want to march. More like rest, feel pleasure. . . .[49]

Their logo features a hammer and sickle: the handle of the hammer becomes a penis that pierces the blade of the sickle, distorting obscenely the legendary symbol. The modification denounces the imposition of an authoritarian power onto an unwilling subject and simultaneously performs symbolic violence against the official signs of power as revenge. This operation is systematically and humorously repeated with everyday images and revolutionary iconography: the slogan of the national brand of cigarettes Popular, "I'm Cuban, I'm Popular," becomes "I'm Porno, I'm Popular." The parody of official slogans that are part and parcel of routine language in schools, workplaces, mass mobilizations, and state media is also prolific, such as "Pioneers for communism, long live ideological divergence!" and "Don't self-medicate, break your TV set!" Like the historical punks, who had their own share of slogans—"Never trust a hippie," "Punk's not dead," "No future"—the band's mock slogans and choruses offered the members' own responses to official mottoes as generational rallying cries: "Don't be such a cocksucker, Commander," "I don't like politics but she likes me, comrade," and "The cultural police is a censorship laborer" were all part of refrains as important as the songs themselves.

PPR did not belong to a preexisting punk scene, though the harmony and rhythms of most songs, the DIY collages of the band's visual materials, and its nonconstructive institutional iconoclasm were punk enough. The meaning of their style, to borrow Dick Hebdige's phrase, was rather an antagonistic language against the established order that used obscenity as the basis of political and creative autonomy, understood as independence from the state and from acceptable forms of political and social critique and as disinterest in professional commercial success. Scandal as the performance of a mythical autonomy was the band's signature (fully undressing during shows). The end of the song "Tipo normal" (Normal guy) from the album *Rock para las masas . . . cárnicas* (Rock for the meaty masses) features the following dialogue between Gorki and Ciro, founding members of the band:

>Gorki: Oye, asere, no vamos a decir tantas malas palabras en este disco.
>Ciro: ¿Y por qué es que no vamos a decir malas palabras?
>Gorki: Asere porque mira, si tú dices pinga y cojones no te ponen en la radio y es de pinga que no te pongan en la radio, es tremenda perra mariconá. . . .
>
>(Gorki: Hey, dude, we are not going to say so many bad words in this album.
>Ciro: ¿And why is it we are not going to say bad words?
>Gorki: Dude, look, if you say cock and balls they don't play you in the radio and it's fucked not to be played in the radio, it fucking sucks.)

When all the legal and professionally equipped means of music production and distribution have been historically managed by official organizations—rendering these state agencies comparable to the tentacles of a single giant record company before the formal and informal expansion of the Cuban music market through digital media and the internet—making sure the band was preemptively unplayable on the radio (and anywhere else, for that matter), as PPR did from the onset, complicated even further any shot at local success. The band's music circulated informally through digital peer-to-peer copies and a limited release of CDs self-produced in Mexico. Despite their international (but fleeting) notoriety, the kind of provocation that attracted media attention to the band did not generate profits. International coverage does not secure a reliable audience for the music; neither is the targeted criticism of local figures—the minister of culture at the time, the local party representative, etc.—sustainably translatable. As of 2023, they have 1,090 monthly listeners on Spotify, and, as is the case with most non-English lyrics, streaming platforms reproduce their "bad words" uncensored and unannounced.

Their use of sexually explicit imagery, insults, and bad words became a strategy of affirmation of an otherwise unrepresentable individual autonomy, further defined by virtue of not belonging to any institutional sphere of cultural production. The independent production of albums, the home recording studio, the illegal performances, and self-exclusion from cultural organizations were necessary preconditions to continue to criticize the government without recourse to indirect or metaphorical language. Their rhetoric did not indicate aspirations to construct a future democratic civil society, but PPR flaunted in very loud terms the desire to break from the orders of representation of the present political moment; the boorish, rustic tunes capture and give shape to a nonlinguistic frustration, a bodily excess irreducible to the narrowly constituted frameworks of political subjectivity in place. More than a simple epiphenomenon of punk indiscipline, the use of the bad word—that unmistakable sign of impropriety in the public sphere—constituted a premeditated act of self-exclusion from the political and social body, while the band's radical political stance and stylistic choices prevented it from catering to a wider audience. Here, too, was its limited portability: the members took the protest *pachanga* with them, performing in Miami and in the Czech Republic for politically (though not always musically) sympathetic audiences. But because of the specificity of their immediate antagonist—the Cuban Communist Party—their discourse gravitated increasingly toward political positions heavily influenced by the Cuban diaspora and the more activist, right-wing groups within it that support, celebrate, and promote their activities in Cuba and abroad. Following this line, Ávila has criticized antigovernment positions that are at the same time politically and socially progressive and in 2018 released a song titled "Voté por Trump" (I voted for Trump), even though he lives in Cuba. While the name of the band's home studio, La Paja Recolds, is a tribute to the legendary Basque punk group La Polla Records, PPR's political imaginary shares little with La Polla's political profile in depth, breadth, or coherence, or with that of Russia's Pussy Riot, whose own command of punk iconoclasm in another postsocialist context has been more compellingly nuanced in its critique of state, capital, and patriarchy.[50]

Nonetheless, at the moment PPR emerged the band critically addressed the avenues of professionalization opened with the Cuban Rock

Agency by a Ministry of Culture invested in showing itself open to cultural initiatives previously unthinkable within official spheres. After constant run-ins with the police and other urban tribes, rowdier spaces like El Patio de María—a historical meeting place for rockers in Havana—closed or were repurposed—like the Rock Agency's new Maxim Rock theater and the puffed-up club El Submarino Amarillo (Yellow Submarine) that has been built in place of the dingy Atelier. Established rock groups in the local scene and emerging bands have thus been brought in under the auspices of the newly created institution and its subsidized festivals, gigs, and touring and recording opportunities.

Claudia Cadelo's post titled "The Rock Agency" in the independent blog *Octavo Cerco* reported that, shortly after the agency was created, it unveiled a set of behavioral norms that appeared to be designed almost exclusively with PPR in mind. The very bureaucratic title "Guidelines for the New Cuban Rocker" (*Estatutos del nuevo Friki*) verged on the absurd: "No bad words. No public nudity. No indecency. No invitations for banned bands to perform." PPR's churlish revenge to this and similar confrontations came in the shape of castigating songs with titles such as "Agencia del Rock" and "Comunista Chivatón." Through these and other songs, its illicit concerts, and public nudity, PPR explicitly objected to the restrictive parameters of the institutionalization of rock music in Cuba and made visible the new pact between rockers and the state. Considering the historical tensions between rockers and the state, on the one hand, and rock's nonconformist identity on the other (as perceived by devotees in any case), the band criticized the new alliance between such strange partners.

PPR's targets included the *trova* movement as well. Their subversion of *trova* aesthetics speaks further to their attempts to rewrite the sonic memory of the relationship between revolution, song, and youth. As discussed above, the weight of the song in the revolutionary soundscape can hardly be underestimated, as the enthusiastic choruses of omnipresent political songs played alongside slogans in schools, parades, and official events. The new song movement (*nueva trova*) from the 1970s onward had a vital role as the leading voice of the revolutionary cultural project: this was the musicalized poetic vanguard that put its didactic voice at the service of the political transformation underway. The transformation of the singer-songwriter and the marriage of poetry, protest, commitment, and song were achieved along the way. The choruses of the protest song, as mirrors of the political slogans, became simultaneously symptoms and motors of collective attitudes and desires: "La era está pariendo un corazón" (The times are giving birth to a heart), "Hasta siempre Comandante" (Until forever, Commander), "Amo esta isla" (I love this island), and "¡Cuba va!" (Go Cuba!) are just a few examples. In other words, this function of the song fully committed its refrain as the sensual double of the political slogan.⁵¹ PPR exploited that relationship by parodying those songs as much as by chastising directly *trova* as an institution of protest song. In this fashion the bandmates positioned themselves as the disillusioned sons of the legendary guitar-carrying poets too, breaking loudly and publicly with the tradition that conceives of the revolutionary song as a privileged place of social critique. PPR's jejune and boorish tunes were designed to startle the aural immunity to shock those decades of endless repetition—of the same political slogans, of the same disciplined refrains—produced in the listeners.

PPR rejected lyrical opacity but preserved the idea of the protest song in whose death the intentionally obscuring metaphoric language of the classic troubadours became an accomplice. This position contrasted starkly with even the most critical and sophisticated of the performers of later generations. From the end of the 1980s onward, singer-songwriters like Frank Delgado and Carlos Varela rehearsed their own biting political and social criticisms, which were also met with suspicion by the authorities and with equal enthusiasm by a public that had come of age during the 1980s without a publicly critical voice. Despite the audacity of their break with official and revolutionary *trova*, however, their poetics maintained a certain faith in filtering the real through the songs' witty lyricisms, whether as exegesis or as catharsis, but bound to the place of enunciation of the singer-songwriter as a special truth-teller with a professional mission.

With their public image and actions, but also with words, PPR denounced the disciplined and privileged critical registers of the *trova* singers:

> You like Rock and Roll now
> before you liked trova.
> You like to live off what's in.
> You used to write convoluted lyrics
> to Latin-sounding melodies.
> And now you got a distortion and a delay
> and make it sound like Alice in Chains.⁵²

The description of a first epoch in the *trova* song invokes the climate of Latin American solidarity in the first decades of the Cuban Revolution. Indirectly, it also comments on the way in which the national cultural field functioned as an agglutinating space and as an aesthetic laboratory for an entire generation of Latin American intellectuals. That "you" who wanders through the first verses is doubtlessly the synthesis of a multigenerational figure: the second-person pronoun does not call on a particular artist but the trajectory of the singer-songwriter as an archetype. Along the same lines, "that which is fashionable" does not refer to a complicity with the musical market or the taste of the consumer as much as it does to a structure of ideological conformism that allowed the protest song to betray its own function as the poetic voice par excellence of the Latin American left. They then invite the artist to desist, to "drop that *trova* with distortion," using a colloquial connotation of the word *trova*, which in addition to referring to the traditional song form also means a narrow-minded spiel of moral or disciplinary tone that attempts to persuade someone of something. "*Trova* with distortion," in the newer generations of troubadours, presents the instrumental update—the use of electric guitars with pedals and amplifiers—into something contradictory: the incorporation of the apparently rebellious component of rock music is canceled by lyrics that are ultimately domesticated. PPR's stand suggested instead that, as long as the changes in discursive modality can be subsequently assimilated within the official cultural landscape and its spectacles of tolerance, even with "distortion and delay" the conciliatory role of the troubadour remains intact. In other words, the *trova*'s song form has outlived its critical potential, denounced by PPR as a sterile criticism unable to question the institutional bonds that ultimately determined its conditions of possibility.

This is the postsocialist punk's version of *pachanga* without socialism: an aggressively improper hedonism rather than simple withdrawal or witty critique. This combination of punk attitude, parody of officialdom, systematic insult, and pleasure in obscenity therefore results in the impossibility of negotiating entrance into the public sphere even under the new rules of increased tolerance. PPR did not adopt its antisocial opposition from the idea of punk understood as a nebulously rebellious subculture, because this would simply amount to reinsertion in a known category. Instead, the emphasis on drugs, sex, and punk rekindled the idea of an undisciplined, consuming body, but the band's targeted insults, source materials, and performance antics—once playing from the balcony of an apartment out to the street, until authorities disconnected the electrical supply—drew its institutional antagonists into its own debased, graphic, socially unacceptable symbolic space.

No wonder the band's best-known song was "El Comandante." It carried out the unthinkable task of insulting Fidel directly; "the Commander" was one of Fidel's many epithets. While the private humor around the figure of Fidel is prolific, the song, in addition to giving private irreverence a public voice, engages in a direct insult that threatens Fidel's authority in different ways from how popular humor tended to reinforce the revolutionary leader's image as an evil genius or mad king.[53] That distinction resides in the structure of the insult around which the song is built. A metallic voice begins the first lines of "El Comandante" in a circuslike atmosphere, and a group of voices intervenes to finally converge in a catchy refrain: "No coma tanta pinga Comandante!" ("Don't be such a cocksucker, Commander!" in the grammatical second-person formal address). Instead of only mocking Fidel's person, however, the speaking subject opts for using the vulgar colloquialism to refuse to comply with what is demanded of him:

> The Commander wants me to work
> paying me a miserable salary.
> The Commander wants me to clap
> after he speaks his delirious shit.

The insult disarticulates the symbolic authority of Fidel's command that the subject join the revolutionary project as a low-paid laborer and obedient cheerleader, thereby shifting the hierarchy organizing the discursive space of each of the song's imaginary interlocutors: the song's singing voice (that of a common citizen) and the addressee (a political figure, an unquestioned revolutionary leader). Their improper hedonisms put front and center the sonic legacy of a state-led productivism that accumulated profit by extracting value from coerced labor.

Under the song's terms, the band addresses the highest revolutionary icon with the same rude colloquialism that any two youths would use to tell each other to "fuck off" in the street, hinting at a social equivalence that is unheard of in the public square. At the same time, the grammatical formality with which the second-person formal address is used highlights the recognition of the authority in question and underscores the contradiction of the insult launched from the precarious authority of an obscure punk band. "Don't be such a cocksucker, Commander" is an aggravated version of the one directed at the *trova* singers: "desmaya esa trova con distorchón" (drop that *trova* with distortion). Toward the end of the song, another icon is brought into the spotlight: the singer's voice is artificially modulated until it blends with a familiar one, that of Silvio Rodríguez, arguably the archetype voice of the revolution. This "song within a song" parody of Rodríguez's "Te doy una canción" questions the lyrical education received and reclaims for itself the prerogative to denounce the youth idols of another era, to expose their present sterility.

The official responses to phenomena like PPR are no less significant and can be grouped into three categories: (1) the design of exclusion strategies by limiting access to mass media; (2) the direct intimidation of participants (especially flash mobs, citations, interrogations, and short-term arrests); and (3) the setup of equivalent cultural responses and the selective support of some actors over others under the rubric of the spectacle of tolerance. These strategies are favorably exploited in turn to cultivate an image of opening, of increasing flexibility, projected by the authorities to please global audiences, old-school sympathizers, and foreign political leaders and think tanks in the Cuban democracy watchlist. In this sense, Porno Para Ricardo's aesthetics were able to speak to the specificity of the postsocialist subject precisely through its simultaneous anachronism, conjunctural relevance, and relative commercial unviability: punk as such has disappeared as a current musical genre (though not perhaps as an ethos); their singularly focused thematic antics have meaning only as long as the political order they rise against remains in power; and the absence of a committed, long-term audience for punk anywhere meant unlikely sustainable success. Whatever the ambivalent and problematic legacy of the band itself, a reading of Porno Para Ricardo's poetics and the response by political and cultural authorities showcased how different voices responded to, and denounced, the discursive hollowness of the political imaginary sustaining the state's old slogans and the old songs of the *nueva trova*: the band made visible the representational crisis that pervades that imaginary through the use of parodic obscenity and performative autonomy as forms of political protest.

The PPR phenomenon shared common technological, political, and aesthetic conditions of emergence with the explosive rise of reggaeton: the dramatic expansion of the means to produce and disseminate music, as well as the popularity and appreciation for genres of music—and the stories they told, the spatial and sonic experiences they offered—that did not require formal schooling, instrumental and compositional virtuosity, or professional networks of management and accreditation to get started. As Ernesto Castro also suggests in his book on Spanish *trap*, new urban music genres and punk share deep aesthetic, technical, and political affinities despite their apparent differences and historical divergences. Both of them present models of non–state mediated, subversive *pachanga* that reject revolutionary *pachanga*'s call for cheerful sacrifice and synchronized labor even if these models are themselves bound to hypermasculine identities shared with the revolutionary state. The hedonism and consumerism inherent to punk and reggaeton are imaginaries that respond to economic hardship and political distrust articulated within the social rhythms and aesthetic values of the communities where they take root, who hear in them their hopes of some measure of success—however trivial, frivolous, and ideologically problematic the terms in which they are expressed may seem—whether it be romantic success, economic success, or social self-determination; each popular song becomes the authentication of the DIY ethos, a chance for upward economic mobility, and the legitimation of self-made dignity and recognition.

Coda: *Patria o Muerte/Patria y Vida*

According to his accounts of the incident, on August 31, 2018, PPR's singer was physically attacked backstage in the Miami Cuban channel Canal 41 by the *reggaetonero* El Chulo, who was accompanying the popular reggaeton *reparto* group El Kokito, El Negrito y Manu Manu. Ávila asked what they thought about the anticipated implementation of the Decreto Ley 349, which explicitly extended government control over independent culture. When the *reggaetoneros* did not want to discuss politics, Ávila questioned how they could come to Miami and perform without positioning themselves in any critical way. The question of whether reggaeton was problematically apolitical has long haunted the meteoric popularity and subsequent internationalization of Cuban reggaeton, as incidents involving Gente de Zona, la Srta. Dayana, and other Cuban musicians who have been publicly confronted about their political silence have shown. Typical complaints regard their success as an obstacle to confronting authorities in the way their counterparts have done in hip-hop and rock. With their popularity, so the argument goes, *reggaetoneros* had the potential to reach audiences on an entirely different level. Many *reggaetoneros*, after all—e.g., Alexander Delgado from Gente de Zona and El Micha—began in the gritty, underground, explicitly politicized hip-hop scene. But remaining apolitical generally protected the performing, financial, and travel benefits they enjoyed domestically, even if they live primarily abroad. This is not a problem unique to Cuba: J. Balvin in Colombia faced questions about whether successful Latin American urban musicians can remain apolitical or moderately critical when confronted by state-sanctioned violence during the 2019 and 2021 protests in Colombia.

The YouTube release on February 16, 2021, of the song "Patria y Vida" (Fatherland and Life), a collaboration between Yotuel, Descemer Bueno, Maykel Osorbo, el Funky, and Gente de Zona, shifted dramatically that understanding, and the song became an overnight sensation. Becoming a street anthem in Cuba and the diaspora—with over 12 million views in YouTube as of 2023, and countless reproductions via alternative media in the island—the song has become a media phenomenon in its own right.[54] "Patria y Vida" and other songs that followed it—most notably El Micha's "Un sueño (Cuba grita Libertad)"—are not only an effect of the success of "Patria y Vida"; they are also symptoms of the worsening economic crisis during Donald Trump's presidency first and the COVID-19 pandemic later. They marked a shift to more public displays of general discontent in mainstream popular music, which historically favored coded social criticism of everyday struggles over explicitly political statements such as

> people suffering others taking decisions
> an urgent change is what people want
> things are bad and even the president knows it. . . .
> they tightened the shoe threw away the sock
> between (food) queues and covid things are serious. . . .
> I dreamed people were in charge.[55]

Unlike PPR's underground mock slogans, "Patria y Vida" chants featured prominently in the 11J street protests.

"Patria y Vida" had an earlier version that, like PPR itself, targeted directly *trova*'s legacy as protest song. "Ojalá pase" (with two meanings: hopefully it comes to pass, hopefully it passes away) by Yotuel and Beatriz Luengo remixed "Ojalá" by Silvio Rodríguez, who complained his song had been plagiarized and used in a work that was critical of the government to boot. "Ojalá pase" was released in January 2020 on the sixty-first anniversary of the Cuban Revolution and introduced verses and melodies that would become some of the most sung in "Patria y Vida" as a slogan capturing the anxieties of Cubans about change and continuity like few others:

Tu 59 yo doble 2 (2020)
60 años trancado el dominó

(You 59, I double two [2020]
Sixty years, domino gridlocked)

The fact that all these artists came together—especially Gente de Zona and Descemer Bueno, who had been criticized for performing in state-sponsored events in Cuba—and the inclusion of the persecuted Movimiento San Isidro *artivists* Funky and Osorbo, was unprecedented. So much so that two weeks later the government responded with its own song, "Patria o Muerte por la Vida," released on YouTube's *Cubadebate* channel on March 1, 2021. The memesphere and social media lit up with complaints and derision about a progovernment tune seriously lacking in flow that accused the "Patria y Vida" artists of being traitors and mercenaries. Interestingly, the government's response uses a supporting cast of women around the male *trova* singer-composer Raúl Torres to contrast with, without subverting, the male-dominated cast of urban music and the "Patria y Vida" video clip.

This war of songs was a war of slogans, a struggle over symbolic and real spaces as markers of hegemonic power: the "Patria y Vida" phenomenon has effectively emptied out any remaining aura of seriousness left in the official, omnipresent "Patria o Muerte" (Fatherland or Death) war cry born at the height of the Cold War. This slogan is the symbol of an official culture of deathly sacrifice and siege mentality far from the classic images of dancing socialism advertised by "*Revolución y pachanga*." In contrast, "Patria y Vida" fills that empty semiotic space by offering an alternative that does not demand the impossible, ultimate sacrifice, as does the classic revolutionary slogan that it aims to substitute. Beyond its intended circle of listeners, it had an impact, too: the most-viewed episode of the US-based Dominican YouTube offering "El Show de Valentín"—a Christian conservative right-wing vlog—is a reaction to the song as evidence of communist failure. Similarly, the conservative Uruguayan president Luis Lacalle Pou saw fit to quote the song's lyrics to address the Cuban president at the September 18, 2021, meeting of the Community of Latin American and Caribbean States. Red-washing and red-baiting, old bedfellows, are never apart in the postsocialist mediascape.

Barthes's classic *Mythologies* opens with an aphorism derived from a verse of Horace's *Ars Poetica*: *bis repetita placent* (things that are repeated are pleasing). Slogans and songs both are ontologically dependent on that very principle. Repetition as an aesthetic procedure, whichever kind of pleasure it generates—including negative pleasure, as in earworms—succeeds by playing and preying on the affective economy of recognition. The impact of "Patria y Vida" on the Cuban soundscape builds on the hypothetical interchangeability between the political slogan and the chorus or refrain as rhetorical forms that give shape to the body politic—through repetition, familiarity, portability, and aesthetically mediated social communion—and posits the possibility of subversion of the former by the latter, though what it means with its call for "homeland and life" remains open enough to be filled by each individual demand. "Patria y Vida" was welcomed as both a personal and a national anthem in this mediascape, challenging the socialist sonic past and its present. During the brief, serial temporality of each singalong—in a kitchen, on the streets, around the world—amplified by digital media and made portable and common through voices and devices alike, a changing body politic sought an alternative collective sound and a critical language of its own.

CHAPTER 3

Postsocialismos de Bolsillo
Women and Fashion in Secondhand Time

July 16, 2018: After consulting the Donde Hay app, I head to Galerías Paseo, a hard-currency shopping center in Havana, to buy Vietnamese toilet paper, bottled water by Nestlé's Cuban affiliate outfit Ciego Montero, condensed milk from Lithuania, and a Mexican laundry detergent. *Dónde hay* roughly translates as "where is it?," meaning which store has what. The app was launched in the summer of 2018 by the state trading corporation CIMEX to help consumers better navigate what was a daylong trek to find what government store stocked which needed product—or if it did at all: one may have cooking oil but no soap, another may have tomato paste but no spaghetti, and so on. Two women stand in an aisle where the transition from household cleaning to beauty products is seamless and abrupt. "What does this say? Is this conditioner?" I sneak a peek. They are talking about an Argan oil moisturizing mousse imported from Italy but without Spanish instructions. I, too, had spent some time deciphering the proper use and place of origin of products that, newly available (albeit at exorbitant markups at hard-currency state-run stores), did not have Spanish-language labels but remained in the original Portuguese, Italian, Vietnamese, Persian, Russian.

The 2014 restructuring of the national debt, the development of the Mariel Free Trade Zone, and new or expanded economic trade agreements since 2000 increased the number of available consumer products from Vietnam, former Soviet republics, Iran, Brazil, Spain, Mexico, and Italy. The government's Donde Hay app was one of the efforts undertaken by Cuban institutions to compete in a crowded market, following state initiatives like Oferta.cu and its print version (2015–present), promising a "secure road" to classifieds. These state-owned platforms have long-established, nonofficial counterparts, such as porlalivre.com and Revolico—the most popular but locally blocked website for classified ads in Cuba—or La Chopi, one of the many local apps advertising and connecting local businesses with consumers in the nonstate sector. They are accessed by proxy or via offline versions, distributed through digital sharing networks, and updated weekly. (*La chopin*, or "the shopping" in English, was the popular name given to the select consumer stores that opened in the late 1980s, where goods were sold in dollars and access was reserved for foreigners, diplomats, and other special personnel.)

Such locally developed offline apps and proxy access to platforms for nonstate and informal economies offer a peak into the digitalization of what Jorge Pérez-López ([1995] 2018) has called Cuba's "second economy": the black, gray, and informal markets that have become, with the retreat of central planning, a rapidly growing sector of nonstate economic activity. These sellers reach their customers through social media as well, and Telegram and WhatsApp groups double as virtual stores and marketing platforms. They all supplement the offering of the official hard-currency stores with cheaper or otherwise unavailable merchandise. New consumers thirst for information in an opaque and still unstable market environment. While Cuba remains an international object of political desire, the global market emerges as a national object of desire instead, a localized desire that is codified and managed differently within and beyond Cuban borders by different constituencies and stakeholders.

If the Cuban postsocialist context, as I contend in this book, is better understood by the explosion of images and narratives that chronicle continuities and transformations in everyday life at the meeting point of digital cultures and informal economies, what are these new media images? How and by whom are they generated? And how do they differ from top-down images of postsocialist Cuba? The aesthetics of what I call "portable postsocialisms" and the media agents that produce them further challenge persistent visions of a reality that many Cubans no longer recognize as their own: the sordid, eroticized apocalypticisms of the post-Soviet years (the 1990s of the Special Period), the siren song of a historically exotic location ripe for emotional and commercial investments as promoted by the foreign gaze, and the identity of abiding underdog of principled humanist socialism projected by official state discourse.

Beyond the perceptions of imminent change projected from outside Cuba, and against the relentless appeal to historical continuity and monolithic unity voiced by the party and its state apparatus, the postsocialist mediascape features the exploration of other values, identities, and concerns, both old and new, in response to those double pressures from global markets and local political leaders. Cubans, like most of the world, are also increasingly involved in the creation of media images of themselves as producers, consumers, citizens, and spectators. Looking at the postsocialist mediascape at the meeting point of culture, digital media, and informal and nonstate economies, this chapter zooms in on images of the Cuban "woman of fashion" as one of its iconic subjects. These images engage the new economic and media landscapes, but they specifically challenge simplified dichotomies pitting the heroic socialist revolutionary past, the Cuban government, and the nation-state against the postsocialist-cum-capitalist present, imported consumerisms, and world markets. Those dichotomies, I maintain, are no longer useful (if they ever were). The postsocialist Cuban woman of fashion, and the discourses around her practices of consumption and beautification, synthetize but also update these anxieties about the end of the national socialist project and its trials with altered economic and media landscapes.

The Aesthetics of Portable Postsocialisms and the Cuban Woman of Fashion

Taking stock of the multilingual shelves at Galerías Paseo I recall Reina María Rodríguez's poetry collection on women, fashion, and the art of dressmaking, particularly these verses: "Who learned to read by looking at (in passing) / the signs of other nations?"[1] Boris Groys contends that former Soviet citizens learned to navigate the sudden predatory privatizations of the 1990s by reading nineteenth-century novels, their last cultural memory of actually existing capitalism. It could be similarly argued that Cubans—and Cuban women in particular—learned about fashion and entrepreneurship from the 1990s telenovelas that accompanied their crash course in postsocialist survival. The telenovela *Vale tudo*, for example, pitted Raquel, an honest rags-to-riches mother entrepreneur against her impatiently greedy daughter, Maria de Fátima. While Fátima steals from her mother and schemes to marry into an old-money family, Raquel goes from selling sandwiches to opening the restaurant Paladar (Palate) and later a chain and food emporium. *Vale tudo* explored upward social and economic mobility from the periphery to the center by pitting (the fiction of) free-market competition against (the certainties of) primitive accumulation. This trivia is significant less because *Vale tudo*, like other Brazilian telenovelas, exposed Cubans to stereotypes of capitalist life at a crucial juncture, than because its plot interrogated whether it was possible to be successful in capitalism while remaining honest. As Fidel put it: "A certain amount of money will accumulate among the people, it's inevitable; there will be accumulation, but that's a logical outcome in a special period situation. What is to be done?"[2] To remain honest—if not to remain socialist—was something with which the official government discourse and everyday Cubans struggled at the time, especially as the exploitative extractivism of foreign capital investments and privatization, the collapse of public services, rising inequality, mass migration, and the growth of corruption, black-market speculation, and subsistence economies became ever more palpable. The other significant, common text in survivalist entrepreneurship was furnished by *Oshin*, the epic soap opera and rags-to-riches story of a Japanese woman struggling through the history of modern Japan, broadcast on Cuban state television in 1990. *Oshin* (1983–1984, NHK network) was a global hit, and the protagonist became a role model of incorruptible perseverance, known for her skills as a professional hairdresser but also working a variety of jobs throughout her life in defiance of traditional expectations against working women. *Oshin* may well have influenced a popular imaginary where hairdressing and self-care became essential tools to face a national crisis with dignity.

The collective perception of looking out from the inside, of living in secondhand historical time, to borrow Svetlana Alexievich's unrivaled phrase, was for too long embedded in the material realities of secondhand fashion and (whether accurate or not) nurtured a sense of embodied outdatedness that compels the Cuban postsocialist consumer, and women in particular, to want to catch up. Nieve, the Cuban protagonist of Wendy Guerra's novel *Everyone Leaves* (2012 [2006]), recollects a similar sentiment:

> I told her that the weirdest thing about my childhood was my closet. If I open it and examine my old wardrobe, it can tell the story of my life and of my friends. One by one they've left me something to wear. Before leaving to Miami, Dania bequeathed me two pairs of blue jeans that I used well into adolescence, patching and fixing them along the way. Luckily, the most recent fashions didn't arrive here on time, and we could wear almost anything and get by. Now it's different, because we care more about what's in style out in the rest of the world. The news reaches us through the people who come and go.[3]

The year is 1987 in the novel, a bildungsroman told through succinct, often harrowing entries from the diaries of Nieve, whose first-person account of a childhood and adolescence in Cuba from 1970 to 1990 narrates the oblique ways in which individuals experience a collective history. The reader is invited to peak into the private, gendered dimensions of contradictory national politics by what is told as much as by what is only hinted at or not told at all. At seventeen, out of a rural town first, and out of the urban slums finally, Nieve leaves those mended, inherited clothes behind, doubly seduced by a glamorous older lover and by the illusions of distinction offered by the mass image of the fashion system: "We went into a store for diplomats. . . . I'd never imagine that any of these things could be found in Cuba. In fact, today is the first time I've ever bought anything off the rack, the first time I don't have to tailor things."[4] In the Cuban discourses of and about the postsocialist woman of fashion, consequently, beauty is not merely a *promesse du bonheur* but the aesthetics of experimentation with the promise of political change, of leaving behind secondhand clothes and secondhand time along with it.

This perception is externally reinforced as well. A middle-aged American intellectual on her way to Romania, Sylvie, the main character of Chris Kraus's novel *Torpor*, embodies that gaze, connecting the perceived outdatedness of postsocialist subjects with their status as media agents. Citizens of former communist regimes "have been deprived of media images of themselves for thirty years," according to Sylvie, remarking on the recognizably outdated fashion of the "Easties" while passing through East Berlin in 1991.[5] Guerra's chronicles of historical abandonment, and Kraus's dramatization of the Western intellectual's engagement with the postsocialist milieu, help to frame the broader questions I would like to pose here: how the relationship between media and their audience in actually existing socialism has been portrayed and conceptualized by different actors and how it is remediated in the postsocialist context. In other words, the issue is not whether citizens in historical communisms were deprived of media images of themselves; the issue is what kind of media images of themselves they were offered and by whom. How new media agents engage this contested visual archive in the process of representing themselves and the nation is particularly relevant given the symbolic weight attached to revolutionary Cuba by multiple constituencies that claim its historical legacy within and beyond its national borders.

These transformations are particularly evident in the aesthetics of the emergent advertising and entertainment offers that circulate primarily through offline mobile apps, DIY wi-fi networks, and sneakernets that make domestic and international audiovisual content available to the general public outside official media channels. This new media ecology is characterized by the portability, digitalization, and massification of the former analogue networks sharing underground bootleg content. Now partly monetized and home to the first comprehensive, countrywide system of commercial advertising for local consumers since the elimination of commercial publicity and private enterprise, the most well-known of these sneakernets is *El Paquete*.

No discussion about digital media in Cuba can avoid *El Paquete*, a weekly release of about 1 terabyte of multimedia data. Users subscribe for home delivery throughout the week or meet carriers (colloquially known as *paqueteros* or *transportadores*), sellers, or generous friends to download all or part of it. And there is much to say about it: it is the first and, as of 2023, the only nationwide nonstate mass media distribution platform in Cuba since 1959. It is the largest repository of the advertising system for local businesses and informal circulation of national and international news, entertainment, digital tools, and textual and audiovisual materials. *El Paquete* digitized, centralized, and monetized its predecessors in the underground cultural economy: private video and game rental banks, illegal satellite antennas, and organized communities for bootleg copying and sharing. It is the unofficial platform for the consumption of the official global culture industry, but it is also the vehicle for the expansion and legitimation of the informal and emergent local economies, which exist in permanent tension with state enterprises and official discourse as much as with transnational capital and its images of Cuba.

El Paquete is not, however, an offline "internet in a hard-drive," the next phase in the struggle against communist Big Brother, or the harbinger of corrupting McDonaldizations of national media consumption, as some of the most extreme coverage portrays it to be. It is the Cuban media phenomenon that had gained the most traction and attention, making it a privileged object of study, reportage, and aesthetic intervention: from Julia Weiss and Néstor Siré's comprehensive art and digital installations, to sensationalist coverage by *The Guardian*, HBO Vice, and Vox Media, to a growing number of scholarly papers addressing its impact from the viewpoint of various disciplinary frameworks. In fact, the kind of international and scholarly attention *El Paquete* has generated says as much about the assumptions that outsiders project onto Cuba and the supposedly liberating role of media technologies as it does about *El Paquete*'s rise to prominence as a local phenomenon and socioeconomic tool.

The postsocialist "woman of fashion" is featured regularly in these window-pages where hybrid economies and digital cultures meet. Her presence in this mediascape underscores the political stakes and technological challenges of new media agents producing images of themselves and the degree to which an emerging consumer culture caters to a changing image of the Cuban woman. One of the most representative examples of this phenomenon consists of intervening international publicity with local advertising and promotion. For example, the category Revistas Internacionales (International Magazines) in *El Paquete* holds modified .PDF files of fashion and gossip magazines like *Cosmopolitan* and *¡Hola!*. Along with their original ads—largely irrelevant for most Cuban consumers—these digital copies include publicity for local businesses and services. A similar procedure applies to pirated TV shows, which likewise feature lower-third ads for local businesses and services. Full-page ads for three local photography studios, one hair salon, and a party-organizing service stand between the cover of a .PDF version of the Spain *Cosmopolitan* issue for May 2015 and the original publicity included in the magazine, for Chloé perfume and Clinique lotion.[6] When the file opens, the subtly made-up, inviting bashful smiles of the actress Paula Echevarría, the cover model, and Clémence Poésy, the perfume model, framed by floating tresses in deliberately impromptu poses, share the spotlight with provocatively dressed anonymous Cuban teens looking directly at the camera, with half-open mouths and tilted heads, brightly colored makeup, extravagantly dyed and curled hair, gem-studded acrylic nails, and hips and pelvises angled prominently forward and sideways.

The advertised hair salons and photography studios offer long-lasting, bedecked evidence of *quinces* (short for *quinceañera*, the celebration of girls, and sometimes boys, turning fifteen), weddings, and other special events. Their forms of representation and their kindred media practices index the irruption of what George Yúdice has called *el pueblo feo* (the ugly nation) in the generation of aesthetic content. Authorship and ownership of one's own image, both individual and collective, determine when such vernacular media literacies are in play, defined not only by active spectatorship but also by active participation in the production of culture at large. The sheer number of photography studios and hair salons advertised on these platforms may strike the casual observer as disproportionate. And the prominence of ads for photography studios would seem to contradict the thesis that digital producibility puts the authorship of their own images in people's hands. But this would be a simplistic way to understand these forms of authorship, the enduring inequalities in access to technology and know-how, and the way these factors and knowledges are organized within a specific social context and local economy.[7]

With smartphones and tablets, with preset filters and image-editing software, with online and offline sharing networks and platforms, Cubans have become adroit producers of images of themselves. The fast-growing numbers of cell-phone lines in use reported by the state telecommunications company ETECSA since the service began in 2008 (7 million lines registered in 2021 and counting) indicate that Cuba has followed the leapfrogging logic of most Latin American countries and developing regions, adding first-time mobile users before PC users who access social media and the internet primarily, and even exclusively, via portable devices. Wireless telephony in Latin America accelerated the access of three key demographics to mobile communication networks and digital content: the rural, the poor, and the very young. Bypassing the long and oftentimes fruitless waiting line for a fixed telephone number, a large sector of cell-phone users are first-time phone owners. The country's multiple digital divides persist due to the US economic embargo as much as the government's centralized monopoly on all other mass media; the state's dawdling on infrastructure upgrades also means that the longer the wait to give up political control of the media the less it is able to respond to exponential growth and to the versatility and innovation of uses and workarounds. Internet access is slow and expensive, with highly regulated traffic. First only available in fixed hot spots throughout the country, home and mobile web access were rolled out in 2017 and 2018, respectively.

However, equipment and know-how are unevenly distributed and inconsistently regulated: modems are available only on the black market, the legally sold Huawei phones remain prohibitively expensive, and GPS devices are technically illegal to import even if nearly every arriving passenger has one embedded in a smartphone. The business of unlocked or used phones and prepaid credit supports the growth of mobile telephony, a sizable, transnational informal sector dependent on the established Cuban diasporas and the new forms of travel available to Cubans. *El Paquete*'s business model relies on the specificity of this mediascape, that is, on the inequality of individual literacies, on uneven access to web content and media infrastructure, and on the state monopoly of mass media. (For example, as of 2018, the ETECSA hot spots I connected to blocked port 80 and other data transfer internet protocols, which in the standard HyperText Transfer Protocol of the World Wide Web normally allow the transmission of linked content and files between a client computer and the web host, making straightforward downloads impossible.) As such, sneakernets are lucrative at various levels: not only copying and distributing existing content but also, as with established private digital media conglomerates elsewhere, producing original material and publishing advertising for local businesses.

This emerging advertising network and its effective use of .PDF manipulation is another example of what Lisa Gitelman asserts are the ways in which born-digital texts question the "intrinsic reliability" and fixedness of print media and establish new standards of publishing by redefining what counts as publishing.[8] These practices highlight discrepancies between the uses for which a technology is designed and the purposes for which it is deployed by everyday users. In doing so, emergent producers and consumers also realize the collective desire to participate in a global economic logic, creating a virtual leveling space where, in turn, local businesses and the emerging advertising industry seek legitimation among well-established brands and their consumer imaginaries while expanding a national presence. They also shift the importance from cover to content: the political importance of both the magazine/journal format and the poster charged front covers with great symbolic weight in Cuban literary culture. The digital file, with its search function and easy scrolling, equalizes the value of the pages for readers more interested in useful, quickly accessible information than on the politics of the front page.

The aesthetics of this popular economy are closer to what Hito Steyerl calls "poor images," discussed earlier in the introduction. The poor image does not offer direct access to the reality of the subjects that produce and consume it. Rather, it conceals the lucrative platforms and the structural inequalities on which it depends. Its fundamental ambiguity—the logic of disorganized consumerisms and the disobliging forms of participatory consent that sustain it—remain nonetheless the keys to its interpretive value: "Its quality is bad, its reputation substandard. . . . The poor image has been uploaded, downloaded, shared, reformatted, and reedited. *It transforms quality into accessibility.* . . . It mocks the promises of digital technology."[9] From the material infrastructure and political energy behind the virtual economy of communicative capitalisms to the new structural and social inequalities introduced by and amplified through the veil of digital democratization, questions remain about who produces and profits from the logic of "the poor image.[10]" However, while democratized access to the aesthetic, technical, and technological means of production was at the forefront of earlier theories of new media as part of a broader project of liberation, the poor image is hardly asking to be emancipated.[11]

A poor image might not be worth a thousand words, but a poor image is better than none at all: the Cuban digital ecosystem favors smaller files to facilitate dissemination; quick access to practical information; and a promotion and production pipeline via platforms that restage the illusion of choice of, and participation in, the high-end, glossy, capitalist culture industry within the bounds of Cubans' own material reality. The postsocialist digital environment is full of those image files described by Steyerl, which nonetheless find expression in new aesthetics languages that stress their real-timeliness, pragmatism, and nonchalance: grainy videos, low-resolution and pixelated pastes, jarring colors, and stretched-out, nonaligned, and mismatched typography. However, in the higher-quality culture, fashion, and entertainment magazines made by Cubans on the island or abroad, primarily for Cuban audiences on the island and in the diaspora (*Vistar, OnCuba, elTOQUE*), the production value is visibly higher, showcasing the work of younger designers, reporters, and editors catering to a versatile audience with its own aesthetic demands and conversant in international styles and design industry standards.

These practices also highlight other ways in which Cuban postsocialism has become portable: renewed Miami and Latin American exchange flows have left their own marks on the transformation of *quinceañeras* in Cuba, as in every other aspect of popular culture and fashion. A "born again" tradition, it is deeply marked by immigration as Julia Álvarez documents in *Once Upon a Quinceañera* and as the groundbreaking bilingual sitcom *¿Qué pasa USA?* humorously addressed in its very first episode. The increasingly fashionable lavish celebration of *quinceañeras* in Cuba again is a prime example of the remixes of national customs, international fashion, personal aspirations, and media cultures that prop up a growing sector of the private economy and mark the rites of adult womanhood as initiations in an emergent consumer culture. Expensive and elaborate photo and video sessions, property rentals and hired bands for parties, and costuming and hairdressing reinforce the well-established trope of representing social success via the enactment of consumption. These updated rituals of womanhood have been the subject of analysis of several photographic series (Niurka Barroso's 1999 *Vestidos de ilusión* [Dresses of illusion], Frank Thiel's 2014 series *15*, and Diana Markosian's *Quince* from 2018) and, in the national press, of at least two highly critical articles in the long-running magazine *Bohemia*, "Vals de las apariencias" (Vals of appearance) and "Historias detrás de un abanico" (Stories behind the fan). The latter reports that some of the latest fashions involve *quinceañeras* exchanging traditional hairdos for those seen on the TV series *Vikings* and *Game of Thrones* and posing in commercial establishments with shopping bags from international brands without local stores such as Victoria's Secret. A new local magazine, *Primavera* (Spring), circulating in *El Paquete* and fashioned after international outlets whose target audience is the teen, promises to equip the Cuban *quinceañeras* with the latest tools to navigate adult femininity and the logistics of its celebration.

In contrast, the state-produced made-for-TV film *Fotos* illustrates further the inadequacy of the official response to these moral panics. It is a story of what happens to good girls who participate in the underground economy of reggaeton; it was broadcast under the División de Programas para Jóvenes y Niños (Programming Division for Youth and Children) of the Institute of Radio and Television. The film begins when the casting team of a reggaetón video clip lures a teenager, Giselle, with promises of fame and money, then copies nude pictures from a flash memory where her official headshots are; the entire school finds out. The filming team counts a stalking pervert among them. She is eventually saved by her boyfriend, her father, and the police: Giselle and her saviors then unproblematically conspire to plant drugs to make it easier to facilitate the arrest of the underground producer. The main problem that drives the didactic gaze of the film is not a critique of the dangers of posing nude, or of the insecurity of the digital information for young audiences; the morale of the plot relies entirely on the repetition of the links between underground cultural networks and informal digital media practices, on the one hand, and crime, sexual exploitation, and drugs on the other. From the perspective of an overprotective model of state media monopoly, Giselle's story is not simply a warning about the dangers of digital media illiteracy and the allures of underground economies to Cubans youths; it is also an ideologically suitable allegory of Cuba's own digital coming-of-age story.

As the site of historical experiments in media, cultural, and political democratization—whatever their heterogeneous legacies are today—the production of images of Cuba, and of images by Cubans, always takes place under a hypervigilant gaze through which its media subjects are routinely reduced to testaments of foreign-inflected consumerisms or state-sanctioned cultural policy. This was most recently illustrated by legal language enforcing Decreto Ley 349 (2018), which seeks to expand official jurisdiction over the cultural politics of the private sector. The portable, self-produced images of an emergent consumer culture often serve as easy ammunition in arguments across the political spectrum. This could mean denouncing the corrupting cultural and economic influences arriving from abroad and in detriment of hard-won socialist and nationalist values or showing the failures of the Cuban revolutionary project to transform the (vulgar, hedonistic) working masses in the long term.[12] These are attempts to convert postsocialist images into mere scapegoats of political arguments or to reduce them to sensationalized and flattened objects of curiosity. Images that inhabit the informal media economy and straddle the dubious zones of economic reinvention, those that are left outside of the pacts between the Cuban state and the global markets, can be easy evidence to decry and diagnose the supposed decline of Cuban society or the existential dangers of consumerist imaginaries.

These concerns dovetail with a revolution that was always as much a historical process as a media phenomenon: filmed, televised, radioed, photographed, narrativized, in short, *overproduced* as a planetary event. As such, the burden of representing postsocialist Cuba in all its ruinous glory weighs heavy not only on most of the literature published in and about Cuba but also on the classic outside observer, just as it did before on the "tourists of the revolution" who were called to give accounts of the extraordinary nature of the foundational political project during the early 1960s. As evidenced in the media writings of the Cuban filmmaker and theorist Jorge García Espinosa and the poet and essayist Hans Magnus Enzensberger, in Cuba there converged the global midcentury revolution in audiovisual and print media technologies with a local political will that provided fertile terrain for aesthetic experimentation and heavily subsidized investments on mass cultural and education programs. Taking as their points of reference the Cuban media experience in times of political revolution, Espinosa and Enzensberger reconsidered earlier Marxist interpretations of mass culture to outline the promises and challenges of a democratization of the technical means of cultural production when technologies of mass producibility were being developed in the 1960s and 1970s.

The mass commercialization of portable technologies that amplified the productive, and not just the reproductive, capacities of media users— such as the Xerox 914 photocopier machine in 1959 and the Kodak Super 8 camera in 1965—brought technological possibilities to bear on the long-running tension running within an "emergent" socialist media theory that revised earlier assumptions of the Frankfurt school and kindred Marxist approaches to mass culture: the question of how to democratize access to the material means and aesthetic techniques of cultural production, and also of returning ideologically appropriate images of the masses onto themselves as subject/object of history. The proposal was to use the technologies of mass reproducibility for shaping revolutionary consciousness and not, as the standard critique of mass culture in capitalism would assert, to maintain hegemonic consent and manipulate and discipline the working classes.[13]

Portability, connectivity, and producibility are now defining values for a digital culture that retools the postmodern economy of the image; value resides in our capacity to produce, exchange, and access polished images of ourselves in real time. Miniaturized, networked technologies repeat the promise to hand over authorship to the former subjects of mass media and the broadcast model. But the emancipatory implications of "going public," of a changed sensibility toward the image from (institutionally mediated) aesthetic contemplation to (commercially motivated) poetic execution, are much less clear.[14] If the socialist theory of media was preoccupied with (a) the author as producer and the political functions of the cultural worker, (b) seizing and democratizing cultural and communication means of production, and (c) the reciprocal transformation of life and culture, then what defines a postsocialist theory of media or the challenges it must contend with? What if socializing the means of production is necessary but not sufficient to deliver its emancipatory promises? What if the subjects to be emancipated continue to choose ideologically problematic representations of experience or make political choices seemingly "against their interests"? Social media and socialization of media are, of course, two quite different, even opposed things insofar as social media is corporately organized and reliant upon the exploitation and surveillance of users and data. But they offer related, if not convergent, spheres where producibility, emancipation, and the representation of political subjectivities are at stake for everyday users.

A key element of this unfolding constellation of cultural responses and media practices to the postsocialist paradigm is the budding creative industry that cuts and blends traditions of clandestine and informal culture under "actually existing socialism" with new peer-to-peer and shared-economy values, which can be as successfully antiestablishment as they are inconspicuously exploitative. For instance, technical ingenuity and cultural agency coexist within *El Paquete* and other sneakernets with unchecked exploitation and unfiltered prejudices: its editorial policy of "no porn, no politics"—a self-protective measure against state censorship—does not prevent the circulation of Christian evangelical materials in which hate speech against the enemies of traditional family values goes hand in hand with the condemnation of any form of sexual desires and behaviors outside church-sanctioned heteronormativity. The cover of a pamphlet on pornography found in the "Christian" folder reads

"Pornography reserves you a place here [in hell]" and describes pornography as a form of visual adultery and therefore a sin against marriage. More interesting, the material originates from the United States (whose Protestant missions in Cuba were among the first established people-to-people exceptions to the embargo), produced by Lámpara y Luz publishers in Farmington, New Mexico. Article 68, one of the most hotly debated (and eventually abandoned) provisions proposed by the new constitution in 2018, was recognition of marriage among persons regardless of sexual orientation and gender. The Cuban government's fraught history with homophobia and gender rights, and its selective reversal on LGBTQ+ issues, positioned the communist leadership (temporarily, in what some might argue was a carefully calculated act) as a seemingly socially progressive force with its proposal to include an amendment for marriage equality. It was defeated by a combination of widespread homophobia—once a Cuban revolutionary principle—and so-called Christian family values.[15] Furthermore, as the abortion debate in Latin America finally breaks new ground, the anti-abortion movement in Cuba—one of the few countries in the region where abortion is legal and free as a public health guarantee—has gained steam, influenced by new coalitions roaming unchecked in an alternative media ecology.

Emergent, participatory media practices cannot be automatically identified as building blocks for emancipation. For cultural studies of postsocialism, this is both a political and a conceptual challenge, as Enzensberger maintained in his theorization of socialist media in 1970 after his visit to Cuba: "The attractive power of mass consumption is based not on the dictates of false needs, but on the falsification and exploitation of quite real and legitimate ones without which the parasitic process of advertising would be redundant. . . . Socialists and socialist regimes which multiply the frustration of the masses by declaring their needs to be false, become the accomplices of the system they have undertaken to fight."[16] Several decades later, Colin Sparks's analysis of postcommunist media transitions impugns any critical project that cannot let go of the image of the state as "a kindly, if regrettably bureaucratic, agency of social regulation," and does not investigate seriously alternative forms of "self-activity and self-emancipation."[17]

These are some of the key questions posed to any postsocialist theory of media by the contemporary demands of its new constituents. These issues cannot be folded into or reduced to an economic determinist analysis of the logic of accumulation in communicative capitalism or countered with party-led statist modes of centralized control. We can no longer discuss the society of the spectacle without considering such demands expressed in new forms of cultural and media-making agency. As participatory digital media practices expand with increased access to social media and the internet, the struggle between emancipatory and exploitative dimensions of networked communication systems wrestle with remediated forms of existing social inequality that pit the amplification of dominant identities and values against counterhegemonic and emergent ones.[18]

The figure of the postsocialist woman of fashion synthesizes a series of national anxieties and desires organized around the expansion of a consumer economy in this new media context, in dialogue with such challenges. Their differentiated demands for cultural, social, and political agency, which characterize the mobile network society and are always geopolitically situated practices, generate competing, dynamic mediascapes (though not on equal footing), no longer in dialogue only with the nation-state as a sovereign force.[19] These dynamics are not unique to Cubans. But embodying the newly introduced forms of consumer culture, the woman of fashion has been an emblematic subject of a postsocialist "restructuring of feeling"—that is, caught between allegorizations of the national economy, the exercise of unsanctioned social agencies, and the pressure of performance under pervasive conservative, contradictory, and patriarchal expectations of womanhood.[20] From very different angles, the trap-reggaeton artist Señorita Dayana, the artwork and performances of the multidisciplinary artist Susana Pilar Delahante Matienzo, the poetry of Reina María Rodríguez, and the fashion label Clandestina, respond to these challenges of navigating the postsocialist Cuban mediascape from the intersection of nation, markets, and gender by creating their own images of the Cuban woman of fashion. Their interventions facilitate spaces of social and political subjectivity that are not reducible to the consumer market practices in which they are necessarily embedded, problematizing as well the normative gazes—male, white, straight, statist—that frame their own takes.

Cuban Women, Economic Crisis, and Consumer Imaginaries: Images of Themselves

Before hard-currency stores were established in Cuba (state-organized stores for small-scale, unrationed commerce of consumer goods steeply priced in dollars or their equivalent in Cuban convertible currency), consumer markets were nonexistent outside the informal economy. In fact, within the socialist bloc, Cuba occupied an extreme position in debates about the role of material incentives in the period of transition to full communism.[21] For the majority of the population, basic goods were subsidized, rationed, and distributed to the family unit, and the possibility of acquiring higher-end commodities (refrigerators, bicycles, cars, TVs) was an incentive tied to state employment and ideological performance as a *trabajador de vanguardia* (vanguard worker).

Consequently, consumption remains a problematic site for the articulation of postsocialist identities, disproportionately burdening women. Historically, "woman" has been the object/subject of consumption par excellence. Whether satisfying the traditional constructs of the male gaze, as resignified practices of sexually assertive self-empowerment, or articulating a notion of common and narrowly defined experience of womanhood, the "Woman of Fashion" endlessly reproduced in the advertising system specifically, and in culture more broadly, "is simultaneously what the reader is and what she dreams of being."[22] At the same time, all consumers are also increasingly involved in the creation of media images of themselves as producers and as participatory spectators. Like other new social types, the postsocialist woman of fashion makes a spectacle of defying and reflecting on the expectations placed on revolutionary men and women: the modesty, sacrifice, constancy, industriousness, self-effacement that characterized representations of the worker/hero and the worker/mother as ideal-types. (The protagonists of the films *Retrato de Teresa* [Portrait of Teresa] from 1979 and *Una novia para David* [A girlfriend for David] from 1985 are classic representations of those revolutionary female values.) Her emergent representations constitute popular irruptions into the space formerly occupied by the state women's magazines. The Cuban artist Gertrudis Rivalta's exquisite oil-and-sequin canvases in the *Mujeres Muchacha* (Woman Girl) series (2021–2022), reworking covers from the magazines *Mujeres* and *Muchacha*, astutely capture this moment of ongoing aesthetic deconstruction of the legacy of sanitized, ideologically appropriate images of Cuban women and of the media infrastructures and dominant gazes that sustained them.

The idea of mass access to mainstream fashion catering to women did not suddenly emerge after the 1990s crisis.[23] Despite Fidel's perennial military uniform and beard as the ultimate icon of 1960s guerrilla fashion, and undeterred by the antimaterialist *guevarism* of the early revolutionary economic policy, the mass modern will to beauty had its temples in socialist everyday life: in state-owned beauty parlors and in

Suchel and Juanita Mateo products. (Juanita Mateo, a Spanish cosmetic company whose presence in Cuba dates from 1984, was among the first foreign companies to operate in the country.) As the government moved to develop its own investments and control a sizable share of the market of beauty and cleaning products, Suchel became a mixed foreign–state enterprise in partnership with the British and Dutch conglomerate Unilever, whose market investments in Cuba began in the mid-1990s, though not without problems with labor productivity, pilferage, governmental obstacles, and the overall restrictions of the US embargo.[24]

As one of the most affected demographics by the economic crisis of the 1990s, it is not surprising that (the representation of) women has been one of the privileged sites of a collective reckoning with an uncharted national destiny. The Special Period stoked gendered stereotypes, especially of the prostitute (or *jinetera*) predicated on allegorical representations of a Cuban socialism in crisis, and on anxieties of male inadequacy confronting an economic and sexual competition with a foreign (usually European) and well-to-do male other.[25] Textbook artifacts of these specifically postsocialist forms of sexism abound, such as the musically groundbreaking NG La Banda's *La bruja* (The witch) and Frank Delgado's "Ambassador of Sex" from the perspective of a Cuban male who cannot afford sex workers' rates:

> Brothel sisters
> Show class consciousness
> Be proletarian whores
> Don't let a foreigner
> Soil your merchandise.

These lines are followed by an encouragement to offer a "unified" rate—one that doesn't distinguish between foreign and national currencies—and to be honest about their motivations: that they are acting not out of hunger but out of natural-born inclination and good business sense. Cubans were challenged by forms of female empowerment, recognition, and sexual agency in the pursuit of material independence that went beyond the double burden of the socialist woman, whom the Cuban Revolution—through the Federación de Mujeres Cubanas (Federation of Cuban Women) in particular—had recruited in large numbers into the workforce but whose primary role in household and child-rearing responsibilities remained rooted in traditional social norms and reinforced by cultural stereotypes.[26] Furthermore, the tendency toward a feminized representation of the Cuban nation has a long tradition in literary and visual culture. Its origins date to the history of the representation of the new world and to Cuba as the key port to the Hispanic Americas and has been reinforced as a "foundational fiction" of the modern nation ever since.[27] This image of the island as a woman has also existed in symbolic tension with its counterpart: the patriarchal chauvinism and militant masculinities that underwrite Cuba's modern and revolutionary nation-building discourses.

When the Cuban government pursued tourism and dollarization as a way out of economic collapse, the *jinetera* became an immediate target of social criticism, the most recognizable dramatic character in allegorical representations of the national crisis, and a testament to the declining morality—or long-term ineffectiveness—of the socialist project. The semantic effect of this tendency updated sexist assumptions that have resurfaced as part of a system of signification in which consumption, Cuban women, and sexual (im)morality became frequent bedfellows in the social text.[28] The postsocialist woman of fashion participates in these imaginaries where consuming images of women stand for the dangers of the broader consumerism paradigmatic of the transformations of economic, cultural, and media practices underway.

In popular music, for instance, the core tropes around the Cuban woman of fashion have not changed much from the 1990s, but key details of the plot have: Los Van Van's musical hit "La moda" (Fashion) and its video clip stage a compelling combination of these updated elements. The song lyrics of "La moda" tell the story of two professional women—"La China has a Ph.D. in science and Dolores in economics"—who want to get keratin treatment and hair extensions. The song sounds two alarms: that hair treatments are dangerous if applied by the wrong hands and that the price of beauty treatments and the popularity of new fashions are astronomically inflated and breaking the men's bank accounts. The song points to a subtle change in the discourses around the postsocialist woman of fashion and to her role in the representation of consumer anxieties in Cuban popular culture; whereas a weak will and material interest previously drove Cuban women into the arms of dollar-wielding foreigners, the dangerous element now is consumer culture proper:

> It's just that today's prices
> Are not those of the past
> How expensive is keratin!
> And extensions, even more . . .

. . .
Men want to get a divorce.

Wielding a vast repertoire of tricks and products deployed in the pursuit of (mass-produced) ideals of female beauty, youth, and grace, her spending habits, frivolous or enfranchising, alternatively fuel the economy or deplete pockets of men in the process of becoming worthy of their possession or their gaze.

Filmed in the privately owned Darocha hair salon, which advertises in *El Paquete*, the video clip tells a parallel story about a dishonest woman entrepreneur: a hairdresser who, seen taking cash from her clients—and from the men in their lives who pay for their hair treatments—extracts a surplus by selling hair products and extensions of questionable provenance, and goes from having a studio in her living room to an upscale locale, while the global stock prices of keratin are shown to surpass those of oil. Besides the jabs at the stock market's and sole trader's winning bets on Cuba's hybrid economy, the social and regulatory costs of the self-employment model is a common trope in critiques of Cuba's new consumer culture that highlight the ensuing restoration of classes and the growing economic inequality but skirt the structural and historical roots of these problems. As doubles of each other's consumerist frivolities, the entrepreneur and the woman of fashion are portrayed as suspicious, corruptible, and corrupting subjects of the postsocialist economy.

Looking at these examples, it would also seem that Cubans are overwhelmingly concerned with hair. Like cleanliness, hair has a long history as a social marker of race, class, and gender in the national imaginary and remains an important cultural signifier. (Cleanliness as national virtue, and the inescapable gendered images it mobilizes, becomes a subject of parody, for example, in the third vignette of Arturo Infante's 2007 short *Gozar, comer y partir* [Enjoy, eat, and leave] and in the Cuban-American lifestyle blog "My Big Fat Cuban Family.") The images of socialist apocalypse and (self-)eroticized sordid survival that predominate in the dirty realism aesthetics of 1990s cultural production had their everyday counterparts in a collective preoccupation second only to food scarcity: lack of water, shampoo, soap, deodorant, menstrual pads, and cleaning supplies. Or as Frank Delgado captures in his 1996 song "La Habana está de bala" (Havana is a bullet): "Havana is very dirty, Havana has lice, Havana has parasites." Consequently, the cult around hair products and treatments and the popularity of hairdressing are as much historical sociocultural phenomena as they are the result of concrete economic decisions: the licenses for hairdressers were among the first authorized forms of self-employment, and they partly redressed a collective preoccupation with grooming and cleanliness that was a signature of the 1990s economic crisis. Cleanliness, and beauty and cleaning products, remained overwhelmingly the concern of the (post)socialist woman as manager of the household.

I want to discuss briefly four very different projects that address the postsocialist Cuban woman of fashion at the intersection of media and markets, where her double, *la emprendedora* (the woman entrepreneur), appears as a cultural producer, subversive to different degrees and scales. These works put into circulation this double figure, yet again, as the obscure object of national desires for the market: like the *jinetera* before, it functions as a scapegoat for male and statist anxieties and simultaneously can be perceived as a figure of self-representation and empowerment, even if her agency remains limited by the established gendered dynamics of power and economic imbalance. In other words, these practices of self-representation take on, and take place within, consumer imaginaries and the racialized, gendered matrix of domination, but their aesthetic choices and self-produced images make it clear they are not, or at least do not desire to be, reducible to them.

During the 2015 Havana Biennial, Delahante Matienzo organized a beauty contest named *Lo llevamos rizo* (We wear it curly) that brought attention to the links between the disciplinary modes of racialized sociability and expectations of beauty, on the one hand, and the hair treatments and procedures, like keratin, aimed at subduing the natural, curly growth of Afro hair into straightened locks, on the other. Delahante Matienzo's installation *Dominadora inmaterial* (Immaterial dominatrix, 2012–2013), in turn, documented her online activity as Flor Elena Resident in Second Life during an artist residency in Germany. As Flor Elena, Delahante Matienzo became the financial dominatrix of as many as twenty virtual slaves who paid real money that was then cashed in through the platform. The avatar is a dark-skinned, curvy, big-haired woman; Flor engages with a long line of archetypical—and allegorical—representations of the Cuban woman as object of desire of both national and international imaginaries, from Cirilo Villaverde's foundational 1839 novel of cross-racial and cross-class romance, *Cecilia Valdés*, to a controversial 2007 Iberia Airline advertising video depicting its flights to Cuba as a place where white European males would be pampered by curvy, brown-skinned Cuban women.

As a study of an extreme—and virtual and temporary—inversion of the more familiar dynamic of Cuban sexual tourism, *Dominadora inmaterial* functioned as an art fundraising project as much as it did an ethnographic document of internet and capitalism. This work also called attention to the aesthetic expectations of the national in the art market and to those who find pleasure in financial punishment via the digital sociabilities where capital can be resignified and redistributed otherwise. It highlights the dilemma of a society founded on women's roles as objects of exchange among men, which in this case intersects with the racial and geopolitical properties of Flor Elena as an avatar. As Luce Irigaray puts in her seminal critique of Lévi-Strauss's theories of kinship, "*A fortiori*: why are men not objects of exchange among women? It is because women's bodies—through their use, consumption, and circulation—provide for the condition making social life and culture possible, although they remain an unknown 'infrastructure' of the elaboration of that social life and culture."[29] The social order depends on the exploitation of their reproductive use value, and their symbolic desirability is built on the falsified perception of their scarcity, which completes the process of women's commodification. Responding to a similar preoccupation, *Dominadora* demonstrates the capacity of the situated work of art to complicate our assumptions about media, capital, and image and to make visible the libidinal, gendered economies underwriting commodity exchange.

For her part, Señorita Dayana is arguably the most successful female Cuban singer of urban genres to date. Also known as *la que no tiene ni perro ni gato* (she who has neither dog nor cat), with this signature persona and the popularity of songs like "Soltera" (Single), "La mentira" (The lie), "Te Choca" (It shocks you), and "Tenemos el control" (We have control), Señorita Dayana gained visibility in one of the most male-dominated areas of Cuban culture: popular dance music. Using this calling card, she joined the growing international roster of popular music icons whose celebratory images of womanhood are the main commodity, a market-mediated representation of female agency, or "commodity feminism," that promotes empowerment through consumption and that conceals the exploitative mechanisms intrinsic to production and circulation of those values and images.[30] This model provides a space of agency—symbolic and economic—that works in the gap between the supposed achievements of gender equality discourses and the remaining structural obstacles and social values that remain in place to prevent its full exercise.[31]

With "La mentira," for example, a song about the necessity of lying to men (and, incidentally, a 2017 commercial for a cosmetic surgery clinic in Miami), she recasts the stereotypical female subject presented as manipulative and a spendthrift ("*No me digas que soy mala ni calculadora*" [Don't tell me that I'm bad or calculating]) as a strategy for survival in a world structured by the expectations of male desire: "*Las mentiras que te digo son las que a ti te enamoran*" (The lies I tell you are those that make you fall in love). In a context of unequal power dynamics, where the burden of emotional labor takes the form of de-escalation and pacification, she offers:

> A lot of lies, so that you don't get stressed
> So that you are happy, and not upset
> So that you are an addition, and not a subtraction
> You want to subdue me and I don't think so.

This is Señorita Dayana's response to Cuba's foremost cha-cha classic, the hit "La engañadora" (The liar), composed by Enrique Jorrín for the Orquesta América and released in 1953 by Panart Studios. The song tells the story of a woman who, having padded her clothes to seem more voluptuous, is found out and shunned as a result ("how silly women are, trying to lie to us"). Señorita Dayana shows the tactical effectiveness of certain forms of lying within the context of an old game that still promotes models of courtship where the expectations placed on women require them to be at once disinterested but impressed by male economic success, ever-present tropes in popular music hits, from La Charanga Habanera's "El temba" (The middle-aged man), to Los Van Van's "La shopimaníaca" (Shopping addict), to El Micha's "Con dinero y pasmao" (With money and without). "La mentira" sets to music a form of female agency that mobilizes effectively the structure of lying even as it reaffirms the myth of the deceptive female archetype as a sociological reality.[32]

In "Te Choca," her take on the song about success against all odds—an obligatory genre in the repertoire of any urban singer—is somewhat different in tone from those of her most popular peers. Praising one's natural talents, boasting of audience popularity and street credibility, and claims of being number one or pioneers in one thing or another are staples of the genre, as showcased by hits like Gente de Zona's "El animal" (The animal), El Micha's "Único en mi peso" (The only one in my weight), Los 4 with La Charanga Habanera's "Lo que tengo yo" (What I have), and Yomil y Dany's "Me imagino" (I imagine). "It shocks you," Señorita

Dayana ripostes to the figure of a former detractor addressed throughout the song, "that now you have to copy even my clothing style." While also framed as a story of hard work and having finally made it, "Te Choca" highlights the role of supporters and collaborators, a subject enjoying the spoils of her triumph that is always plural, and the inordinate hostility and verbal violence she has faced in a cutthroat music industry and in a predominantly male genre.

A very different proposal, the fashion label Clandestina began in 2014 as a design initiative by women under the direction of the artist Idania del Río and gained press coverage during a Q&A with Barack Obama during his March 2016 visit. Since 2018, the company advertises as the first "made in Cuba" design and clothing company to sell its products online. Their 2018 collection, Made in Cuba: País en Construcción (A country in construction), was developed in collaboration with Google and unveiled in a fashion show at the Museo Nacional de Bellas Artes in Havana, Cuba's leading art museum. Clandestina illustrates the complexities of representation and creativity in the postsocialist context, where the combination of cultural projects and commercial ventures has a fighting chance at success. The project shows that being independent and alternative no longer automatically translates as antiofficial and underground (thereby provoking the concomitant state repression), denoting a changing relationship among Cuban local producers (artisans, entrepreneurs, and *cuentapropistas*), global markets, and the heretofore all-controlling state.

Clandestina designs feature cheeky slogans like "99 percent Cuban design," "Actually, I'm in Havana," and "vintrashe" (trashy vintage) that play with but also incorporate global fashion trends, local referents, and recycled materials, playfully trafficking in ambiguously deployed political symbols. The brand name capitalizes on a synthesis of several historical and political traditions in the nation without distinction, remixing symbols of prerevolutionary republican modernism, socialist iconography, and eco-friendly tropicalism. It presents itself as a social and ecologically conscious project for the promotion of world-class design by Cuban women and as a trendy fashion label and clothing company startup. Clandestina illustrates the porous frontier between the sole traders, artistic projects, and nonstate economic and social actors and the necessary rhetorical (and political) strategies for successfully representing themselves, and the idea of a rebranded Cuba, within a global mediascape. Its hard-currency prices put them at the same level of other global brands, highlighting that the label's work is, and should be, valued on par with those of any other international designer, that it must provide a living wage to their creators. However, that also makes its products unaffordable for most working Cubans.

More important, Clandestina is an exceptional project that eclipses a dark trove of other "clandestine" popular fashions: the massive informal market for cheap clothes and the cleaning and beauty products with which they coexist and where most Cubans satisfy these necessities. Because state stores, which also sell secondhand clothes bought abroad in bulk, cannot fully satisfy the demand for basic consumer goods, a parallel market of clothing resellers and traveling bulk buyers is thriving. They import mostly Chinese-made products and counterfeit goods brought from Mexico, Ecuador, Brazil, Miami, Russia, and other common shopping destinations targeted by Cuban "mules." This submerged economy sustains the aspirations of everyday Cubans to be, and remain, worldly fashionable. Indeed, in Reina María Rodríguez's *The Book of Clients*, secondhand clothes, confiscated and inherited clothes, and containers of cheap clothes become opportunities to reflect on how fashion, like poetry, compensates for the horrors of the everyday. Poem by poem, the indulgence of the woman of fashion is remade as a tactic in which the pursuit of beauty can be a form of self-knowledge, survival, and (in)sanity. These are themes explored, for example, in the poem "The Dress": "*¿Quién puede traspasar la pasión de un vestido?*" (Who can pierce the passion of a dress?); and in the text "La pacotillera" (The materialist): "*Déjenla mentir. Que crea en la negación del tiempo.*" (Allow her to lie. Let her believe in the negation of time.).[33] *Pacotilla* refers to merchandise of inferior quality, and *pacotillero/a* is one who either peddles it or likes to buy a lot of it indiscriminately. This connotation in Cuban Spanish refers to a female consumer of cheaply made goods in large quantities, someone whose agency is recognized and validated in Rodríguez's poem. In popular culture the *pacotillera* often consumes at the expense of her man's money, and she is the subject of popular *timba* songs like Los Van Van's "La shopimaníaca" and Maykel Blanco y su Salsa Mayor's "La pacotillera."

In the poem "*¿Una cara de reina?*—dices" (The face of a queen?—you say) the corporeal estrangement of wearing secondhand clothes captures the reluctant resignation of a woman in a consignment store: "Hoy ha sido frívola y se ha comprado una blusa/ para la premiación de lo que no le han dado/ni le darán" (She was frivolous today and bought herself a blouse/for the award ceremony [of the prize] they didn't give her, and never will).[34] Rodríguez, reading Barthes, renders the dress as artisanal commodity, as status symbol, as shroud of gendered obligations, and as metaphor for the aesthetic effect of the poem upon the body politic.

Rodríguez's investigations into the zones where images of a public Cuba intersect with the intimate and with the representation of (its) women are explicitly developed further in *Variedades de Galiano*, where Rodríguez's own photographs and poems close with a commentary on recent work by Cuban women photographers: "This is how we pee subject to the undertow.... The nation is also woman and gives births, disguises herself, camouflages with the colors of dusk, with the clouds passing through the sun and the blood."[35] In a largely unchanging world of sun and blood—as far as cycles of structural injustice and inequality go—fashion has never failed to provide the illusion of change, but even illusions have a performative impact in the imagination: they nurture and camouflage the genesis—the birth—of the unexpected.

This survey across diverse cultural forms—a teen magazine, a performance artist, a reggaeton singer, a fashion brand, a poet—showcases forms of play and pleasure with gendered imaginaries of change filtered through dress and self-image embedded in the digital, symbolic, and hybrid economies of the postsocialist context. Delahante Matienzo, Señorita Dayana, Clandestina, and Rodríguez each provide singular and contrasting counterarguments about the roles that the Cuban woman has been asked to play in these postsocialist consumer imaginaries and portable mediascapes. They offer a corrective to the sense of abandonment, dependency, and secondhand pleasure that Guerra's protagonist Nieve wrestles with in the novel through the successive betrayal and loss of male authority figures, and those of the revolutionary state as their sublimation. Their aesthetic proposals do not rely on the business of (revolutionary) disenchantment; neither do they easily fold into the usual demonization of the woman as paradigmatic subject/objects of consumer culture and foreign fashion. Their chosen names and the titles of their works—*señorita, clandestina, dominadora, pacotillera*—already point to the rejoinders that reshape their public images in their own terms while simultaneously embodying the structural, mediatic, and social contradictions in which they operate. These names and the projects behind them not only authorize the desires to be single, subversive, domineering, and consumerist but also actualize productive models of self-fashioned agency within the broader structural limitations they inhabit.

The woman of fashion can also be understood as a stand-in for the desire to be fully integrated in a national narrative of postsocialist mobility, redressing symbolically (but also performatively) its gendered limitations. The double of the woman of fashion is the *emprendedora* (woman entrepreneur) celebrated in the Brazilian and Japanese soaps. This figure has become particularly visible as a result of the deepening of the economic crisis after 2019 and the government's attempts to revamp (within limits) the nonstate sector as a temporary palliative. Official media outlets like *Prensa Latina*, *Cubadebate*, and *Telesur* have featured profiles of business enterprises led by women, at the same time that independent media focused on developing and catering to emergent market literacies also foreground women entrepreneurs as untapped national resources of economic growth—as is the case with the woman-led consulting agency La Penúltima Casa (The House Before Last) and its *El pitch* podcast, or the digital magazine *Negolution* (a portmanteau of the Spanish word for "business" and the English suffix for "revolution").

Official and unofficial narratives of entrepreneurship engage, though quite differently, the perception that Cubans are catching up. While the official coverage repurposes the sacrificial ethos of crisis-driven ingenuity, national identity, and needs-based design in their framings, sleek and original branding, social media literacy, and unique offers are the highlights for prospective and current *emprendedoras* in independent media outlets instead. What these two celebratory versions of the *emprendedora* figure obscure are the legal, social, and material barriers to women in the hybrid economy, which range from less available financing, to less reliable social networks, to racial, regional, and class privileges, to being effectively pigeonholed in a few of the authorized activities of self-employment. Despite the more evenly distributed professional and educational backgrounds of the labor force along gender lines, and despite the sustained growth in women-owned businesses, men are significantly more likely to start and own businesses and be self-employed, and the state lacks any targeted support policies.[36]

The availability of internet plans on mobile devices, launched in December 2018, has also continued to transform the mediascape: Facebook, Instagram, Telegram, and WhatsApp are more relevant than ever for both legal nonstate businesses and the informal economy, as well as for setting the pace of collective perceptions of change and fashions. Any official attempt to remediate a homogenizing image of the national woman is open to instant interrogation. For example, President Díaz Canel's digital Mother's Day card on May 9, 2021, unleashed a meme chain reaction targeting the new Cuban first family's official image of women. Posing in a faux-rural tableau, the family photo was criticized for its poor design as much as for a foreign-inspired look that underscored their blondness and whiteness. It set off in reply a Twitter series of user-generated countermemes that matched Cuban or Cuban-sounding institutions with photos of foreign celebrities, e.g., the dean of chemistry at the University of Havana with *Breaking Bad*'s Bryan Cranston as Walter White.

Images do not reflect the world; they reflect upon it. By combining pictorial, textual, aural, and spatial properties, images denote and connote, evoke, combine, and communicate multiple functions and meanings simultaneously. They do not reflect the social reality; they constitutively organize it as lived meaning. In so doing, they refract the (in)visible seams of established narratives about their object of reflection. In Cuba, a change in fashions signals very specific economic, social, and political transformations, even if it is not the change most needed or the one many Cubans hope for. Looking more closely at narratives of transformation across a range of these media practices can provide a measure of changed social concerns and cultural meanings that avoids simplified dichotomies. The focus of these stories has shifted from migration to upward mobility; from marketability of tropical sexuality to the desire for recognition of racial and gendered subjectivities; from epic futures (never) to be built to immanent presents (always already) under construction.

I want to avoid reducing citizenship to consumerism, but any serious critique of the culture industry and the expansion of consumer culture in Cuba cannot forget that the state has had a very successful run with its own commodification of Cuban culture. Those who look to the Cuban state, in its current form, as a possible ally against consumer culture and capitalist exploitation rely on binary oppositions such as socialism versus capitalism or local versus global that no longer obtain. Emerging debates around entrepreneurship and *emprendedoras* underscore a pending subject of postsocialist imaginaries, namely, redefinitions and reinventions that resist both the traditional Marxist and neoliberal orthodoxies that conflate (desires for) independent economic activity with (the exploitative designs of) market capitalism.

Without being an icon of radical emancipation, the postsocialist woman of fashion invites us to think beyond binary critiques wherein Cuban images of change and continuity and consumerism and socialism, and incommensurable claims to authenticity, are reduced to the neoliberal and national(ist) hegemonic strategies that channel legitimate desires and needs onto the narrow spheres of privatization and statecraft. The pocket here—in *postsocialismos de bolsillo*—is both metaphor and material reality: it describes the portability of the mobile, digital media in which these artifacts and practices thrive, their connection to participatory processes of identity formation and reinvention, and the burdensome, out-of-pocket investments that the pressures of the informal and hybrid economy, the global market, and the state impose on everyday Cubans to feel and remain connected, up to date. Like everywhere else, they respond with strategies and agencies that are never one-dimensional and that are simultaneously responses to a shared geopolitical and technological present and locally tailored interventions.

CHAPTER 4

Cuban Screen Cultures

Postsocialist Cuba is a place and a symbol; it is also a digital media object. The Cuban social reality, and the meanings and experiences it gives rise to, are mediated by screens. Contested imaginaries of change and continuity are alternatively created for, concealed by, projected in, accessed through, and made portable via screens. Screens, and portable digital screens especially, are a key medium of the postsocialist social text. These practices and artifacts, and the social networks and material infrastructures that make them possible, speak to the battles over the meaning of continuity and change as politically expedient signifiers in the Cuban postsocialist context. I use the phrase "screen culture" here as shorthand, signifying media practices and artifacts whose production, circulation, and reception are made possible by digital technologies but where different senses of the screen as object and/or metaphor are in play.

Portable screens, affordable connectivity, and digital storage are objects of desire for Cubans: they are in high demand as practical tools of upward mobility, learning, entertainment, employment, sociability, and worldly connection. In turn, Cuba—and Cuban screens—are global objects of desire in the postsocialist condition: from Hollywood films to media studies, whether as digital detox destination, emerging market, or privileged observatory of an alternative model of digital penetration, the informatization of Cuban society is a cause célèbre. That is to say, Cuba itself functions metaphorically as a screen—shielding, framing, reflecting local transactions and global imaginaries—a role it has played before.[1] Screens simultaneously connect and set apart the local postsocialist context with and from the global postsocialist condition. Screen cultures thus mediate the interaction of competing narratives, constituents, and stakeholders and the different ways in which Cuban postsocialism as state capitalism is concealed or made visible.

The significance of the screen as a key site of collective political identity and social transformation is tied to revolutionary nation-building, concurrent as the 1959 revolution was with the audiovisual revolution of the 1960s. The Cuban Institute of Cinematographic Art and Industry (known as the ICAIC, its Spanish acronym), a national cinema engine and a platform for Third Cinema, was created in 1959, and the Cuban Institute of Radio and Television (the ICRT) was created in 1962. With his characteristic theoretical bluntness, Marshall McLuhan singled out Fidel as representative of a new type of TV-enabled politician "who rules his country by a mass-participational TV dialog and feedback . . . giving the Cuban people the experience of being directly and intimately involved in the process of collective decision making."[2] Fidel's screen persona cemented his status as a revolutionary master signifier, as a personal repository of transformative collective libidinal energies, a presence in every family's living room TV during his hours-long speeches:

> Even if we did not know
> what he was going to tell us
> just to see him
> to feel him behind the screen.[3]

In the twenty-first century, digital media—from a presidential Twitter account to Cubadebate.cu, the official news and opinion portal to combat "enemy propaganda"—remediates and invokes that mass-mediated revolutionary iconicity to project national unity and continuity beyond its historical leaders.[4]

But this technologically amplified symbolic unity in the service of power consolidation was only one face of the revolutionary pursuit of hegemony via screen culture; the other aspired to actualize anti-imperialist and socialist theories of cultural and media democratization: "The ICAIC is the only laboratory of experimental cinema in the world, a factory of [the] vanguard," the Brazilian filmmaker Glauber Rocha remarked in 1973, writing to Alfredo Guevara, then the ICAIC's director, while in exile in Rome. The letter supports the revolutionary process in Cuba for what it could do for world cinema: "The ICAIC must assert itself exporting to any possible market a model that competes with Hollywood from the most advanced center of the third world."[5]

By far the most influential theory of Cuban revolutionary screen politics, and at a time when the Kodak Super 8 camera and Xeroxing promised to transform DIY media cultures, Jorge García Espinosa's

For an Imperfect Cinema went even further to argue that more user-friendly technologies, combined with a revolutionary political will, would finally turn over the means of cultural production, including specialized aesthetic and technical know-how, to the masses.[6] This process would dislodge the grip of alienating commercial culture and achieve the radical democratic promise of the old avant-gardes: merging art and life, with art (cinematic art in particular) being understood as a vehicle of revolutionary political transformation of the masses, and revolutionary politics being understood as a vehicle of transformation of the hitherto exclusionary, elitist institution of art itself. Yet only in 2019, and after considerable struggles, was independent cinema formally legalized in Cuba, forcing a reconsideration of how communal and individual modes of audiovisual creativity engage or reject standardized state and market models of aesthetic representation, financing, and/or distribution.[7]

Coming of age with the expansion of TV, the Cuban Revolution was fully televised, as Simone Lueck documents in the photo-essay *Cuba TV*: a domestic, material remainder of this love affair with the television set. TV programing was generally more ideologically conservative, technically inferior, and more pedagogically inclined than ICAIC's productions for the big screen. Luis Trápaga and Alfredo Hevia's "Mass media" from 2011 (fig. 4.1) reflects on the affective remainders of this broken trust in an art installation consisting of a TV set fully covered with a collage of

Figure 4.1. Luis Trápaga and Alfredo Hevia, "Mass media" (2011), installation and video exhibited at the independent gallery El Círculo. State security did not allow some of the participating artists to travel to the exhibit. Image courtesy of Luis Trápaga.

mismatched socks and a playful mistranslation for title: while "mass media" translates as *medios masivos*, "media" in Spanish means "sock." A television set broadcasts a didactic, English-language nature program. A colorful patchwork effect cites the custom of covering electronic devices with ornamental fabric while not in use as protection from dust and saltpeter, given the high cost of devices for average working families and the long stretches of daytime during which there was little or no broadcast transmitted. Trápaga and Hevia go beyond the technique of concealing an everyday object by wrapping it in order to bring attention to it or to offer a different mode of seeing the ordinary. The quiltlike impression of the socks coming together to block the device suggests a potentially adversarial reaction toward the apparatus and/or its programming, if the sock pile is to be thought of as the result of a collective, aggregate effort. The installation took place in the home-based, independent exhibition space El Círculo in Havana, further emphasizing the role of a private-public agency, of a bottom-up yet homebound collective subject that rejects official, top-down media images of the nation.

The artwork, and its censored residential exhibition, negate the totality of any media system in shaping a subject that was never a passive spectator to begin with, and who, within her conditions of possibility, retains forms of subjective and practical agency, however modest. Layered onto this standard critique of TV as mass media, whether as an ideological mouthpiece of politicians or for capital, are readings specific to its context: the enduring control of the media by the Cuban Communist Party as self-appointed ideological guardian of the people and the increasing irrelevance of the small screen in the era of even smaller, portable ones where the bootleg audiovisual offer is richer, highly personalized, and available on demand. To a bilingual speaker (English and Spanish), the wordplay in "mass sock/mass media" further signals the unstoppable expansion of the various local sneakernets as well. Given the limited access to high-speed, affordable internet connections and digital storage capacities in Cuba, most of the demand for foreign and digital content is satisfied through bootleg DVDs, CDs, and external hard drives as local alternatives to online peer-to-peer file-sharing methods, which travel "on foot" via couriers around the country.

Cuba's postsocialist transformation began to appear on screens nationwide via Cuban-made TV shows and films in the early 1990s. The first episode of the hit detective series *Day and Night* features an illegal bar where an Afro-Cuban religious drumming party and a meeting of delinquent hustlers is happening simultaneously. Two cops stumble into the bar after breaking up a fistfight over a woman, and one tells the other: "In these clandestine beer bars we always find surprises."⁸ These racial and class allusions, tied to the portrayal of new economic activities and emergent social identities in a negative light as always suspicious, reinforced patterns of exclusion and selective tolerance of new social and economic activity in public life that have affected disproportionally, and in different ways, Black Cubans, women, the LGBTQ+ community, and political dissidents.⁹ A long history of criminalizing misfits and nonconformists—in the legal figure of "pre-criminal dangerousness"—served also as a scapegoat for the generalized moral bankruptcy characteristic of the "late Socialist subject," who complies in public with the performance of ideological loyalty to the revolution while engaging in the black market and voicing dissent in private.¹⁰ Its counterpart was a state that reserved the right to participate in and profit from legal and *alegal* (unregulated)

Figure 4.2. Decorated room of a *dorama* fan and reseller. She is in her seventies and belongs to a group of friends who trade *dorama* titles among themselves, though she sells copies from her collection to others outside the group. The group of friends, all women of similar age, meet regularly to discuss the soaps and all things South Korean. Author's photo, July 2018.

markets to bureaucrats and foreigners (e.g., importing articles via diplomatic channels and reselling them in the black market during the economic collapse of the 1990s). The widespread perception that economic openings have overwhelmingly benefited those with previous political capital has also deepened a sense of collective mistrust of the government-managed transition to a hybrid economic model of state and nonstate activity.

But from the 1980s onward, it was foreign telenovelas that codified most profoundly postsocialist imaginaries of change, a process Ana M. López describes as "a funky Caribbean glasnost."[11] The first family-operated restaurants took their name from a Brazilian soap opera, after those of a self-made heroine in the wildly popular telenovela *Vale tudo* (Anything goes). A cautionary tale about old money, greed, and hard work, its 1993 transmission in Cuba could not have been more propitious, as the spread of *paladares* was concurrent with the airing of the program. These small-scale food services, from snack kiosks to bootleg bars based in private homes, were formally authorized in 1995.[12] The first private businesses to be officially allowed by the government in three decades, they had been operating clandestinely as makeshift responses to an economic collapse whose national impact has been compared to the Great Depression of 1929. When it came to the cherished prime time of the soap, national screen time was divided in the era of fixed-time programming: Cuban-made soaps (*la novela nacional*) were usually period pieces that explored the social injustices of colonial and prerevolutionary society and were broadcast Tuesdays and Thursdays, while Brazilian soaps (*la novela brasileña*) usually took place in contemporary settings and were broadcast Mondays, Wednesdays, and Fridays, both at 9 p.m. On the one hand, the strict management of screen time and space, and the different production and thematic values, signaled important differences between local audiences and the fictional subjects portrayed: the us and them, the here and there, the then and now. On the other hand, these soaps and their consumption signaled real-life transformations happening all around, as screen-time compartmentalization was eroded and cultural meanings reworked to analyze national events through foreign media objects. In a similar vein, Cuban audiences renamed the popular German film *Das Leben des Anderen* (The life of others, about an East Germany spy). They changed the Spanish title, *La vida de los otros*, to *La vida de nosotros*, since the Spanish word *"otros"* (others) rhymes with *"nosotros"* (us).

In the twenty-first century, where screen time is no longer compartmentalized yet the sense of not being fully part of the global mediascape remains, Korean *doramas* (fig. 4.2) have gained a significant following among soap-opera spectatorship in postsocialist Cuba, just as it has among other Latin American publics. For fans, "different," "romantic," and "beautiful" define *dorama*'s appeal against the backdrop of their everyday experiences, as apparent windows of desire into the lives of global others were opened wider still by digital technology, as if *doramas* were not themselves the hyper-stylized, marketable emplotment of those global others' own parallel imaginaries of upward mobility, melodramatic catharsis, and social change. Attuned to these shifts, the Cuban government announced the closing of the ICRT in 2021 and its reorganization into a more comprehensive, up-to-date media regulatory body subordinated to the central administration of the state. Meanwhile, across the Florida Strait, América Tevé Channel 41 and Radio Caracol employ many former ICRT actors and producers, with programming targeting Cubans in the homeland and diasporas. Carlos Vasallo, the CEO of the parent network America CV, has called for a multimedia outreach to Cubans in a future "free Cuba" as part of a company expansion strategy in the Hispanic market.[13]

The polemics around Cuban digital screens in the twenty-first century build on these competing interests between the revolutionary state, the global culture industry, capitalist and market desires—as distinct, if entangled, imaginaries—and local constituents. Two lines of inquiry have consequently dominated the discussion from the outset: (How) does the digital turn transform the relationship between (authoritarian) state power and citizens? And can the revolutionary state still be thought of as a counterhegemonic actor against the inroads of colonial communicative capitalisms at the global level and as the guarantor of equitable redistribution at the domestic one?[14] The Cuban government describes its policies on digital information and communication technologies (ICTs) as part of an alternative model privileging quality over quantity content, and collective over individual access, in line with its paper models for public health, education, and culture. How terms like "quality," "collective," and "access," however, are deployed and defined, and by whom, casts doubt on the binary choice between individual and collective models of access as presented and between state- and market-led access and development as they actually exist in Cuba.

Another question is whether and how digital screens and ICTs support, or not, counterhegemonic, community-grounded practices and discourses in the context of a revolutionary hegemonic crisis and whether and how the postsocialist mediascape can allow for a redefinition of alternative political imaginaries and praxis. Beyond cultural and media representations of postsocialism, I am interested in multimedia practices, narratives, and agents that engage with digital screen cultures to problematize established binaries (inside/outside, national/international, state/market, socialist/capitalist). The art projects, media artifacts, and digital narratives and agents discussed below critically address select aspects of infrastructure and state policy, networked sociability, and digital public spheres to map national and international imaginaries of postsocialist change and continuity. We continue to explore how postsocialist culture as lived experience makes sense through and in new, portable media, in intimate dialogue with how Cubans see themselves and how they want to be seen as cultural producers and political agents in a digital mediascape that privileges self-publication and more horizontal, if not always more equitable, forms of communication.

(Dis)connected Cubas

July 12, 2018: I am sitting in John Lennon Park in Havana, trying to get online. A wi-fi card from a black-market reseller connects my device to the internet via one of the state telecom's hot spots (there were none for sale at the official kiosk). The website for *14ymedio*, the first digital independent newspaper produced from Cuba, is blocked. Thankfully Revolico, the classified ad forum for the informal and nonstate sector, is available. It was Cuba's first and most popular Craigslist-style website, hosted in Spain. It was blocked between 2008 and 2016, available only via proxies and offline mirrors until then. I need a plumber and find one available. Before Revolico, it could have taken days through word of mouth alone. Nearby, two self-employed *almendrón* drivers enumerate to their Miami family and co-investors the pieces and exact sums needed to keep the business going. The car has not moved in two weeks, and they are losing business. It's not quite eavesdropping: the wi-fi spots in public parks encourage loudly shared intimacies over videoconferencing and VoIP apps, a new type of public/private hybrid space; this is not unusual in a city where windows and doors are often open, dissipating the tropical heat and connecting street and domestic space through the sounds of everyday life. There are specific ways of accessing and using ICTs in the context of slow speeds, high prices, the US embargo, and total surveillance: data- and signal-sharing apps like Zapya and Connectify, VPN networks, proxy addresses, and a dynamic offline/online hybrid media ecosystem, where the latest curated online content is rapidly available offline for less than its equivalent online cost.[15]

Digital, networked, portable media transformed the state's media monopoly. The state's economic reliance on tourism and remittances demanded it, as both require reliable, real-time transnational electronic communications and transactions. So did a citizenry eager to connect to the world and each other. The launch of commercial cell-phone lines in 2008 by the state telecommunications company ETECSA marked the exponential adoption of portable, internet-capable communication technologies and fueled myriad grassroots initiatives. Informal and gray-market technical experiments have flourished along with the proliferation of digital screens—from dissident bloggers to Instagram influencers, from local mobile apps that work offline to internet-sharing hacks—while high-caliber negotiations between state and market actors (ETECSA, Telecom Venezuela, Huawei, Google) divvy up the digital real estate, balancing the state's need for maximum political control, the logistic requirements of a global economy and professional workforce, and the pursuit of a profitable and up-to-date media and communications industry in light of the increasing demands of everyday users as producers, consumers, citizens. Just who will control this expansion, and who is better poised to benefit from it in the long run—the PCC, transnational capital, new elites, everyday citizens, dissidents, or the Cuban diaspora—are issues yet to be decided.[16]

The politics of the portable has many angles, but none is as far reaching and less visible than the infrastructures of the digital, which our everyday modes of engagement with portable screens, and the persistence of national frameworks of analysis, tend to conceal. The first Latin American country to connect to a submarine telegraph cable system in 1867, Cuba was the last one to connect to the underwater fiber optic system, which links the country to the internet in addition to satellite. But this connection, operating a Venezuela–Cuba–Jamaica link since 2013 (ALBA 1), did not jump-start wider, cheaper, and faster broadband internet access as expected. Investment priorities have been channeled toward portable connectivity instead, wherein models of navigation, pricing, data collection, and customization limit significantly the agency and experience of everyday users within the closed architecture of small smart screens. Cuba therefore follows the same leapfrogging connectivity patterns observed elsewhere in Latin America of comparative "high growth, low (total) penetration," where the biggest asymmetries are observed between urban and rural areas and where the backlog of fixed-line connectivity demand, endemic corruption, political interests, and economic limitations shape the prevalence of mobile prepaid systems and the lack of socially oriented broadband investments.[17] Chinese telecom companies Huawei, ZTE, and TP-Link provide the national network infrastructure and the devices available for sale in the domestic market, though a vast black and gray market powered by the Cuban diaspora supplies citizens with unblocked phones at more affordable prices and with remittances in the form of prepaid data. Meanwhile, the Cuban and US governments play the blame game for the country's low levels of internet connectivity and its prohibitively high prices, even though both share responsibility.

Connectivity is subject to internal and external embargoes and a highly unstable regulatory environment. On April 13, 2009, President Obama signed a memorandum to the secretaries of commerce and the Treasury modifying parts of the trade embargo on Cuba that, among other things, introduced two key measures that affected Cuban communication technology development and investment: authorization to offer Cuba telecommunication services like the installation of fiber optics, roaming, and satellite by US companies, and the lifting of restrictions on family travel and remittances to Cuba imposed on Cubans and Cuban Americans living in the United States. Yet the language used in the press release by the White House press secretary's office ("SUBJECT: Promoting Democracy and Human Rights in Cuba") confirmed the Cuban government's claim that any offer of contracting US companies for infrastructure and large-scale connectivity would be coupled to a political destabilization program. Restrictions imposed by the United States Treasury block direct access to the services of many US technology companies, which also find the regulatory instability and ambiguity in US-Cuban relations an impediment to further investment. The architecture of surveillance and censorship layered onto domestic networks by the Cuban state in turn caters to the party's perceived ideological threats: blocking websites and portals, disciplinary measures and confiscations, import bans on networking equipment, and internet blackouts are part of a larger effort to police the national mediascape based on vaguely defined parameters like "social interest, morality, good customs, and personal integrity" and to retain the technical means of social communication "in the hands of the people" as defined by the state (Decreto Ley 370/2019). A sweeping cybersecurity law, Decreto Ley 35/2021, was issued after antigovernment street protests were amplified by and convened on digital media. The law reaffirms the state's digital sovereignty and stipulates that all ICT users are to refrain from offensive, false, and politically destabilizing speech and from unauthorized technical equipment uses and modifications. A new 2022 provision in the Penal Code further criminalizes offensive public speech against those holding political office.

The first legal, free wi-fi spot in Cuba illustrates the play between the state's spectacle of tolerance and the performativity of public access, on the one hand, and its practical inequalities and regulatory overreaches on the other. It was a pilot project in Havana at the art studio and community initiative Museo Orgánico de Romerillo (MOR, 2014–2017). In line with the performative tolerance that independent blogger Claudia Cadelo called, following Fidel's famous dictum to intellectuals, "Within art everything, outside of art nothing," MOR was a Kcho (Alexis Leyva Machado) project with special authorization from ETECSA, paid by the artist at a reported cost of $900 per month, beginning in March 2015. Adjacent to the historically underserved neighborhood of Romerillo, to the notorious architectural complex the Instituto Superior de Arte, and to the Paradero de Playa—a crucial transportation connection node in the capital city—the studio and its surrounding streets immediately drew crowds from all corners of the city and beyond. It was, significantly, inaugurated in January 2014 with what would be one of the last public appearances of Fidel Castro after a mysterious absence of nine months.

MOR invested in public works in the neighborhood that featured collaborations between visiting artists and Romerillo residents and included street lighting, a rich cultural offering and audiovisual programming, and the rehabilitation of building façades. The main draw of Kcho's project among locals and visitors both was the amplified wi-fi signal from his private, state-provided DSL connection, a privilege assigned at the time to a limited number of professional and foreign workers. There were originally three PCs installed in the small, air-conditioned library (the Biblioteca Comandante de la Revolución Juan Almeida Bosque), surrounded by Cuban art books and by the collected works of Lenin, Fidel, and Martí. In this sense, the promise of a connection was couched in revolutionary terms via performative allegiances. Users had to respond with the classic call-and-response structure of the revolutionary soundscape (described in chapter 2) by typing official political slogans as passwords to the network before connecting to the web and social media communities: "Aquí no se rinde nadie" (Nobody surrenders here) and "Abajo el bloqueo" (Down with the blockade). A few months later, in the summer of 2015, ETECSA's wi-fi "street spots" began to operate with a system using a prepaid, per-hour navigation model. In March 2016, access to the DSL connection and wi-fi signals were greatly boosted by the installation of Google equipment at MOR, including a second, larger navigation room with eighteen Chromebooks, in a deal negotiated as part of the US-Cuban rapprochement period of 2014–2016 and announced during Obama's visit to the island. MOR closed to the public in 2017 amid rumors of personal and financial scandals. ETECSA's DSL home service, Nauta Hogar, was announced and implemented that same year.

MOR showcased Google's pitch to participate in Cuba's mass connectivity, a gesture eventually lost to Chinese investment in ETECSA's rollout of home and mobile internet plans. As a performance of egalitarian access, MOR demonstrated that the internal embargo was as decisive an obstacle to public connectivity as was the US embargo; that unrestricted access to the web was a politically and economically privilege reserved for progovernment, high-profile artists like Kcho; and that the demand for affordable connectivity beyond the restrictive Cuban intranet and ETECSA's expensive navigation tariffs was overwhelming. Crowds connecting from all neighborhoods in the capital occupied the studio's surroundings at all hours, and the queues to use the indoor studio were over an hour long despite the scorching tropical heat. Its exceptional and short-lived model of connectivity contrasted with that of the nationwide Joven Club de Computación (Youth Computing Club), created in 1987 as a network of computer navigation rooms and education programs and associated with the Communist Youth Union (UJC). While the clubs' cost to connect tends to be a fraction of the dollar-per-hour average of an ETECSA internet session, access is restricted to the national intranet and email—featuring its own, highly politicized version of Wikipedia (Ecured) and social network (The Clothesline)—but no connection to the web. Still, even the Google-backed MOR was subject to the country's overall internet controls.[18]

A take on how digital media art can denounce, instead of compound, the silent complicities and structural limitations of existing state- and capital-led approaches to connectivity, Rodolfo Peraza's artwork since 2003 has explored what "public" means, and what it could become, in digital information and communication technologies. Peraza's ethnographically informed *Pilgram* installations stress the resilient desires of everyday users to connect with each other and the world, as well as the invisible links that simultaneously facilitate and interrupt them. *Pilgram 1.0* monitored user practices in exchange for free navigation in the first hot spots in Cuba, demonstrating that users prioritized their connections to use social media and messaging apps. It also staged the inescapable model of exchanging services for personal data that until then had been largely irrelevant to Cubans. *Pilgram 2.0* mapped the packet-data traffic between

Miami and Cuban IP address blocks allocated from 1995 to 2014, looking at the path of information as it traveled to and from Cuba via satellite and cable. Data moved around the world but inevitably passed back and forth the United States, given the borderless network infrastructure of transnational providers like Tata, Intelsat, and NewCom International through which Cuban traffic ultimately travels. *Pilgram 2.0*'s abstract, colorful visualizations of network movement invited spectators to decipher the "un-embargo-able," the otherwise invisible data links that are monetized, interrupted, and politically exploited in their names.

At the same time that these art projects confronted the transnational continuities of media monopolies and data colonialisms, they invited users to participate in the production of that critique while they navigated the web and, through the curated visualization and exhibition of navigation practices and infrastructure architecture, to reflect on their own interventions as customers and citizens of both actually existing and speculative networked communities. By setting up "guerrilla hot spots" in Fanguito Studio in Havana and in Miami's Wynwood district, two neighborhoods that are historically poor and predominantly Black, Peraza's work also disputed Cuba's and the United States' mutually reinforcing yet illusory exceptionalisms by mapping mirror practices of surveillance and privatization across the Florida Strait.[19]

The dismantling of Havana's underground mesh networks in 2019 put into stark relief other dimensions of the struggles over connectivity, statization, and consumerism. Streetnets (SNETs) began around 2010, evolving from LAN-based gaming communities to become large neighborhood mesh networks for online multiplayer gaming with their own social media apps and chats, forums to advertise events and services, and peer-to-peer hosting and sharing. The estimated number of users was significant (20,000–40,000), distributed among nine server nodes connected via perforated antennas, routers, and signal amplifiers (fig. 4.3). Because importing or even selling modems is prohibited, devices were acquired on the black market. The network thrived in a legal limbo for almost a decade, helped by a strictly self-enforced policy of avoiding political and pornographic content and of never connecting to the internet. Administrators pledged all revenue would go toward equipment and network maintenance, though this was not without internal controversy, including acrimonious competition among nodes with higher user bases (and thus higher revenues).

The laws and provisions that informed the closure of SNETs (Decreto Ley 370; Resolutions 98/2018 and 99/2018 of the Ministry of Communications) also affected independent digital platforms and publications and

Figure 4.3. A rooftop in Havana with a slotted unidirectional antenna that propagates wi-fi signals amplified by Ubiquiti Bullets or similar devices. Author's photo, August 2016.

thus were widely perceived as another typical move by a government that explicitly embraced censorship as a homeland security issue. But the closing in July 2019 of the SNETs—which were absorbed by the Joven Club de Computación, the government's internet literacy program—cannot be framed only, or even primarily, as a repressive measure in the traditional sense. Much like *El Paquete* the SNETs had successfully put in place self-censorship checks. This was just as much an economic and cultural competition issue: throughout 2019 ETECSA rolled out 3G services for the first time. A growing network of offline social media was a direct competitor to these services. In contrast with ETECSA's pay-per-data model, SNET users could navigate without restrictions for the equivalent of a dollar per month. The discussion within SNETs about such confrontations with authorities also showed the aggregate disobediences of a community of users who did not come together for the same reasons or were fighting for the survival of the network with the same goals. For some, SNETs were their livelihood; for others, an entertainment and information source. And for others still, they represented a utopian glimpse of an autonomous, community-built space free of market and state interference: by hosting their own servers these multiplayer gaming communities circumvented the subscription paywalls of their favorite games (*Defense of the Ancients*, *World of Warcraft*, and *Call of Duty*), otherwise unavailable in Cuba because of the embargo and because of the difficulties of obtaining and paying for a reliable internet connection. Above all, such confrontations showed a state apparatus interested in keeping its policing and surveillance capabilities—like all states everywhere—but also interested in preserving a local monopoly on lucrative services while fully engaged in the same fights against end-to-end encryption, net neutrality, and municipal networks that take place in the United States and elsewhere.[20]

From abroad, these difficulties and their workarounds are selectively sensationalized in traveling images of Cuban postsocialism and its media cultures. The director of the first Hollywood movie filmed in Cuba in five decades, for example, retold his most memorable filming experience there as a "first contact" story in which a technologically advanced civilization dazzles the natives with gadgets that offer images of themselves and the modern marvels that await:

> We brought in our helicopter with this huge camera on it. It looks like a spaceship to the locals and is flying 50 feet above our heads at top speed, chasing the two cars driving through the streets. I set up this big screen for the locals to see what the helicopter was shooting. We're sending the video signal back to this monitor, and they're watching their city from the sky. A lot of them have never been on a plane. You start seeing tears stream. Then we start to cry, because they're crying, and it's this moment you share where you realize how special it is and how much we take for granted.[21]

Why were these Cubans crying? Likely not because they had never seen a helicopter, themselves, or their city on a screen. Nobody asked them, yet the director, F. Gary Gray, seemed perfectly assured as a witness/traveler to a socialism frozen in time reporting on his findings (this trope is explored in chapter 1). On display is the traveler's own self-image: the satisfaction of seeing himself perceived as savior, a pilgrimage of authentic spirituality achieved through an unspoiled other that has been lost in the technologically advanced self. As seen in some of the global media responses to the July 11, 2021 protests, this gaze has a political counterpart in the desire among global progressives for Cubans to perform as virtuous revolutionary subjects, much as in the United States, where techno-solutionist, free-market conservatives imagine that parachuting "free internet" and "free markets" to Cubans would bring about instant regime change and economic advancements.[22] Another plausible explanation for crying: here was palpable evidence of a long-awaited change—US-Cuban rapprochement—coupled with the excitability of commonplace Hollywood fandom.

In "Compañero Obama," Patricio Fernández's account of Obama's 2016 Cuba trip, this spontaneous crying appears precisely as a cathartic outpouring of concrete expectations:

> La afirmación de que "El futuro de Cuba tiene que estar en las manos del pueblo cubano" que Obama pronunció en español, fue entendida por la mayoría de los viandantes con que conversé desde el hotel Inglaterra hasta la escalera de la universidad, atravesando todo Centro Habana, no como un llamado a la democracia, sino más bien a una agilización del libre mercado. Que los negocios se arreglen entre ellos, no siempre a través del Estado. . . . En su caso no se trata de una demanda ideológica, sino enteramente práctica."[23]

Despite Fernández's misleading reference to the "free market," the key agent here is the self-employed entrepreneur/artisan in structural opposition to both global capitalist expansion in search of cheap labor and consumer markets and accumulation and control via bureaucratic statization. As such, the digital innovations and media practices of users, while shaped by the context, respond less to the transcendental political frameworks that characterize discussions of Cuban informatization and more to the concrete needs of everyday economic survival, socialization, and entertainment, what Verónica Gago calls "the desire for popular prosperity" that is then doubly exploited by transnational capital and local elites.[24]

Domestically, the protective overreach of the state's media policy goes well beyond policing connectivity and sensitive information, compounding user frustration. For instance, the most popular TV series in Cuba, as in much of the world, *Game of Thrones* was broadcast by the state's own Cubavisión channel beginning in 2012 as part of its adult-oriented midnight programming in the summer. But this broadcast cut the scenes of sex and nudity that constitute one of the show's biggest selling points and are essential to its plot integrity. Generalized chagrin and mocking bemusement soon followed, affecting those unable to pay for the unabridged bootleg copies through one of the peer-to-peer networks and thus reliant on state TV to keep up. Meanwhile, the sneakernet *El Paquete*, like all other major global networks of alternative and peer-to-peer media distribution—from *The Pirate Bay* to *Cuevana*—offered the subtitled installment in full on the Monday after its Sunday transmission. In

Memorias del subdesarrollo (Memories of underdevelopment), one of the most iconic filmic manifestos of ICAIC's revolutionary cinema, there is a scene in which filmmakers jokingly imagine a montage with all the nude scenes cut by the bourgeois censors in their hypocritical prudishness. An irony explored by Jesús Díaz as well—in the novels *Las iniciales de la tierra* (The initials of the earth) and *Las palabras perdidas* (The lost words)—the cultural vanguards of the 1960s, rising against bourgeois Catholic mores and Soviet-style socialist realism simultaneously, hardly scraped the top-down tutelary paternalism and moral puritanism that ultimately endured in the Cuban state's cultural and media policies regulating content.

The promise to sweep away the vices of the capitalist nightlife of the republican era anchored the endurance of socially conservative social values instead, utilizing cultural wars in the service of political policing. This prudishness, repackaged as proper socialist values from the 1960s onward, remains a counterproductive tool of hegemonic representation of the state as a guardian of national identity, good customs, and morality against capitalist corruptibility. Sneakernets bypass all this, just as they redress the low bandwidths and high cost of devices characterizing network connectivity in the country, dominating the massive yet informal modes of dissemination of information and entertainment. They combine the sharing and self-publishing capabilities of digital and electronic portable technologies with a physical network of street barter that originated with cassette and videotape cultures in the late 1970s and early 1980s against the artificial scarcity created by external and internal constraints.

In fact, the rise and consolidation of the nationwide sneakernet *El Paquete* (2010s–present) can be tracked to the explosive demand for the four specific things that neither state mass media nor the conditions of connectivity could satisfy: foreign TV series, reggaeton, app and software updates, and local economic information. *El Paquete* offers other things, too—movies, magazines, software, apps—but it is the element of seriality in these genres that *El Paquete* caters to (episodic for series, high turnout of fashionable "hits" for music, and real-time, horizontal communication among citizens in expanding, globalized nonstate economic and cultural sectors). Neither the state media structures in place nor the preexisting informal avenues of access to global media industry products that preceded *El Paquete* can compete with its weekly reliability.

The official response to *El Paquete* was *La Mochila* (The backpack), an entertainment platform with none of the attractive features of *El*

Paquete, including its very name: while *El Paquete*'s name refers to how the hard drives were packed for quick travel across the country, the word also invokes the packages of wondrous, locally unavailable goods sent from abroad. But few would want to carry the burden of a backpack offered by a government with a history of recruiting youths for labor-intensive tasks in agriculture and social services under grueling conditions. *La Mochila* is distributed through the youth computing clubs. Its early versions were still heavily skewed toward official political content and state-produced audiovisual entertainment, and the platform lacked an effective distribution network. Its 2021 version, including an online streaming portal at mochila.cubava.cu, featured less politically curated content and more from international platforms like Netflix, HBO, and Disney+.

Official state piracy is a long-established practice, premised on the collectivization of intellectual property and the decolonization of knowledge. Yet both alternative and state-sponsored consumption of mass media and popular culture before digital media tend to be eclipsed by a focus on perceived cultural isolations before the 1990s and on the exaggerated newness of digital media. The forgotten case of OmniVideo illustrates these gaps. Before illegal private satellite antennas and underground movie banks became the main source of underground entertainment for Cubans in the 1990s, OmniVideo videotapes—first in Betamax and later VHS—circulated copies of new and unreleased Hollywood and international films that looked like factory copies (complete with sleeves and copyright notices) and were available for rent in municipal *videotecas* (video stores). Allegedly, OmniVideo was a commercial piracy scheme created by top counterintelligence officers and incorporated through shell companies in California and Panama active in the 1980s.[25] Unlike *libros fusilados* (Xeroxed books published without copyright in the 1960s for universities), OmniVideo had no claims to emancipatory cultural politics. Instead it highlighted once again the many dimensions of Cuban state capitalism well before the Special Period, a heterogeneity of actors, and contradictory interests within the state apparatus itself.

Consequently, there can hardly be consistent policies about sneakernets. Criticisms range from seeing them as a threat to accepting them as an unavoidable, necessary outlet in response to the state's policy failures. However, even *El Paquete*'s sympathetic critics reify its exceptionality—and thereby Cuba's—by maintaining the distinction between imperfect but socialist Cuban reality and the capitalist one out there. The poet and cultural critic Víctor Fowler's reflections on *El Paquete* are worth quoting in full:

> From this perspective, the *paquete* is one more link in a large chain of consumption-related activities across the almost six decades of the revolution that represent a kind of holdover resistant to almost all attempts at assimilation or extinction by socialist culture.... The *paquete* represents a (consumption-based) vehicle as well as a fugitive space in the face of political and ideological pressures: a space of imaginaries of otherness in opposition to the normative designs in the different strata of the Cuban state's apparatus of cultural and ideological reproduction; a territory in dispute, not infrequently ferocious, which challenges the reach, effects, meaning, and importance of the life changes entailed in identifying with the Cuban Revolution.... The *paquete* is an extremely complex sociocultural fact, a kind of mirror that reflects the desires and the shortages in our lives and, by extension, in the Cuban socialist project.[26]

The unspoken assertion of the perfectibility of the revolutionary project—which Fowler has expressed elsewhere—and the unquestioned break between the here and there supposed by its socialist character, reinsert Cuba in a self-exoticizing, exceptional socialist logic. The analysis does not, however, carry out a socialist, materialist critique of the revolutionary state and its media apparatus or of an official narrative where the supposed anticapitalist, noncommercial character of the state institutions is part of the revolutionary brand and itself a cultural commodity.[27]

These positions dismiss the very practices of that state, the structural continuities between local and global audiences, and the many ways in which all publics consume and reappropriate cultural and media content. Similarly, the great many dissertations, news articles, and academic papers focused solely on *El Paquete* are a welcome recognition of its complexity and reach as a nonstate employer, as "the internet of the poor" (Fowler), and as an engine of local talent. But this oversized attention is also predicated on the exotic exceptionality of Cuban informatization; the digitized materials included there are also produced and circulate in the broader underground cultural industries of Latin America and the world. The focus on the distribution aspect in turn tends to overlook how *El Paquete* became an increasingly pyramidal, monetized, and centralized model for producing and disseminating audiovisual content dominated by two "matrixes," or curating groups: Odisea, focusing mostly on music, and Omega, specializing in series.

While Latin American cultural and media studies have long looked at consumption as a sphere of active renegotiation of power and identity, such an approach is generally absent in Cuba because of the predominance of state cultural institutions, its politico-economic structure, and its apparent lack of direct participation in the global culture industry and markets before the 1990s. This popular desire for the satisfaction of material and cultural needs and for participation in the global market is not a phenomenon introduced after the Special Period with transnational capital and tourism or as a foreign influence that has strained and taunted a still perfectible socialist revolutionary project.[28] The consumption of difference is not born out of a mythical capitalist/socialist divide but out of the same mediated gap between everyday life everywhere—dominated, alienated, and desiring—and the multimedia stories we tell ourselves, and are told, about it. It bears repeating that particularity and exceptionality are not the same thing. Williams's point about British working-class consumption of American TV remains useful here: "In many parts of the world this apparently free-floating and accessible culture was a welcome alternative to dominant local cultural patterns and restrictions."[29] That these practices are ultimately embedded in exploitative, corporative interests does not cancel out the context-specific exercise of a relative agency, even if this agency is exercised through a double fetishism concealing the mode of production of the cultural commodity and of its global dissemination that characterizes mass-culture consumption in Latin America.[30]

In a media context where the only other means of acquiring desirable goods are the underground sneakernets, where overregulation, surveillance, and censorship are routinely justified by the supposed social benefits of the statization of information and communication technologies, even seemingly nonpolitical, regulatory actions, like the *Game of Thrones* and SNET cases, erode public trust in the absence of legitimate alternatives. They discredit public institutions' legitimate regulatory roles as much as they reinforce the sense of marginalization and isolation of the most underserved audiences, on behalf of whom state institutions are supposed to intervene as equalizers. While independent cultural and media production and dissemination, whether or not it is authorized, is widespread, as long as most of it remains *alegal* and informal it is subject to arbitrary restrictions and pressures to self-police as much as it is to unregulated exploitation. *El Paquete* and all similar curated archives and networks, whether or not they are monetized, in Cuba as elsewhere, are not a necessary evil or a quirky novelty. They illustrate the failures of state-led and market-let initiatives to meet demand and to empower community-led solutions. Sneakernets are hardly a sustainable solution to structural inequalities in access to information and entertainment but yet another built-in feature of the inequities of the global mediascape in all its complexity. Cultural black markets reach customers that neither states nor markets consider worth investing in, which opens them to all forms of exploitation, from fraud to disinformation. But this underground economy represents less a revenue lost to so-called piracy (as the notion of loss implies that these customers would otherwise be able to purchase these goods) and more another form of free advertising and market dominance (by spreading and standardizing some goods over others).[31] This is what a project like Néstor Siré's *El Paquete* interventions aims to make visible and minimally redress, showcasing contemporary Cuban art and culture and embedding access to a variety of cultural offerings that follow neither official nor mainstream commercial logic.[32] The "Literature" folder, for example, curated by Cuban writers and included in *El Paquete* by Siré, contained an expansive digital collection of canonical and experimental national literature as well as Latin American and world literatures in translation (fig. 4.4).

A postsocialist critical project ought then to distinguish public, collective, and communal forms of agency from their statist institutionalization, to recognize the long and uneven practices of self-determination and self-emancipation, and to distinguish those desires and demands from privatization and/or statization. As Colin Sparks states, "It is no longer possible to imagine that state institutions are constituted as mechanisms for sustaining a culture. They are not, naturally and inevitably, the enemies of the market. They are not, naturally and inevitably, the expression of popular will."[33] This is all the more important considering that the role of the state and the regulation of community media have been at the center of Latin American populist politics in this century, challenging the dominant media studies' almost exclusive focus on transnational globalization and classic neoliberal privatization processes, which overlook the way state-owned media and public-private partnerships in the region engage with and shape the local mechanisms of media globalization.[34] The rise of Venezuela's Telesur and Russia's RT in Spanish and English, their offerings of an "alternative" viewpoint—supposedly anti-Western and anti-imperialist—along with an amplifying transmedia circuit that caters to Latin American and global audiences alike is as much a source of illiberal, national populist, and socially conservative narratives as other private media conglomerates.

Returning to *La Mochila* and the Joven Clubs, the once-powerful image of a national youth cadre with backpacks on a revolutionary

Figure 4.4.
Paquete-literatura.
Image courtesy of
Lizabel Mónica.

mission against inequality and exploitation, whose first test was the Literacy Campaign of 1961, is equally in crisis. An effective mobilizing strategy in the early 1960s, it offered young teachers from urban centers an unprecedented socializing experience across the gender, race, and class barriers of the old republican order and a meaningful place in a credible process of revolutionary transformation.[35] Government attempts to re-create that model in the Battle of Ideas launched digital literacy campaigns and employment and education opportunities for computer literacy and art instructors but were unable to project a similar horizon of credible change and individual fulfillment for a new generation of youth whose only experience of immobility, censorship, and hardship has been tied to that same revolutionary government.

Octavio Cortázar's 1968 documentary *Por primera vez* (For the first time) explored these early promises of participatory media literacy, while Sandor González's 2013 *3D por primera vez* (3D for the first time) reflects a troubled legacy. A documentary about the *cinemóviles* (portable cinemas) and the reactions of first-time cinema audiences, Cortázar's film begins by explaining to viewers the task and material challenges of the project, a government-funded program that mounted film projectors onto trucks that then traveled to remote rural areas. These audiences had rarely if ever seen a movie before. General access to the moving image was a revolutionary promise. Not by chance did the documentary's director choose to capture the reaction of these audiences to Charlie Chaplin's *Modern Times*: revolutionary screens were harbingers of a coming, but alternative modernity, of the production of a cultural offering that could compete with the stupefying frivolities of the capitalist culture industry, as Rocha wrote in 1971. "For the first time" implied it would not be the last, anticipating dozens of cinemas marking the urbanization of the rural countryside carried out by the revolutionary government in the following decades.

A 2013 sequel to Cortázar's classic, González's *3D por primera vez*, was filmed in the rural community of Soplillar, deep in the Ciénaga de Zapata. In November 2013, the same year this work was filmed, the government announced the closure of private, makeshift 3D theaters and videogame parlors for profit. While categories for self-employment statutes have since expanded, independent cultural and media production has been an uphill battle. Again the argument behind these periodic clampdowns was that they eroded Cuba's national culture by promoting bad taste and frivolous consumerism. *3D por primera vez* reveals a Soplillar where revolutionary modernization never quite arrived, though the Cuban Revolution certainly did: the iconic posters behind the interviewers, the comments of the townsfolk, and the suspicious local officials all frame the efforts to set up the screening. González arrived in Soplillar with the Martha Machado Brigade, another Kcho project, whose most recognizable footprint included the nationwide public artworks in support of the five Cuban spies sentenced in the United States in 2001. But González developed his own relationship, both artistic and personal, with the remote town. His work in Soplillar is social work and cultural project in equal measures. His commitment to a noncommercial, utopian artwork evokes the original revolutionary promise: the documentary was shown only to Soplillar residents and remains unexhibited.[36] Like Kcho's MOR, and despite its stated commitments to cultural democratization, *3D por primera vez* is also an unintended document of a state abandoning its promises of alternative, egalitarian informatization and modernization for all. The differences with *cinemóviles* are telling: there are no grand public projects behind it, no promises of a cultural or economic transformation to come. The notion of film and visual literacy as cultural capital convertible to political capital, to be reinvested in emancipatory or hegemonic processes—as Tomás Gutiérrez Alea and García Espinosa theorized—has been replaced by the more modest promise of amusement by and curiosity for updated ways of passing the time.[37]

Spheres of Publicity: Amateurs, Intellectuals, and Memelords

Digital and web technologies expanded everywhere the capabilities for widely disseminated self-publications, independent journalism, locally oriented content production, and organizing in spaces outside the direct control of the state or the market, even as most platforms for self-publication and social networking become monopolies trafficking in personal data, advertising, surveillance, and disinformation. In addition to the diversification, globalization, and fragmentation of Cuban screens, the twenty-first century has also seen the intensification of explicit debates around definitions of "civil society" and "public sphere" in relation to this new mediascape. These conversations have expanded the discursive field of Cuban (cultural) politics significantly, calling into question once again what "public" means and who the public *is* in narratives of inclusive public access to new media technologies. From *la guerrita de los emilios* (The little email war or little war of emails) in 2007—the first public digital discussion among intellectuals about state censorship—and the independent blogosphere to the *directas* (livestreams) and the memesphere, new media practices, technologies, and artifacts made technically possible those debates and forced the reconceptualization of the terms and participants of the political and cultural debates themselves.

For the purposes of this discussion, the *public sphere* includes the practices, media, and artifacts, institutional and informal, that make possible the production and exchange of meaning and ideas of common concern in a given community. Several issues render any normative claims about the relationship between democracy and public spheres theoretically suspect: how "common concern" is defined and contested; who is included and excluded from the community being addressed; the precarious links between public sphere participation and sociopolitical change; and the gap between formal and substantive rules of participation in a discursive space that is not homogenous or contiguous but rather results from the uneven interaction between several and different publics in conditions of unequal power.[38] Yet despite the theoretical inconsistency and sociological inadequacy of terms like "public sphere" and "civil society"—as explored in a vast scholarship ever since these terms became dominant in media studies and democratic theory—the highly policed and narrowly politicized history of public speech and action in Cuba confers upon them significant symbolic weight as well as tactical, organizing potential, that is, they are important for the social actors themselves.

In Latin America, the translation of Jürgen Habermas's influential work on the public sphere to English and Spanish in the 1980s coincided with the process of democratic transitions in the region. As such, paradigmatic discussions around the public sphere centered on the postdictatorial processes to address historical memory and human rights in their juridical and socio-cultural dimensions, the privatization and expansion of media conglomerates and communication technologies, and state and nonstate censorship and violence faced by activists and journalists in the region.[39] But it was the reception of the public sphere debates in the context of the postsocialist transitions in Eastern and Central Europe, with the main focus on the influential role of a civil society clearly differentiated from political society in the promotion of a democratic discourse, that had the most direct impact in the Cuban debates.[40] While Ted Henken has described the differences between the four major actors who contend for influence and recognition emerging from this digital public sphere ("dissidents, millennials, critical revolutionaries, and the diaspora"), I'm interested here in how the arguments and artifacts they put forth engage, politically but also aesthetically, narratives of postsocialist change and continuity, state and market pressures, and Cuban exceptionalism.[41]

Like any emancipatory imaginary, the concept of the *public sphere* functions as a regulative utopia that informs and channels the concrete practices and desires of these media and cultural agents as much as those of the state and the market through a battery of policy, investments, official narratives, and more or less repressive gatekeeping models aimed at shaping communities as a public in their own image. The question here is less what the socialist public sphere was and what comes next or whether a political theory of democracy depends on a theory of the public sphere.[42]

It is a far more modest, situated enterprise: What models of the public sphere operate in these political imaginaries and why? How do their potentials and limitations, their successes and failures, and their convergences and conflicts help us understand the Cuban postsocialist mediascape and, through it, our own techno-cultural, political conditions of possibility as global postsocialist subjects in medias res?

Few cultural figures have embodied and theorized the public and digitally mediated role of the Cuban Marxist intellectual as a "critical revolutionary" like Desiderio Navarro. An academic *paquete*, *A Thousand and One Texts: Volume 1* was a scholarship dissemination project by Navarro's Centro Teórico–Cultural Criterios, consisting of a digital archive of a thousand and one academic articles on a range of topics and disciplines: critical theory, cultural studies, literary theory, media studies, semiotics. These articles were published by journals largely unavailable to Cuban academics, who access them either via peer-to-peer websites and networks (libgen, academia.edu), when they travel abroad, or by means of direct peer-to-peer exchange with a foreign scholar with institutional subscription privileges. The expansion of internet connectivity in 2015 brought improvements, but these were and remain unreliable avenues of access and cannot substitute comprehensive access that responds in real time to research needs. The project minimally redressed what Sparks has underscored as a pending subject of de-Westernizing/decolonizing media studies: beyond thematic issues and modes of critique, it must reckon with uneven material resources and access in the global division of academic labor as much as with Western media assumptions about "communist media systems."[43] More significant, Navarro stressed, there was no sustained space in the national public sphere either for the circulation of, and engagement with, these materials.[44]

The original 560MB digital file was given to attendees of the launch event on Friday, November 2, 2007, and it has been in circulation in CD or USB formats ever since, passed from hand to hand. It was followed by four other volumes. This collection, as many of the offline digital archives that circulate informally in contexts of low connectivity or constrained access, is curated, no matter how comprehensive it may be. An important cultural editor, translator, and theorist, Navarro founded the cultural center mentioned above and the journal *Criterios* in 1972. That work has been central to ongoing debates about the degrees of state censorship in Cuba's public sphere (and in the intellectual and cultural fields in particular) and the degree of political participation of, and spheres of public intervention open to, Cuban intellectuals and cultural producers. Two issues are at stake here: first, the historical and theoretical tension between an established tendency toward vanguardism and didacticism in revolutionary cultural politics in relation to the stated democratizing and socializing ends of the state cultural apparatus; and second, how those same tensions are playing a role now in debates about media and information democratization, especially as other social actors and desires—born out of generational shifts as much as responsive to changing technical and political conditions—engage with and create their own global and public screens.[45]

Surprisingly, there is digital marginalia in file 929: Madina Tlostanova's "The Imagined Freedom: Post-Soviet Intellectuals Between the Hegemony of the State and the Hegemony of the Market." Someone using .PDF annotation tools registered to Navarro has highlighted what that reader arguably considers key moments of Tlostanova's argument. It does not mean this was Navarro behind the screen, only that someone was using his software; we will call that user "DDN" (Digital Desiderio Navarro). The annotations date from October 25 and 26, 2006, before the release of the files. They also contain a time stamp of when the logo was added for publication of the file the month before the event (October 10, 2007).

DDN's annotated file is important. Tlostanova's work moves on two fronts: the theorization of a critical function for post-Soviet intellectuals, and the critique of the post-Soviet condition vis-à-vis Russia's neo-imperial project from a decolonial, postsocialist framework that revisits the tensions between colonialism, nationalism, Europhilia, and xenophobia in the region. These critiques are relevant to the Cuban present: Tlostanova interrogates, as we do here, the ways in which both state and market power are exercised through and reinforced by cultural meaning and intellectual practices, sketching the particular discursive forms these acquire in postsocialist contexts. On page 20, DDN highlights Tlostanova's argument that the role of the intellectual is by definition a risky one. Tlostanova contends that intellectual critiques involve two inherent dimensions of hazard: a positive one, from the Arabic etymology of "hazard," or (throwing) "the dice" as acting on the chance that things will end well; and a negative one, which captures both the possible political and economic risks to the scholar as a person and those affecting disciplinary fields as a whole. In DDN's annotations, only the negative aspect is highlighted: "Along with the danger of physical hazard, political persecution, and imprisonment, we have to take into account other repercussions of the 'scholars at risk' situation—from the loss of one's own social and economic status, to the general loss of prestige within the humanities and social sciences, and consequently to the loss of the opportunity (and the ability) to think critically." More significant, the sentence that precedes this passage, sandwiched between two highlighted passages, is *not* emphasized: "However, in order to do that [i.e., *taking the risk* of expressing an independent and critical opinion, counter to the pressures of state power and to the seductions of the market] it is necessary to *have* or be able to *shape* such an opinion, which does not seem to be possible in Russia."[46] Inasmuch as this dilemma is also faced by Cubans, why would DDN single out this sentence as not worthy of attention in a section otherwise underscored, especially in the context of Navarro's "In Medias Res"?

In that influential article, Navarro absolves Cuban intellectuals and himself of being complicit in gatekeeping, elitism, and censorship, placing the blame entirely on Cuban bureaucrats, as if the distinction between the two social actors were a given. It locates bureaucratic censorship in the general climate of populist anti-intellectualism, making the labor of the scholar a lonely, besieged one. Navarro accepts the myth of the construction of socialism already volunteered by the party/state to explain the reasons for censorship while taking distance from its methods. Despite the stated aim of the article, the actual intervention in the public sphere to demand political accountability is postponed to redefine the role of the intellectual and reconcile it as a class with the "party" and "the people," those safe subjects of Cuban official ideology, by naming the negative tendencies that ought to be rectified. This is a classic trope of the committed critic.

Purged by a healthy dose of socialist criticism, intellectuals reemerge as pursuing the same goals as the party/state, and thus Navarro is immediately repositioned as "dentro," the safety zone of Fidel's original cultural guidelines: within or against. Critical revolutionary intellectuals demand academic freedom for themselves only and as defined by the state, not freedom of speech as a civil right, much less the kind of radical democratization of knowledge that C. L. R. James would identify as the main task of postcolonial left intellectuals in the 1968 Cultural Congress of Havana—to abolish themselves as a class—to the consternation of his Cuban hosts.[47] The misappropriation of Gramsci's notion of civil society and hegemony by Cuban intellectuals since the early 1990s has shaped this perspective, allowing the intellectuals to characterize the Cuban public sphere as socialist and democratic. Navarro's article closed a decadelong debate about whether or not Cuban socialism featured a democratic (albeit state-led) civil society (in the context of the 1990s celebratory discussions about the role of civil society in postsocialist transitions taking place simultaneously in and about Eastern and Central Europe) and prefigured the next debate about the intellectual's functions and autonomy in the Cuban public sphere that took place during the famous *guerrita de los emilios* in 2007. This digital debate took place among cultural producers and intellectuals over email and was unprecedented in several ways: in its having taken place digitally, in addressing more candidly than usual political questions about censorship, in including voices from the diaspora, and in having been made public.

The unemphasized passage brings into relief the political and/or epistemological inability of Cuban Marxist theorists to distinguish between socialism and its different theoretical and political corpuses, on the one hand, and the specific institutional, militaristically hierarchical, and ideologically dogmatic party/state politics of Cuba on the other. Working to expand their own autonomy while also defending the democratic character of Cuban socialism, Cuban Marxist intellectuals did not carry out a Marxian, materialist analysis of their own. As I contend in chapter 1, the conditions of possibility to make those distinctions are not only a matter of domestic (self-)censorship. They are tied to Cuba's legacy in New Left thought: these views are not just a question of personal choice and of hazard as much as they are the effects of "the field of the sayable," reinforced by and shared in a wider discursive field that includes a still dominant imaginary in Latin American and global left thought, where Cuban socialism is defined by a mix of a rebellious nationalist tradition, anti-American imperialism, and egalitarian longings rather than by theoretico-empirical parameters.[48]

Navarro's reductionist account of Cuba's political topography creates a flawed framework of analysis for the Cuban socialist public sphere because it defuses potential antagonisms between very different forms of socialist thinking by bracketing the distinguishing features of Cuba's political order: party/state, militarism, and personal leadership. Rafael Rojas has similarly recognized that Navarro, and others like Rafael Hernández, Víctor Fowler, and Fernando Martínez Heredia, stand for a socialism that sounds very different in tone and content from that of the PCC and its more propagandistic outlets (e.g., *Granma*, *Cubadebate*), a difference largely mediated by their defense of cultural and aesthetic pluralism within the single-party system. Yet their inability to define unambiguously their own place of enunciation in the field of power implicates their discourse in the dynamic of a spectacle of tolerance as official cultural politics: "Neo-Marxism is a theoretical position that, adopted in Havana without a clear signal of opposition [to the PCC], loses all critical value."⁴⁹ The work of dissemination and translation carried out by Desiderio Navarro and *Criterios*, although individually admirable, thus commits an oblique editorial violence: it betrays its own proposals and theoretical context by disavowing—by *not* highlighting—the political and social reality in which it circulates. In their solitary and decontextualized reading, the problems discussed in works of contemporary neo- and post-Marxism showcased by the journal signal a world elsewhere, one out in the "capitalist" world. This goes to the heart of Tlostanova's argument (and my own) about the problem of parsing out a critique capable of taking on both communist past and capitalist present, state and market, in their specific forms of dominance in the postsocialist context.

The discourse of intellectuals like Navarro historically legitimized an official double screen that is largely still operative: the screen upon which the state's spectacle of tolerance is projected (tied to the protection of Cuba's symbolic legacy as a viable socialist alternative), a screen that attempts, and fails, to conceal other explicit demands for political, economic, social, and cultural participation and self-determination. The state politics of the spectacle of tolerance, combined with a socialist tradition of culture conceived as a political tool, fashioned a Cuban cultural field traditionally burdened with the task of social critique and with expanding and contracting cycles of critical permissibility.⁵⁰ But it was the independent blogger movement that most forcefully and publicly challenged the idea that domestic political critique ought to be left exclusively to artists and intellectuals between 2008 and 2014. Two of the most widely read blogs, *Generación Y* and *Octavo Cerco*, did this in three specific ways: confronting the spectacle of tolerance by narrating online the offline experiences with censorship and exclusion by the supposedly tolerant intellectual establishment; presenting themselves as part of the very same culturally engaged public that socialist theories of aesthetic democratization once proposed to usher in; and actively maintaining alternative spaces, networks, and alliances with independent artists, writers, and musicians. This work of cultural criticism did not merely supplement but served to legitimize their more mundane daily reporting on everyday hardships and their solidarity with more traditional activists from the independent civil society organizations.

The autobiographical tone of these posts, coupled with the density of the data allowed by technology (photos, video, audio, facsimiles, and so on) provided an unusual and disproportionate visibility to the opinions of otherwise regular citizens; that is, not as artists or intellectuals or writers or any other official position recognized by the proper institutional channels and/or protected by ideological loyalty to a particular order. Concerned authorities thus found it more difficult to discredit the bloggers' personas given bloggers' ability to produce and articulate a competing narrative from the inside. Furthermore, these narratives circulated (however limited) much more than previous attempts at open confrontation by traditional dissidents. By putting in play their cultural capital and their technical know-how, these bloggers tried to disentangle precisely the two options given by official cultural policy in the public sphere: to be within or against. Compare, for example, Navarro's digital project above with digital samizdat. In "Bibliography in a Flashdrive," the blogger Claudia Cadelo documents the transformation of reading networks brought on by portable memories:

> Lately the best books arrive digitally . . . what one can find in the street is explosive:
> —*From Dictatorship to Democracy* and *The Relevance of Gandhi to the Modern World*, both by Gene Sharp.
> —*Russia: Something Less than Democracy*, [an] interview with Alexander Podrabinek.
> —*Live Not by Lies*, by Alexander Solzhenitsyn.
> —*Countdown*, by Jakub Karpinski.
> —*Regime, Opposition*, "Solidarity," by Marek Tarniewski.
> —*The Controversy of Purification*, by Petruška Šustrová.
> —*The Power of the Powerless*, by Václav Havel.[51]

Through their publicized, private screens, bloggers practiced a form of Habermasian Publizität (calling publicly on political society to respond to their demands) and made visible a sociopolitical actor via literary and media production, a subject I call "amateur citizen."[52] That subject publicly reckoned with the shortcomings of the old revolutionary state's promise of cultural and media democratization for all, effectively deploying her literacies against the state's own informational monopoly and repressive screens. In the process, the alternative blogosphere displaced the language of the traditional opposition groups to mobilize in its place an imaginary organized around the needs of an informed, global, tech-savvy citizen of the twenty-first century: a political subject whose relationship to government and civic participation was not entirely regimented by grand narratives of national teleology and red-baiting anticommunist abstractions but who sought to reconstitute the public realm instead as a negotiated aggregate of plural interests and for whom access to information and digital technology was conceived as another inalienable right. This would later change from a demand voiced in public only by a handful of bloggers (publicized in events like the blogger popularity contest "Una isla virtual" [A virtual island] in 2009) to massively popular and openly voiced complaints against state telecom ETECSA's service, as the online campaign #BajenLosPreciosDeInternet (#LowerInternetPrices) illustrated in 2019. These demands have intensified and diversified since: from independent bloggers movement in 2008–2014 to digital left dissidents, from the livestreaming of the police interruption of the hunger strikes of the activist art collective Movimiento San Isidro (MSI) to the street protests of July 11, 2021, along the other myriad screens—personal, commercial, transnational, communal—that make up an important part of the portable postsocialist mediascape.

Yoani Sánchez's *Generación Y* and the blogs that emerged around the *Voces cubanas* (Cuban voices) project in 2008 and 2009 articulated an unprecedented debate about the role of new media in the development of political and cultural agency in Cuba. By the same token, the governmental responses with which they were met—blocking domestic access to their websites, discrediting campaigns through state media, personal and professional harassment through detentions and interrogations, overt surveillance, propagandist counterparts like *Yohandry's Blog* (an anonymous defender of the Cuban government whose name sounds close to Yoani's)—would serve as models for the government's responses to other digital media and cultural initiatives that followed later, in which public identity would be built on similar strategies to those of the independent bloggers: on professing autonomy from state institutions, on having a strong cultural component (using art, literature, music, performance, photography, etc.), on criticizing the ruling party in their capacity as everyday citizens, and on the production and dissemination of data- and media-rich narratives claiming a more authentic representation of the Cuban social reality. This alternative media sphere with a strong antigovernment, cultural component survives in projects like *el paketito*, a regularly updated digital trove of multimedia content that, unlike *El Paquete*, does not shy away from explicitly political materials.[53] The blogosphere was an early test case for the shifting relationship between the political, cultural, and public spheres in a postsocialist digital mediascape increasingly reliant on peer-to-peer networks of production and dissemination.

Conversely, the right-wing counterparts of the critical revolutionaries—whether they be based in Cuba, Spain, or Miami—also try to shape, monopolize, and monetize the political imaginary of opposition to the government, responding to red-washing with an equal dose of red-baiting: "La naciente sociedad civil cubana habla de ecología, de racismo, de machismo tóxico, de protección de gatitos, de «todes» y «tod@s» porque ha recibido adiestramiento de los asesores de sensibilidad social de la izquierda *woke* norteamericana."[54] Another impasse emerges here: the pull of this ultraconservative, traditionalist opposition, often allied with the rise of Christian evangelicals in Cuba as in the rest of Latin America, and who in turn take their cue from American conservatives, has been rekindled in the digital ecologies that connect local initiatives with the transnational digital spheres in which they circulate and on which they often depend for protective visibility and for economic, political, and symbolic support. When I open the Instagram account of the MSI activist and artist Luis Manuel Otero Alcántara (the target of Díaz de Villegas), the algorithm suggests similar accounts to follow: Alexander Otaola (whose artistic/influencer name is simply Otaola), Eliecer Ávila, and other prominent hardline figures of the Cuban conservative diasporic opposition. These algorithmically mediated continuities blur important ideological differences and the lines between what we could call "commodity activism" and citizen demands for change that commodity activists claim to represent yet push to codify and appropriate, cashing in on the diasporic Cuban nostalgia industry as well as on a host of US-based financing dedicated to the promotion of regime change in Cuba.

Platform visibility rewards those with the best resources and bigger networks to produce and disseminate content regularly and widely. Worst, the decolonial critique of platform capitalisms, along with the arbitration of what counts as "fake news," are co-opted in turn by the Cuban government and its professional pundits, who exploit legitimate critiques of algorithmic mediation and data colonialism to deauthorize and discredit social media discontent and independent media producers altogether. Thus in both print and digital media state institutions invest in the remediation of two old rationales for repression as an ideological defensive necessity: any political critique, even if voiced by a good friend in social media, is part of a US-led media war against Cuba; and Cuban socialism as defined by the government is still part of a historic Latin American struggle against imperialism.⁵⁵ Thus the hegemony of the market and the propaganda of the state here, bolstered by the deeply influential Cold War frameworks of anticommunist propaganda in Latin America and the Cuban diasporas, not only promote an apparent chain of equivalence between opposition to the Cuban government and conservative neoliberalism but also dismiss, suppress, or simply eclipse critiques that deviate from that script, further limiting the conditions in which independent opinions, to use Tlostanova's terminology, become possible.

These dynamics are obscured in different ways. A Netflix meme about the Elpidio cartoon arrives via WhatsApp. In 2015, Netflix was the first US company to announce the availability of its service to Cubans under Obama's flexibilization of the embargo, a symbolic move given that access to the platform required access to international payment mechanisms and a reliably fast internet connection. The most famous national animated character, Elpidio, is an independentist rebel of the nineteenth century fighting Spanish colonialism. The original cartoon promotes the national rebelliousness and anti-imperialism that has long bolstered an official mythology in which the 1959 revolution completes the original nineteenth-century independent project. The meme stages several remediations: the remediation of political humor itself now socialized via the meme as genre; of a revolutionary cultural icon (Elpidio Valdés's relaunch marketing campaign featured an Instagram account and a WhatsApp sticker pack); and of the conservative suspicion of identity politics in global consumer culture, perceived as an imposition on national values as cultural markets expand, with parallels in earlier revolutionary fears of American cultural imperialism. The original picture used for the meme was released on Facebook as part of the cartoon's relaunch campaign in 2020.⁵⁶ Elpidio has become Elpidie, a gender-neutral name, and is now black; his band of rebels now includes a trans person, one in a wheelchair, and other modifications (fig. 4.5). A version of the "woke casting" memes, it appeals to the hardline conservative position who criticizes neoliberalism not because of its exploitative economic logic but because of its supposed dissemination of the woke values of global urban elites, portraying inclusivity and diversity as imposing caricatures. From a progressive perspective, these memes speak to the tokenization strategies of corporate diversity efforts as well. Unwittingly, the meme also calls attention to colorism and the lack of onscreen diversity in Cuban state media, topics that have surfaced in national conversations about race since the 1990s.

The rise of a discourse tapping into the economic neoliberal failures from socially conservative, national populist perspectives everywhere has

Figure 4.5. Elpidie. Cuban meme published by the Twitter user @Globo_03 circa 2020.

found its Cuban mouthpieces via right-wing readers of Spanish-language media platforms like *infobae* (infobae.com) and *PanAm Post* or consumers of viral videos like the Guatemalan libertarian influencer Gloria Álvarez's "Why Are Millenials Socialists" (#SocialismoPaMilenials), reproduced on the YouTube channel of the Cuban dissident group Unión Patriótica de Cuba. Arguing against the adoption of a proposed new Family Code that would have legalized same-sex marriage and adoption rights in September 2022, evangelical religious groups have not only expressed their opposition to equal rights legislation but also gone so far as to exalt the common ground between their views and the discriminatory record of Cuba's military and PCC on the subject, rejecting the "ideology of gender" as foreign to national culture.[57] It is ironic that they are often the ones importing exclusionary and misleading language from North America, a phenomenon not exclusive to the region but solidified by north-to-south evangelical movement toward Latin America.[58]

The shared social conservatism of PCC cadres and the party's neoconservative opposition has also shined a light on the emergence of a young and heterogeneous dissident left with a strong digital presence and markedly different positions from the classic revolutionary critics discussed above. They comment on contemporary topics as independent voices on their social media accounts and/or collaborate on media platforms like the *Havana Times*, *Joven Cuba*, and *Comunistas de Cuba*. Looking in tandem at their support for the Family Code and their rejection of a Penal Code that goes further in its criminalization of political dissidence, for instance, illustrates another change: an understanding of participation in what we could call a strategic statism, different from previous forms of dissidence that view any government legislation as fruit of the poisoned tree and any participation as a legitimation of its repression. Along those explicitly self-identified as dissident leftists, a host of progressive voices work to shift the public imaginary around intersectional social identities and issues.

The feminist and LGBTQ+ activist Hasta El Coño @MelaSuda91 tweeted "no to the penal code" and "yes to the family code" while using a new and widely adopted Latin American feminist slogan to characterize the Cuban government: "El estado cubano es un macho violador" (The Cuban state is a rapist male).[59] The feminist platform @YoSíTeCreo in turn described the proposed family code as progressive but cautioned that its application could not be guaranteed as written so long as state institutions were not politically autonomous, noting the absence of comprehensive laws against gender-based violence and the unavailability of femicide statistics and reporting.[60] The animal-rights and environmental activist @unguajirocubano lamented how the domestic press discussed only the controversial family code but not the penal code, and all of them have condemned the imprisonment and lengthy sentences of participants in the 11J protests. Among others, @DaltonLiebknec1 described the family code as the result of activism achieved after considerable repression: "Antes de 11J y 27N hubo un 1M" (Before 11J and 27N there was 11M), referring to the 2019 march in favor of LGTBQ+ rights broken up by the police, the July 11, 2021, street protests against the government's economic and COVID-19 policies, and the November 27 artist sit-in at the Ministry of Culture to protest repression and censorship. Like bloggers before, these new media agents link and document their online and offline activities to a broader project of participatory citizenship linked to digital Publizität. They often make their way to official media screens that are forced to "debunk" or discredit them on state TV programs like "Mesa

Redonda," "Razones de Cuba," and "Con Filo," ultimately giving them the visibility originally denied by the official media structure.

The arrest of the university student Leonardo Romero, whose picture carrying the sign "Socialismo Sí, Represión No" (Socialism yes, repression no) went viral in 2021, and the Russian invasion of Ukraine in 2022 further spotlighted the distinguishing marks of these digitally mediated, dissident, progressive voices vis-à-vis local and global issues. Much like the 1968 Soviet invasion of Prague, Cuba officially sided with Russia despite its stated commitments to nonalignment and to anti-imperialist self-determination. As a reminder of the October Crisis, the president of the Russian Duma was in Cuba at the time of the invasion. The independent journalist and feminist activist Marta María Rodríguez tweeted "Antiimperialista debería escribirse con S mayúscula al final" (Anti-imperialist ought to be written with a capital S at the end) along with a condemnation of *Granma*'s front-page piece supporting Russia's deceitful self-defense narrative for invading Ukraine.[61] Others from this Twittersphere—several of whom follow, like, and retweet one another—condemned Russia's invasion and Cuba's tacit support but refocused the discussion on Luxembourgian antiwar positions. Some among these digital-left dissidents still identify ambiguously as *fidelistas* and/or *guevaristas*, that is, as critical revolutionaries (*revolucionarios críticos*) rather than left dissidents proper, historicizing the deterioration of the revolution more squarely in its twenty-first-century transformations.[62] Nonetheless, their calls for systemic change, their disavowal of the government's monopoly on definitions of socialism, their engagement in the digital public sphere, and their commitment to socially progressive values and explicit antigovernmental critiques set them apart from the earlier generation of critical revolutionaries like Navarro. Their comments, retweets, and networks of followers show a clear continental feedback loop with the Latin American shift from the Pink Tide to a new "Green Tide"—the color that predominates in the environmental and the feminist protest aesthetics—in which Indigenous, feminist, environmental, LGBTQ+, and community-based issues are becoming the central hegemonic axis of a novel left coalition long in the making and intimately tied to popular culture and mass media processes of identity formation.[63]

Reflecting on these shifts, the cofounder of the investigative journalism and digital storytelling outfit *El Estornudo*, Carlos Manuel Álvarez, penned a piece looking at Gabriel Boric's 2022 election in Chile alternatively as a generational test for a progressive Latin American statecraft, which until recently was still trapped in traditional populist referents and unable to look beyond Fidel, Chávez, and the Pink Tide experience as "leftist" models.[64] In the aftermath of the 2021 protests, and with the prominent role of digital media in organizing and documenting these and the government's repressive responses—including a seventy-two-hour internet blackout—a parallel rupture took place in online discussions between international left-wing supporters of the Cuban government and its left-wing critics.

While the Cuba question has been a permanent fixture for the global left from the start, this new round of discussions is revealing for several reasons. Criticism of Cuba (in Latin American fora and online from the left) is far more visible than it used to be, though still polemical, particularly regarding the role of the US embargo, as evidenced in the North American Congress in Latin America's dossier on the topic and the controversy generated by LASA's 2021 statement on Cuba.[65] A new generation of politically influential progressive voices has to wrestle again with the Cuba question as well, as the exchange surrounding the 11J protests between the Black Lives Matter Instagram account (supporting the Cuban government) and Danielle Pilar Clealand (a scholar of race relations) demonstrated.[66] More sophisticated materialist critiques, as opposed to superficial demands for less political repression, are also taking root. The New York–based writer and editor John Michael Colón's Twitter thread about the Cuban currency issues, and the Spain-based environmental anthropologist Emilio Santiago Muiño's thread about the difficulties of left critique in the wake of 11J are representatives of a digital, public-facing, global left group of dissidents keen to carve a more discerning critical space of left international solidarity that avoids the reductive limitations of Cold War Third Worldism alliances on display in posts like the Democratic Socialists of America's message of support for the Cuban government during the protests. A critical postsocialist solidarity in this sense would distinguish between internationalism and interventionism so as to avoid ceding the space of solidarity to the neoliberal pairing of freedom and market and other opportunistic cheerleaders of the Cuban opposition who are then perceived as the dissident's only international allies.

Back at home, whatever the heterogeneous positions of the different Cuban voices on local and global issues, the most significant change in this still minoritarian yet increasingly diverse digital public sphere is the appearance of dissident voices that are no longer purely oppositional (i.e., abstractly anticommunist or antiauthoritarian) or organized around pre-existing Christian and classically liberal democratic groups but that seek a progressive dissident space that challenges in words and deeds the revolution's symbolic monopoly on social and economic justice. While the majority of readers of independent blogs were located outside Cuba, Twitter and other social media platforms are much more accessible and attractive to a younger domestic readership cohort. Moreover, tweets often recirculate as screenshots via messaging apps like WhatApp and Telegram. Widely read or not, their very public presence constitutes a transformation in perceptions of the public sphere and is a symptomatic indicator of shifting political imaginaries and possible counterhegemonic alliances that do not simply capitulate to the postsocialist neoliberal consensus that ruled the ends of "actually existing socialisms" in Eastern and Central Europe.

Manuel Castells has described the counterhegemonic significance of technologies of mass self-communication as symptoms of "a culture that emphasizes individual autonomy[] and the self-construction of the project of the social actor."[67] In the case of Cuba, new media technologies initially provided user-friendly spaces and networks that did not require institutional support to thrive and thus were not accountable to direct government interference (other than through personal intimidation). The digital age reconfigured those dynamics by allowing public participation by these new actors in spaces of relative autonomy and where, as the intelligence officer Eduardo Fontes pointed out, doing "prohibited things" became not only logistically easier but also contagiously attractive. Fontes, known as the "cybercop," appeared in a 2011 leaked video instructing military personnel about new technologies and their use by dissident groups. He recognized their "cool" factor and the dangers to the ideological commitment of the young cadres posed by indiscriminate socialization on the web. The conference was widely distributed, especially through Facebook and YouTube, and was covered by news sources like *El Nuevo Herald*, *Diario de Cuba*, and *Penúltimos Días*. Another leaked video from 2017 of the current president, Díaz-Canel (who took office in 2019), speaking about the proliferation of alternative and independent fora thanks to the expansion of digital media and the internet showed the Cuban leaders' position has not evolved much in six years, similarly complaining about "websites, platforms, magazines with a low profile, seemingly harmless, but many of them firmly anchored in proven stereotypes of the culture war. These media pay our journalists more money than we can pay, so they also attract our young journalists. They conceal their real intentions behind the supposed ideas of critical attitudes and freedom of expression." The external funding of these initiatives is neither a secret nor a smoking gun, but the government uses it to discredit independent reporting; under current Cuban laws (2019 Decreto Ley 370 and 2021 Ley 35), receiving funding may come dangerously close to ambiguous charges of collaboration with a foreign power. Tracey Eaton's US-based Cuba Money Project critically tracks US government's investments in regime change in Cuba through a variety of programs. In turn, independent news platforms like *Periodismo de Barrio*, for example, dedicate concrete efforts to make explicit and transparent their sources of external funding and the reasons why they are necessary.

Foreign financial and logistic support for independent political, cultural, and media activity in Cuba has been historically provided via the National Endowment for Democracy, USAID, Open Society, the Swedish and Norwegian embassies, and embassies and foundations from Poland, Czechia, and Serbia through initiatives like Kafka Novels, People in Need, and the Exit Festival.[68] However, parallel to these funding opportunities, the infamous case of Zunzuneo uncovered the continuity of US-led initiatives to extend previous programs of ideological influence and disinformation to the digital realm. An investigation by the Associated Press uncovered Zunzuneo, a USAID-financed plan to create a social media platform through third-party contractors that looked Cuban-born, attracted a youthful audience, and could foster a climate of unrest similar to the Arab Spring; it was active between 2010 and 2012.[69] These top-down efforts end up undermining the credibility of legitimate Cuban grassroots projects and, much like the economic embargo, give the Cuban government the benefit of the doubt in claiming media manipulation every time a significant challenge to its official narrative emerges. The 2010 Wikileaks diplomatic cables also showed contact and various levels of support between US officials in Cuba and dissident groups, though the nuances of who is using whom, and the degree of negotiations between transnational actors with temporary alliances but different end goals, are lost in such decontextualized correspondence.

These two dimensions of foreign support inescapably evoke the different modes of cultural and mediatic investments established during the Cold War: the covert financing of cultural projects in Latin America promoting the implicit kinship between economic liberalism and artistic freedom, and the covert but explicitly interventionist media projects like Radio Swan and Sherwood. Moreover, as Tlostanova cautions, even in cases of NGO financing and similar "postideological" forms of support, there are deeper theoretical and political questions about the expectations and pressures created regarding grant recipients and beneficiaries to mold their project missions to fit narrow parameters of aesthetic value, democratic discourse, and critique designed elsewhere. Equally, many of these funds function not only as long-term tools of soft power but also to legitimize the democratic illusions of liberal capitalism. However, from the perspective of situated demands for autonomy, information, and real-time access to global mediascapes, and faced with no other possibilities for domestic publicly or independently funded alternatives, compounded with the loss of job opportunities and ostracism that may accompany dissident activities, those concerns are doubly academic questions for activists on the ground. Additionally, accusations of foreign support have to contend with state-owned media and troll farms, which oftentimes are paid actors engaged in digital counterinsurgency and propaganda campaigns undertaken by the government. In Cuba these are pejoratively known as *ciberclarias* (cybercatfishes), after an invasive species of catfish imported from China that has become a staple referent of failed state food policies and citizen frustration.

Therefore, it is less pertinent to ask where funds come from than about the nature of the relationship between the funded project and the funds in question. How do these initiatives connect with broader citizen demands for participation and change? And how do they interpellate—and become interpellated by—state and market forces? My objective here is not to romanticize voices of political dissent or of emergent and informal consumer and media cultures so as to recuperate and uncritically celebrate spaces of symbolic resistance and digital citizenship. My intention is merely to highlight key components of the reticular network of local screen practices that are transforming public discourse and forms of dissent deemed unacceptable by dominant stakeholders (figs. 4.6a–b.).

Since the official professional status for artists and journalists is tied exclusively to state institutions, claims to narrative, investigative, or interpretive authenticity are mediated less by institutional credentialed parameters and more by each project's capacity to protect and project their grassroots commitments and editorial independence. When blogs like *Generación Y* and *Octavo Cerco* broke into the scene in the mid-2010s, they combined in their posts genres like *testimonio*, *crónica*, and journalistic reports to create an online persona that effectively captivated the reading public through an intimate approach to public concerns. The evidentiary multimedia that accompanied the posts (videos, photos, leaks, documents, art, music) as much as their writing styles offered a charismatic, informed, and verifiable dissenting voice that was unambiguously critical of the political establishment and cultivated an unrehearsed model of participatory politics

Figure 4.6a–b. Memes questioning whether the sources of financial support for alternative and independent Cuban media should matter to their claims of authenticity and legitimacy.

that became especially relevant after a government crackdown on independent journalists in 2003 (known as the "Black Spring"). Straddling multiple experiments with citizen journalism, digital media, and aesthetic representation, independent blogs were indebted most to the Latin American tradition of the *crónica*.

Since the decline of blogging, the most compelling postsocialist storytelling found a home in a fully fledged digital *crónica*. Cuban postsocialist *crónicas* are published in digital platforms like *Periodismo de Barrio*, *elTOQUE*, and *El Estornudo*, deliberately engaging in the continuing battle over who gets to tell the stories of life in contemporary Cuba and through what means and media. The shift from individual blogging projects to the digital *crónica* showcases the back-and-forth between the professionalization of the amateur and the amateurization of the professional: Sánchez, who started as a blogger with a background in literature and philology but not in journalism, founded the digital daily *14ymedio* with her partner Reinaldo Escobar, a journalist who became a blogger; *14ymedio* was the first independent digital newspaper produced from Cuba. This trajectory can be compared to that of Elaine Díaz, who polemicized with Sánchez and other alternative bloggers from her previous platform in *La Polémica Digital* and as a state-employed journalist. Díaz, whose position then was that of the "committed critic," ended up leaving state employment to pursue independently financed, in-depth local reporting. Her web portal and reporting team at *Periodismo de Barrio* have faced the same accusations by official authorities once faced by *14ymedio*, despite focusing more on local in-depth reporting than on national politics.

The growth and impact of *Periodismo de Barrio*, *elTOQUE*, and *El Estornudo* placed the figure of the amateur citizen that emerged with the Cuban blogosphere into a conversation with the postsocialist *cronistas*. As *El Estornudo*'s Abraham Jiménez Enoa put it, "Professions belong . . . to those who practice them."[70] A foundational genre of Latin American literary modernity, the *crónica* provided the material and institutional vehicle for the training and professionalization of journalists and for the financial support of modernist writers (e.g., Darío and Martí, pioneers of the genre) in the absence of an autonomous field of literature and a stable market and reading public and thus helped usher in the professionalization and modernization of literature itself. Several of the most widely read and recognized new voices in these platforms, such as Monica Baró, Carlos Manuel Álvarez, and Abraham Jiménez Enoa, trained in the writing workshops of Onelio Jorge Cardoso. Their stylistic, thematic, and institutional approaches to long-form and investigative journalism places them squarely within the corpus of their Latin American *cronista* peers. These affinities were further explored and crystalized with the Taller de Periodismo de Investigación (Investigative Journalism Workshop) in Tania Bruguera's International Institute for Artivism Hanna Arendt; the first iteration included the participation of household *cronistas* like Cristian Alarcón (Argentina), Óscar Martínez (Salvador), and Marcela Turati (Mexico).

Like its colonial and modernist predecessors, the *crónica* at the turn of the twenty-first century remains committed to emergent structures of feeling. With an eye toward "knowledge rather than data," the *crónica* has eclipsed other historically significant Latin American literary genres like *testimonio*, and the essay as the most dynamic nonfiction writing published today.[71] If the *crónica* at the turn of the twentieth century was a response to industrial modernization, mass media, and the professionalization of literature, the *crónica* at the turn of the twenty-first is where the violence of neoliberalism, the struggles for political recognition, and the precarizing digital remediation of literature and journalism have found constant attention. However, though the national hero José Martí was among the genre's pioneers, and revolutionary cultural institutions such as *El Caimán Barbudo*, *Prensa Latina*, and Casa de las Américas furnished support to key Latin American *cronistas*, including Rodolfo Walsh and Gabriel García Márquez, in the mid-1960s, Cuban writers have been conspicuously absent from the continental *crónica* boom of the turn of the twenty-first century.

In the 2010s, external and internal catalysts pushed the production and circulation of a new Cuban postsocialist *crónica*: the forays and, in some cases, decline of other national journalistic and literary projects that preceded it; a new generation of writers and journalists with access to other influences, publics, and media; digital publishing and social media platforms to promote them; and a market eager for new Cuban stories after the death of Fidel, the financial crisis of 2008, the Obama rapprochement, and the rise and fall of the Pink Tide. As Esther Whitfield demonstrated, this interest, fostered since the 1990s, reflects endless variations of a commonplace literary aesthetic that "pits representations of authenticity (what Cuba is now) against stimuli of nostalgia (for what Cuba once was or might have been), thereby exposing ideological fissures in both the Cuban Revolution itself and outsiders' interests in it."[72]

But it can be asserted that Cuban literature as a whole was a victim of its own success and is still recovering from its market boom in the 1990s. With the exhaustion of "dirty realism" as the dominant aesthetic of that decade—self-exoticizing, allegorical, and monothematic—and the reception challenges facing the various postnationalist, postrealist, and experimental digital literary projects of Generation Zero and beyond (the generation of writers active circa 2000 and after), the Cuban *crónica* has found new footing in Spanish-language readerships by satisfying this demand. In this sense, the circulation of the Cuban contemporary *crónica* coincides with the reemergence of the trip to Cuban socialism discussed in chapter 1, satisfying a reading gaze that finds an audiovisual equivalent in YouTube influencers strolling around Havana to show the world "the real Cuba," with a global counterpart seen in the *crónicas* of foreigners traveling to the end of socialism.[73] These literary journalism projects have been welcomed and promoted within the established fora for the Latin American *crónica*, like the García Márquez and Ortega y Gasset prizes, and magazines and publishers that sustain the genre, like *Gatopardo*, in which Jiménez Enoa publishes a column.[74] In addition to the affordances of digital platforms and social media, grants and prizes, and an established publishing market for the genre in Latin America, an upward trend in the global appetite for human-interest stories fuels this renewed interest in Cuban stories about the end of socialism.

Crónicas no doubt satisfy demands for authenticity delivered through literary pleasure, but they also subvert the established ideological coordinates of that consuming desire by producing a polyphony of first-person narratives that challenge stereotypical expectations about what postsocialist subjects look like and desire. The *crónica*'s intimate, immersive, multiperspectival aesthetics binds topics, subjects, narrator, and readers in a storytelling experience that disavows the rhetorical comforts of emotional distance, of binaries, of grand narratives, of official histories. In tension with official or mainstream journalism (i.e., against news outlets' supposed neutrality, their short-term outlook, their call to shock, their superficial analysis, their drive to be first with a scoop), "the *crónica* requires and imposes alliances, a horizontal procedural logic, to achieve the text; its aesthetic is political in that sense."[75] Despite continued repression, what could be written about only as fiction in the 1990s can be written about today as nonfiction (though not without repercussions). But unlike the blogs, where a global readership beyond the diaspora and a hunger for local news were limited to those with niche interests in Cuban digital dissidence, the new *crónica* is read by a more diverse public. Even investigative journalism pieces that are not strictly *crónicas* underscore the influence of the genre, featuring literary descriptions of the scenes where the events in question take place, attentive profiling of interviewees, and metacritical references to investigative methodologies and political limits in this specific context.

The platforms that publish *crónicas* have a stake in the domestic public sphere in ways that isolated literary works did not, even if the Cuban literary sphere historically has been a space of surrogate practices for unofficial histories, unsanctioned sociologies, and disguised dissidences. An activist who identifies as a hardline right-winger described *elTOQUE* (a digital platform for cultural and social criticism, news, and investigative journalism with an antigovernmental social-justice bent): "Young 'progres' are the only ones who read that." But as the founder of the digital platform *La Trinchera*, Miguel Alejandro Hayes, put it, even or especially for progressive youths, "El gobierno es incapaz de ofrecer un proyecto, un horizonte, una esperanza" (The government is incapable of offering a project, a horizon, a hope).[76] *La Trinchera*, for example, began as a digital debating space to explore other Marxisms beyond Marxism–Leninism and became a transmedia platform reflecting on a wide range of social issues that includes materialist critiques of Cuban socialism. Though not strictly a space for *crónicas*, it seeks public recognition for a unique political perspective via transmedia, locally situated narratives told by first-person individual and collective voices as well. Similarly, digital platforms like *Tremenda Nota* (specializing in LGBTQ+ communities) and *Alas Tensas* (feminist issues) explore and expand activist and progressive horizons in Cuba, discussing external pressures as much as internal struggles. These perspectives are especially important in postsocialist Cuba, where the primary functions of public revolutionary iconography and of the state's media policies are not to rebuild the hegemonic consensus around a socialist state project but to prevent any counterhegemonic convergence from taking its place so that no alternative horizon (other than immigration) becomes credible as a project of radical social transformation. This is the case to such a degree that even seemingly nonoppositional causes are obstructed and discredited by the authorities as soon as they reach visibility and credibility. The suspicion with which authorities view civil society initiatives (like the growing animal rights movement, which works online and offline to promote animal welfare, including pet adoption, in the absence of serious public attention to animal control and protection) exemplifies these dynamics.

Simultaneously, these new media agents diverge from and counter the narrow, enduring patterns of government criticism of the right-wing Cuban exile community, historically amplified by their outsized dominance in US-based media systems.[77] As was the case with independent bloggers, it is hard to quantify how publicly effective this diversification of civil society is and whether it tests or threatens the limits of the state's demonstration of tolerance for a privileged few. Nonetheless, the gradual emergence of this more pluralistic digital sphere has never been divorced from offline activisms, solidarities, and real risks, having already proven to be a successful training ground for new forms of narrating and making sense of postsocialist Cuba with little to no representation in traditional opposition fora. *elTOQUE*'s legal analyses and how-to sections, for instance, add important practical resources to the platform's narrative ones. They are especially important avenues for mutual recognition and the articulation of a shared social project in the absence of the legal right to independent political assembly in an opaque and unreliable media environment. Regardless of whether they effect political change in the short term or the long term, they are symptomatic of transformations that have already taken place, that signal change in other scales and spheres, building community, expanding and codifying imaginaries of the possible, openly investigating government power, and questioning social dogmas.

In fact, the public dissemination of political demands and subjectivities aligned with the socially progressive values of a new generation of Cubans on these platforms has produced telling public confrontations that illustrate their challenges to the government's symbolic monopoly on social and economic justice, on the one hand, and to its conservative opposition on the other. As the top official in matters of public sexual health and LGTBQ+ and women's rights, and as the daughter of Raúl and the FMC (Federación de Mujeres Cubanas, or Federation of Cuban Women) founder Vilma Espín, Mariela Castro has been at the center of many public controversies on these matters, not the least for using sexist language against women dissidents. In a 2008 post later erased from the CENESEX website, Castro called blogger Yoani Sánchez a female cock, implying that her speech and behavior in public was out of bounds with gender-conforming roles. On March 10, 2021, Castro again shared a post on Facebook, written by Raúl Escalona Abella of *La Tizza*, that toyed with the idea of detailed violent acts against well-known cultural figures critical of the government, like Tania Bruguera, Luis Manuel Otero Alcántara, Mónica Baró, and denounced *Rialta* magazine (produced in Mexico), *El Estornudo*, and *elTOQUE* as counterrevolutionary media. One of Cuba's best-known independent journalists and *cronistas*, Baró called out (as Sánchez had before) the disconnect between Mariela Castro's official stated mission and her speech, as well as the justifications for state-sanctioned sexist violence when dissident women are on the receiving end.[78] Like *Yohandry's Blog* before, *La Tizza* is a publication platform that presents itself as an independent socialist response to projects like *elTOQUE* and *El Estornudo*, though some of its editors are graduates of the diplomatic school within the Cuban Ministry of Foreign Affairs (at least according to their linked Facebook bios), which suggests a more porous official relationship than the platform advertises. Baró's post also underscores the role of alternative and independent media in forcing a public conversation on the realities of gender-based violence in Cuba beyond insufficient rhetorical commitments by state institutions to equal justice and protection. A few months before, an article published in *Granma* blamed specifically the increasing but misleading visibility of gender-based violence in Cuba on the recent surge of storytelling as "a device that doesn't report an event through information but through emotional narrative," of the kind promoted by counterrevolutionary digital media platforms "disguised as independent journalism."[79]

In Cuba, as elsewhere in Latin America, nationalist conservatives and traditional leftists have sought to neutralize the demands and critiques of feminists, LGTBQ+ communities, and other marginalized groups by suggesting they are dividing the nation and discrediting the government using imported frameworks of human rights.[80] While Global South feminists have always stressed the necessity to decolonize Western feminisms, the anti-imperialist rhetoric is mobilized in this context instead to deflect criticism and avoid responsibility and to continue to reserve the symbolic and institutional spaces of progressive social justice only for the single-party state and its authorized agents: "The mediatization of femicide in social media has become one of the most exploited resources by the digital media machine financed by the [United States] in the media wars against Cuban society . . . [illustrating] the forced import of initiatives that originated in other countries."[81] In its more subtle forms, official rhetoric condemns gender-based violence but either negates or minimizes the existence of the problem (Mariela Castro has publicly denied the existence of femicides in Cuba) or acknowledges it as a sociocultural issue that the government is keenly aware of but unable to do more about.[82]

The contemporary Latin American *crónica*, whether in Cuba or elsewhere in the region, combats state censorship and violence, on the one hand, and the predatory demands of the attention economy and the defunding of media conglomerates who have divested from investigative journalism and invested in twenty-four-hour cycles of headlines and clickbait, on the other. In this sense, despite the overall marketization and standardization of the *crónica* in Hispanic literary markets, it remains a peripheral genre with respect to the centers of power and information in the region, whether they are serving political elites and governments or the commercial media conglomerates. While the national readership is hard to quantify (*El Estornudo* has been blocked inside Cuba since 2018), these texts reshape public discourse, in Cuba as they do elsewhere, sustaining a wider spectrum of political commitments and cultural imaginaries and generating content by and about women, the precariat of the subsistence and informal economies, rural outposts, urban misfits, environmental defenders, and Indigenous, Black, and diasporic communities. All these figures belie the classic, homogenizing discourses of traditional party politics in Cuba and Latin America that have been heavily skewed toward anti-imperialist and nationalist populisms. From a Cuban-focused perspective, these experiences are featured in *Periodismo de Barrio*'s "Vulnerable Communities" series and in *El Estornudo* and *elTOQUE*'s profiles, *crónicas*, and investigative reports. These stories circulate in the Spanish-speaking world, redrawing a symbolic map of structural oppressions and local solidarities that challenges the promises and pitfalls of the nation-state model and Cuba's mythical exceptionality.

Beyond born-digital literary journalism and digital Habermasian Publizität, the portable screens of postsocialism chronicle change and continuity in myriad ways. Like many others, Cubans have found the language of memes to be joyful (in the sense of Barthes's *jouissance*); memes represent efficient ways to remain connected and informed, to complain, and to reshape public discourse in their own terms. As the product of a participatory process (making a meme involves modifying an existing template or photograph, and its dissemination reflects the meme's suitability, ingenuity, and persuasiveness), political memes necessarily involve users in critical "deconstructions" not only with respect to the media-making process but also vis-à-vis public speech and politics at large.[83] As opposed to oral political humor that is shared only in complicit intimacies, social networks and interpersonal communications open undetermined spaces of exchange in which humorous dissidences, like humor itself, lower the stakes of political participation and opinion formation and make the risk of going beyond the intimate circle of trusted friends or the protection of oral ephemerality attractive to reap social rewards—the pleasure of offering the best joke, the drive to be first, the prospect of more arriving in barter.

Postsocialist Cuban memes build on the topics and genres of classic socialist humor, but they also introduce new formal and thematic elements that showcase shifting preoccupations and frameworks of reference as much as the growing influence of and desire to participate in global internet cultures (figs. 4.7a–c). Significantly, meme topics go beyond the 1980s and '90s humor standards about censorship, corruption, absurdity, scarcity, and contrast comparisons with a mythical capitalist world out there. Instead they react in real time to local and global news, incorporate more pointed critiques of the state's economic policy and its monopolies (especially ETECSA), and succinctly communicate how everyday Cubans navigate the informal and hybrid economies and the state media monopoly. A broader range of ideological positions has begun to emerge in popular political humor, including the rejection to be "political" and "factional" in the narrow, binary frameworks of the traditional polarization: "Ni comunistas, ni gusanos," yet both are affected by and unable to escape the discursive and ideological terms established by these poles. Cuban memelords with large followings like @YoUsoMiNasobuco and @SanMemero also use their channels, whether or not they are monetized, for social awareness: retweeting amber alerts, calling for mutual aid, and fund-raising for various causes. In Cuba the risks are real: Ariel Falcón, the meme maker and influencer behind @YoUsoMiNasobuco, who streamed his participation in the 11J protests, was arrested and left the country shortly thereafter.

This postsocialist memescape brings into play the remediation of classic socialist humor with the emergence of a similar phenomenon that I call "capitalist humor," or perhaps more accurately "anticapitalist humor," as a symptom of the postsocialist condition. This new type of humor (in the United States, at least) follows a similar formal joke structure. It not only measures the gap between the political promise and its actual, everyday delivery but also underscores that such a gap is the result of the deliberate and all too often absurd self-interested actions of political elites who are evil and incompetent in equal measures. This humor invokes a collective subject comprising those who have now realized the game is rigged, who find humor in their shared suffering with a resigned, critical distance with respect to the possibility of corrective justice in the short term. On December 29, 2020, for example, the US Department of the Treasury announced a COVID-19 relief and economic stimulus check for all citizens, for an amount of $600. A popular meme captured the general frustration with the government's handling of the pandemic and the related economic impact by combining the guillotine as a revolutionary symbol with the apparent rise of DIY projects during the initial pandemic lockdowns. It suggested that the low purchasing power of the amount offered could be maximized otherwise, listing prices of a guillotine's

Figure 4.7a–c. Memes on political economy and polarization.

components at a major home improvement store, allowing recipients to stimulate the economy, as the check was meant to do, while also using it to provide the raw materials to dismantle the system itself.

These types of jokes used to be the sole domain of "actually existing socialism" and a privileged site of Cold War discourse, so much so that President Ronald Reagan loved to tell "Soviet Jokes." In the absence of a legible difference between actually existing socialism and actually existing capitalism today, the obvious butt of the joke behind the Iron Curtain removed, part of the argument of this new anticapitalist humor is that "the Right can't meme" despite the alt-right's otherwise effective use of digital media campaigns and networks. In the Cuban memescape, the equivalent political class that cannot meme, in this sense, is represented by the Communist Party and the state apparatus, in which the equivalent loss of cultural and political hegemony (though not power) means that "the (nominal) Left can't meme."[84]

Memelords are "amateur citizens." Jorge, the meme maker and page administrator of La Coyuntura, one of the most popular Facebook meme pages, had no previous experience in graphic design, digital media, or politics. Based in Florida, he started making memes in 2019 as a reaction to the treatment of the Movimiento San Isidro activists by the Cuban government. After one viral meme (featuring Captain Jack Sparrow struggling to figure out an economy with three different currencies, it had over 2 million views on Facebook alone), he saw the subscription to his pages grow exponentially (about 56,000 followers in Facebook from 2019 to 2021). La Coyuntura memes are also shared through WhatsApp, Telegram, and text messages. According to his page statistics, 60.9 percent of visits came from Cuba, followed by 23.4 percent from the United States, 3 percent from Spain, and 2 percent from Mexico.[85] Portable postsocialisms travel—through screens, through trips, through economic flows, through translation, through communicative and aesthetic exchanges—as "the imagined nation" is maintained and contested by Cubans everywhere.

These practices are also embedded in the exploitative circuits of the digital attention economy and its global division of labor. The personal costs of these ordinary insurgencies are bound to the exploitation of personal data and to the emotionally predatory forms of competition for our gaze, on which these platforms depend.[86] They are not immune to forms of media engagement that actively disempower and disinform the participant/citizen, especially in contexts of rapid change in media ownership and models, as in postsocialism.[87] Moreover, globally recognizable memes tend to originate on the anglophone internet and are adapted later to the local situation at hand. Cuban-originated memes are not immediately translatable in their use of hyperlocal referents, slang, and situations.[88] Even when this one-way legibility is reversed, it relies overwhelmingly on preestablished media brokers to become amplified. For example, #DiazCanelSingao, a hashtag that casts the president as a bastard, briefly became a global trend through a viral video of the influential media maker and former adult-film star Mia Khalifa, who used the catchphrase to show her interest in and support for Cuban protesters and to deny the Cuban president's claims that she was another media mercenary.

Private and public platforms of digital communication extend competing claims to the past as well in ways that link collective memory to political claims to the future. A popular, collaborative remediation of national history and cultural identity is carried out along with scholarly and artistic labors, which are coordinated in Facebook and WhatsApp groups formed around shared experiences and in digital archives like El Archivo de Connie and Cuba Material and informally shared in social media and the comment sections of digitized analog materials. The task of historiographical remediation here is not only participatory but also paratactic (tactical parataxis). It does not simply present a syntactic alternative to Official History; its outcome remains underdetermined. Nonetheless, given the outsized participation of the Cuban diaspora in the generation of this content, it remains to be seen how (or whether) the digitally mediated experience of a diasporic archive might transform the preexisting relationship of those communities with Cuba as symbolic space and material place, and with their places of residence, in coming decades.[89]

Cuba's apparent geopolitical exceptionality and isolation have transformed into situated forms of engaging with world events, where the local reality is not illegible with respect to a global mediascape but represented and disseminated through it, as illustrated in two memes: the NASA 2021 and the "Here's Johnny" memes (figs. 4.8a–b). The scorched landscape of the NASA meme remits us to the postapocalyptic dimension of postsocialist culture and politics. It is an invitation to explore whether and how the competing discourses of survival anchored in the experience of the Special Period have changed or continued in the twenty-first century and the degree to which the new economic collapse (dubbed by the government as "conjunctural" to rein in a panic about the return to the 1990s but mocked and denounced with increasing desperation by citizens as "La

Figure 4.8a–b. A meme reaction to news of the February 18, 2021, landing of NASA's Mars rover that began circulating soon after in social media (received on February 20, 2021, through a WhatsApp group). The Cuban version of the popular "Here's Johnny" meme and a video remix series is based on Stanley Kubrick's film *The Shining* (1980).

Coyuntura") has shifted once again competing narratives of what survives in Cuban socialism and how those stories are produced, disseminated, and received, and by whom.

The composite social text of Cuban screen culture rebuffs images of the country as an exceptional political experiment, disconnected and frozen in time, resisting any approach to its alternative digital ecosystems that reduces them to its revolutionary legacies. These practices and artifacts attest not only to the continuities of state power and capitalist expansion and to the complexities of postsocialist change but also to the resilient agencies of everyday citizens. Above all, they problematize statization and privatization as unexamined opposites and underscore how issues of (de)regulation and censorship cannot be divorced from their milieus. To understand the wagers of both market and state in the postsocialist context, the different dimensions of the Cuban postsocialist screen (as a heavily regulated and highly disputed realm, as the vehicle for the articulated demands of emergent political subjects, as refuge and refuse of popular cultural imaginations) must be analyzed together, including from the necessarily distant, modular, and interactive reading modes that our screen cultures impose on us. In a time of ubiquitous, networked screens, we all carry these competing postsocialisms in our pockets, at the tips of our fingers, at the mercy of a like or a share and even perhaps as the occasional objects of self-reflection. These portable postsocialisms include more than ever self-produced but not unmediated participatory narratives, relying on vernacular media literacies as much as on institutional and corporate gatekeepers for their public articulation and dissemination. The struggle over informatization therefore reproduces inequalities in some spheres and breakthroughs in others, but its public battles allow us a more careful examination of both dominant and insurgent narratives of change and continuity, of state control and of market expansion. Even against the odds, the postsocialist mediascape can offer moments of critical redefinitions (of what Cuban socialism was, of what postsocialism is) for the local and global constituents of a revolutionary past alike and for the stakeholders of a present permanently under construction.

CONCLUSION

Cuban Mediascapes after the End of History

Marx sabe el diablo por viejo que por diablo.

El que Marx anda, Marx acaba.
CUBAN PUNS[1]

Postsocialism brings into relief *the ends* of "the end of history."

In the 1990s "the end of history" became synonymous with the end of actually existing socialisms. The dissolution of Eastern and Central European socialist governments allowed Francis Fukuyama to infamously declare "the end of history," only not as Marxists had imagined it. Marx and Engels reasoned that if the history of all hitherto existing society was the history of class struggle, if communism was not a state of affairs to be achieved but the historical movement of modern humanity toward a classless society, and if capitalist class struggle was the final form of this economic battle against exploitative conditions of labor waged since the beginning of history, then surely the end of class struggle would also deliver the end of history in this sense.[2] Instead, Fukuyama claimed, capitalist democracy had been the victorious midwife of this final chapter of human emancipation.[3] Controversial from the outset, this version of the end of history nevertheless resonated with the end of a millennium on the Gregorian calendar, dovetailing with other narratives the period produced about itself. This triumphalism was the perfect alibi to the uncertainty, hunger, and death that characterized the 1990s elsewhere, from Sarajevo to Havana. Postsocialist contexts legitimized this reinterpretation of the end of history, informing the conditions under which it became politically useful as explanatory model. But postsocialisms, whether local or global, also had to contend with the return of history: financial collapse, statist renewals, antiestablishment and antiglobalization politics on the left and right.[4] Katherine Verdery's classic question must then be posed anew: What was postsocialism, and what comes next?

Fukuyama's assertion, despite its philosophical crudeness, endured because it resonated with an entire epoch in which failure and triumph were routinely, systematically, and unquestionably linked to socialism and capitalism, respectively. This alloy was part of a semantic field of serialized duos, naturalized in popular culture as much as in scholarly circles throughout the 1990s:

capitalism/socialism
triumph/failure
good/evil
democracy/totalitarianism

These binaries suppressed and obfuscated any challenges to the narrative that the human political imaginary has been exhausted, amplifying what David Graeber calls a "machinery of hopelessness . . . the weird ideological contortions by which we are constantly told that 'communism just doesn't work.'"[5] Against this backdrop, the very possibility of speaking about the left as a loose international coalition of organizing and thinking united against capitalism toward a common path of social and economic justice was once more at stake. For all varieties of socialist thought, the end of the Cold War catalyzed long overdue critical engagements with the legacies of the revolutionary takeover of the state apparatus in the name of socialism.

This same binary allowed Cuba to be represented at home and abroad as the exceptional survivor and museological guardian of a revolutionary legacy in danger of extinction.[6] As I have discussed throughout this book, it gave meaning to the politically transgressive round trip to the allegorical ruins of twentieth-century history, to the allure of an untapped territory for capitalist expansion, and to the Cuban ruling class's investment in the political continuity of a revolutionary state apparatus linked to the signs, slogans, heroes, and tropes that allow for the aesthetic experience of an out-of-history place, dissimulating the Cuban state's pursuit of foreign capital and its retreat from public investments. This is a narrative that insists on its own version of the end of history, one immune to further revolutionary transformation. Consider the 2021 PCC Congress, which declared the necessity of carrying out changes in order to maintain continuity, keeping with the 2002 constitutional stipulation that

Cuban socialism was "irrevocable."⁷ But is it redefinable? The defining symbols of the Cuban Revolution—Fidel, the Cuban Communist Party, the national heroic past, rebellious hypermasculinity—would first have to be vacated of their signifying monopoly, of their institutionalized organizing functions, as the exclusive representatives of the very real demands for political change that once gave them popular legitimacy but remain unfulfilled today.

It is no coincidence that "the end of history" and its aftermath—the bankruptcy of triumphant neoliberalism, the failed promises of its democratic transitions—were met with the explosion of apocalyptic and postapocalyptic tropes. They constitute what Hrvoje Tutek calls "one of the central spaces for the imaginary enactment of the 'epochal' questions of the 'End of History,' or capitalist universality."⁸ A thriving contemporary (post)apocalyptic culture industry maintains the question posed by Fredric Jameson and seized on later by Slavoj Žižek in the affirmative: Has it really become easier to imagine the end of the world than to imagine the end of capitalism?⁹ The provocation is that, as long as socialism and all other political projects of radical transformation are consistently and pejoratively associated with the specific experiences of the revolutionary state takeovers of the twentieth century by single-party rule, the total disruption of the capitalist system and its governing institutions can be imagined only as the aftereffect of a freak accident or as the collateral damage of a natural catastrophe. After all, apocalyptic and postapocalyptic fictions are to neoliberal end-of-history ideology what Robinson Crusoe was to classical, liberal capitalism.¹⁰ Whereas the apocalyptic plot—when the action takes place in medias res—re-creates the conditions under which humanity pulls together at the last minute to save itself (or its best parts), the postapocalyptic narrative derives its dramatic tension from being faced with the possibility to completely reorganize society differently and from ultimately failing to do so. The (post)apocalyptic genre can be read simultaneously as the invitation to imagine, and as the preemptive neutralization of, the prospects of a radical social transformation. It naturalizes our self-made catastrophes while it mimetically registers our collective desires for change.

But our apocalyptic obsession is not just another regulative dystopian dispositif, a narratively compelling ideological sleight-of-hand. In its contemporary mode, it also stands instead for a political unconscious casting modern state projects as dysfunctional disaster managers and all too often as disaster catalysts themselves. This question of the state animates an apocalyptic universe that is appropriately a Hobbesian revenge fantasy:

solitary, poor, nasty, brutish, and short. This is because, if the popularity of the (post)apocalyptic shows how difficult it is to imagine the end of capitalism as something other than the destruction of the world, then it also consistently shows how easy it is to imagine the failure of the modern nation-state to rise to global challenges. In addition, the problem of the state is specifically where end-of-history and end-of-the-world narratives meet head-on, because if postsocialism stands for the death of (a certain understanding of) the state, then postsocialist thought and (post)apocalyptic imagery must be examined together. In this sense, Cuban (post)apocalyptic tropes address the shared revolutionary legacy of fully centralized bureaucratic statization. They speak to the core political questions—the possibilities and pitfalls of a reinvented imaginary of social justice—that postsocialist fictions of the end of history and its aftermath demand of us.

Cuban End-times

A detour through Cuban representations of the end of history in apocalyptic and postapocalyptic keys can illustrate how the political specter of statism remains at the center of the postsocialist condition and its contexts at the end of the end of history. At the same time it can sketch a tentative shift in Cuban survivor tropes after the Special Period.

The end of history was experienced as disaster or liberation depending where and who one was in the 1990s. "The Fall" was indeed a catastrophe experienced in Cuba at multiple levels and was decidedly world-ending, too.[11] Its economic impact on the island has been compared to that of the 1929 Great Depression. It was the end of the socialist state (as they knew it), the end of history (they were told), and possibly the end of the world (evidence is never lacking). Waves of impromptu seafaring migrants languished in the ocean and in the US Guantánamo Bay Naval Base, ears pricked up for news in endless blackouts, between an agonizing bureaucratic order barely able to sustain itself and collective expectations of structural change that never crystallized.

When the end of the socialist world was imminent, the Cuban government wanted no part of it. After the dissolution of the socialist bloc and the Soviet Union (1989–1991), Cuba followed neither their transition model nor the aggressive market socialism of China and Vietnam. The long-standing nationalism of the 1959 Cuban Revolution facilitated this singular course. If the early official historiographies of the revolutionary event retroactively read its epic insurrectionary origins in the colonial past (as a way to absorb internal factions and as a way to assert its relative autonomy at the height of the Cold War), half a century later it was that same teleological interpretation of national history that eased Cuba's divorce from the socialist bloc. This operation began in earnest with the Rectification of Errors and Negative Tendencies (1986), an aggressive response to curtail any influence from, and expectation of, Soviet-style perestroika and glasnost. The official story of Cuban socialism thus gained another exceptional twist as a survivor of the end of history. By 1990, Cuba's global field of action was decomposing in real time, while simultaneously its national but internationalist sense of a historical mission was thrown into a crisis and into the spotlight throughout the decade, as "the first trench of the independence of America" and as "the last bastion of communism":

> Actually, all those *catastrophic problems* happening in the socialist bloc in recent times, they were not foreseen, those events happening in the countries with whom we had established solid economic links, and who helped us defend ourselves from the imperialist blockade, and which furnished the base of [Cuba's] development.[12]

> Your Holiness: I think we have given the world a good example: You, visiting what some insisted calling the last bastion of communism; us, receiving the religious chief to whom the responsibility of destroying socialism in Europe has been attributed by some. There was no shortage of those predicting *apocalyptic events*. Some even hoped for it.[13]

While Cuba officially cast itself as the heroic survivor of a historical catastrophe, Cubans confronting a harsh material reality and a sudden ideological vacuum saw themselves as survivors of an entirely different order. These were two completely antagonistic accounts of what survival meant and of the role played by the Cuban revolutionary state in each of them.

As such, popular Cuban jokes from the 1990s thrived with variations on national hunger and survival:

> Two friends are standing in the bread queue talking:
> "You know what I was thinking the other day? I think Adam and Eve were Cubans."
> "Why do you say that?"
> "Well, they had no clothes, went around barefoot, were not allowed to eat apples, and were constantly told they lived in Paradise."

202 Conclusion

> Three gifts gave Fidel to Cuba, and three things he took away: He gave us education, sport, and health, but he took away breakfast, lunch, and dinner.

Hardly the funniest in the repertoire, these two jokes underscore several key themes of the vast trove of Cuban Special Period humor: the worsening of the economic embargo, the commodification of the (national) body, the reinvention of cultural politics, the return of religion to public life, the scarcity that made visible the extent of Cuba's dependence on Soviet subsidies and the real cost of its socialist humanism, and the sense of being stuck in time and isolated. What sometimes has been called the "late socialism" of the 1990s was squarely apocalyptic (how to survive without knowing what's next? when and wherefrom is the change coming?), whereas the postsocialism of the twenty-first century is fully postapocalyptic, the changes that made survival possible were neither the expected nor the desired ones.

The representations and critiques inspired by the sudden end of the Second World must be reconsidered after the end of the Special Period, when the Venezuelan trade and oil agreements signed in 1999 kicked in, followed by the comprehensive (albeit insufficient) economic and political reforms of the following decades. Images of apocalyptic survival produced throughout the 1990s and associated to the long-lasting, transformative effects of the economic and ideological crises of the Special Period (ca. 1990–2000)—animalistic hunger, sexual and racial exoticism, primitive ingenuity, political defiance, and above all allegorical urban ruin—have given way to new cultural practices and media images in the face of changed socioeconomic, technological, and political landscapes. Themes of national and individual survival remain central to postsocialist imaginaries, but they are increasingly explored from critical viewpoints that effectively deconstruct official state narratives and the testimonial burden of exotic survivalism so often found in those of the Special Period. Postapocalyptic and postsocialist subjectivities share a similar affect with respect to the promise of good things to come—that constitutive element of all radical politics of emancipation. The only safe assumption of the postapocalyptic/postsocialist imaginary in this particular context is that the promise of good things to come for all is the mark of the false messiahs, so that distrust and particularistic interests replace disillusion and collective concerns as the predominant affective responses (figs. 5.1a–b).

The return of an economic crisis starting in the summer of 2019, which began with widespread fuel shortages accelerated by the Venezuelan crisis (though by 2013 Cuba's economy had already diversified from

Figure 5.1a–b. "My grandpa was eaten in [the crisis of] '94. This time no one will eat cat. Ready for this conjuncture in its second phase." This meme combines the soldier-cat meme with a reference to the return of the 1990s Special Period crisis and the anecdotal claims that some Cubans ate cats for lack of other animal proteins available. A meme comparing the catastrophic penalty failures of last-minute substitutes to the English team during the 2021 European Championship soccer finals to the failures of the policy changes introduced by the Cuban government in early 2021 (Tarea de Ordenamiento) to prevent the deepening of the economic crisis, which led to the street protests that broke out the same day the soccer match was played, July 11.

Venezuela significantly), were intensified by the changes to US policy toward Cuba under President Trump and electoral victories in Latin America that curtailed beneficial trade programs (such as the end of the Mais Medicos program in Brazil under Jair Bolsonaro), all of which were compounded by the devastating effects of the COVID-19 pandemic on the tourist industry.[14] The *"coyuntura"* (conjuncture) label, suggested by President Díaz Canel to prepare Cubans for a coming economic recession under the headline "without fear," was widely mocked as an empty promise and as a distraction from the ongoing structural crisis that had led to that moment, from the blaring economic inequalities and disconnect between the ruling elites and the general population.[15] The memescape, social media networks, and independent press pushed back quickly with widespread preoccupations about a return to the 1990s but with an entirely different tone: no amount of official window-dressing would distract Cubans from the gravity of what was to come, and they might not be any better prepared materially or politically speaking, but at least they were prepared affectively speaking and knew the state would not come to their aid this time around, either.

Because what is the postsocialist subject to do, like a Mad Ma(r)x, after a relatively anticlimactic, even underwhelming apocalypse? What is to be done *after* the end of history when reinsertion in global capital, in business as usual, clashes against the idea of a radically new historical project, a mortgaged future that must now be left behind:

> Up there are the space stations, the satellites with nuclear warheads, the servers of the Global Neural Net, the *Russian way of life*, as they say among the Florida sea-migrants. Illegal immigrants who sleep in the halls of the [hospital/building] Amejeira and make four *kopec* working in the Underguater platforms. All for a chance to board one of those and get to the Romanenko station. Or to any other. An entire life of trying to be like the Russians. Just another *tavarish*. . . . Now you are legal in Autonomous Havana. When you left you were just a Cuban citizen. Today you have a Russian passport that lets you enter and leave this city-state you barely recognize anymore.[16]

This is the alternative universe of the Cuban science-fiction writer Erick J. Mota, many of whose stories take place in the future polity of what used to be Cuba, now Underguater (a creolization of "underwater"), a dystopian territory under Russian control and the casualty of unforgiving oceanic wrath.[17] As Rachel Price asserts, Mota's submerged chronicles explore the futuristic fantasies of this shared socialist past; more important, they stage the rudiments of a critical decolonial subjectivity beyond disaster survival, one trained to grasp the aftereffects of stepping out of linear time, beyond a scripted collective history.[18] In Underguater, the familiar Soviet signs are recontextualized in the logic of competing global empires foreclosing on socialist utopias: the "American way of life" and the "Russian way of life" are finally interchangeable. The directions of Cuban migration change to and from the Florida Strait, and the underlying exploitation of labor and nature remain in place. Mota's fictional postapocalyptic Cuban future makes the environment the principal, ultimately unfathomable agent of historical change instead of the nation-state, becoming not just the true main character of the *Underguater* novels and stories but determining in the last instance the very conditions, not of their own choosing, under which humanity must again learn to make their history.

This short story, "Asuntos pendientes" [Unfinished business/Pending subjects], is included in the "Literatura cubana de ciencia ficción" (Science Fiction Cuban Literature) folder in *El Paquete*, the peer-to-peer literary archive described in chapter 4. Mota's literature, like that of many of his contemporaries, does not circulate exclusively in the form of books published by state editorials or by Spanish-language editorials abroad. It is also disseminated through the self-published or collaboratively published alternative and informal modes of distribution that range from hand-to-hand USB circuits to digital cultural projects that publish new literature and long-form cultural journalism. These are spaces that survive parallel to, and against, the remnants of the state publishing industry and the whims of the global literary industry.

Carlos Manuel Álvarez's novel *Los caídos* (The fallen ones, 2018) stands out as another dramatization of this postapocalyptic, postsocialist sensibility inasmuch as it critically engages some of the classic tropes of "dirty realism" and postrevolutionary melancholy that powered the Cuban literary boom of the 1990s.[19] The novel recounts a Cuban family's trials and tribulations with the postsocialist mixed economy, allegorizing the reorganization of social and political values after the Special Period through the generational clashes between an aging couple and their young adult children. Álvarez's literary and journalistic output situates him squarely in the post-Special Period generation of Cuban writers both in age and in ethos, and this novel consciously pursues historiographical and formal concerns—multiperspectival, defamiliarizing aesthetics—honed in the new literary journalism of digital platforms and in *El Estornudo* in particular.[20] When the mother of the family tries to recollect the hardships of the 1990s and sift from her memories a narrative that explains the family's survival during the hungry years, she stumbles against the collective epistemological crisis at the center of Cuba's survivalist tropes:

> I don't know where people got their food. No one knows, in reality. Now that I think about it, we only remember a circle of hunger, a state of siege in which there was nothing, a hole in the plates, a hole in the stores, a hole in the freezer of the refrigerators, a hole in the fields and the factories and a hole, the biggest hole of them all, in our hearts and our stomachs. But it is clear that hole was neither as big or absolute as we remember it, because if we let ourselves be guided by memory we should not have survived.[21]

The ethos of survival during the Special Period was reinforced by a strong narrative of how creative and innovative Cubans were in finding ways to ride out or escape the crisis, a kind of exotic virtuousness, which Álvarez's novel problematizes. Notwithstanding its overreliance on the family-as-nation trope, *Los caídos* fleshes out two modes of the Cuban postsocialist ethos, highlighting the difference between the apocalyptic and postapocalyptic approaches to socialist end times: the epic, heroic mode of survival ultimately indebted to mythical revolutionary fictions (witnessing the end of history, concerned with participating in it), and the pragmatic, hedonistic, unheroic, and necessarily self-absorbed mode of a present without a future but without a clear image of the past to inform it. In this second variant, represented by the economically savvy and unscrupulous daughter and by the impractical and sadistic son, the absence of a collective teleology gives rise to a zone in which all possible individual stories, or the potential self-realization of autonomous life projects, are at once possible and improbable.

Zombie States

Two different versions of the zombie apocalypse in Cuba can further illustrate the local and global imaginaries in which Cuban postsocialism is thought about, and thinks itself, as it negotiates its place within reconfigured historical timelines. The zombie genre, in film and literature in particular, is a commonplace analysis of late capitalism. At the same time, the heralded end of socialism and its many returns, the death of something that refuses to die, have consequently distinguished a turn toward eschatology and hauntology as privileged frameworks of political and cultural interpretation since the 1990s.[22] My interest here is not to belabor those points. To the degree that the zombie trope presents a unique challenge to political hauntology—it does not rely on the figure of a specter whose nonpresence haunts the future of those who survived it, as in Derrida's reading of *Hamlet* for postsocialist times, but on the real-time turning of your fellow humans into unmanageable threats to our collective institutions and ways of life—my concerns here are limited to a concluding sketch of the zombie apocalypse as an apt imaginary of the survival of state socialism after the end of history.

In Max Brook's *World War Z: An Oral History of the Zombie War,* Cuba becomes the world's foremost destination in a not-so-distant future. As we learn from the narrator of the Cuban account, aptly named Seryosha García Álvarez (the Russian diminutive of "Sergei" indicates a Cuban born in the 1970s or later, when mixed intersocialist families and Slavic-inspired baby names were most common):

> Cuba won the Zombie War; maybe that's not the most humble of statements, given what happened to so many countries, but just look at where we were twenty years ago as opposed to where we are now. Before the war, we lived in a state of quasi-isolation, worse than during the height of the Cold War. At least in my father's day you could count on what amounted to economic welfare from the Soviet Union and their Comecon puppets. Since the fall of the communist bloc, though, our existence was one of constant deprivation. Rationed food, rationed fuel . . . the closest comparison I can make is that of Great Britain during the Blitz. . . . This was the Cuba I grew up in. That is, until the dead began to rise.[23]

In this North American version, in a kind of perverse apocalyptic Trotskyism, Cuba was spared the worse of the zombie epidemic precisely because of its anomalous and, until the collapse of the world order, anachronist dysfunctionality of centrally planned authoritarian socialism. Aided by its geographic and political isolation, by the patiently deviant political calculus of Fidel—who, the narrator explains, so aptly exploited the counterproductive policies of the US economic blockade to his advantage—by the high number of doctors per capita, and by the discretionary level of government control and decision-making powers, Cuba's structural luck was matched by a strong state's effective political response to the crisis (a rhetoric of statist protectionism that has reemerged globally with the 2020 Covid-19 pandemic). After the Zombie War, the island became an exceptional haven for a large number of international refugees, among them its own Cuban American diaspora. Cuba also turned into a democracy with Fidel's reluctant but eventual blessing: "Of course our new Latin superpower is anything but idyllic. We have hundreds of political parties and more special-interest groups than sands on our beaches. We have strikes, we have riots, we have protest, it seems, almost every day."[24] Very loosely adapted into the blockbuster film *World War Z* (released in 2013, just before Hollywood could legally shoot in Cuba), that subplot, and much of the book's political punch and plot nuance, did not make the script.

Mota's short story "That Zombie Belongs to Fidel" is in many ways a response to Brook's post-WWZ world map. In Mota's version, we meet a worker at the Center for the Investigation and Development of Zombies who suspects with growing alarm that the state experiment to develop a serum that controls the zombies has gone horribly wrong. "It had been the serum all along. . . . We wanted to create a less voracious, more manageable zombie. Like in the legend of the Haitian Bokor. Friendly zombies, easy to order around. Revolutionary zombies."[25] In this near-future, the "Zombie Period" followed the Special Period. Deemed a politically safer alternative to economic recovery—harnessing the power of zombie labor without dealing with the autonomous subjectivity of a worker—the zombie program backfired with a vengeance. As the narrator's family and neighbors cope with what appears to be a mutated strain of the Z virus, resistant to the state-developed chemical mollification, the zombies multiply unchecked in the streets; the noninfected go along, pretending to be zombies so as to collect the additional food rations allocated to these new ideal revolutionary subjects gone awry.

In contemporary pop culture, extracted from their Afro-Caribbean roots, zombies have become the paradigmatic undead of North American capitalism in their unbridled consumerism, their accumulation by dispossession, and their uncontrollable proliferation. They are often read as apt metaphors for alienating, othering discourses, and as allegories of involuntary servitude with a dash of false consciousness: they are the very personification of dead labor returned in all its monstrosity.[26] Against the background of Cuba's international medical programs and their sizable investments on biomedical research, the crown jewel being Tarará's hospital for children affected by radiation after the nuclear catastrophe of

Chernobyl, Mota's story plays with the idea of Cuba as a neglected "hot zone" of biomedical research instead and provides a counternarrative to both American-style zombie tropes and to the possibility of survival, let alone renewal, of revolutionary subjectivity as defined by the Cuban state. The tactic of pretending (pretending to be zombies, pretending to work, pretending to be revolutionaries), which becomes the strategy of survival for the narrator's family and others who have not yet turned, slips in the ways in which compliance and noncompliance are blurred in everyday life, thereby compromising any attempt to exist squarely outside of the system.

Mota's rendering of the zombie outbreaks in the Cuban context highlights the structural similarities between the North American zombie trope and twentieth-century state socialism's own misadventures with capitalist modes of production, that is, with the history of the revolutionary state's own designs to produce loyal, disciplined bodies of labor. The zombies initially work in the sugarcane fields, attend the political parades, and are celebrated in *Granma* as weapons of the revolution. In his critique of Cuban statization, Dumont, the socialist agronomist whose travelogues we discussed in chapter 1, highlights the degree to which wage labor directly controlled by the state negates the democratic socialization of the means of production. Denying workers material incentives while intensifying their labor power with volunteer or overtime work became another form of capital accumulation, this time by the state, producing a surplus value that relied on the elimination or distortion of real wages.[27]

While the emphasis on volunteer and forced overtime decreased over time, one of the most contentious issues of Cuba's economic opening to foreign investment is the state's reluctance to give up its role as broker of local labor. This equivocation of the revolutionary state as something other than an extractivist (albeit inefficient) employer finds its most absurdist illustration in the permanence of a famous but misquoted socialist slogan in the new 2019 constitution, inherited from Cuba's first socialist constitution from 1976 (Article 19.1). The well-known phrase, foregrounded in Marx, is changed from "from each according to their abilities, to each according to their needs" to "from each according to their capacity, to each according to their labor."[28] The phrase appears a year earlier in the Theses and Resolutions of the First Congress of the PCC in 1975. Its source, the Soviet constitution of 1936, was famously denounced by Trotsky in *The Revolution Betrayed* as a Stalinist, nonsensical theoretical falsification of unknown authorship.

Mota's zombie serum is not only an apt metaphor for the coercive and ideological methods through which state as the organizer of labor power exerts control over, and extracts surplus value from, its citizens. It can also be read as the fictional double of a series of highly publicized and sometimes suspect government incursions into pharmacological and nutritional fads like Policosanol (PPG), soy, and *moringa*. Starting in 1991, Cuba began promoting PPG, a natural supplement derived from sugarcane wax that supposedly lowered cholesterol and improved blood circulation. Later dubbed the "Cuban Viagra," PPG sparked a national trend and a legendary black market for European tourists who followed the rumor that the blood-flow med had a more alluring off-label use.[29] More recently, the Centro Nacional de Investigaciones Científicas (National Center for Scientific Research), where PPG was developed, announced it was testing its efficacy as a palliative for COVID-19. The wonders of soy and *moringa* have also occupied the national press and imaginary at times. Soy products became a staple during the 1990s, when animal protein and dairy became even scarcer—including the infamous *picadillo de soya*, a ground mixture of soy and animal blood and entrails sold in state markets as a substitute for protein rations. Starting in 2012, *moringa* was praised by Fidel and later the official press as a wonder supplement and as a possible source of employment and economic development. *Moringa* has been another staple not only in the press releases but also in the memescape critical of the Cuban government.[30] And while promotion of the benefits of soy protein and *moringa*, in fact, are not exclusive to the Cuban government, the problem of context is again inescapable: beneficial things that have become either promoted or imposed by the Cuban state are tainted by association among large segments of the public.

Mutatis mutandi, a parallel can be drawn between the popular backlash and skepticism against soy and *moringa*, on the one hand, and the absence of general platforms and the cause-specific trends of the most vocal oppositional stances to the government, on the other (from abstract demands for freedom to specific demands for freedom of the press or LGBTQ+ rights). For instance, Cubans might want substantial changes to their free education and universal health programs, but there is little political will to redefine a notion of public good that can shed its attachment to single-party statism. In other words, despite the erosion of the hegemony of the Cuban Communist Party, its monopoly on the vocabulary of social justice, still deployed effectively by the government, is manifest in the absence of robust counterhegemonic proposals that wrestle it away from that terrain. This is why the visible but minoritarian presence of a progressive Cuban generation (discussed in chapter 4), critical of the government but supportive of social and economic justice goals, contends with the difficulties of a postsocialist redefinition of an egalitarian, inclusive political project.

The key to Mota's intervention in the broader context of the zombie genre as an exploration of a global systemic crisis is that this version does not simply situate the zombie within the domestic and historically specific forms of hunger that populate the Special Period's national survival narratives and their aftermath. Mota's Zombie Period highlights ingenuity and dissimulation as forms of agency and resistance, but it also foregrounds the embodied traces of the revolutionary government's extractivist productivism. (Its theoretical obfuscation and sonic permanence were explored in chapters 1 and 3, respectively.) In the North American version, Cuba is always (still) a space of exception, even when it participates in the global zombie outbreak. But in this Cuban version of the zombie apocalypse—and we could add here the popular movie *Juan de los Muertos*—not only is Cuba as vulnerable to zombification as anywhere else on the planet; the socialist state is also impotent, collapsed, or complicit in worsening, or even in setting off, the crisis.[31]

Postsocialist End-Times: Beyond Disenchantment and Defeat

The problem of the state is where end-of-history and end-of-the-world narratives meet head-on. It is also where the disjuncture between the postsocialist condition and the different contexts through which it is experienced finds its most decisive and tense articulation. It is no accident that the debates about Marxist theories of the state and of single-party state-led transitions to socialism resurged in the second half of the 1970s at the same time that postsocialist thought as a radical critique of the communist past and of the neoliberal present began to crystalize.[32] If Jean-François Lyotard argued that "simplifying to the extreme, I define *postmodern* as incredulity toward metanarratives," might we then say that, simplifying to the extreme, the *postsocialist* can be defined as incredulity toward the state?[33]

In the nineteenth century the idea of the postsocialist enjoyed a previous life as a secular prophecy of sorts, running through all currents of socialist thought, Marxist and non-Marxist alike: "The time will come when states will exist no more—and all the efforts of the social-revolutionary party in Europe are being bent to their destruction."[34] Put bluntly: if the state was only an instrument of (bourgeois) class domination, then a future classless society would have no need for a class-based apparatus of repression. A view of human history proceeding from lower to higher stages of development, combined with mechanistic views of social change, predicted that the socialist transformation of the forces and relations of production, after its revolutionary takeover by the working classes, would inevitably result in "the withering away of the State," even if no one agreed how and when exactly that would come about. The dilemmas of that postsocialist state, or of its foretold evanescence, resided in the intractability of the temporality of revolution, the unpredictable forms of the future socialist polity, and the epistemological gap between theory and practice. All were pending questions to be settled through further elaboration grounded in political action. This is what Mandel identifies as Marx's fundamental theoretical insight in the relationship between the state and society, namely, "that the functions performed by a State need not necessarily be transferred to an apparatus separated from the mass of the members of a society, but only become so in historically determinate and specific conditions."[35] The Marx*ist* theories of the state, on the other hand, or the sins thereof, are a separate topic of contention altogether.

The late 1970s saw important (albeit marginal) critiques of traditional Marxism and actually existing statization by Latin Americans like Juan Carlos Portantiero and José Aricó. Their engagement with Gramscian hegemony in a regional context defined by brutal right-wing dictatorships and the shortcomings of the revolutionary experience directed them toward a more radical democratic critique of Marxism. Their rediscovery of Gramsci furthered trends to reject the economic determinism and the bureaucratic vanguardism of earlier Marxisms and bolstered their recognition that solely reorganizing the material base or the state apparatus would not entail social transformations. The truly democratic articulation of collective political, social, and cultural demands became as important and necessary as any economic plan (both prior to and after political victory) whether or not it was revolutionary.[36] Democracy, Portantiero would go on to write, "is not a fact that emerges out of a structure, but a social production. Neither formal democracy is coextensive with capitalism, nor does the statization of the means of production generates automatically a 'true democracy'; democracy is, rather, a popular construction."[37]

These conversations produced a valuable reformulation of Gramsci. They criticized the narrow economism of certain historical materialisms and revised the idea that an organizational change in the material base of a given society would carry with it, necessarily and sufficiently, the seeds of the social and political transformation or that the work on social and cultural articulation of political demands (what Gramsci called the "war of position") was not as important and necessary and even prior to the revolutionary event proper, that is, the shift to a war of maneuver. But the bigger issue here is not the value of the idea that democracy will not simply emanate from the socialization of the means of production by the state. It is the reluctance to engage with socialization of the economy understood as fully centralized bureaucratic statization, an inability to show how it not only did not produce democracy but actually prevented it. The key difference between these earlier departures, and the more comprehensive kind of postsocialist critique I have invoked throughout the book, is that, while they rejected the idea that economic statization had produced a "genuine democracy," they did not foreground statization as carried out in the Cuban case study (which was foremost in their writing) in specifically economic terms.[38]

Merely ten years earlier the notion of postsocialism as the period to follow a transitional socialism still meant an entirely new historical stage (perhaps communism proper). Che Guevara writes about the transition to full communism (*comunismo plenamente desarrollado*), and the lessons to be learned from the Soviet Union, in the crucible of the 1963–1964 economic debates in Cuba, studying (and misrepresenting) Marx's *Critique of the Gotha Programme*, in direct contact with Mandel's thought. Mandel's assessments of Cuban economic paths defended the central planning that Guevara was initially advocating (and for which Guevara had enlisted Mandel's help) but encouraged greater trade-union and worker participation than the guerrilla theorist was willing to concede.[39] At this time, the success of the Cuban transition from the revolutionary takeover of the state to the building of a different kind of socialism still seemed to hold the keys to the project of the New Left: "Humanity's hope of one day achieving a more humane form of socialism will to a large extent rest on these socialisms of the Third World. Should they fail completely, it is hard to see who else in our time could reasonably take up the torch."[40] The original vision of a period after socialism in which the withering of the state stood for the final horizon of human emancipation has gone over to the domain of the transition ideologies of the postsocialist, liberal capitalist consensus.

"Transition," up until the Spanish and Latin American turns from right-wing military dictatorships to neoliberal democracies with multi-party elections (Spain 1975, Uruguay 1980, Argentina 1983, Chile 1989, Brazil 1989), meant something altogether different than it does today. In fact, the terms "transition" and "alternative" belonged exclusively to left-wing imaginaries: transitions to political and economic democratization, to the withering of the state. "Alternative" (referencing alternative modernities, Third World Marxisms, and Rudolf Bahro's alternative in Eastern Europe from 1977) sought a third path divergent from the US-Soviet divide. Since the 1980s, "transition" refers almost exclusively to models of transition to liberal capitalism, whether from state socialist or right-wing dictatorships—the setting for what Buden calls "transitologies" and Naomi Klein described as "shock doctrine." And now the word "alternative" has been reformulated yet again (e.g., Alternative für Detschland, the "alt-right"). Stuart Hall's investigations of the cultural and political imaginaries of Thatcherism's neoliberal brand in the 1980s summarized their ideological essence as a revival of classic liberalism's emphasis on individual freedom combined with an aggressive, social-Darwinist approach to social and economic inequality: "However anachronistic it may seem, neoliberalism is grounded in the 'free, possessive individual,' with the state cast as tyrannical and oppressive."[41] Thus it is hardly a surprise that to many contemporary readers that is exactly what the historical experience of Marxist communist parties (which more or less successfully carried out revolutionary takeovers of the state apparatus in the last century) stands for: the strong role of a centralized state in the planning and development of a national but market-oriented economic policy.

These debates are not only relevant to abstract Marxist theorizing; they allow us to examine how the afterlives of this earlier sense of postsocialism (preoccupations with the "withering of the state") survive in postsocialist sensibilities. How can we reconcile the socialist critique of the state with the reality that, in our time, the erosion of the state as a guardian of public interest is understood as one of neoliberalism's identifying marks? As Moishe Postone points out, only a comparative framework can illuminate the convergence of several processes in the historical decline of the modern nation-state's capacity to represent, and intervene on behalf of, the constituencies it claims:

> Two apparently opposed historical tendencies have contributed to this weakening of the central institutions of the state-interventionist phase

of capitalism: on the one hand, a partial decentralization of production and politics, and with it the emergence of a plurality of social groupings, organizations, movements, parties, subcultures; and on the other, a process of globalization and concentration of capital that has taken place on a new, very abstract level, far removed from immediate experience and apparently, for now, beyond the effective control of the state.[42]

Thus the challenge in postsocialist contexts, when unfettered global markets and the natural rights of man are constantly portrayed as emancipatory forces and when it is increasingly impossible to untangle the interests of transnational capital and those of nation states (total surveillance, unbridled extractivism, and unchecked inequality), might be to understand the postsocialist imaginary as a critique of the modern state's performance in the twentieth century but not to take postsocialism as the celebration of the state's regulatory capture.

In this context, radical imaginaries to overcome the shortcomings of the state as an idea are at a disadvantage, as Pierre Bourdieu has explained: faced with "the efforts to dismantle the welfare state . . . one is led to defend programs or institutions that one wishes in any case to change, such as public services and the national state, which no one could rightly want to preserve as is, or unions or even public schooling, which must be continually subjected to the most merciless critique."[43] In post-neoliberal times, after all, the strong state can return only as a ghost of itself: it has finally shed its assumed role as a guarantor of common good and social welfare to perform its repressive functions with impunity. From a postsocialist perspective, Susan Buck-Morss has investigated furthest the epistemological implications of these sensibilities for critical thinking. While she proposes to call it the "post-Soviet condition," the core idea remains the same. Seen through this lens, our common present bears the mark of the triumphalist rhetoric and the responses to the supposed defeat of the left in the wake of the Cold War, of the eroded monopolies of the vocabulary of social justice, and of an incomplete conceptual apparatus to deliver us from it.[44] Graeber characterizes it as a qualitative transformation in the reconstitution of radical politics: "We are at a moment, after all, when received definitions have been thrown into disarray. It is quite possible that we are heading for a revolutionary moment, or perhaps a series of them, but we no longer have any clear idea of what that might even mean."[45] The semantic pairs of failure and triumph during the 1990s have been thrown into disarray, but in their place a host of regressive fundamentalisms have gained even more ground.

After "the end of history," when one can speak increasingly of a postneoliberal paradigm (a mounting collective suspicion of the established and corrupt political classes, the lingering effects of the 2008 world financial crisis, the observable effects of the climate emergency, and a keen awareness of the failure of the much-touted promises of neoliberalism, multiparty democracy, and multicultural globalization), a surge of insurgency politics with new profiles has emerged. The maturation of anticapitalist struggles of the turn of the twenty-first century (*indignados*, Occupy, Extinction Rebellion) coexists with the neofascist and alt-right movements that combine racial and ethnoreligious supremacy with social conservatism, and vow a return to economic and political policies that are nationalist, protectionist, and often seek to reorganize the state apparatus to protect the short-term goals of a local elite. What all of these antiestablishment discourses and protests have in common is not substance but form. They may include repugnant, incongruent ideologies, but they are unleashing collective intuitions and cumulative resentments that result from an accumulation of disappointment and suspicion.

Thirty-plus years after the fall of the Berlin Wall, a wave of socially conservative, nationalist, protectionist, and xenophobic sentiment sweeps through Eastern and Central Europe, headed by politicians who have weaponized resentment over the status of former communist countries as second-class citizens in the process of regional integration and transition to market economies. That Russian postsocialist imperialism (perhaps we can call it "Putinism") is aligned to nationalist right-wing conservatism makes sense to the extent that these responses to the failures of multicultural globalization and the liberal democratic capitalism of the 1990s find fertile ground in the zones hit harder by their promises *and* their detrimental effects. Madina Tlostanova contends that the post-Soviet condition is precisely the framework that allows Vladimir Putin to play and profit from a Janus-faced role in this context: as a domestic and regional expansionist strongman, on the one hand, and as a "weaker" counter-hegemon to American political hegemony on the other, exploiting a collective sense of victimhood and resentment among the losers and the latecomers to the end of history on the peripheries of Western liberal capitalism.[46] Meanwhile, in Latin America the ebbs and flows of the Pink Tide responded to a set of continentwide political crises that were the legacy of right-wing dictatorships and neoliberal privatizations, though that regional framework obscures the fundamental differences and local dynamics that set apart presidential figures like Kirchner, Lula, Mujica,

Morales, Correa, Moreno, Maduro, López Obrador, and Castro—or Bolsonaro, Piñera, and Macri for that matter.

In the wake of these experiences, and confronting the real effects of state-sanctioned and paramilitary violence, Latin American critical thought has not been a stranger to a pervasive rhetoric of defeat at the turn of the twenty-first century. But since 1959 Cuba has been a site usually defined not by defeat but by triumph, by victory against a dictatorship and against the designs of US imperialism, and by a victory of sorts against the sense of political defeat in the left after the disappearance of the socialist bloc. Just as it was thought to be an exceptional event in the early 1960s, at the height of de-Stalinization, as a Western, humanist alternative to the Soviet Union, Cuba is widely considered to be a survivor of that defeat, the one exception to that collapse, as much as to the total capitulation to the market, as in China or Vietnam—in short "a historical peculiarity."[47] Throughout the foregoing pages, I have examined alternative takes on Cuban postsocialism as a social text, one that emerges in its local, contemporary cultural media production to represent popular imaginaries of change. I have also shown the persistence of Cuban socialism as a media object that circulates globally and that responds to particular desires in this specific historical moment.

These exchanges between the Cuban postsocialist context and the global postsocialist condition occur at a time when the haunting defeats of socialism coexist with the resurgence of an anticapitalist ethos, especially after the financial crisis of 2008, and in Latin America with the rise and fall of the Pink Tide governments. From this perspective a disjuncture appears between the postsocialist condition and the postsocialist context, which was evident to me in the link between two apparently divergent phenomena: At the turn of the twenty-first century, Cuban socialism—its signifiers, its legacies—was reactivated as an international object of political desire in the postsocialist moment; at the same time, the global market became a national object of desire in postsocialist Cuba, but that desire meant different things to different social actors. However, these imaginaries of change challenge both the traditional Marxist and neoliberal orthodoxies that conflate (desires for) independent economic activity with (the exploitative designs of) market capitalism.

During a panel discussion (via Zoom) on feminisms, the pandemic, and antiestablishment politics, Rita Segato remarked that *"they will crucify me* for saying this, but the Cuban model does not work anymore as a political referent for the Latin American left."[48] A lot of remarkable scholarly work has emerged recently in ecological, feminist, and *indigenista*[49] critiques of the Pink Tide governments, from Chávez to Morales, for their neoextractivist developmentalisms and for their record on Indigenous communities, women, LGBTQ+ rights, and state-sanctioned violence. This ongoing work addresses what Raquel Gutiérrez Aguilar has called, speaking of Bolivia, the *machopartidismo pseudoplurinacional* (pseudo-plurinational maleparty-ism) of the established Latin American leftist parties. And yet, as Segato lamented, to say that Cuba is not an exception now (or has ever been), and to say that Cuban socialism represented (then as now) not the absence of capitalism but the presence of a differently organized form of capital accumulation, somehow remains a heretical proposition even when we are several decades into the emergence of a rigorously anticapitalist postsocialist theoretical corpus.

Why Cuba still functions as a "final girl" in a metaphorical historical horror flick is the implicit question in Laura van den Berg's novel *The Third Hotel*. An understated thriller with Havana's film festival as backdrop, the novel investigates the subjectivity of travel literature, marriage, guilt, and horror film theory through a story of deeply individual, solipsistic grief that amplifies the disorienting effect of the text's unique treatment of place. Muses Clare, the protagonist, a middle-aged American sales representative, recently widowed, a deconstructed version of a final girl herself: "A photographer, and she had seen many people taking photographs, could arrange this city to look however they wanted: nostalgic, luxurious, devastated, avant-garde."[50] Far from finding this misleading legibility comforting, van den Berg's protagonist will find postsocialist Havana, ultimately impenetrable in its duplicitous permutations and endlessly disseminated in mass media images of its many selves, the optimal quasi-cinematic setting to face an unspeakable, unrepresentable personal horror instead. Van den Berg's readings of the city and of the way its multiple curated identities refract, rather than reflect, the subjective states of those who inhabit it (permanently or temporarily) suggest that, in the tension among received image, memory, and the approximation to the real, our (aesthetic) judgments reveal us to ourselves more than they reveal anything about the artifacts that occasion them. The Cuban postsocialist mediascape might offer an opportunity to allow some artifacts to read back to us our own desires in the postsocialist condition. Taking a cue from Cuban zombie film *Juan de los Muertos*—in which the protagonist devises a small business scheme designed to kill beloved family members turned zombies—and in as much as Cuba is persistently portrayed as some kind of "final girl" in a metaphorical horror film of twentieth-century history, one of the tasks of (post)socialist critique could be to sacrifice it, as a beloved family member of the New Left, once and for all, as an undead alternative, as a zombie socialism that has irrevocably turned into something unrecognizable and irredeemable.

I have contended that narratives about what exactly triumphed in 1959 and what has survived since as Cuban socialism (and their cultural and media representations and social and political afterlives) hinge on, among other things, the theoretical failure of the left broadly speaking and of the New Left in particular to critically engage with "actually existing socialism" in the Cuban case. Here we are still very much knee-deep in what Stuart Hall called "the crisis of the left" vis-à-vis the apparent defeat of socialism elsewhere. The overarching question is: How do we rethink defeat and victory in the postsocialist moment from and with the postsocialist context when the postsocialist condition is understood as a time of searching for vocabularies critical of the neoliberal present and critical of the communist past and the postsocialist context as the place where the direct experience and memory of twentieth-century state socialist projects still organize cultural, political, and social imaginaries?

Taken as a whole, the Cuban mediascape after the end of history illustrates the specific preoccupations of its local postsocialist context as much as it inhabits the temporality of the global postsocialist condition. It presents multipronged critiques to party-led, state-centered solutions still strong in Latin American progressive politics, to the logic of accumulation and growth as an elite ruling project built on precarity and inequality, and to the culturally mediated fetishism of a Cuban revolutionary vocabulary that monopolizes definitions of socialism and critiques of capitalism. These coopted definitions equivocate a Pyrrhic victory with socialist survival and (to return to Enzensberger's poetic description of an "Old Revolution") lead to the exhaustion of that particular revolutionary model of change: "After me nothing will follow."[51] The attendant romances of (dis)enchantment this generates cater to the desire to see the remnants of a project not reproducible elsewhere ever again, we are always told. Even as, or precisely because, insurgent politics of disparate brands bring into question at the beginning of the twenty-first century the celebrated triumph of liberal democracy and capitalism in the 1990s, they do so along a radically open and deeply fractured horizon of political responses to the new status quo: permanent war, ecological collapse, ubiquitous surveillance, distrust of institutions, political deadlock, and distributed economic recessions.

In addition to thinking about the postsocialist present as an opening-up to other intellectual genealogies of, or parallel to, the New Left, contemporary cultural and media representations that engage with Cuban postsocialism are another site where I have contended that Cuban (post) socialism makes itself visible as state capitalism, showing breaks as well as continuities, then as well as now, between actually existing socialisms and actually existing capitalisms. I argue that only from this perspective can a critique of Cuban postsocialist culture capture the tension between two seemingly contradictory phenomena: the continued relevance of Cuban socialism as an object of international political desire, and the unfolding of national desires to participate in the capitalist global market.

Cuba is not a regional exception when it comes to recent economic, social, and technological changes, but it is crucial to understand the role its exceptionalism plays domestically and abroad and how this exceptionalism is construed and reproduced as a traveling cultural media object. Its demystification, I conclude, opens up future critical possibilities and past intellectual genealogies alike. Consequently, nothing less than our capacity to unpack and rebuild our political imaginaries for the future is at stake in the discursive and representational battles for political meaning that are taking place in this locally situated yet globally significant cultural and media landscape. This speaks directly to a postsocialist, postcolonial present that strives to find vocabularies of social justice after modern revolutionary conceptions of historical change have lost credibility, a process in which Cuba is depicted all too often as the paradigmatic survivor. Looking at the way this ideologically charged space has been culturally exploited, nationally and internationally and across the political spectrum, also asks scholars to examine their own positionality and gaze. Scholars must engage with the dreams and demands of constituencies that toil beneath and between the pressures and alliances of global markets and the nation-state, especially when they do not appear as recognizable political interventions, when they do not follow the familiar aesthetics of radical utopian horizons, when they do not invoke the canonical tropes of antihegemonic resistance or even occupy the more familiar positions of anticommunist political dissidence.

David Graeber proposed that we rethink the very notion of revolution by redefining what revolutionary demands might look like today, pointing to debt cancellation as an example. I would add that we need to rethink not only our imaginaries for alternatives (now that Cuban socialism as an alternative cannot furnish them) but also the very notion of social change that the concept of alternative as regulative utopia mobilizes. The old political idea of an alternative conveys a calculated choice, a choice between mutually exclusive but available options. It enlists a temporality of social change where all marches in step. If the notion of alternative is bound to eschatological and messianic philosophies of history and the political that no longer obtain, that are dead (though not buried) with the grand narratives of modernity and universal emancipation, then what is the future of the idea of an alternative? I do not know what the answer is. But we might as well redouble our efforts to reflect, yet again, on what it does not look like. This means finding comfort in an apophatic political ontology (*via negativa*), one invested in vocabularies of social and ecological justice that are critical of the communist past, critical of the capitalist present, and responsive to the recalcitrant demands of a future that hails us to do better. This is where the work of postsocialist critical theory remains most alive.

Notes

Introduction

1. Buck-Morss, "Theorizing," 23.
2. For theoretical research on postsocialism as a critical category, see Buck-Morss, *Revolution* and "Theorizing Today"; Chari and Verdery, "Thinking Between the Posts"; Shih, "Is the Post- in Postsocialism the Post- in Posthumanism?"; Buyandelgeriyn, "Post-Post-Transition Theories"; Carpentier, "Reading Back Beyond the 'Post' Prefix"; Tlostanova, *What Does It Mean to Be Post-Soviet?*; and Bailyn et al., *The Future of (Post)Socialism*.
3. Chari and Verdery, "Thinking," 11.
4. Scott, *Omens*, 22.
5. The terms "post-Soviet" and "postcommunist" are also employed, but the "postsocialist" terminology highlights historical and philosophical kinships with "the postmodern condition" popularized by Lyotard's 1979 eponymous tract. Alain Touraine's *L'après-socialisme*, for example, was published in 1980, with Spanish and Japanese translations in 1982. It also corrects a Soviet-centric postsocialist thinking and its approximations toward, and from, other (socialist) worlds.
6. For the concept of mass utopia and its standing in capitalist and socialist imaginaries of the twentieth century, see Buck-Morss, *Dreamworld*, x–xi, 43–45. I refer to "desire" here as a culturally mediated, political category differentiated from, but meaningfully articulating, individual and collective needs, in dialogue with post-Lacanian notions of desire that emphasize its constructed, discursive dimensions and its possibilities as a politically productive investment, while recognizing its locations and transpositions in specific matrices of power and representation.
7. This use relies on the etymological roots of these terms: "condition," from the late Latin mergers of *condicio* (as the prerequisite state of things and persons, as discursive agreement *con+dicere*) and *conditio* (to make, to put together, to condiment, to compose, as the thing without which the whole cannot be, as prerequisite, reinforcing and confusing itself with *condicio*); and

"context," from *contextere, contextus*, as the weaving together of several elements, as that which accompanies, surrounds, anchors, gives concrete meaning to a network of symbols, discourses, and experiences. For context as a methodological and theoretical concept in cultural studies, see Grossberg, *Cultural*, 20–27, 252, and Restrepo, "Estudios culturales" (for its intersections with Latin America as scholarly object and location).
8. See Castoriadis, *The Imaginary*, 95–101, 369–373, and Buck-Morss, *Dreamworld*, 11–13. Castoriadis develops the imaginary as an autonomous, politically creative force of social self-institution, while Buck-Morss emphasizes the relational topography of forces and values in the political imaginary conceived as a landscape, "a concrete, visual field in which political actors are positioned."
9. For theoretical and historical accounts of post-Marxist hegemonic theory and its centrality to the project of cultural studies, see Hall, "Gramsci and Us," Colpani, "Two Theories," and McRobbie, *Postmodernism*, 44–49.
10. Alexievich, *Secondhand*, 6.
11. Loss, *Dreaming*; de Ferrari, *Comunidad*.
12. See the special editions of the Documents of the Seventh Congress of the Communist Party (Tabloids I and II, 2017) and "Foreign Investment Opportunities Portfolio," www.granma.cu/especiales/cartera-de-oportunidades-de-inversion-extranjera. Parallel to this pursuit of foreign capital investment, the 2018 guidelines for self-employment were widely perceived not only as a political move to reaffirm strong centralized control over the growing nonstate economic sector but also as measures that largely missed the larger structural issues afflicting overall economic growth and diversification and, above all, national food security. See *Gaceta Oficial* 35. Since 2018, the most significant measures affecting the nonstate sector expanded the small and midsize private enterprises sectors in response to the COVID-19 pandemic and the crisis that sparked the 11J protests in 2021.
13. Gago, *Neoliberalism*, 3.
14. Gago, *Neoliberalism*, 5.
15. Appadurai, "Disjuncture," 298.
16. Krasznahorkai, *The Melancholy*, epigraph.
17. See @E_Santiago_Muin, Tweet, https://twitter.com/E_Santiago_Muin/status/1415253820511301632, July 14, 2021, 6:16 a.m. EST. All translations from Spanish and Portuguese are by the author unless otherwise noted.
18. See Vidmar Horvat, "Sociology," and Hall, "Cultural Studies."
19. Williams, "Culture," 4–5.
20. Couldry, "Afterword"; Szurmuk and Waisbord, "The impasse," 19. Beyond these specific lines of inquiry, and depending on particular institutional and disciplinary histories, there are different practices associated with Latin American cultural studies, each with their attendant metacritical debates. See, for instance, Restrepo, "Cultural Studies," and Moreiras, *The Exhaustion*.
21. Postone, *Time*, 391–392.
22. For theoretical and historical background of the concept of state capitalism (and of state socialisms as state capitalisms), see Postone's discussion of the

Frankfurt school economist Friedrich Pollock in *Time, Labor, and Social Domination*, Sperber's "The Many Lives of State Capitalism," the corpora of the Johnson–Forester tendency by Raya Dunayevskaya and C. L. R. James, and the Socialisme ou Barbarie group by Claude Lefort and Cornelius Castoriadis.

23. Non-Aligned Technologies Movement, "What Is It?", www.tierracomun.net/en/natm.
24. Lefebvre, *Key*, 88.
25. Lefebvre, *The Production*, 54.
26. Lefebvre, *Rhythmanalysis*, 56.
27. As it appears here, this mediascape is fairly Havana-centric, but the capital city should not be seen as a stand-in for the entire country. This selection bias is partly due to the people and spaces I had access to as a researcher and partly due to the fact that Havana is the gravitational center of the cultural institutions and media industries discussed here.
28. See Laclau's distinction between floating and empty signifiers in *Emancipation(s)*, 37. While floating signifiers are unfixed in the hegemonic chain of signification (e.g., "change"), an empty signifier is the sign of hegemonic representation par excellence (e.g., "the people"), that which stands for the totality it cannot fully represent but without which the necessarily incomplete representation of that totality could not become a political possibility in the first place. Empty signifiers constitute identities assumed to be fixed in a stable frontier of popular representation, while the logic of floating signifiers wrestles with its destabilization (*On Populist Reason*, 133). Laclau's work on hegemony moved increasingly toward an abstract, discursive view of hegemonic mechanisms as coextensive with populism and with the political as such. But Laclau's final ontology of the political is only one way to understand Gramscian hegemony from a post-Marxist perspective. While Laclau's terms here are useful to unpack change and continuity as signifiers of the revolution's crisis of hegemony, I remain more indebted to Hall's insistence on conjunctural and materialist approaches to hegemony and representation as mechanisms of social (re)constitution that do not disable other terrains of the political. For alternative responses that elaborate on post-hegemony as a logic counter to totalizing understandings of hegemony, see Arditi, "Populism Is," and Moreiras, *Against*, 9–10, 29.
29. Laclau, *Emancipation(s)*, 36.
30. The environmental, regulatory, and debt dimensions of these infrastructural investments and often secret partnerships with individual nation-states have made Latin American reception of the initiative a thorny issue. For an overview, see *Nature*'s special report on the BRI at www.nature.com/immersive/d41586-019-01127-4/index.html. Arturo Escobar's work on developmentalism, and more recently works by Thea Riofrancos, Alberto Acosta, Eduardo Gudynas, and Macarena Gómez-Barris, have underscored the new extractivist paradigms underlying state-led investments couched in classic developmentalist language of economic justice in the region.
31. The gravity of lead contamination and the absence of publicly available environmental and health studies and regulation came to light in a special

report by Mónica Baró for the citizen journalism project *Periodismo de Barrio*, a piece awarded by the Gabo Foundation in 2019. Projected investments in the Minas de Matahambre project for expanded zinc and lead extraction have also continued in an otherwise impoverished, underserved community in Cuba's westernmost province, Pinar del Río.

32. See Fidel Castro's speech of January 28, 1991. For a comparative analysis of the various economic models of postcommunist transitions and the ways in which political, social, and economic capitals play different roles in capitalist accumulation during these large-scale reorganizations of the state-owned economic sector, see Szelenyi, "Capitalisms after Communisms."
33. International medical missions and other professional services are among Cuba's top export goods. The state retains a large percentage of the salaries paid to doctors by host countries and has a set of punitive measures on family travel and salary collection in place to prevent defection, arguably disproportionate to the cost of their publicly funded education. For a summary of *raulista* reforms, see Mesa-Lago, *Cuba en la era*, 221–275.
34. Postone, *Time*, 40.
35. Rachel Price's *Planet/Cuba* undertakes such a project by analyzing how contemporary Cuban literature and visual arts engage the postindustrial, eschatological precarities of its most precious resources: land, sea, and free time. In *Opción cero*, Emilio Santiago Muiño also queries Cuba's so-called zero option and the international interest in Cuba's extreme survivalist cultures, analyzing whether the state responses to rapid deindustrialization after 1989 can be said to be sustainable or exportable as ecological models when forced or indirect greening practices responded more to the collapse of supplies of energy, fertilizers, and economic networks than to political will and deliberate planning.
36. The 2020 US election cycle illustrated this problem with the media coverage of Congresswoman Karen Bass's and Senator and presidential candidate Bernie Sanders's past histories with, and comments about, Cuba. See Dovere, "When Karen Bass," and Gessen, "What Bernie Sanders."
37. Gray, *Intersectional*, 170.
38. Wittel, "Toward," 51–52.

Chapter 1: Cuban Travels

1. Ronaldo Menéndez recounts a similar experience in *Rojo Aceituna*, the Cuban writer's travelogue through former socialist enclaves, as does José Manuel Prieto in *La Revolución Cubana explicada a los taxistas*.
2. After the reactivation of US tourism to Cuba in December 2014 (later curtailed in 2019), news outlets began to report in 2015 the increased volume of Canadian and European visitors also rushing "to see it before it changes," wary of the specific transformations that an American rapprochement would bring to the island. See Wetherall, "Cuba"; Zabludovsky, "Americans"; and Hamre, "Surge."

3. The political sensitivity of the Angolan War in Cuba and the unavailability of archival access have made study of this event from the Cuban perspective fraught with difficulties. Literary accounts of Cuba's military engagements in Africa have been more forthcoming. See Gleijeses, *Conflicting Missions*, and Millar, *Forms of Disappointment*.
4. Portela, *El pájaro*, 146. *Cronopios* are fictional creatures from Argentinian writer Julio Cortázar's literary universe known for their whimsicality, sensibility, idealism, and care-free character, contrasting with their counterparts: the industrious, strict, disciplined social types Cortázar baptized as *famas*. Cortázar, a frequent visitor to Cuba and one of the cardinal references of Latin American literature in the mid-twentieth century, credits his political awakening to his contact with the Cuban Revolution. See his interview in *Paris Review* 83 and an account of one of his trips, "Itinerario cubano," for the Mexican journal *El Sol*, reprinted in the collection *Papeles inesperados*.
5. For pilgrimage and discovery as place-making narrative frameworks, see Zamora, *Reading*, 100.
6. Enzensberger, *Tumult*, 270.
7. The original meaning of "fellow traveler," or попутчик [poputchik], described intellectuals in the wake of the 1917 October Revolution who were not opposed to its goals but were not fully committed or politically integrated into the cause. "Fellow traveler," "political pilgrim," and "tourist of the revolution" have all been used since to describe, usually negatively, the discourse and travelogues of the New Left trips in the 1960s, in particular those from Western Europe and North America to the countries undergoing decolonization and socialist revolutions in Asia, Africa, and the Americas, then known as the "Third World."
8. See Artaraz's *Cuba and Western Intellectuals Since 1959*; de la Nuez's *Fantasía roja*; Rojas's *Fighting Over Fidel*; Young's *Soul Power*; Kalter's *The Discovery of the Third World*; Latner's *Cuban Revolution in America: Havana and the Making of a United States Left, 1968–1992*; and Garland Mahler's *From the Tricontinental to the Global South*.
9. Wallerstein, *World-Systems*, 84–85.
10. Wallerstein, 12–13.
11. Williams, *Culture*, 255.
12. Marcuse, *The New Left*, 123.
13. See Revueltas, "So That Mayakovsky's."
14. Rocha, *Cartas*, 432. Letter to Cacá Diegues from Havana.
15. See *The Dunayevskaya–Marcuse–Fromm Correspondence* and Dunayevskaya, "The Cuban Revolution."
16. Dumont, *Cuba*, 41.
17. Dumont, *Cuba*, 56.
18. Dumont, *Cuba*, 208.
19. Dumont, *Is Cuba*, 130.
20. Dumont, *Is Cuba*, 146–147.
21. Dumont, *Cuba*, 207.

22. Farber, "Cuba in 1968."
23. Postone, *Time*, 43–44.
24. Postone, *Time*, 44.
25. Guevara, "Algunas reflexiones."
26. For a dedicated discussion of different socialist humanisms in conversation with the Cuban Revolution, see Artaraz, *Cuba*, 98.
27. Williams, *Culture*, 255–256.
28. Hall, "When Was the Postcolonial," 258.
29. "Cuba, la CIA et M. René Dumont," *Le Monde* (March 4, 1971), www.lemonde.fr/archives/article/1971/03/04/cuba-la-cia-et-m-rene-dumont_2470034_1819218.html.
30. CIA, Directorate of Intelligence, "Castro and His Critics."
31. "Castro and His Critics," 1.
32. Hosek, *Sun*, 136.
33. Enzensberger, *Tumult*, 111–112.
34. Enzensberger, *Tumult*, 110–113.
35. Enzensberger, *Tumult*, 225–226.
36. Enzensberger, *Tumult*, 153.
37. Enzensberger, *Tumult*, 224–225.
38. Enzensberger, *The Sinking*, 81.
39. Hosek, *Sun*, 136.
40. Enzensberger, *The Sinking*, 12.
41. Jonathan Monroe in "Between Ideologies" points to the poetics of a "utopian pragmatist" at work in Enzensberger's oeuvre. This very same wording and ethos—rooted in the Gramscian appeal to "pessimism of the intellect and optimism of the will" (and a phrase quoted by Enzensberger himself in "Constituents of a Theory of the Media")—has been recovered by David Graeber to redefine large-scale (and we might say postsocialist) revolutionary goals that, for example, shift the focus from violent state takeover to other systemic issues and structural targets like debt cancellation and general strikes. See "A Practical Utopian's."
42. Written a year after the publication of the poem, "Two Notes on the End of the World" is partly addressed to a left seemingly unable to cope simultaneously with the need for positive utopia and the perception of historical defeat.
43. Laclau, *Emancipation(s)*, 10.
44. The first version of the poem might have sunk, too. Enzensberger was unable to copy the work because carbon sheets were scarce in Cuba at the time, sent the only original copy to Europe, and it was lost in transit.
45. Enzensberger, "Tourists," 185.
46. Álvarez, *La tribu*, 21–22.
47. According to the Cuban National Office of Statistics and Information, the total foreign travelers to and from Cuba were 5,262,302 in 2014, 6,202,574 in 2015, and 6,988,877 in 2016, of which 3,021,872, 3,556,354, and 4,035,577 were tourists. The increased numbers of visitors were due largely to travelers from America, with Canadians, the Cuban diaspora, and the United States heading the count: the number of non-Cuban US tourists tripled from 2014 to 2016. The same study reports earnings for both state and

nonstate sectors of 1,988 and 378.9 million convertible pesos in 2014, 2,115.6 and 485.2 in 2015, and 2,369.8 and 537.3 in 2016.
48. *Transformers: The Last Knight* (2017) and *Fast & Furious 8* (2017) were the first Hollywood movies to be filmed on location in Havana after the diplomatic thaw. Their filming in April and May 2016 was a veritable sensation and an unprecedented opportunity for local audiovisual producers as much as for hopeful extras and celebrity-watchers.
49. Enzensberger, "On Leaving America."
50. One of the top-earning artists of urban music, whose public persona moderately appeals to social justice causes, Jay-Z writes in *Decoded* that those verses originated in a journalist's observations about the ideological incongruity of one of his outfits, namely, a Che tee-shirt and a crucifix pendant.
51. In the 2008 Seventh Congress of the National Union of Writers and Artists of Cuba, the Cuban writer Víctor Fowler proposed the need for a "socialism with swing," the idea that rethinking socialism as an attractive, culturally desirable destiny had to involve the search and open debate for truth, with the capacity to include different lifestyles, sexual identities, subjectivities, modes of entertainment, and more. See Fowler, "Somos." For more on "socialism with swing" and its older incarnation *socialismo y pachanga* (socialism with a festive spirit), see the discussion on revolutionary soundscapes in chapter 2.
52. Pérez Jr., "Visit," 658.
53. Fisher, *Capitalist*, 2.
54. See www.cubadebate.cu/noticias/2021/07/06/matanzas-que-medidas-se-implementan-para-enfrentar-la-compleja-situacion-epidemiologica.
55. Larsen, "Havana's Symphony of Sound."
56. British Pathé Archive of Pathé News, 1910–1970. Rafael Rojas's *Fighting Over Fidel* pores over the corpus of the 1960s New York radical press to show how these affinities played out on the North American intellectual scene. And while the global appeal of Fidel as a revolutionary icon for left intellectuals and activists has been well documented and studied, this particular YouTube footage reminds us of the true fascination that captured the American popular imaginary. Abel Sierra Madero has explored this aspect of Fidel's public persona in the US press and in *Playboy* magazine specifically as a sex symbol of the 1960s in *El Comandante*.
57. Marable, "Race," 16.
58. Casamayor-Cisneros, "Obama," 39. See also Clealand, *The Power of Race in Cuba*.
59. Casamayor-Cisneros, 39–40.
60. "Remarks by President Obama."
61. Steyerl, *The Wretched*, 32–33.

Chapter 2: Portable *Pachanga*

1. Pérez de la Riva, *La Isla*, 125–126.
2. Popularized by R. Murray Schafer, the term "soundscape" has invited objections by Stefan Helmreich for its conceptual limitations for sound

studies in nonurban or entirely technologically mediated listening environments, like the forest or the ocean, and by Steven Feld for its connotation of an already given sonic scene that does not take enough into account the listeners' agency. But this same connotation can be understood as a precise referent to the logic of production and reproduction of a given sonic environment, that is, as landscaping *stricto sensu*: the creation of apparently fixed features behind which lies a constant work of maintenance, the production of a scene that must incorporate and discipline simultaneously the aesthetic and practical needs of its intended audience and yet can never fully control the process of listening from end to end, giving rise to the sound equivalents of desire paths. In this sense, soundscape describes a revolutionary sonic culture and its afterlives heavily informed by a history of deliberate curatorship and unruly receptions.

3. In rap and other urban music styles, "flow" refers to the skillful combination of rhymes and beats. Conversation, July 24, 2018; follow-up email to author April 4, 2019. LOWE is his stage name.
4. de la Nuez, "Teoría."
5. Conversation with author; follow-up email, October 6, 2020.
6. Padilla, "El hit."
7. The Chilean band Los Bunkers covers "El necio" in their tribute album to Rodríguez, *Música libre*, a best-seller that became one of the most-bought albums in Chile in the twenty-first century. Online footage of live versions of this song in concerts around Latin America shows audiences cheering and singing along. Rodríguez, who was deputy to the Asamblea Nacional Popular from 1993 to 2008 and has also been a blogger since 2010, has repeatedly come under fire among critics of the Cuban government for his overzealous and unqualified support for its leadership.
8. See González, "24 horas."
9. According to Spotify statistics (as of July 9, 2020; see https://open.spotify.com/artist/4rUyBlggM5tZUH5QZn9ZuO), Rodríguez's listeners come in decreasing order from Santiago de Chile, Mexico City, Buenos Aires, Bogotá, and Guadalajara. Cuban listeners are not counted, since Spotify does not operate there.
10. Gago, *La potencia*, 49–51, 205–206.
11. Lefebvre, *The Production*, 54.
12. Dopico, "Picturing," 481. See also Ogden, "Instagram."
13. Bruno, *Surface*, 213.
14. Kalter, *The Discovery*, 262.
15. Francos, *La fête*, n.p.
16. Žižek, *Did Somebody*, 130–131.
17. Jameson, *The Political*, 45.
18. Tom McEnaney's research on radio in the Americas offers a poignant example of the ebbs and flows of the symbolic and the real in that sonic landscape, particularly through the example of Robert F. Williams's *Radio Free Dixie*, a program broadcast from Havana by the exiled civil rights leader targeting African American communities in the American South. *Acoustic Properties*, 148.

19. Žižek contends that the formal though catastrophic institutionalization of the communist ideal guaranteed the preservation of a symbolic space of confrontation between the real and the imaginary, one where the very failures of that experience kept alive the possibility of a utopian critique, forcing as it did the measurement of the gap between delivery and expectation. Whether or not one agrees with Žižek's specific framework of analysis on this issue—that Stalinism is politically significant not only on account of its failures or horrors but also because it preserved a space of opposition to capitalism, that there is a "formal aspect" separate from its political praxis— is a different matter altogether. Conversely, one could argue that, by monopolizing the space of anticapitalist dissent and by actively suppressing other forms of radical and progressive thought, Stalinist and other "Left" orthodoxies did as much damage to that very same imaginary space of opposition as did capitalism itself.
20. Leary, "Communique"; Bartra, *The Mexican*, 141–142.
21. Guevara, "Socialism," n.p.
22. Guevara, "Algunas reflexiones," n.p. (emphasis added).
23. Fanon, *The Wretched*, 19.
24. Carbonell, *Cómo surgió*, 32.
25. Guerra, *Visions*, 169.
26. Guerra, *Visions*, 157–162.
27. See Moore, *Music*, and Manuel, "Marxism."
28. Miljački, "Classes," 235.
29. P.M.M. PRODUCTION EVENTS USA, LLC, filed in Division of Corporations, Florida Department of State, https://dos.myflorida.com/sunbiz/search.
30. Bourdieu, *Distinction*, 7.
31. Rivera et al., *Reggaeton*; Baker, *Buena Vista*, 133–134.
32. Padura, *La transparencia*, 85.
33. See Guillermina de Ferrari and Vicky Unruh's "Padura después del vendaval" and Žižek on Padura's literary project of melancholic conformity in *Living*, 58–59.
34. Hernández-Reguant, "Inventor."
35. Chapters 3 and 4 examine in more detail *El Paquete* and other informal digital media spheres.
36. Kant, *Critique*, 206–207.
37. Ramos, *Divergent*, 131–133.
38. NG La Banda, "Los Sitios Enteros,"*Nueva Generación*.
39. As stipulated in the building ordinances of 1861, *repartos* were modern residential zones built outside the colonial city walls, from the second half of the nineteenth century to the urban development boom of the 1950s, by dividing farmlands and holdings in the outer perimeters of the old city. Sandoval y García, *Ordenanzas*, 9–18; Scarpaci et al., *Havana*, 160.
40. Perna, *Timba*. See also Quiroga, *Cuban*, 172.
41. For a Latin American perspective on how the emergence of the category "World Music" from the 1990s onward has restructured the music market and disciplined and diversified the aesthetic experience of the global

listeners, see Ana María Ochoa, "Músicas locales," and George Yúdice, "Músicas plebeyas."
42. Triana, "El 349."
43. See Planas, "Ella Guachinea," and Loss, "Socialism with Bling" (a reading of Cimafunk's retrofuturistic vintage aesthetics as a contrast to *reparto* culture).
44. Vázquez, *Listening*, 10–11.
45. González-Seligmann, *Writing*, 56–59.
46. Lefebvre, *Rhythmanalysis*, 50.
47. Greene, *Punk*. See also the special issue of *Social Text* 116 (2013).
48. Punk was not generally favored by Cuban rock listeners and produced relatively few homegrown bands.
49. Porno, "Comunicado Manifiesto," *A mí no me gusta*.
50. Bernstein, "An Inadvertent Sacrifice."
51. See Barber-Kersovan's "Music as a Parallel Power Structure," which argues for music as a sensual double of politics.
52. Porno, "Trova con Distorchón, versión 0.2," *Rock para*. As Geoffrey Baker argues, *trova*'s critical role was also challenged and taken up by hip-hop artists. See Baker, *Buena Vista*, 45.
53. Lambe, *Madhouse*, 3.
54. See Levine, "Sounding," for a detailed look at reggaeton *reparto*'s alternative media ecology.
55. Michael Fernando Sierra "El Micha," "Un sueño (Cuba Grita Libertad)," YouTube, March 31, 2021, www.youtube.com/watch?v=pKTWTCzjpg8.

Chapter 3: *Postsocialismos de Bolsillo*

1. "¿Quién aprendió a leer mirando (al pasar) los letreros de otros pueblos?" Rodríguez, "En el camerino," *El libro*, 58.
2. Castro, "Discurso pronunciado en el acto de inauguración," January 28, 1991.
3. Guerra, *Todos*, 164.
4. Guerra, *Todos*, 190.
5. Krauss, *Torpor*, 185.
6. *El Paquete Semanal*, June 1, 2015.
7. For an in-depth ethnographic account of the phenomenon of *quinceañeras* and digital photography studios, see Pertierra, "Quinceañera."
8. Gitelman, *Paper*, 117–118, 131.
9. Steyerl, *The Wretched*, 32 (emphasis added).
10. Dean, *Democracy*.
11. Mitchell, *What*.
12. Duong, "Amateur," 287–289.
13. Benjamin, "The Author"; Buck-Morss, *Dreamworld*. For the global circulation of theories of film and image as part of a broader critical project of capitalist modernity, see Salazkina, *Moscow*.
14. Groys, *Going*, 14–15.

15. For more detailed analyses of the revolutionary state's historically fraught relationship with the LGBTQ+ community and its afterlives, see Negrón-Muntaner's "Mariconerías de estado," Tenorio's "Havana's Last Conga," and new-media discussions on reproductive rights and gender violence in chapter 4.
16. Enzensberger, "Constituents," 24–26.
17. Sparks and Reading, *Communism*, 191.
18. Nakamura, "Gender," n.p.
19. Castells et al., *Mobile*, 51.
20. Jelača et al., *The Cultural*, 4.
21. Mesa-Lago, "Ideological," 50–51.
22. Barthes, *The Fashion*, 261; McRobbie, *Feminism*, 69. See also Santa Cruz and Erazo, *Compropolitan*, for an overview of women fashion magazines and consumerism in Latin America.
23. For a material history of early revolutionary fashion in Cuba, see Cabrera Arús, "Beauty and Quality for All."
24. Feinberg, *Open*, 119.
25. See Whitfield, *Cuban*, and Bobes, "Las mujeres."
26. For a history of women in revolutionary Cuba, see Chase, *Revolution*.
27. Sommer, *Foundational*.
28. For a reading of *La bruja* along similar lines, see Gámez-Torres's "Hearing."
29. Irigaray, *The Sex*, 175.
30. Goldman, Heath, and Smith, "Commodity," 333–334.
31. More substantial but less mainstream critiques of Cuban images of womanhood from the perspectives of class, race, and gender identity appear in the corpus of hip-hop groups like Krudas Cubensi and Obsesión, for example. See Saunders, *Cuban Underground*.
32. Guillermina de Ferrari identifies a similar sensibility in the characters of Ena Lucía Portela's novel *A Hundred Bottles*, set in the Havana of the 1990s. *Comunidad*, 111.
33. Rodríguez, *El libro*, 71, 115.
34. Rodríguez, 83.
35. *Variedades*, 201.
36. Díaz-Fernández and Echevarría-León, "El emprendimiento."

Chapter 4: Cuban Screen Cultures

1. Amaya, *Screening*, 2.
2. "The Playboy Interview." Without endorsing McLuhan's underlying theory of media, this is an example of the far-reaching significance of Cuban revolutionary screens and of the state's production of a popular perception of direct democracy, modernization, and political change mediated by mass media technologies in ways that expanded and intensified the work of radio and cinema before. For a critique of McLuhan's media determinism, see Williams, *Television*, 129–132.

3. Rodríguez, "Hoy," 52–53. For the importance of foreign reporting and photography in this multimedia process, see Guerra's *Visions of Power in Cuba* and Sierra Madero's *El Comandante Playboy*.
4. McEnaney, "The Digital."
5. Rocha, *Cartas ao mundo*, 165–166.
6. García, "Por un cine."
7. Decreto Ley 373/2019, *Gaceta Oficial* 43 (27 June 2019). The rise of independent cinema is an important field of study on its own, including the different ways in which independence from the state and its ideological apparatus, and/or the global market, is understood and practiced. The film critic Jorge Antonio García Borrero published an important collective reflection on the subject, "El cine independiente en Cuba," in his blog *Cine cubano, la pupila insomne*, a key resource and live archive of film criticism in Cuba along with his project *Enciclopedia digital del audiovisual cubano* (endac.org). See also Reyes, *El gobierno de mañana*.
8. *Día y noche: Su propia lucha*, E01. Estudios Taínos del ICRT, 1990.
9. See Casamayor-Cisneros, "Obama," and Farber, *Cuba*.
10. Žižek, *Did Somebody Say Totalitarianism*, 90–91.
11. López, "Our Welcomed," 264.
12. Henken, "Vale."
13. See www.elnuevoherald.com/entretenimiento/article250452346.html.
14. Venegas, *Digital*.
15. For a history of digital media in Cuba, see Venegas, *Digital*. See Babbs, "Robinhood of Internet," and Boza, "Mobile Data," for examples of local DIY solutions to the context-specific shortcomings of the Cuban digital media and technology infrastructure. Larry Press's blog *The Internet in Cuba* remains an indispensable resource for technical commentary on Cuban Internet and digital technology infrastructures: http://laredcubana.blogspot.com.
16. Henken and García, *Cuba's*, 2.
17. Castells et al., *Mobile*, 16–17, 29.
18. See Open Observatory of Network Interference's 2017 assessment of Cuban network censorship at https://ooni.org/post/cuba-internet-censorship-2017.
19. Interviews with artist in Miami (August 2014) and via WhatsApp (January 2022).
20. Cuba reacquired the remaining 27 percent stake held by Telecom Italia in 2011. ETECSA's revenues and shares have been used in the past to restructure sovereign debt, at least in the case of Mexico. According to Telecom Italia SEC filings, Cuba paid approximately $2 million combined for telephony and mobile telephony technical support services for a number of years. See Telecom Italia's SEC filings on EDGAR and *Bancomext v. Etecsa* EWHC 2322 (Comm); [2007] I.L.Pr. 59, a case on ETECSA's defaulted debt that was tied up in international courts for years.
21. See www.nytimes.com/2017/04/14/movies/the-fate-of-the-furious-f-gary-gray-interview-cuba.html.
22. Rubio-Scott amendment (#3097) to Senate Budget Resolution, August 10, 2021. See also US Department of State Cuba Internet Task Force reports, 2017–2019, www.state.gov/cuba-internet-task-force.

23. Fernández, *Viaje*, 241. The assertion that "Cuba's future must be in the hands of the Cuban people," which Obama said in Spanish, was not understood by the majority of the passersby I spoke to from the Hotel Inglaterra to the university steps, crossing all of Centro Habana, as a call for democracy, but as an acceleration of the free market instead (that businesses may sort out things between them, not always through the state). In their case it is not an ideological demand but an entirely practical one.
24. Gago, *La potencia*, 32; Jennifer Cearns, "'A Una Cuba Alternativa'? Digital Millennials, Social Influencing, and Cuentapropismo in Havana," in Henken and García, 262–284.
25. Fuentes, *Dulces*, 428–430; "Cuban Involvement in International Narcotics Trafficking," Hearings Before the Committee on Foreign Affairs House of Representatives, July 25 and 27, 1989.
26. Fowler, "El paquete," in *Cuba Reader*, 669.
27. De Ferrari, "Cuba," 235.
28. See Fidel's key speech on the cultural achievements of Cuban socialism—and how those would have to confront a connected world—during the fortieth anniversary of the Second Declaration of Havana, April 16, 2001, www.cuba.cu/gobierno/discursos/2001/esp/f160401e.html.
29. Williams, *Television*, 136.
30. Zolov, *Refried*, 97.
31. Karaganis et al., *Media Piracy*; Nicolas Maigret and Maria Roszkowska, eds., http://thepiratebook.net/.
32. See www.nestorsire.com and Lizabel Mónica, "Literatura."
33. Sparks and Reading, *Communism*, 191.
34. Waisbord, "Media," 134.
35. Guerra, *Visions*, 157.
36. WhatsApp conversation with González, January 21, 2022.
37. Televisión Serrana (TVS), a public project with combined public and international financing where audiovisual producers work with the rural communities to document and narrate local knowledges and ways of life, is perhaps the most salient living example of this theoretical legacy. See Stock, *On Location*.
38. Fraser, *Justice*; Dean, *Democracy*; Negt and Kluge, *Public*.
39. See Piccato, "A esfera"; Avritzer and Costa, "Teoría."
40. Hoffman, "Civil"; Duong, "Amateur."
41. Henken, "Cuba's," 453.
42. Fraser, "Rethinking."
43. Sparks, "Media theory after the fall of communism." See also Sparks, "Hegemonic Shadows."
44. "Por una circulación internacional de las ideas," HTML file 0 PRESENTACION Y RELACION DE LOS 1001 TEXTOS.
45. DeLuca, M., & Peeples, J., "From public sphere to public screen."
46. Tlostanova, "The Imagined Freedom," 656.
47. González-Seligmann, "Caliban." See also Rojas's *El estante vacío* and Hernández Salván's *Mínima Cuba* for an intellectual history of this Cuban post-Soviet milieu.
48. Gilman, *Entre*; Gordy, *Living*, 2.

49. Rojas, "Diáspora, intelectuales y futuros de Cuba," 147.
50. Fusco, *Dangerous*.
51. Cadelo, "Bibliografía en flash." For a prehistory of digital samizdat literature from the 1990s onward, see Hernández Salván and Dorta.
52. Duong, "Amateur Citizens."
53. Escobar, "El 'paketito.'"
54. Díaz de Villegas, "Luisma." The translation is: The emergent Cuban civil society speaks of ecology, of racism, of toxic masculinity, of protecting kittens, of "everyone" (todes) and "all" (tod@s) because it has been trained by the social sensibility advisers of the North American *woke* left.
55. See, for example, the documentary *La dictadura del algoritmo* (dir. Javier Gómez Sánchez, 2021), broadcast by *Cubadebate*'s YouTube channel and on state TV, accompanied by a book of interviews on the subject published by Ocean Sur, a state editorial house created in 2011 with a Latinamericanist, left-wing, and progressive mission statement but with an obvious official editorial policy, organized around Fidel Castro and Che Guevara's canons. Available at https://www.oceansur.com/quienes-somos.
56. See https://elpais.com/cultura/2020-08-30/elpidio-valdes-vuelve-a-la-carga-medio-siglo-despues-de-su-creacion.html.
57. Cabrera, "El Minint y la iglesia."
58. Perreau, *Queer*.
59. See https://twitter.com/MeLaSuda91/status/1487252551078748161; https://twitter.com/MeLaSuda91/status/1495417223699128322; https://twitter.com/MeLaSuda91/status/1495417225834020866.
60. See www.facebook.com/yositecreoCuba/posts/pfbid0EzZDQ7ykuNauBXCrQS5JUZy4AiCCZWUXDXARjfUqtKGc4LCwZVKufmVVNsLsy-6iRl (February 2, 2022).
61. Marta María Rodríguez, *Twitter*, February 24, 2022, https://twitter.com/Martamar77/status/1496861895810330627.
62. See interview with Frank García Hernández from *Comunistas de Cuba* in *En defensa del Marxismo* no. 58 (February 2022), https://revistaedm.com/edm/58/en-cuba-hay-un-antes-y-despues-de-las-protestas-del-11-de-julio.
63. Martín Barbero, *De los medios*, 225–226.
64. "Boric y la deuda de la gente joven," *El País*, December 31, 2022, https://elpais.com/opinion/2022-01-01/boric-y-la-deuda-de-la-gente-joven.html?event_log=go.
65. Dilla, "¿Qué se discute . . . ?"
66. @ProfClealand, Twitter, July 15, 2021, https://twitter.com/ProfClealand/status/1415656732072808449.
67. Castells, "Communication," 249.
68. See, for example, the Czech Foreign Ministry's "Transition Promotion Program" established in 2005, www.mzv.cz/jnp/en/foreign_relations/human_rights/transition_promotion_program/index_1.html.
69. Buckwalter-Arias, "*Cuban Studies* en la época de Trump." See also Tracey Eaton's digital web portal tracking down the money spent by the US federal government in "fostering democracy" in Cuba, *Cuba Money Project*, http://cubamoneyproject.com.

70. Jiménez Enoa interview with Ted Henken, *No Country Magazine*, August 23, 2021, https://nocountrymagazine.com/abraham-jimenez-enoa-professions-do-not-belong-to-those-who-study-them-but-to-those-who-practice-them. See Henken and García, *Cuba's Digital Revolution*, for several studies on the emergence of digital watchdog journalism in Cuba.
71. Villanueva Chang, "El que enciende."
72. Whitfield, *Cuban Currency*, 22.
73. Nadia Nava Contreras, "Así está Cuba hoy: YouTubers, the Commodification of Urban Narratives and the Quest for Virtual Agency in Havana," New Directions in Cuban Studies Conference, University of Miami, October 27–29, 2021. See also Eltit, "¿Voy bien Camilo?"
74. Nuevo Periodismo Iberoamericano awarded prizes to both Jorge Carrasco, for *El Estornudo*, and Mónica Baró, for *Periodismo de Barrio*.
75. Carlos Manuel Álvarez, Zoom interview, September 3, 2021.
76. See @mayahescuba, https://twitter.com/mahayescuba/status/1495983980063117313. @mayahescuba, February 21, 2022.
77. Mwakasege-Minaya, "Exiled Counterpoint."
78. See Mónica Baró, www.facebook.com/monabarosanchez/posts/10158107863681395, March 10, 2021.
79. Gómez Sánchez, "Revictimizada mil veces."
80. Segato, *La escritura*, 39; Frances Negrón-Muntaner, "Mariconerías."
81. Gómez Sánchez, "Revictimizada."
82. See www.cubadebate.cu/especiales/2021/05/18/mujeres-tras-las-sombras-desafios-del-femicidio-en-cuba-i.
83. Shifman, "The Cultural Logic of Photo-Based Meme Genres," *Journal of Visual Culture* (December 16, 2014), https://journals.sagepub.com/doi/full/10.1177/1470412914546577.
84. For more on Cuban diasporic humor, see Laguna, *Diversión*.
85. Zoom interview, May 7, 2021.
86. Srnicek, *Platform Capitalism*.
87. Mejías and Vokuev, "Disinformation and the Media."
88. Zidani, "Messy on the Inside."
89. For the politics and aesthetics of archival remediation, see Gordon-Burroughs, "The Pixelated Afterlife"; Bustamante, *Cuban Memory Wars*; and Andy Alfonso, "Un/exceptional Shadowlands: Space, Memory, and Archives in the Wake of the Cuban Revolution," MS.

Conclusion

1. *Marx*, *more* (Sp., más), and *badly* (Sp., mal) sound somewhat similar in Spanish, forming near rhymes. These are classic Spanish proverbs where *more* and *badly* have been substituted with Marx, roughly resulting in "Devil knows more/Marx because he is old, not because he is the devil" and "Whoever walks badly/Marxist, ends badly/Marxist."
2. What Marx meant by "the end of history," giving new meaning to Hegel's phrase, has its own chapter in the scholarly debate. Étienne Balibar suggests

that one clue can be found in an unpublished chapter of *Das Kapital*, when Marx runs against the aporia of the end of the state as the end of "the political" as he understood it. Balibar, *Citizenship*, 109.
3. Fukuyama's "The End of History?" and the follow-up book was one of several thinly veiled revivals of the *translatio imperii* dogma of the 1990s combining the end of history with the triumph of neoliberalism.
4. For a take on the returns of the state and its left-wing and right-wing models of post-neoliberal protectionism, see Gerbaudo, *The Great Recoil*.
5. Graeber, *Revolutions*, 36.
6. See, for example, Morris, "Unexpected."
7. Raúl Castro, "Informe."
8. Tutek, "Dwelling," 33.
9. See Jameson's *Seeds of Time*. In "Future City," Jameson adds another twist: What would it look like if we began to think about the end of the world through capitalism instead of the end of capitalism through world-ending apocalyptic fantasies?
10. Ian Watt's classic *The Rise of the Novel* delves into an extensive analysis of Robinson Crusoe as the literary archetype of the utilitarian, self-made *homo economicus* whose productive activity seems to be realized, mythically, in the absence of a social link. Watt argues that the shipwreck trope conceals and facilitates at once the degree to which Crusoe as a capitalist benefits from the accumulated labor of others—exclusive access to leftover artifacts, knowledge, and tools—while presenting his activity on the island as a successful example of self-interested, independent, free enterprise (87–88).
11. Blackburn, *After the Fall*.
12. Fidel's speech in January 1990 announced the Special Period in Times of Peace and the coming political and economic crisis to the CTC at the Karl Marx Theater. Emphasis added.
13. Fidel's 1998 reception of John Paul II—a Polish pope and the first pontiff to visit Cuba. Emphasis added.
14. "Cuba y los nuevos desafíos del sector privado, en el marco de las actuales transformaciones de la nación," data presented by Cuban economists Omar Everleny Pérez Villanueva and Pavel Vidal at the David Rockefeller Center in Harvard University, May 23, 2019.
15. See www.granma.cu/discursos-de-diaz-canel/2019-09-27/sin-miedo-a-la-coyuntura-27-09-2019-23-09-41.
16. "Asuntos pendientes," El Paquete, circa 2016.
17. A dystopic reversal of the great flood, or *inundación*, that Virgilio Piñera used to describe the eve of the revolutionary triumph is found in "The Flood": "And the flood began. At the beginning, and in spite of the overwhelming impetus that it carried in itself, it seemed like a thread of water, quick and zigzagging, but which at the same time a child's foot could divert from its course. Everyone, if they are not inhuman, must have something to say about revolutions. The range is extremely varied. For one person, they will have reached their high point in the moment of clandestine struggle, for someone else, when we have achieved the social victories for which men have fought and died" (128–129).

18. Price, *Planet*, 80–90.
19. Birkenmeir, "Dirty," 489–490.
20. Reporting for the *Washington Post* and *El País*, Álvarez joined and documented the Movimiento San Isidro's 2020 hunger strike and house-in, demanding artistic freedom and the release of the rapper Denis Solís. Álvarez was detained by Cuban authorities and placed under house arrest and police surveillance before leaving the country.
21. Álvarez, *Los caídos*, 63.
22. Balibar, *Citizenship*, 110. Laclau's *Emancipation(s)* takes on Derrida's hauntology as it unfolds in *Specters of Marx*, addressing deconstruction's problem in grounding the ethics of total emancipation and proposing the basis—conceptual, organizational—for a possible reaggregation of those ghostly, unfulfilled, incongruent demands around reconstituted, intersectional political projects, where the pursuit and occupation of power and of the state must be continually renegotiated but not necessarily renounced (79).
23. Brooks, *World*, 229.
24. Brooks, 235.
25. Mota, "That Zombie," 145.
26. Capital is "dead" labor because it is the accumulated extraction of surplus value from the living worker who is forced to sell her only possession, her (labor) time, which is why Marx famously compared capitalist extraction of value from labor as vampiric. See Shaviro, *The Cinematic Body*.
27. Dumont, *Is Cuba*, 91–94. For an early history of concrete state initiatives to shape citizenship through labor, see Hynson, *Laboring*.
28. *Constitución de la República de Cuba*, Artículo 65, www.gacetaoficial.gob.cu/es/constitucion-de-la-republica-de-cuba-proclamada-el-10-de-abril-de-2019.
29. In 2019, Cuba announced an accord to provide the sugarcane derivative for the production of PPG in Japan. Most of the comments in the announcement complain about the disappearance of PPG from the national establishment and the double-dealing of the state facilities that cannot supply the national demand yet are able to supply foreign markets. See www.cubadebate.cu/noticias/2019/08/08/ppg-medicamento-cubano-sera-producido-en-japon. An archive article from 1998 in the Spanish daily *El mundo* delves into the early fury of PPG in Europe: www.elmundo.es/salud/276/15N0055.html.
30. Reflexiones de Fidel, June 17, 2012, "La alimentación y el empleo sano," www.14ymedio.com/cuba/cooperacion-Cuba-Venezuela-extiende-moringa_0_3054894482.html.
31. For different interpretations of the Cuban zombie apocalypse, see Cardentey Levin's "La Revolución," Maguire's "Walking Dead in Havana," and Arroyo's "Cities of the Dead," all close readings of *Juan of the Dead*.
32. See Balibar's account of the French Communist Party's debates on "the dictatorship of the proletariat" in 1976, and Cornelius Castoriadis's response in *Le Monde*, republished as "On the Possibility of Creating a New Form of Society" (1977) in *A Society Adrift*. Castoriadis broke in the late 1940s with the French Communist Party to develop, along with Claude Lefort and others in the Socialisme ou Barbarie group (1949–1966), a theory of

comparative bureaucratic capitalisms. They were foundational to noncommunist or dissident left currents of thought, forerunners of the contemporary critical postsocialist response to our own present. See "Marx Today," a special issue of *Social Research* 45, no. 4 (Winter 1978), featuring essays by Claude Lefort, Cornelius Castoriadis, Jean Cohen, Moishe Postone, Agnes Heller, and Mihaly Vajda on these topics.

33. Lyotard, *The Postmodern*, xxiv.
34. Bakunin, *Statism*, 90.
35. Mandel, *Late*, 474.
36. Aricó, "Ni cinismo," 15.
37. Portantiero, "La democracia," 6.
38. Aricó, "La crisis," 13.
39. Mandel, who was invited to Havana in 1964, did not go as far as Dumont in his critique of Cuba's economic centralization and militarization. See Mesa-Lago, "Ideological," 61, 110. Marx's *Critique of the Gotha Programme* famously addresses this problem: "What transformation will the state undergo in communist society? In other words, what social functions will remain in existence there that are analogous to present state functions? . . . Between capitalist and communist society there lies the period of the revolutionary transformation of the one into the other. Corresponding to this is also a political transition period in which the state can be nothing but *the revolutionary dictatorship of the proletariat*" (n.p.; emphasis in the original). See Guevara, "Algunas reflexiones."
40. Dumont and Mazoyer, *Socialisms*, 336.
41. Hall, "The Neoliberal," 10.
42. Postone, *Time*, 12.
43. Bourdieu, *Firing*, 23.
44. Buck-Morss maps out what this may mean for the reconceptualization of the political in postsocialist times: "What is called for is an exact inverse of the Marxist global discourse of the twentieth century, which was a universal discourse differently articulated. [. . .] If I speak today of the 'post-Soviet condition,' it is to say that 'post-Soviet' refers to an ontology of time, not an ontology of the collective" ("Theorizing," 29–30).
45. Graeber, *Revolutions*, 41.
46. Tlostanova, *What Does*, 12.
47. Mosquera and Oroz, "Interview."
48. "Pensar en Presente. Diamela Eltit and Rita Segato in Conversation." September 30, 2020, Princeton University. I am paraphrasing her statement; emphasis added.
49. The term comes from the specific indigenous tradition of critique from Latin America, *indigenismo*, and is not easily translatable into English.
50. van den Berg, *The Third*, 37.
51. Enzensberger, *Selected*, 223.

Bibliography

Ahmed, Azam. "Cuba on the Edge of Change." *New York Times*, March 19, 2016.
Álvarez, Carlos Manuel. *La tribu: Retratos de Cuba*. Mexico City: Sexto Piso, 2017.
Álvarez, Carlos Manuel. *Los caídos*. Mexico City: Sexto Piso, 2018.
Amaya, Héctor. *Screening Cuba: Film Criticism as Political Performance During the Cold War*. Urbana: University of Illinois Press, 2010.
Anderson, Kevin, and Russell Rockwell. *The Dunayevskaya-Marcuse-Fromm Correspondence, 1954–1978: Dialogues on Hegel, Marx, and Critical Theory*. Lanham, MD: Lexington Books, 2012.
Appadurai, Arjun. "Disjuncture and Difference in the Global Cultural Economy." *Theory, Culture & Society* 7, no. 2 (1990): 295–310.
Arditi, Benjamin. "Populism Is Hegemony Is Politics? On Ernesto Laclau's *On Populist Reason*." *Constellations* 17, no. 3 (2010): 488–797.
Arellano, Jerónimo. "Introduction: Comparative Media Studies in Latin America." *Revista de Estudios Hispánicos* 50, no. 2 (2016): 281–291.
Aricó, José. "La crisis del marxismo." *Controversia* 1, no. 1 (1979): 13.
Aricó, José. "Ni cinismo ni utopía." *Controversia: Para un análisis de la realidad argentina* 2, nos. 9–10 (1980): 15–17.
Arroyo, Jossianna. "Cities of the Dead: Performing Life in the Caribbean." *Journal of Latin American Cultural Studies* 27, no. 3 (2018): 331–356.
Artaraz, Kepa. *Cuba and Western Intellectuals Since 1959*. New York: Palgrave Macmillan, 2009.
Avritzer, Leonardo, and Sérgio Costa. "Teoria crítica, democracia e esfera pública: concepções e usos na América Latina." *Dados* 47, no. 4 (2004): 703–728.
Babbs, Morgan. "Robin Hoods of Internet Access in Cuba." *Medium*, June 30, 2020. https://medium.com/the-contrasts-blog/robin-hoods-of-internet-access-in-cuba-66a8f17d3f68.
Bailyn, John F., et al. *The Future of (Post)Socialism: Eastern European Perspectives*. Albany: State University of New York Press, 2018.
Baker, Geoffrey. *Buena Vista in the Club: Rap, Reggaetón, and Revolution in Havana*. Durham, NC: Duke University Press, 2011.
Balibar, Étienne. *Citizenship*. Cambridge, UK: Polity, 2015.

Balibar, Étienne. *On the Dictatorship of the Proletariat*. Translated by Grahame Lock. London: New Left Books, 1977.
Barber-Kersovan, Alenka. "Music as a Parallel Power Structure." In *Shoot the Singer! Music Censorship Today*, edited by Marie Korpe, 6–10. London: Zed, 2004.
Barthes, Roland. *The Fashion System*. Berkeley: University of California Press, 1990.
Bartra, Roger. *The Mexican Transition*. Cardiff: University of Wales Press, 2013.
Birkenmeir, Anke. "Dirty Realism at the End of the Century: Latin American Apocalyptic Fictions." *Revista de estudios hispánicos* 40, no. 3 (2006): 489–512.
Blackburn, Robin, ed. *After the Fall: The Failure of Communism and the Future of Socialism*. London: Verso, 1991.
Bobes, Velia Cecilia. "Las cubanas ante el periodo especial: ajustes y cambios." *Debate Feminista* 23 (2001): 67–96.
Bourdieu, Pierre. *Distinction: A Social Critique of the Judgement of Taste*. Translated by Richard Nice. Cambridge, MA: Harvard University Press, 1987.
Bourdieu, Pierre. *Firing Back: Against the Tyranny of the Market 2*. Translated by Loïc Wacquant. New York: New Press, 2003.
Boza Ibarra, Glenda. "Mobile Data Packages and Cubans' Connection Strategies." *elTOQUE*, March 22, 2019. https://eltoque.com/mobile-data-packages-and-connection-strategies.
Brooks, Max. *World War Z: An Oral History of the Zombie War*. New York: Penguin, 2006.
Brown, Jayna, Patrick Deer, and Tavia Nyong'o. "Punk and Its Afterlives." *Social Text* 31, no. 116 (2013): 1–11.
Bruno, Giuliana. *Surface: Matters of Aesthetics, Materiality, and Media*. Cambridge, MA: MIT Press, 2014.
Buck-Morss, Susan. *Dreamworld and Catastrophe: The Passing of Mass Utopia in East and West*. Cambridge, MA: MIT Press, 2002.
Buck-Morss, Susan. *Revolutions Today*. Chicago: Haymarket Books, 2019.
Buck-Morss, Susan. "Theorizing Today: The Post-Soviet Condition." *Log* 11 (2008): 23–31.
Buckwalter-Arias, James. "*Cuban Studies* en la época de Trump: Recordando la 'normalización' y sus narrativas." *A Contracorriente* 15, no. 1 (Fall 2017): 287–306.
Buden, Boris. "Children of Postcommunism." *Radical Philosophy* 159 (2010): 18–25.
Bustamante, Michael. *Cuban Memory Wars: Retrospective Politics in Revolution and Exile*. Chapel Hill: University of North Carolina Press, 2021.
Buyandelgeriyn, Manduhai. "Post-Post-Transition Theories: Walking on Multiple Paths." *Annual Review of Anthropology* 37 (2008): 235–250.
Cabrera, Yoandy. "El Minint y la iglesia ante el matrimonio igualitario en Cuba." *Rialta*, June 3, 2021. https://rialta.org/dios-y-el-minint-la-iglesia-ante-el-matrimonio-igualitario-en-cuba/.
Cadelo de Nevi, Claudia. "Bibliografía en flash." *Octavo Cerco* (blog), March 28, 2009. http://octavocerco.blogspot.com/2009/03/bibliografia-en-flash.html.
Carbonell, Walterio. *Cómo surgió la cultura nacional*. Havana: Yaka, 1961.

Cardentey Levin, Antonio. "La revolución zombificada. La alegoría del trauma cubano en Juan de los Muertos, de Alejandro Brugués." *Alambique: Revista académica de ciencia ficción y fantasía/Jornal acadêmico de ficção científica e fantasía 2*, no. 1 (2014).
Carpentier, Nico. "Reading Back Beyond the 'Post' Prefix: The Politics of the Signifier Post-socialism and Its Opportunities for the Enrichment of Participatory Media Theory." *Mediální studia/Media Studies* 1 (2010): 7–30.
Casamayor-Cisneros, Odette. "Obama in Havana and the Racial Politics of Contemporary Cuba." *Transition* 126 (2016): 39–45.
Casamayor-Cisneros, Odette. *Utopía, distopía e ingravidez: Reconfiguraciones cosmológicas en la narrativa postsoviética cubana*. Madrid: Iberoamericana, 2013.
Castells, Manuel. "Communication, Power and Counter-power in the Network Society." *International Journal of Communication* 1 (2007): 238–266.
Castells, Manuel, et al. *Mobile Communication and Society: A Global Perspective*. Cambridge, MA: MIT Press, 2007.
Castoriadis, Cornelius. *The Imaginary Institution of Society*. Cambridge, MA: Polity, 2005.
Castoriadis, Cornelius. "On the Possibility of Creating a New Form of Society." *A Society Adrift: Interviews and Debates (1974–1997)*. New York: Fordham University Press, 2010 [1977].
Castro, Fidel. "Discurso pronunciado en el acto de inauguración del cosultorio-vivienda 'Antonio Guiteras.'" January 28, 1991.
Castro, Fidel. "Discurso pronunciado por Fidel Castro Ruz, Presidente de la República de Cuba, en la clausura del XVI Congreso de la CTC." January 28, 1990. http://www.cuba.cu/gobierno/discursos/1990/esp/f280190e.html.
Castro, Raúl. "Informe Central al 8vo Congreso del Partido Comunista de Cuba." *Granma*, April 17, 2021 (Special Supplement). www.granma.cu/file/pdf/2021/04/17/G_2021041717.pdf.
Castro Córdoba, Eduardo. *El trap: filosofía millennial para la crisis en España*. Madrid: Errata Naturae, 2019.
Central Intelligence Agency, Directorate of Intelligence. "Castro and His Critics." Weekly Summary Special Report, July 16, 1971, No. 0379/71A, 1. www.cia.gov/library/readingroom/docs/CIA-RDP79-00927A008900040002-1.pdf.
Chari, Sharad, and Katherine Verdery. "Thinking Between the Posts: Postcolonialism, Postsocialism, and Ethnography after the Cold War." *Comparative Studies in Society and History* 51, no. 1 (2009): 6–34.
Chase, Michelle. *Revolution within the Revolution: Women and Gender Politics in Cuba, 1952–1962*. Chapel Hill: University of North Carolina Press, 2015.
Colpani, Gianmaria. "Two Theories of Hegemony: Stuart Hall and Ernesto Laclau in Conversation." *Political Theory* 50, no. 2 (2022): 221–246. https://doi.org/10.1177/00905917211019392.
"Conversation with James Baldwin, A; James Baldwin Interview." WGBH Media Library & Archives, June 24, 1963. http://openvault.wgbh.org/catalog/V_C03ED1927DCF46B5A8C82275DF4239F9.
Cortázar, Julio. *Papeles inesperados*. Edited by Aurora Bernárdez and Carles Álvarez Garricá. Madrid: Alfaguara, 2009.

Couldry, Nick. "Afterword." In *Latin American Media Cultures: Key Concepts and New Debates*, edited by Anna Cristina Pertierra and Juan Francisco Salazar, 181–189. London: Routledge, 2021.
"Cuban Involvement in International Narcotics Trafficking." Hearings Before the Committee on Foreign Affairs House of Representatives, July 25 and 27, 1989. Washington, DC: US Government Printing Office, 1989.
Dean, Jodi. *Democracy and Other Neoliberal Fantasies: Communicative Capitalism and Left Politics*. Durham, NC: Duke University Press, 2009.
de Ferrari, Guillermina. *Comunidad y cultura en la Cuba postsoviética*. Madrid: Verbum, 2017.
de Ferrari, Guillermina. "Cuba: A Curated Culture." *Journal of Latin American Cultural Studies* 16, no. 2 (2007): 219–240.
de Ferrari, Guillermina, and Vicky Unruh. "Padura después del vendaval." *A Contracorriente* 15, no. 1 (2015).
de la Fuente, Alejandro. *A Nation for All: Race, Inequality, and Politics in Twentieth-Century Cuba*. Chapel Hill: University of North Carolina Press, 2001.
de la Nuez, Iván. *Fantasía roja: Los intelectuales de izquierdas y la Revolución Cubana*. Barcelona: Debate, 2006.
de la Nuez, Iván. "Teoría del reggaetón." August 10, 2016. ivandelanuez.org.
Delgado, Frank. 1996. "La Habana está de bala." *Trova-Tur*. Mutis. CD.
DeLuca, M., and J. Peeples. "From Public Sphere to Public Screen: Democracy, Activism, and the 'Violence' of Seattle.'" *Critical Studies in Media Communication* 19, no. 2 (2002): 125–151.
Derrida, Jacques. *Specters of Marx: The State of the Debt, the Work of Mourning and the New International*. Routledge Classics. London: Routledge, 2006.
Díaz de Villegas, Néstor. "Luisma, ¿hombre sincero o snowflake?" *Revista El Estornudo*. May 6 2021. https://revistaelestornudo.com/luisma-hombre-sincero-o-snowflake.
Díaz-Fernández, Ileana, and Dayma Echevarría-León. "El emprendimiento en Cuba: un análisis de la participación de la mujer." *Entramado* 12, no. 2 (2016): 54–67. https://doi.org/10.18041/entramado.2016v12n2.24239.
Dilla, Haroldo. "¿Qué se discute . . . ?" *Rialta*, June 6, 2021. https://rialta.org/declaracion-lasa-derechos-humanos-en-cuba/.
Dopico, Ana María. "Picturing Havana: History, Vision, and the Scramble for Cuba." *Nepantla: Views from South* 3, no. 3 (2002): 451–493.
Dorta, Walfrido. "Without Initiation Ceremonies: Cuban Literary and Cultural Ezines, 2000–2010." In *Cuba's Digital Revolution*, edited by Ted A. Henken and Sara García Santamaría, 323–344. Gainesville: University Press of Florida, 2021.
Dovere, Edward-Isaac. "When Karen Bass Went to Work in Castro's Cuba." *The Atlantic*, July 31, 2020. www.theatlantic.com/politics/archive/2020/07/karen-bass-cuba-venceremos-brigade/614662.
Dumont, René. *Cuba: Socialism and Development*. Translated by Helen R. Lane. New York: Grove, 1970.
Dumont, René. *Is Cuba Socialist?* Translated by Stanley Hochman. New York: Viking, 1974 [1970].
Dumont, René, and Marcel Mazoyer. *Socialisms and Development*. Translated by Rupert Cunningham. New York: Praeger, 1973.

Dunayevskaya, Raya. "The Cuban Revolution: The Year After." *News and Letters*, December 1960. http://www.marxists.org/archive/dunayevskaya/works/1960/cuba.htm.
Duong, Paloma. "Amateur Citizens: Culture and Democracy in Contemporary Cuba." PhD diss., Columbia University, 2014.
Eltit, Diamela. "¿Voy bien Camilo?" *The Clinic*, July 24, 2018. https://www.theclinic.cl/2018/07/24/voy-bien-camilo/.
Enzensberger, Hans Magnus. "Constituents of a Theory of the Media." *Critical Essays*. New York: Continuum, 1982 [1970].
Enzensberger, Hans Magnus. "On Leaving America." *New York Review of Books* 10, no. 4 (February 29, 1968). www.nybooks.com/articles/1968/02/29/on-leaving-america.
Enzensberger, Hans Magnus. *Selected Poems*. Translated by Michael Hamburger and H. M. Enzensberger. Newcastle upon Tyne, UK: Bloodaxe Books, 1994.
Enzensberger, Hans Magnus. *The Sinking of the Titanic: A Poem*. Boston: Houghton Mifflin, 1980.
Enzensberger, Hans Magnus. "Tourists of the Revolution." *Critical Essays*. New York: Continuum, 1982.
Enzensberger, Hans Magnus. *Tumult*. Translated by Mike Mitchell. London: Seagull, 2016.
Enzensberger, Hans Magnus. "Two Notes on the End of the World." *New Left Review* 1/110 (1978). https://newleftreview.org/issues/i110/articles/hans-magnus-enzensberger-two-notes-on-the-end-of-the-world.
Escobar, Luz. "El 'paketito,' un rival clandestino para el 'paquete.'" *14ymedio*, May 5, 2017. https://www.14ymedio.com/cienciaytecnologia/paketito-rival-clandestino-paquete_0_2211978784.html.
Espinosa, Jorge García. "Por un cine imperfecto." *Cine Cubano* 66–67 (1969): 46–53.
Farber, Samuel. "Cuba in 1968." *Jacobin*, April 29, 2018. https://jacobinmag.com/2018/04/cuba-1968-fidel-castro-revolution-repression.
Farber, Samuel. *Cuba Since the Revolution of 1959: A Critical Reassessment*. Chicago: Haymarket Books, 2011.
Feinberg, Richard. *Open for Business: Building the New Cuban Economy*. Washington, DC: Brookings Institution, 2016.
Fernández, Patricio. *Cuba: Viaje al fin de la Revolución*. Santiago de Chile: Penguin Random House, 2018.
Fisher, Mark. *Capitalist Realism: Is There No Alternative?* Winchester: Zero Books, 2009.
Fowler, Víctor. "Somos unos sobrevivientes." *La Jiribilla*, no. 361 (April 5–11, 2008). www.lajiribilla.co.cu/2008/n361_04/361_13.html.
Francos, Ania. *La fête cubaine*. Paris: Julliard, 1962.
Fraser, Nancy. *Justice Interruptus: Critical Reflections on the "Postsocialist" Condition*. New York: Routledge, 1997.
Fraser, Nancy. "Rethinking the Public Sphere: A Contribution to the Critique of Actually Existing Democracy." In *Habermas and the Public Sphere*, edited by Craig Calhoun, 109–142. Cambridge, MA: MIT Press, 1992.
Fuentes, Nortberto. *Dulces guerreros cubanos*. Barcelona: Seix Barral, 1999.
Fukuyama, Francis. "The End of History?" *The National Interest* 16 (1989): 3–18.

Fusco, Coco. *Dangerous Moves*. London: Tate, 2015.
Fusco, Coco. "Who's Afraid of Yoani Sánchez?" *Huffington Post*, March 27, 2013.
Gaceta Oficial 35 Extraordinaria. July 10, 2018. http://www.fgr.gob.cu.
Gago, Verónica. *Neoliberalism from Below: Popular Pragmatics and Baroque Economies*. Durham, NC: Duke University Press, 2017.
Gago, Verónica. *La potencia feminista, o, el deseo de cambiarlo todo*. Madrid: Traficantes de Sueños, 2019.
Gámez-Torres, Nora. "Hearing the Change: Reggaetón and Emergent Values in Contemporary Cuba." *Latin American Music Review* 33, no. 2 (2012): 227–260.
García Borrero, Jorge Antonio, ed. "El cine independiente en Cuba." *Cine Cubano, la pupila insomne* (blog), May 4, 2019. https://cinecubanolapupilainsomne.files.wordpress.com/2019/05/el-cine-independiente-en-cuba-1.pdf.
Gerbaudo, Paolo. *The Great Recoil*. London: Verso, 2021.
Gessen, Masha. "What Bernie Sanders Should Have Said about Socialism and Totalitarianism in Cuba." *The New Yorker*, February 25, 2020. www.newyorker.com/news/our-columnists/what-bernie-sanders-should-have-said-about-socialism-and-totalitarianism-in-cuba.
Gilman, Claudia. *Entre la pluma y el fusil: Debates y dilemas del escritor revolucionario en América Latina*. Buenos Aires: Siglo XXI, 2003.
Gitelman, Lisa. *Paper Knowledge: Toward a Media History of Documents*. Durham, NC: Duke University Press, 2014.
Gleijeses, Piero. *Conflicting Missions: Havana, Washington, and Africa, 1959–1976*. Chapel Hill: University of North Carolina Press, 2002.
Goldman, Robert, Deborah Heath, and Sharon L. Smith. "Commodity Feminism." *Critical Studies in Mass Communication* 8, no. 3 (1991): 333–351. doi:10.1080/15295039109366801.
Gómez Sánchez, Javier. "Revictimizada mil veces." *Granma*, August 18, 2020. www.granma.cu/cuba/2020-08-18/revictimizada-mil-veces-18-08-2020-22-08-28.
González, Miguel. "24 horas con la candidata (IV)." *El país*, April 29, 2021. https://elpais.com/espana/elecciones-madrid/2021-04-30/24-horas-con-la-candidata-iv-monasterio-una-cubana-contra-el-che-guevara.html.
González-Seligmann, Katerina. "Calibán Why? The 1968 Cultural Congress of Havana, C. L. R. James, and the Role of the Caribbean Intellectual." *The Global South* 13, no. 1 (2019): 59–80.
González-Seligmann, Katerina. *Writing the Caribbean in Magazine Time*. New Brunswick, NJ: Rutgers University Press, 2021.
Gordon-Burroughs, Jessica. "The Pixelated Afterlife of Nicolás Guillén Landrián." *Journal of Cinema and Media Studies* 59, no. 2 (Winter 2020): 23–42.
Gordy, Katherine. *Living Ideology in Cuba: Socialism in Principle and Practice*. Ann Arbor: University of Michigan Press, 2015.
Graeber, David. "A Practical Utopian's Guide to the Coming Collapse." *The Baffler* 22 (April 2013).
Graeber, David. *Revolutions in Reverse*. London: Minor Compositions Autonomedia, 2015.
Graeber, David. *The Democracy Project*. New York: Penguin Random House, 2013.

Gray, Kishona. *Intersectional Tech: Black Users in Digital Gaming*. Baton Rouge: Louisiana State University Press, 2020.
Grossberg, Lawrence. *Cultural Studies in the Future Tense*. Durham, NC: Duke University Press, 2010.
Grossberg, Lawrence. "Pessimism of the Will, Optimism of the Intellect: Endings and Beginnings." *Cultural Studies* 32, no. 6 (2018): 855–888. https://doi.org/10.1080/09502386.2018.1517268.
Guanche, Julio César. "La libertad de creación, la nueva constitución y el Decreto Ley 349." *OnCuba News*, December 6, 2018. http://oncubanews.com/opinion/columnas/la-vida-de-nosotros/la-libertad-de-creacion-la-nueva-constitucion-y-el-decreto-349/.
Guerra, Lillian. *Visions of Power in Cuba: Revolution, Redemption, and Resistance, 1959–1971*. Chapel Hill: University of North Carolina Press, 2014.
Guevara, Ernesto. "Algunas reflexiones sobre la transición socialista." *Apuntes críticos a la economía política*. Havana: Instituto Cubano del Libro, 2012.
Habermas, Jürgen. *The Structural Transformation of the Public Sphere: An Inquiry into a Category of Bourgeois Society*. Translated by Thomas Burger. Cambridge, MA: MIT Press, 1991.
Hall, Stuart. "Cultural Studies: Two Paradigms." *Media, Culture & Society* 2, no. 1 (1980): 57–72.
Hall, Stuart. "The Neo-Liberal Revolution." *Cultural Studies* 25, no. 6 (2011): 705–728.
Hall, Stuart. "When Was the Postcolonial? Thinking at the Limit." In *The Postcolonial Question: Common Skies, Divided Horizons*, edited by Iain Chambers and Lidia Curti, 242–260. London: Routledge, 1996.
Hamre, Jaime. 2016. "Surge of Americans Tests Limits of Cuba's Tourism Industry." Reuters, January 26, 2016.
Harman, Chris. *Zombie Capitalism: Global Crisis and the Relevance of Marx*. Chicago: Haymarket Books, 2010.
Harvey, David. *The New Imperialism: Clarendon Lectures in Geography and Environmental Studies*. Oxford, UK: Oxford University Press, 2003.
Hebdige, Dick. *Subculture: The Meaning of Style*. London: Routledge, 2002.
Henken, Ted A. "Cuba's Digital Millennials: Independent Digital Media and Civil Society on the Island of the Disconnected." *Social Research: An International Quarterly* 84, no. 2 (2017): 429–456. doi:10.1353/sor.2017.0026.
Henken, Ted A. "'The Revenge of the Jealous Bureaucrat': A Critical Analysis of Cuba's New Rules for Cuentapropistas." *Cuba in Transition* 28 (2018): 231–238.
Henken, Ted A. "'Vale Todo' (Anything Goes): Cuba's Paladares." *Cuba in Transition* 12 (2003): 344–353.
Henken, Ted, and Sara García Santamaría. *Cuba's Digital Revolution: Citizen Innovation and State Policy*. Gainesville: University Press of Florida, 2021.
Hernández-Reguant, Ariana. "Inventor, Machine and New Man." In *Caviar with Rum: Cuba-USSR and the Post-Soviet Experience*, edited by Jacqueline Loss and José Manuel Prieto, 199–209. New York: Palgrave Macmillan, 2012.
Hernández Salván, Marta. *Mínima Cuba: Heretical Poetics and Power in Post-Soviet Cuba*. Albany: State University of New York Press, 2015.

Hoffmann, Bert. "Civil Society 2.0? How the Internet Changes State-Society Relations in Authoritarian Regimes: The Case of Cuba." GIGA Working Papers, 156 (2011). German Institute of Global and Area Studies. https://gsdrc.org/document-library/civil-society-2-0-how-the-internet-changes-state-society-relations-in-authoritarian-regimes-the-case-of-cuba/.

Hosek, Jennifer Ruth. *Sun, Sex, and Socialism: Cuba in the German Imaginary.* Toronto: University of Toronto Press, 2012.

Hynson, Rachel. *Laboring for the State.* Cambridge, UK: Cambridge University Press, 2020.

Irigaray, Luce. *The Sex Which Is Not One.* Translated by Catherine Porter and Carolyn Burke. Ithaca, NY: Cornell University Press, 1985.

Jameson, Fredric. "Future City." *New Left Review* 21 (2003): 65–79.

Jameson, Fredric. *The Seeds of Time.* New York: Columbia University Press, 1994.

Jameson, Fredric. *Signatures of the Visible.* New York and London: Routledge, 1990.

Jameson, Fredric. *A Singular Modernity: Essay on the Ontology of the Present.* London: Verso, 2002.

Jank Curbelo, Jesús. "Reparto, el reggaetón de los pobres." *elTOQUE*, July 18, 2018. https://eltoque.com/reparto-regueton-cubanos-pobres.

Jelača, Dijana, Maša Kolanović, and Danijela Lugarić-Vukas. *The Cultural Life of Capitalism in Yugoslavia: (Post)Socialism and Its Other.* London: Palgrave, 2017.

Kalter, Christoph. *The Discovery of the Third World: Decolonization and the Rise of the New Left in France, c. 1950–1976.* Cambridge, UK: Cambridge University Press, 2016.

Kant, Immanuel. *Critique of the Power of Judgment.* Rev. ed. Translated by Paul Guyer and Eric Matthews. Cambridge, UK: Cambridge University Press, 2001.

Karaganis, Joe et al. *Media Piracy in Emerging Economies.* New York: Social Science Research Council, 2011.

Kermode, Frank. *The Sense of an Ending: Studies in the Theory of Fiction.* Oxford, UK: Oxford University Press, 2000.

Krasznahorkai, László. *The Melancholy of Resistance.* Translated by George Szirtes. New York: New Directions, 2000.

Kraus, Chris. *Torpor.* Los Angeles: Semiotext(e), 2015. Distributed by MIT Press.

Laclau, Ernesto. *Emancipation(s).* London: Verso, 1996.

Laclau, Ernesto. *On Populist Reason.* London: Verso, 2002.

Laguna, Albert. *Diversión: Play and Popular Culture in Cuban America.* New York: New York University Press, 2017.

Lambe, Jennifer. *Madhouse: Psychiatry and Politics in Cuban History.* Chapel Hill: University of North Carolina Press, 2016.

Larsen, Reif. "Havana's Symphony of Sound." *New York Times*, March 12, 2018.

Lefebvre, Henri. *Key Writings.* New York: Continuum, 2003.

Lefebvre, Henri. *The Production of Space.* Translated by Donald Nicholson-Smith. Cambridge, MA: Blackwell, 1991.

Lefebvre, Henri. *Rhythmanalysis: Space, Time and Everyday Life.* Translated by Stuart Elden and Gerald Moore. New York: Continuum, 2007 [1992].

Levine, Mike. "Sounding *El Paquete*: The Local and Transnational Routes of an Afro-Cuban Repartero." *Cuban Studies* 50 (2021): 139–160. doi:10.1353/cub.2021.0010.
López, Ana M. "Calling for Intermediality: Latin American Mediascapes." *Cinema Journal* 54, no. 1 (2014): 135–141.
López, Ana M. "Our Welcomed Guests." In *To Be Continued: Soap Operas Around the World*, edited by Robert C. Allen, 256–275. London: Routledge, 1995.
Loss, Jacqueline. *Dreaming in Russian: The Cuban Soviet Imaginary*. Austin: University of Texas Press, 2013.
Loss, Jacqueline. "Socialism with Bling: Aspiration, Decency, and Exclusivity in Contemporary Cuba." *Journal of Latin American Cultural Studies* 30, no. 2 (2021): 291–310. https://doi.org/10.1080/13569325.2021.1937965.
Lyotard, Jean-François. *The Postmodern Condition: A Report on Knowledge*. Translated by Geoff Bennington and Brian Massumi. Minneapolis: University of Minnesota Press, 1984.
Maguire, Emily. "Walking Dead in Havana: Juan de los muertos and the Zombie Film Genre" In *Simultaneous Worlds: Global Science Fiction Cinema*, edited by Jennifer L. Freeley and Sarah Ann Wells, 171–188. Minneapolis: University of Minnesota Press, 2015.
Mandel, Ernest. *Late Capitalism*. Translated by Joris De Bres. London: Verso, 1980 [1975].
Mandel, Ernest. "The Myth of Market Socialism." *New Left Review* 169 (1988): 108–120.
Mandel, Ernest. "On the Nature of the Soviet State." *New Left Review* 108 (1978): 23–45.
Manning Marable, William. "Race and Revolution in Cuba." *Souls* 1, no. 2 (Spring 1999): 6–17.
Manuel, Peter. "Marxism, Nationalism and Popular Music in Revolutionary Cuba." *Popular Music* 6, no. 2 (1987): 161–178.
Marcuse, Herbert, and Douglas Kellner. *The New Left and the 1960s: Collected Papers of Herbert Marcuse*. London: Routledge, 2005.
Martín Barbero, Jesús. *De los medios a las mediaciones: Comunicación, cultura y hegemonía*. Barcelona: Editorial Gili, 1987.
Marx, Karl. "Critique of the Gotha Programme." *Marx/Engels Selected Works*. Moscow: Progress, 1970. https://www.marxists.org/archive/marx/works/1875/gotha/index.htm.
McEnaney, Tom. *Acoustic Properties: Radio, Narrative, and the New Neighborhood of the Americas*. Evanston, IL: Northwestern University Press, 2017.
McEnaney, Tom. "The Digital Revolution? History, Photography, and the Body of Fidel Castro." *La Habana Elegante* (Spring/Summer 2011). www.habanaelegante.com/Spring_Summer_2011/Notas_McEnaney.html.
McLuhan, Marshall. "The Playboy Interview." *Playboy* (March 1969).
McRobbie, Angela. *Feminism and Youth Culture*. New York: Routledge, 2000.
Menéndez, Ronaldo. *Rojo aceituna: un viaje a la sombra del comunismo*. Madrid: Páginas de Espuma, 2014.
Mesa-Lago, Carmelo. *Cuba en la era de Raúl Castro*. Madrid: Colibrí, 2012.

Mesa-Lago, Carmelo. "Ideological, Political, and Economic Factors in the Cuban Controversy on Material Versus Moral Incentives." *Journal of Interamerican Studies and World Affairs* 14, no. 1 (1972): 49–111.
Miljački, Ana. "Classes, Masses, Crowds: Representing the Collective Body and the Myth of Direct Knowledge." In *Making Things Public: Atmospheres of Democracy*, edited by Bruno Latour and Peter Weibel, 234–243. Cambridge, MA: MIT Press, 2005.
Millar, Lanie. *Forms of Disappointment: Cuban and Angolan Narrative after the Cold War*. Albany: State University of New York Press, 2019.
Mitchell, W. J. T. *What Do Pictures Want? The Lives and Loves of Images*. Chicago: University of Chicago Press, 2005.
Mejías, Ulises A,. and Nikolai E Vokuev. "Disinformation and the Media: The Case of Russia and Ukraine." *Media, Culture & Society* 39: 7 (2017): 1027–1042.
Monroe, Jonathan. "Between Ideologies and a Hard Place: Hans Magnus Enzensberger's Utopian Pragmatist Poetics." *Studies in 20th Century Literature* 21, no. 1 (1997): 41–77.
Moore, Robin. *Music and Revolution: Cultural Change in Socialist Cuba*. Berkeley: University of California Press, 2006.
Moreiras, Alberto. *Against Abstraction: Notes from an Ex-Latinamericanist*. Austin: University of Texas Press, 2020.
Moreiras, Alberto. *The Exhaustion of Difference: The Politics of Latin American Cultural Studies*. Durham, NC: Duke University Press, 2001.
Morris, Emily. "Unexpected Cuba." *New Left Review* 88 (July/August 2014). https://newleftreview.org/issues/ii88/articles/emily-morris-unexpected-cuba.
Mosquera, Martín, and Florencia Oroz. "Interview with Álvaro García Linera." *Jacobin*, April 5, 2021. www.jacobinmag.com/2021/04/interview-alvaro-garcia-linera-mas-bolivia-coup.
Mwakasege-Minaya, Richard M. "Exiled Counterpoint: Cuban Exile Reception, Media Activism, Conservatism, and the National Educational Television Network." *Chiricú* 4, no. 2 (Spring 2020): 37–61.
Nakamura, Lisa. "Gender and Race Online." In *Society and the Internet: How Networks of Information and Communication Are Changing Our Lives*, edited by Mark E. Graham, William H. Dutton, and Manuel Castells. Oxford, UK: Oxford University Press, 2014. https://academic.oup.com/book/5264/chapter/147978804.
Navarro, Desiderio. "In Medias Res Publicas: On Intellectuals and Social Criticism in the Cuban Public Sphere." Translated by Alessandro Fornazzari and Desiderio Navarro. *Boundary 2*, no. 29 (2002): 187–203.
Negrón-Muntaner, Frances. "Mariconerías de Estado: Mariela Castro, los homosexuals y la política en Cuba." *Nueva Sociedad* 218 (2008). https://nuso.org/articulo/mariela-castro-los-homosexuales-y-la-politica-cubana.
Negt, Oskar, and Alexander Kluge. *Public Sphere and Experience*. London: Verso, 2016.
NG La Banda. *Nueva Generación*. EGREM, 1992. CD.
Obama, Barack. "Remarks by President Obama to the People of Cuba." Office of the Press Secretary, March 22, 2016. https://obamawhitehouse.archives.gov

/the-press-office/2016/03/22/remarks-president-obama-people-cuba. Ogden, Rebecca. "Instagram Photography of Havana: Nostalgia, Digital Imperialism and the Tourist Gaze." *Bulletin of Hispanic Studies* 6 (2021): 87–108. doi: 10.3828/bhs.2021.6.
Oroza, Ernesto. *Technological Disobedience Project*. https://www.ernestooroza.com/category/technological-disobedience-project.
Padilla Cárdenas, Gilberto. "El 'hit parade' del comunismo." *Hypermedia Magazine*, March 29, 2019. www.hypermediamagazine.com/columnistas/maquina ciones/el-hit-parade-del-comunismo.
Padura, Leonardo. *La transparencia del tiempo*. Barcelona: Tusquets, 2018.
Pérez, Louis, Jr. "Visit Cuba Before It Changes!" In *Cuba Reader*, edited by Aviva Chomsky et al., 657–660. Durham, NC: Duke University Press, 2019.
Pérez de la Riva, Juan. *La Isla de Cuba en el s. XIX vista por extranjeros*. Havana: Ciencias Sociales, 1988.
Perna, Vincenzo. *Timba: The Sound of the Cuban Crisis*. London: Routledge, 2017.
Perreau, Bruno. *Queer Theory: The French Response*. Stanford, CA: Stanford University Press, 2016.
Piccato, Pablo. "A esfera pública na América Latina: Um mapa da historiografia." *Revista Territórios & Fronteiras* 7, no. 1 (2004): 6–42.
Porno Para Ricardo. *A mí no me gusta la política, pero yo le gusto a ella compañero: Soy porno, soy popular*. Havana: La Paja Recolds, 2006. Double album CD.
Porno Para Ricardo. *Rock para las masas . . . (cárnicas)*. Havana: La Paja Recolds, 2002. CD.
Portantiero, Juan Carlos. "La democracia difícil: Proyecto democrático y movimiento popular." *Controversia: Para un análisis de la realidad argentina* 1, no. 1 (1979): 6–7.
Portela, Ena Lucía. *El pájaro: pincel y tinta china*. Havana: Unión (Ediciones Unión), 1998.
Price, Rachel. *Planet/Cuba: Art, Culture, and the Future of the Island*. London: Verso, 2015.
Prieto, José Manuel. *La Revolución Cubana explicada a los taxistas*. Mexico City: Planeta, 2017.
Postone, Moishe. *Time, Labor, and Social Domination: A Reinterpretation of Marx's Critical Theory*. Cambridge, UK: Cambridge University Press, 1993.
Quiroga, José. *Cuban Palimpsests*. Minnesota: University of Minnesota Press, 2005.
Ramos, Julio. *Divergent Modernities: Culture and Politics in Nineteenth-Century Latin America*. Translated by John D. Blanco. Durham, NC: Duke University Press, 2001.
Restrepo, Eduardo. "Estudios culturales en América Latina." *Revista de Estudos Culturais* 1 (2015): 46–73.
Revueltas, José. "So That Mayakovsky's Suicide Not Be Repeated." *International Socialist Review* (January–February 1970): 38–44.
Reyes, Dean Luis. *El gobierno de mañana: la invención del cine cubano independiente (2001–2015)*. Santiago de Querétaro: Rialta, 2020.
Rivera, Raquel Z., Wayne Marshall, and Deborah Pacini Hernández, eds. *Reggaeton*. Durham, NC: Duke University Press, 2009.

Rocha, Glauber. *Cartas ao mundo*, edited by Ivana Bentes. São Paulo: Companhia das Letras, 1997.
Rodríguez, Reina María. *Cuando una mujer no duerme*. Havana: Ediciones Unión, 1982.
Rodríguez, Reina María. *El libro de las clientas*. Havana: Editorial Letras Cubanas, 2016.
Rodríguez, Reina María. *Variedades de Galiano*. Havana: Editorial Letras Cubanas, 2008.
Rojas, Rafael. "Diáspora, intelectuales y futuros de Cuba." *Temas* 66 (2011): 144–151.
Rojas, Rafael. *El estante vacío: Literatura y política en Cuba*. Barcelona: Anagrama, 2009.
Rojas, Rafael. *Fighting Over Fidel: The New York Intellectuals and the Cuban Revolution*. Translated by Carl Good. Princeton, NJ: Princeton University Press, 2016.
Salazkina, Masha. "Moscow, Rome, Havana: A Film Theory Roadmap." *October* 139 (Winter 2012): 97–116.
Sánchez, Yoani. "El Chupi Chupi y el dilema de los límites." *14 y medio*. November 21, 2011. www.14ymedio.com/blogs/generacion_y/Chupi-dilema-limites_7_1017568234.html.
Sandoval y García, Aurelio. *Ordenanzas de construcción para la Ciudad de la Habana y pueblos de su término municipal* [Building Ordinances]. 4th ed. Havana, 1914. Florida International University Digital Library of the Caribbean. http://ufdc.ufl.edu/AA00004236/00001.
Santa Cruz, Adriana, and Viviana Erazo. *Compropolitan: el orden transnacional y su modelo femenino: un estudio de las revistas femeninas en América Latina*. Mexico City: Nueva Imagen, 1980.
Santiago Muiño, Emilio. *Opción cero: El reverdecimiento forzoso de la Revolución Cubana*. Madrid: Traficantes de sueños, 2017.
Saunders, Tanya L. *Cuban Underground Hip Hop: Black Thoughts, Black Revolution, Black Modernity*. Austin: University of Texas Press, 2015.
Scarpaci, Joseph L., Roberto Segre, and Mario Coyula. *Havana: Two Faces of the Antillean Metropolis*. Chapel Hill: University of North Carolina Press, 2002.
Scott, David. *Omens of Adversity*. Durham, NC: Duke University Press, 2013.
Segato, Rita. *La escritura en el cuerpo de las mujeres asesinadas de Ciudad Juárez*. Mexico City: Tinta Limón, 2006.
Shaviro, Steven. *The Cinematic Body*. Minneapolis: University of Minnesota Press, 2011.
Shifman, Limor. "The Cultural Logic of Photo-Based Meme Genres." *Journal of Visual Culture*. December 16, 2014. https://journals.sagepub.com/doi/full/10.1177/1470412914546577.
Shih, Shu-mei. "Is the Post- in Postsocialism the Post- in Posthumanism?" *Social Text* 30, no. 110 (2012): 27–50.
Sommer, Doris. *Foundational Fictions: The National Romances of Latin America*. Berkeley: University of California Press, 1991.

Sontag, Susan. "Some Thoughts on the Right Way (For Us) to Love the Cuban Revolution." *Ramparts*, April 1969. Republished in *La Habana Elegante*. www.habanaelegante.com/Archivo_Revolucion/Revolucion_Sontag.html.
Sontag, Susan. *Trip to Hanoi*. New York: Farrar, Straus and Giroux, 1969.
Sparks, Colin. "Hegemonic Shadows: USA, China and Dewesternising Media Studies." *Westminster Papers in Communication and Culture* 12, no. 1 (2017): 19–20.
Sparks, Colin. "Media Theory after the Fall of Communism." In *De-Westernizing Media Studies*, edited by James Curran and Myung-Jin Park, 35–49. London: Routledge, 2000.
Sparks, Colin, and Anna Reading. *Communism, Capitalism, and the Mass Media*. London: Sage, 1998.
Sperber, Nathan. "The Many Lives of State Capitalism: From Classical Marxism to Free-Market Advocacy." *History of the Human Sciences* 32, no. 3 (July 2019): 100–124.
Srnicek, Nick. *Platform Capitalism*. Cambridge, UK: Polity Press, 2017.
Steyerl, Hito. *The Wretched of the Screen*. Berlin: Sternberg Press, 2012.
Stiglitz, Joseph E. *The Roaring Nineties: A New History of the World's Most Prosperous Decade*. New York: W. W. Norton, 2003.
Stock, Ann Marie. *On Location in Cuba*. Chapel Hill: University of North Carolina Press, 2009.
Szelenyi, Ivan. "Capitalisms after Communisms." *New Left Review* 96 (November/December 2015).
Szurmuk, Mónica, and Silvio Waisbord. "The Intellectual Impasse of Cultural Studies of the Media in Latin America: How to Move Forward." *Westminster Papers in Communication and Culture* 8, no. 1 (2011): 7–38.
Tenorio, David, "Havana's Last Conga: Trans Engagements and Queer Moves in Twenty-First-Century Cuba." *Cuban Studies* 52 (forthcoming 2023).
Tlostanova, Madina V. *What Does It Mean to Be Post-Soviet? Decolonial Art from the Ruins of the Soviet Empire*. Durham, NC: Duke University Press, 2018.
Triana, Alexis. "El 349, un decreto en torno a la circulación del arte." Interview with Alina Estévez, the human resources director of the Ministry of Culture. *Granma*, November 29, 2018.
Tutek, Hrvoje. "Dwelling in the Apocalypse: Capitalist Modernity, Antimodernism, Zombies." *Journal of French and Francophone Philosophy* 25, no. 1 (2017): 27–48.
Vázquez, Alexandra T. *Listening in Detail: Performances of Cuban Music*. Durham, NC: Duke University Press, 2013.
Venegas, Cristina. *Digital Dilemmas: The State, the Individual, and Digital Media in Cuba*. New Brunswick, NJ: Rutgers University Press, 2010.
Verdery, Katherine. *What Was Socialism, and What Comes Next?* Princeton, NJ: Princeton University Press, 2014.
Vidmar Horvat, Ksenija, "Sociology of Culture and Cultural Studies: Towards a Postsocialist Reconciliation." *Revija za sociologiju* 42, no. 2 (2012): 119–140.
Villanueva Chang, Julio. "El que enciende la luz." *Letras libres*, December 31, 2005. https://letraslibres.com/revista-mexico/el-que-enciende-la-luz/.

Villares, Lizabel Mónica. "Literatura por otros medios: Tecnología digital y campo literario en la Cuba contemporánea." PhD diss., Princeton University, 2022.
Waisbord, Silvio. "Media Policies and the Blindspots of Media Globalization: Insights from Latin America." *Media, Culture & Society* 35, no. 1 (2013): 132–138.
Wallerstein, Immanuel. *World-Systems Analysis: An Introduction.* Durham, NC: Duke University Press, 2004.
Watt, Ian. *The Rise of the Novel.* Berkeley: University of California Press, 2007.
Wetherall, Tyler. "Cuba Sees Record Bookings as Tourists Rush to See It before It Changes." *The Guardian,* October 30, 2015.
Whitfield, Esther. *Cuban Currency: The Dollar and "Special Period" Fiction.* Minneapolis: University of Minnesota Press, 2008.
Williams, Raymond. *Culture and Materialism.* London: Verso, 2005.
Williams, Raymond. "Culture Is Ordinary." In *Resources of Hope: Culture, Democracy, Socialism,* 3–14. London: Verso, 1989.
Williams, Raymond. *Television: Technology and Cultural Form.* London: Routledge, 2003.
Wittel, Andreas. "Toward a Network Sociality." *Theory, Culture & Society* 18, no. 6 (2001): 51–76. https://doi.org/10.1177/026327601018006003.
Young, Cynthia Ann. *Soul Power: Culture, Radicalism, and the Making of a U.S. Third World Left.* Durham, NC: Duke University Press, 2006.
Yúdice, George. "Músicas plebeyas." In *Memorias, saberes y redes de las culturas populares en América Latina,* edited by Graciela Maglia, Leonor Arlen Hernández Fox, 105–148. Bogotá: Pontificia Universidad Javeriana, Universidad Externado de Colombia, and Institut français d'études andines, 2016.
Zabludovsky, Karla. "Americans Are Heading to Cuba, but the Europeans Don't Like It." *BuzzFeed News,* July 13, 2015.
Zamora, Margarita. *Reading Columbus.* Berkeley: University of California Press, 1993.
Zidani, Sulafa. "Messy on the Inside: Internet Memes as Mapping Tools of Everyday Life." *Information, Communication & Society* 24, no. 16 (2021): 2378–2402.
Žižek, Slavoj. *Did Somebody Say Totalitarianism?* London: Verso, 2001.
Žižek, Slavoj. *Living in the End Times.* London: Verso, 2017.
Zolov, Eric. *Refried Elvis: The Rise of the Mexican Counterculture.* Berkeley: University of California Press, 1999.

Index

Page numbers in italics indicate figures.

11J protests, 10, 14, 59, 155, 172, 176, 178, 190, 203, 224n12
14ymedio, 148, 183
27N protests, 176

abortion, 126
accumulation, 26, 115–116, 156, 209, 218
Acosta, Alberto, 225n30
advertising, 24–25, 28, 93, 114, 117, 121, 126, 161
African Americans, 62
agency, 160; female, 127, 133; new media and, 172–173; political and cultural, 172–173; public, collective, and communal forms of, 161
agriculture, 41–49
Alarcón, Cristian, 184
Alas Tensas, 186
Alexievich, Svetlana, 7, 116
Algeria, 41, 78
algorithmic mediation, 29, 173
Alliance for the Peoples of Our America (ALBA), 19, 149, 218
almendrones, 76, 90–96, 98, 148
Alonso Olivé, Raúl, 48
"alternative," definitions of, 214, 221
Althusserian school, 38
alt-right movements, 216–217
Álvarez, Carlos Manuel, 55–56, 177, 183, 239n20; *Los caídos*, 205–206

Álvarez, Gloria, 175
Álvarez, Julia: *Once Upon a Quinceañera*, 122
Álvarez, Santiago: *Now*, 62
amateur citizen, 171, 183–184, 192
America CV, 147
América Tevé Channel, 41, 147
Angolan War, 32, 227n3
Anthony, Marc, 93
anti-Black racism, in revolutionary Cuba, 97
anticapitalist struggles, 216, 217, 231n19
anticommunist propaganda, 174
anti-imperialism, 38, 173–174, 177, 188, 189
apocalyptic tropes, 60, 114, 193, 199–200, 204–211, 218
Appadurai, Arjun, 12, 13, 17
apps, 113–114, 117, 138–139, 149; data-sharing, 148; Donde Hay app, 113; informal economy and, 138; signal-sharing, 148; VoIP, 148
Archivo de Connie, El, 193
Arellano, Jerónimo, 12
Arenas, Reinaldo: *Before Night Falls*, 85
Argentina, 24, 38, 73, 214
Argudín Sánchez, Elías, 63
Aricó, José, 212
Arroyo, Jossianna, 12
artistic freedom, 27, 88; economic liberalism and, 180

Associated Press, 180
autonomy, 90, 99, 102–103, 108, 179, 206; intellectuals and, 169, 172, 183; Cuba and, 25, 201
Ávila, Eliecer, 173
Ávila, Enrique, 64
Ávila, Gorki, 99–100, 102, 103

Bahro, Rudolf, 214
Bajanda, 91, 93
Baldwin, James, 95–96
Balibar, Étienne, 237–238n2, 239n32
Balvin, J., 110
Barbero, Jesús Martín, 16
barbudos, 84
Baró, Mónica, 183, 187, 188, 225–226n31
Barroso, Niurka, 122
Barthes, Roland, 111–112, 136–137, 189
Bartra, Roger, 84
Bass, Karen, 226n36
Batista, Fulgencio, 74, 80
Battle of Ideas, 8, 162
Bay of Pigs invasion, 82
Beauvoir, Simone, 58
Benjamin, Walter, 39–40
Berlin Wall, fall of, 8, 216
Bettelheim, Charles, 43, 44, 47
Beyoncé, 57, 58, 61
Black Cubans, 62–63
Black Lives Matters movement, 63, 178
black market, 9, 51, 116, 120, 146, 153, 161, 210
"Black Spring," 183
bloggers, dissident, 149
blogosphere, independent, 164, 170–173, 179–183, *182*
Bohemia, 50, 122
Bolívar, Simón, 19
Bolivia, 19, 38, 218; 2019 street protests in, 73; Alliance for the Peoples of Our America (ALBA), 19, 149, 218
Bolsonaro, Jair, 204, 217
Boric, Gabriel, 177
Bourdieu, Pierre, 90, 215
Brazil, 22, 38, 113, 136, 204, 214
Brooks, Max: *World War Z: An Oral History of the Zombie War*, 207–208
Bruguera, Tania, 184, 187

Bruno, Giuliana, 76
Buck-Morss, Susan, 1, 3, 215, 224n8, 240n44
Buden, Boris, 214
Buquenque, 93

Cáceres, Dolores: *No vendo nada*, 24–25, *24*
Cadelo, Claudia, 151; "Bibliography in a Flashdrive," 171; "The Rock Agency," 104
Caimán Barbudo, El, 184
Canada, 22, 31
Canal 41, 109
Canclini, Néstor, 15–16
capitalism, 16–17, 82, 147, 156, 157, 219, 220, 239n26; "actually existing capitalism," 192, 220; critique of, 219; democracy and, 212; end of, 199; platform capitalisms, 173; rejected by Guevara, 84; socialism and, 198; telenovelas and, 115–116; zombie genre and, 206–211
Carbonell, Walterio, 85–86
Cardenal, Ernesto, 51
Cardoso, Onelio Jorge, 183
Casa de las Américas, 60, 184
Castells, Manuel, 179
Castillo, Pedro, 20
Castoriadis, Cornelius, 37, 224n8, 225n22, 239n32
Castro, Ernesto, 107–108
Castro, Fidel, 22, 31, 50, 57, 79, 99, 107, 151, 178, 188, 199; 1959 trip to New York City, 60–61; on accumulation, 115–116; appeal of, 229n56; cultural guidelines of, 168; death of, 8, 184; Dumont and, 41–42, 48–49; "The First Declaration of Havana," 81–82; Guevara's letter to, 46; Karol and, 48–49; language of state capitalism and, 47; Malcolm X and, 61; McLuhan on, 142; passing of power to Raúl, 9; screen persona of, 142; on Special Period, 238n12; speech of September 2, 1960, 81–82; uniform of, 128
Castro, Mariela, 187, 188
Castro, Raúl, 9, 11, 18–19, 31, 55–56, 217

CENESEX, 187
censorship, 25, 86, 96, 103, 125–126, 150, 154, 160, 164, 169–170, 188–189, 195; bureaucratic, 168; censorship law (Ley 35/2021), 10
Center for the Study of the Americas, 62
Centro Nacional de Investigaciones Científicas (National Center for Scientific Research), 210
Centro Teórico-Cultural Criterios, 166–168
cha-cha-chá, 69, 78–79, 134
Chang, Peter: *Cuba: Journey to the Heart of the Caribbean*, 57, 76
change, 41–55, 141, 195; chronicling of, 189; in Dumont, 55; in Enzensberger, 55; narratives of, 139; periodizing, 6–18
Chaplin, Charlie: *Modern Times*, 163
Chari, Sharad, 2, 3
Chávez, Hugo, 8, 66, 178, 218
Chile, 73, 177, 214
China, 20–22, *21*, 34–35, 38, 42, 82, 150, 152, 200.
Chirino, Willy, 60
Chocolate MC, 75, 93
Christian: evangelicals, 173; family values, so-called, 126
ciberclarias, 181
Ciego Montero, 22, 113
CIMEX, 113
cinema, 144–145; *cinemóviles*, 162–163; documentary, 86; foreign, 146; Hollywood, 141, 142, 158; independent, 143, 234n7
citizens, 149; state power and, 147. *See also* amateur citizen
citizenship, consumerism and, 139
civil society, 127, 168, 170; definition of, 164; diversification of, 186–188; inadequacy of term, 165; postsocialist transitions and, 169
Clandestina fashion label, 135–136, 137
class, 77, 90, 145, 153
classic liberalism, 214
Clealand, Danielle Pilar, 178
cleanliness, 131–132
Clothesline, The, 152

Cold War, 36, 57, 58, 63, 82, 174, 178, 180, 198, 215; "alternatives" to, 214; legacies of, 20; propaganda race, 82
Colombia, 73, 110
Colón, John Michael, 178
colonialism 167, 174; colonial tropical stereotypes, 79, 132; gaze of, 85. *See also* data colonialisms
Coloquio Internacional Patria, 60
commercialism, 15, 70, 76, 96
commodification, 30, 58, 133, 136–137, 139, 202
communication, horizontal forms of, 148. *See also* connectivity
communications technology, 149–50
communism, transition to, 20, 197, 213
Communist Party, 45, 56, 214. *See also* Cuban Communist Party (PCC)
Communist Youth Union (UJC), 152
Comunistas de Cuba, 176
Conde, Mario, 91–2, 96
Connectify, 148
connectivity, 8–9, 13, 23, 88, 125, 148, 148–164, *154*; affordable, 141; DSL, 151–152; expansion of, 166; leapfrogging, 149–150; low levels of, 150; regulatory environment and, 150–151; wi-fi cards, 148; wi-fi, 117, 151–152, *154*. *See also* hot spots
"conspiracy of silence," 85
consumerism, 97, 114; culture and, 90, 98, 119, 122, 174; citizenship and, 139; expansion of consumerist imaginaries, 14–15; women and, 127–140; zombie genre and, 208–209
consumption, 115; of difference, 160; identity and, 159–160; postcolonial identities and, 128; power and, 159–160; women and, 128
continuity, 41–55, 141, 195; chronicling of, 189; periodizing, 6–18
Correa, Rafael, 74–75, 217
Cortázar, Julio, 36, 227n4
Cortázar, Octavio: *Por primera vez*, 162
Cosmopolitan (Spain), 119
COVID-19, 10, 59, 110, 111, 176, 190, 204, 210, 224n12
"*coyuntura*," 193, 204
creative industry, 125–126

Criterios, 166–167, 170
critical revolutionaries, 165, 166, 167–169, 170, 173, 177
critical theory, 23–24. *See also* postsocialist critical theory
Crocker, Frank, 95
crónicas, 181, 183–186; marketization and standardization of, 188–189; platforms publishing, 186–187; and public discourse, 188–189
cronistas, 183–184, 187
Cuba, 19, 24, 81; 1976 constitution, 209; 2014 restructuring of national debt, 113; 2019 constitution, 209; in 2020 US election cycle, 226n36; criticism of, 178 (*see also* critical revolutionaries); embargo against, 81; feminized representation of, 129–130; "frozen in time," 34, 75–76; as international object of desire, 26; isolation of, 81–82, 193–194; as liberated territory, 82; as metaphorical screen, 141; racism in, 62–63, 97; Soviet Union and, 177. *See also* Cuban government
Cubadebate, 8, 111, 138, 142
Cuba: Journey to the Heart of the Caribbean (Chang), 76
Cuba Material, 193
Cuba Money Project, 180
Cuban Afro-descendants, 62–63
Cuban Communist Party (PCC), 10, 12, 18, 19, 20, 48, 144, 149, 192; congresses of, 9, 23, 198–199, 209; LGBTQ+ issues and, 175; social conservatism of, 175–176; socialism of, 169; and vocabulary of social justice, 210–211;
Cuban diaspora, 64, 88–89, 103, 110, 120, 122, 149, 165, 174, 193, 228–229n47; black and gray market and, 150; right-wing, 173
Cuban exceptionalism, 6–8, 13, 15, 23–24, 27–28, 57–58, 63, 165, 193–195, 198, 217, 218; informatization and, 159; as international object of desire, 220; limits of, 220; rebuffed, 195; rhetorical framework of, 82; role of, 220
Cuban government, 147, 215; cultural policy, 77, 86–88, 90, 97, 123, 171;
gender rights and, 126; homophobia and, 126; image of Guevara, 126; LGBTQ+ issues and, 126; media policy, 156–157; Ministry of Culture, 104; Ministry of Foreign Affairs, 188; Ministry of Interior, 64; opposition to, 174; shortcomings of, 215; state apparatus, 70, 71, 86–88, 97, 160, 161, 167, 198, 234n7; state capitalism, 141, 158, 220; state control, 195; state-controlled media, 10, 96, 113–114, 149, 156–157, 172, 181; state digital sovereignty, 150–151; state-organized productivism, 87; state policy, 148; state power, 147; state-sanctioned violence, 218; state socialism, 17
Cuban hip-hop, 15, 90
Cuban Institute of Cinematographic Art and Industry (ICAIC), 142, 143–144, 157
Cuban Institute of Radio and Television (ICRT), 87, 142, 147
Cuban literature, 33, 161, 184–185
Cuban music, 87, 98; brand of, 70, 87; postsocialist remediation of, 77. *See also specific genres and artists*
Cubanness, 76, 95
Cuban postsocialism: alternative takes on, 217; four key transformations of, 13; global postsocialist condition and, 217; mediascapes of, 6–18; New Left and, 220; persistence as media object, 217; portability of, 122–123; as social text, 16, 217; as state capitalism, 141
Cuban Revolution, 5–6, 9, 21, 25, 32–40, 41, 47–48, 55–56, 58, 74, 80, 142, 163; Baldwin on, 96; (dis)enchantment with, 59; dual status as abstract and concrete event, 79–80; Enzensberger on, 52–53; as everyday experience, 79–80; exportability of, 57; fetishization of, 13; legacy of, 198; as media phenomenon, 124; Ministry of Communications, 153–154; music and, 71; nationalism of, 200–201; new itineraries for, 55–67; New Left and, 83–84; online debates on, 73; race and, 61–63; significance of, 57; and Spanish colonialism, 174; symbolism

of, 57, 79–80; televised, 143–144; *trova* and, 106; US civil rights movement and, 61; US imperialism and, 81; versions of, 60; vocabulary of, 219
Cuban Revolutionary Offensive of 1968, 44, 51
Cuban Rock Agency, 103–104
Cubans: images of themselves, 119, 127–140, 132, 137, 155; migration patterns of, 74–75
Cuban socialism, 218; Black American community and, 62; critiques of, 186; definition of, 199; (ex)portability of, 74; as genre, 35–36; global postsocialist condition and, 219–220; as international object of desire, 217–218, 220; as "irrevocable," 198–199; music and, 67–112; New Left and, 46–47, 49–55, 169, 213, 219, 220; "public sphere" and, 169–170; sounds of, 67–112; soundtrack of, 71; state's monopoly on, 98–99; as survivor at the end of history, 201; traveling images of, 5–6
Cuban studies, 24, 71
Cubatón, 93
Cubavisión, 156
Cuevana, 156
Cultural Congress of Havana, 1968, 168
cultural criticism, independent blogger movement and, 170–173
cultural studies, 14–16, 17, 84; Birmingham school of, 16; of postsocialism, 126
Czechia, 103, 180

@DaltonLiebknec1, 176
dance, 69, 83, 84–85
data colonialisms, 153, 173
Dayana, Señorita, 109, 127, 133, 137; "La mentira," 134; "Te Choca," 134–135
Day and Night, 144–146
Debray, Regis, 80
debt cancellation, 220
Declaration of Costa Rica, 81
decolonization, 15, 38, 166, 188
Decreto Ley (Decree Law), 90, 97, 123; 35/2021, 150, 180; 370/2019, 150, 153–154, 180; 373/2019, 234n7

Dedeté, 20
Delahante Matienzo, Susan Pilar, 127, 132, 137
De la Nuez, Iván, 71
Delgado, Alexander, 109
Delgado, Frank, 105; "Ambassador of Sex," 129; "La Habana está de bala," 131
Delgado, Isaac, 93
Del Río, Idania, 135
democracy: capitalism and, 212; culture and, 164, 168, 170–171; democratic transitions in Latin America, 165; grassroots, 13; neoliberal democracy, 214; public spheres and, 164–166; as social production, 212; statization and, 212–213; totalitarianism and, 198
Democratic Socialists of America, 178
democratization, 121, 142, 167; aesthetic, 170; information democratization, 167; promise of, 86; of technical means of cultural production, 124–125
Derrida, Jacques, 207
Descemer Bueno, 110, 111
desire, concept of, 223n6
de-Stalinization, 15, 37–38, 42, 217
developmentalism, 10–11, 15, 21, 24, 218, 225n30
Diario de Cuba, 179
Diásporas, 55
Díaz, Ciro, 100, 102
Díaz, Elaine, 183
Díaz, Jesús, 157
Díaz-Canel, Miguel, 9, 10, 138–139, 179, 204
#DiazCanelSingao, 193
Díaz de Villegas, Néstor, 173
dictatorships, right-wing, 37, 73, 214, 216
difference, consumption of, 160
digital attention economy, 192–193
digital literacy campaign, 8, 162
digital media, 8, 95, 118, 120–122, 142, 149, 183; art, 151–153; cultures, 118, 125; ecosystem, 121–122; informal distribution and advertising networks for, 93; participatory practices, 127; portability and, 77; proliferation of, 13; rise of, 88; soundscape and, 71

digital public spheres, 148, 177–179; emergence of more pluralistic, 187–188
digital technologies, 118; mass commercialization of, 124–125; portable technologies, 157; screens, 147–148; storage, 141; music and, 70. *See also* digital media
directas, 164
"dirty realism," 184–185
discrediting campaigns, 172
disinformation, 164
Disney+, 158
dissidents, 149, 165, 176–177; digital-left dissidents, 176–178; digital public spheres and, 177–179; new media technologies and, 179–183; United States and, 180
División de Programas para Jóvenes y Niños (Programming Division for Youth and Children) of the Institute of Radio and Television, 123
DIY media cultures, 124, 142–143
DJ Hectico (Hector Díaz Yáñez), 89
documentary film, 86
dogmatism, 42–43
dollarization, 8, 130
Dominican Republic, 98
Donde Hay app, 113
Dopico, Ana, 76
doramas, 145, 147
Dumont, René, 35–36, 37, 40, 44, 47, 51, 55, 209; and CIA, 48; *Cuba: Socialism and Development*, 41; expulsion from Cuba, 49; *Is Cuba Socialist?*, 41
Dunayevskaya, Raya, 37, 39, 40, 85

Eastern and Central Europe: "alternatives" in, 214; alt-right movements in, 216–217; nationalism in, 216–217; neofascism in, 216–217; postsocialisms in, 25, 165, 169; social conservatism in, 216–217
Eaton, Tracey, 180
Echevarría, Paula, 119
economic crises, 10; crisis of world capital 2008, 19–20, 184; deepening of in 2019, 138, 202–203; economic recessions, 219. *See also* economic crisis of the 1990s
economic crisis of the 1990s, 34, 93, 115–116, 146, 193–195; dollarization and, 130; fears of return of, 202–204, *203*; tourism and, 130
economy: controlled participation in global markets, 8, 12, 23; decentralization of economic sector, 13; recovery, 89; survival, 156; informal, 93, 128, 138–140; updating of economic model, 10, 12. See also *raulista* market reforms
Ecuador, 136; Cuban migrants in, 74–75; protests in, 73
Ecured, 8, 152
EGREM, 70, 91
El Chulo, 109
El Círculo, *143*, 143–144
El Funky, 110
Elián Affair, 8
elites, 22, 30, 46, 53, 149, 156, 174, 189, 190, 219
El Kokito, El Negrito y Manu Manu, 109
El Mariel, 60
El Micha, 134; "Con dinero y pasmao," 134; "Único en mi peso," 134; "Un sueño" (Cuba grita Libertad)," 110
El Patio de María, 104
Elpidio, 174, 175
"El Show de Valentín," 111
El Submarino Amarillo, 104
elTOQUE, 14, 183, 186, 187, 188, 189
emancipation, 125, 126, 161, 197; radical politics of, 54, 139, 202
emprendedora, 132, 137–138, 139
"end of history," 237–238n2; Cuban mediascapes after, 197–221; Cuban representations of, 200–206; fictions of, 27, 28; postsocialism and, 197–198
Engels, Friedrich, 53, 197
entrepreneurship, 115, 116, 137–138, 139, 156. See also *emprendedora*
Enzensberger, Hans Magnus, 35–36, 37, 40, 41, 49–55, 57, 60, 124, 219, 228n41; "Constituents of a Theory of Media," 51; in Cuba, 126; *Der kurze Sommer der Anarchie: Buenaventura Durrutis Leben und Tod*, 55; *Havana*

Inquiry, 51; "Lachesis Laponica," 51; "Old Revolution," 51; "On Leaving America," 51; "Portrait of a Party," 51; *The Sinking of the Titanic*, 49–50, 51, 52, 53–54; "Tourists of the Revolution," 51, 54; *Tumult*, 49, 50–52, 53–54, 55, 67
Escalona Abella, Raúl, 187
Escobar, Arturo, 225n30
Escobar, Reinaldo, 183
Espín, Vilma, 187
Estornudo, El, 14, 56, 177, 183, 187, 188, 189, 205–206
ETECSA, 21, 120, 149, 151–152, 154, 172, 234n20
European Championship soccer finals, 203
Exit Festival, 180
extractivism, 13, 15, 21, 22, 24, 116, 225n30; neoextractivist developmentalism, 218

Facebook, 28, 138, 179, 187, 192, 193
Falcón, Ariel, 190
"Fall, The," 200
Family Code, 175, 176
Fanguito Studio, Havana, 153
Fanon, Frantz, 41; *The Wretched of the Earth*, 84
fashion, 27, 122–123; mass access to, 128–129; secondhand, 113–140; transformation and, 139; women and, 113–140
Fast & Furious 8, 57, 59
Federación de Mujeres Cubanas (Federation of Cuban Women), 129–130, 187
Feld, Stefan, 229–230n2
femicides, 188. *See also* gender-based violence
feminism, 13, 188. *See also* women
Fernández, Patricio, "Compañero Obama," 156
fidelistas, 177
film. *See* cinema
First Congress of Education and Culture, 49
First Congress of the PCC, Theses and Resolutions, 209

"First Declaration of Havana, The" (Fidel Castro), 81–82
floating signifiers, 18, 225n28
Flor Elena, 132, 133
Florida Strait, 28, 64
Fontes, Eduardo, 179
For an Imperfect Cinema (García Espinosa), 143
Fotos, 123
Fowler, Víctor, 158–159, 169, 229n51
France, 78, 79
Franco, Ania, 85; *La fête cubaine*, 79
Frankfurt school, 124
Fukuyama, Francis, 197, 198, 238n3

Gabo Foundation, 225–226n31
Gago, Verónica, 10–11, 156
Galeano, Eduardo, 80
Galerías Paseo, 113, 115
Game of Thrones, 122, 156, 160
gaming communities, 153–154
García, Osmani, 99; "Chupi Chupi," 89–90, 91, 93, 96; *El Malcriao*, 91
García Borrero, Jorge Antonio, 234n7
García Espinosa, Jorge, 66, 124, 164; *Cuba Baila*, *P.M.*, 86; *For an Imperfect Cinema*, 143
García Márquez, Gabriel, 36, 184, 185
gatekeeping, 168
Gatopardo, 185
gaze, critical 11, 20, 54, 220; male, 127, 128, 131; foreign, 13, 35, 76, 78, 85, 99, 114, 155, 185
GDR, 49
gender, 27, 126; equality, 133; ideology of 175; rights, 126; stereotypes, 129–130
gender-based violence, 176, 188
Generación Y, 170, 181
Generation Zero, 185
Gente de Zona, 93, 109, 110, 111; "El animal," 134; "La gozadera," 93; "Somos Cuba," 93; "Traidora," 93
Germany, 22, 49, 117. *See also* Berlin Wall, fall of
Gilman, Claudia, 85
glasnost, 146, 201
global culture industry, 57, 147, 160
global markets, 88; controlled participation in, 8, 12, 23

Index

Global South feminists, 188
Gómez-Barris, Macarena, 225n30
González, Sandor: *3D por primera vez*, 162–163
Google, 21–22, 57, 61, 135, 151–152
Gorbachev, Mikhail, 66
GPS devices, 120
Graeber, David, 198, 215, 220, 228n41
Gramsci, Antonio, 5, 16, 168, 212, 213, 225n28, 228n41
Granma, 10, 20, 48, 177, 188
Gran Teatro de La Habana, 62–63
Gray, F. Gary, 155
Great Economic Debate, 47, 51
Greene, Shane, 100
"Green Tide," 177
Groys, Boris, 115
Guamá, 20
Guanche, Julio César, 97
Guardian, The, 118
Guatemala, 38, 82
Gudynas, Eduardo, 225n30
Guerra, Lillian, 86
Guerra, Wendy, 137; *Everyone Leaves*, 116–117
guerrillas, 37, 50, 53, 74, 78, 128–129
guerrita de los emilios, la, 164, 169
Guevara, Alfredo, 142
Guevara, Ernesto "Che," 41, 45, 66, 80; critique of Soviet Union, 45–46, 213; *foco* theory, 57; *pachanga* and, 77; sculpture of, 64; Sontag on, 84–85
guevarism: antimaterialist, 128; economic guidelines, 83; rhetoric, 46–47
guevaristas, 177
Gutelman, Michel, 44
Gutiérrez Aguilar, Raquel, 218
Gutiérrez Alea, Tomás, 164
"G y 23," 100

Habana Libre Hotel, 18, 20–21, *21*
Habermas, Jürgen, 165
Habermasian Publizität, 171, 176, 189
hair, 119, 122–123, 131–132
Haiti, 5
Hall, Stuart, 16, 47, 214, 219
Hasta El Coño @MelaSuda91, 176
Hatuey 32; beer, 58

hauntology, 58, 207, 239n22
Havana, Cuba, 62, 76, 113, 148, 225n27; L y 23, billboard at, *19*; reggaeton in, 98
Havana Art Biennial, 24, 25, 132
Havana Times, 176
Hayes, Miguel Alejandro, 186
HBO, 158; *Vice*, 118
Hebdige, Dick, 101
Hegel, G. W. F., 237–238n2
hegemony, 168, 225n28; crisis of, 11, 27, 192, 210; Gramsci's theory of, 5, 16, 168, 212; Laclau on, 225n28
Helmreich, Stefan, 229–230n2
Henken, Ted, 165
"Here's Johnny" meme, 193–195, *194*
Hernández, Rafael, 169
Hernández-Reguant, Ariana, 92
Hevia, Alfredo, *Mass media*, *143*, 143–144
hip-hop, 15, 90
¡Hola!, 119
Hollywood, 141, 142, 158
home studios, 93
Horace, 111–112
Horn of Africa, 32
Hosek, Jennifer, 52
Hotel Nacional, 21, 53
Hotel Theresa, 61
hot spots, 120, 148; "guerrilla hot spots," 153
Huawei, 21–22, 150; phones, 70, 120, 149
human rights, 188
humor, during Special Period, 201–202; socialist humor, 189, 190, 192; remediation of, 174; *See also* memes
Hungary, Soviet intervention in, 50
hybrid economies, 118
hypermasculinity, 90

identity, consumption and, 159–160
Iglesias, Pablo, 73, 74
image(s), 114–115; by Cubans, 123; in informal media economy, 123–124; "poor images," 66, 121–122; postmodern economy of, 125; production of, 120, 123; self-image, 132, 137, 155; of women, 127–140

imaginary, the, 224n8
independent media, 14, 173; financial support for, *182*; independent journalism, 164, 179–183, *182* (*see also* blogosphere); independent press, *203*; self-publication, 148, 157, 164
Indigenous communities, 13, 218
indignados movement, 74
inequality, 116, 219
Infante, Arturo, 131
infobae, 175
informal economy: apps and, 138; hybrid economy, 93, 128, 139–140; images in, 139–140
informal media economy, images in, 123–124
information: democratization of, 167; statization of, 160
information and communication technologies (ICTs), 147–148, 150
informatization, 141, 156, 159, 195
infrastructure, 21, 148, 149–150; infrastructure development, 21, 225n30. *See also* developmentalism
Instagram, 28, 138, 149, 173, 174, 178
Institute for Research in African-American Studies, Columbia University, 62
institutional racism, in the United States, 62–63
institutions, distrust of, 219
Instituto Superior de Arte, 151
insurgency politics, 216, 219
intellectual property, collectivization of, 158
Intelsat, 153
International Institute for Artivism Hanna Arendt, 184
international investment, 10, 12, 21–22, 34, 63, 116, 152, 224n12
internet access: blackouts, 10; internet sharing hacks, 149; performativity of, 151–152; tolerance of, 151. *See also* connectivity; sneakernets
interventionism, 10–11; vs. internationalism, 178; interventionist media projects, 180–181
intranet, 152

Iran, 113
Italy, 22, 113

Jamaica, 149
James, C. L. R., 37, 39–40, 168
Jameson, Fredric, 80, 81, 199, 238n9
Jank Curbelo, Jesús, 95
Jay-Z, 57, 58, 61, 229n50
Jiménez Enoa, Abraham, 183, 185
jineteras, 129, 130, 132
John Lennon Park, 148
John Paul II, Pope, 57, 238n13
Johnson–Forest Tendency, 40
Jones, Leroi, 36
Jorge (administrator of La Coyuntura), 192
Jorrín, Enrique: "La engañadora," 134
journalism: independent, 164, 181, 188 (*see also* blogosphere); literary, 185, 189, 205–206; state, 183
journals, 121. *See also specific publications*
Joven Club de Computación y Electrónica (Youth Computing Club), 8, 152, 154, 161–162
Joven Cuba, 176
Juan de los Muertos, 211, 218
Juanita Mateo, 129
July 11, 2021, demonstrations on. *See* 11J protests
Juventud Rebelde, 20

Kafka Novels, 180
Kalter, Cristoph, 78
Kant, Immanuel, 93–94, 96
Karol, K. S., 37, 44, 48–49
Kcho (Alexis Levya Machado), 151–152, 163–164
Kennedy, John F., 63, 81
Khalifa, Mia, 193
Kirchner, Cristina Fernández de 216
Klein, Naomi, 214
Kodak Super 8 camera, 124, 142–143
Korda, Alberto, 64
Kraus, Chris: *Torpor*, 117

Lacalle Pou, Luis, 111
La Charanga Habanera, 134
La Chopi, 114
Laclau, Ernesto, 225n28

La Coyuntura, 192, 193–195, *194*, 203
Lámpara y Luz publishers, 126
LAN-based gaming communities, 153–154
La Paja Recolds, 103
La Polla Records, 103
LASA (Latin American Studies Association), 2021 statement on Cuba, 178
Latin America: critical thought, 217; democratic transitions in, 165; exchange with, 122; modernity, 16; solidarity, 106. *See also specific countries*
Latin American studies, 24; cultural and media, 12, 17
Lauzán, Alen, 20, 56; El tiempo, el implacable, el que pasó, 20–21, *21*
Law of Foreign Investment, 34
Leben des Anderen, Das, 146
Lefebvre, Henri, 17, 75, 98
Left/leftism, 218, 231n19; "crisis of the left," 219; left populisms, 11, 13; old left, Soviet Union and, 85. *See also* New Left
Le Monde, 48
Lenin, Vladimir, 45–46
Lévi-Strauss, Claude, 133
LGBTQ+ communities, 83, 186, 188
LGBTQ+ issues: Cuban Communist Party (PCC) and, 175; Cuban government and, 126; Cuban military and, 175; homophobia, 126; TV shows and, 145
LGBTQ+ rights, 175–176, 187, 218
liberal democratic capitalism, 214, 216, 219
liberalism, 180; artistic freedom and, 180
libros fusilados, 158
Literacy Campaign of 1961, 162
Locke, John, 44–45
López, Ana, 12, 146
López Obrador, Andrés Manuel, 217
Los 4, 134
Los Bunkers, 230n7
Los Van Van, 65, 87–88, 130; "La moda," 130–131; "La shopimaníaca," 134, 136

LOWE, 70
Lucas Prize, 99
Lueck, Simone, *Cuba TV*, 143–144
Luengo, Beatriz, "Ojalá pase," 110
Lukàcs, Georg, 54
Lula da Silva, Luiz Inácio, 216–217
Lyotard, Jean-François, 211, 223n5

Machado, Alexis Levya. *See* Kcho (Alexis Levya Machado)
machopartidismo pseudoplurinacional, 218
Macri, Mauricio, 217
Madrid, Spain, 74
Maduro, Nicolás, 64, 217
Mafia, 80, 81, 82
magazines, 121, 122; international, 119. *See also specific publications*
Maguire, Emily, 71
Mais Medicos program, 204
Malcolm X, 61
Mandel, Ernest, 44, 45, 46, 47, 212, 213, 240n39
Mandela, Nelson, 32
Manuel, Elvis, 88
Mao, critique of Soviet revisionism by, 45
Marable, Manning, 62
Marcuse, Herbert, 39, 40; "On the New Left," 38–39
Mariel, Cuba, Special Development Zone, 10, 22, 113
Markosian, Diana, 122
marriage equality, 126
Martha Machado Brigade, 163
Martí, José, 19, 184
Martínez, Óscar, 184
Martínez, Rebeca, 87
Martínez Heredia, Fernando, 169
Marx, Karl, 40, 53, 197, 212, 237–238n2, 239n26; *Critique of the Gotha Programme*, 46, 213
Marxism, 16–17, 23–24, 27, 38, 47, 80–81, 86, 169, 186, 214; critiques of, 212; Guevara and, 45–46; Marxism-Leninism, 186; mass culture and, 84, 124–125; reassessments of, 44–45; revolutionary politics and, 54. *See also* Marxist theory
Marxists, 40

Marxist theory, 15, 43–44, 211–212, 214–215
masculinity, 89–90, 128, 129–130; mass media, traditional: parody of, 101; state's monopoly on, 96–97. *See also specific media*
Matanzas Province, 59
materialist critique, 41–55
Matienzo, Delahante, 132, 137; *Dominadora inmaterial*, 132–133
Maxim Rock theater, 104
Maykel Blanco y su Salsa Mayor, 136
McDonald's, 23
McLuhan, Marshall, 142, 233n2
media, competition in, 21–22; infrastructures, 88; literacies, 195; monopolies, 153; networked 29, 149
mediascapes, 13, 15–16, 17, 60–61; as analytical framework, 13–14; coining of the term, 12; at the end of history, 197–221; notion of, 12; "woman of fashion" in, 118–119
media studies, 16, 17, 141; de-Westernizing, 166; focus on transnational globalization, 161
medical programs and missions, 8, 23, 208–209, 226n33
memelords, 192
memes: classic socialist humor and, 189, 190, 192; and economic crisis, *203*; language of, 189–192; memescape, 164, 174, *175*, *182*, 189–192, 202–204, *203*; on political economy and polarization, *191*; portable postsocialisms and, 192. *See also specific memes*
memesphere, 111
Memorias del subdesarrollo, 157
Menéndez, Ronaldo, 226n1
mesh networks, 153–154
Mexico, 22, 113, 136
Miami, Florida, 28, 103, 122, 136, 153
migrants, 60, 200
migration, 9, 13, 28, 74–75, 116, 228–229n47
millennials, 165
Mills, C. Wright, 36, 39
Minas de Matahambre project, 225–226n31
miniaturization, 77, 125

Moa, Cuba, mining in 22
mobile devices, 8, 120, 149; internet plans on, 138–139
Mochila, La, 157–158, 161–162
modernity, 16, 163, 183, 221
Monasterio, Rosario, 74
Monroe, Jonathan, 228n41
Monroe Doctrine, 82
Morales, Evo, 217, 218
moringa, 210
Mota, Erick J., 204–205, 211; "Asuntos pendientes," 205; "That Zombie Belongs to Fidel," 208–210
Movimiento San Isidro (MSI), 111, 172, 173, 192, 239n20
Muchacha, 128
Muiño, Emilio Santiago, 14, 178, 226n35
Mujeres, 128
Mujica, José, 216–217
municipal networks, 155
Museo Nacional de Bellas Artes in Havana, 135
Museo Orgánico de Romerillo (MOR), 151–152, 163–164
music, 27, 70, 87, 98; Cuban Revolution and, 71; Cuban socialism and, 67–112; digital technologies and, 70; labels, 70; markets, 76, 77. *See also* Cuban music; popular music; *specific genres and artists*
Muzak, 94

NASA 2021 meme, 193–195, *194*
National Council of Scenic Arts, 70, 89
National Endowment for Democracy, 180
nationalism, 77, 123–124, 200, 216–217
nation-state, decline of, 214–215
Nauta Hogar, 152
Navarro, Desiderio, 166–167, 170, 171, 177; "DDN" (Digital Desiderio Navarro), 167–168; "In Medias Res," 168–170
neoliberalism, 73, 174–175, 214; conservative, 174, 175–176; neoliberal democracy, 214; privatization and, 161; triumphant, 197–199, 238n3
Nestlé, 22, 113

266 Index

Netflix, 57, 158, 174, *175*
net neutrality, 155
networks, 117, 118, 125, 127, 148; municipal networks, 155; VPN networks, 148
NewCom International, 153
New Economic Policy, 45–46
New Left, 15, 26, 34–35, 36–40, 44, 58, 85, 219, 227n7; Cuban postsocialism and, 220; Cuban Revolution and, 83–84; Cuban socialism and, 49–55, 169, 213, 219, 220; culturalist approaches and, 46–47; image of Guevara, 45
new media: agency and, 172–173; ecology, 117–118; political and cultural agency and, 172–173; technologies, dissidents and, 179–183
newspapers, 101. See also journalism; *specific publications*
New York City, 95; salsa in, 87
New York Times, 60
NG La Banda: *La bruja*, 129
North American Congress in Latin America, 178
Norwegian embassy, 180
nostalgia, 57, 99, 173, 184
Nuevo Herald, El, 179
nueva trova, 71–73, 75, 104–105, 108. See also *trova* movement

Obama, Barack, 31, 55–56, *65*, 135, 150–151; change in relations, December 17, 2014, 64–65, 184; flexibilization of the embargo, 174; "Obama Heroico" meme, 64–65, *65*, 66; speech at Gran Teatro de la Habana, 62–63, 235n23; visit to Cuba, March 2016, 56, 60–66, 152, 156
Ochoa, Arnaldo, 32
Octavo Cerco, 104, 170, 181
October Crisis, 177
Odisea, 159
Oferta.cu, 113
Office of the City Historian, 25
Offlaga Disco Pax, *Socialismo Tascabile*, 30
offline/online hybrid media ecosystem, 148

Ogaden War, 32
Old Havana, 25
Omega, 159
OmniVideo videotapes, 158
OnCuba, 56
One Belt, One Road initiative (BRI), 21
Open Society, 180
Operation Sherwood, 82
Organization of American States, 81
Oroza, Ernesto, 92
Ortega y Gasset Award, 185
Oshin, 116
Osorbo, Maykel, 110, 111
OSPAAL, 80
Otaola, Alexander, 173
Otero Alcántara, Luis Manuel, 173, 187
Otra vuelta de tuerka, 73
Oviedo, Yulién, 56

pachanga, 27, 69–112; as consensus-building tool, 78; *pachanga*-style revolution, 86; postsocialism and, 77–90; state cooptation of, 97–98; state regulation of, 97–98; subversive forms of, 89–90
Padilla, Heberto, 47–48, 49
Padilla Cárdenas, Gilberto, 71, 72
Padura, Leonardo, 15; *La transparencia del tiempo*, 91–92, 94, 96
paketito, el, 172
paladares, 115, 146
PanAm Post, 175
Panart Studios, 134
Paquete, El, 93, 97, 118–120, 123, 125–126, 131, 154, 156–161, 172, 205
Paquete-literatura, *162*
Para Bailar, 87
Paradero de Playa, 151
Para que tú lo bailes, 87
participatory digital media practices, 127
Patria o Muerte, 109–112
"Patria y Vida," 109–112
Pausini, Laura, 57
peer-to-peer networks, 93, 102, 156, 166, 173
Penal Code, 151, 176
Penúltima Casa, La, 138
Penúltimos Días, 179

People in Need, 180
Peraza, Rodolfo, *Pilgram* installations, 152–153
perestroika, 7, 23, 66, 201
Pérez-López, Jorge, 114
Periodismo de Barrio, 14, 180, 183, 189, 225–226n31
personal data, 164; exploitation of, 192
Perú, 2021 electoral campaign, 20
photography, 76, 119
Pinar del Río festival, 99–100
Piñera, Virgilio, 217, 238n17
Pink Tide, 11, 13, 74, 177, 178, 184, 216–217, 218
piracy, 158, 161
Pirate Bay, The, 156
Planet Records, 70
platform capitalisms, 173
Plaza de la Revolución, 64, 81
P.M., 86, 88
P.M.M. (Por un Mundo Mejor), 70, 89
pocket postsocialisms, 28–29
Podemos, 73, 74
Poésy, Clémence, 119
Poland, 180
Polémica Digital, La, 183
Policosanol (PPG), 210, 239n29
politics: political imaginaries, 1, 4–5, 18, 27, 78, 108, 148, 166, 179, 220, 224n8; political subjectivities, 125; of the portable, 149–150
Ponte, Antonio José, 88
popular culture, 122–123
popular music, 56, 60, 65, 69–112, 133. *See also specific musicians*
popular sovereignty, 81
populism, 225n28; left-wing, 11, 13; national, 189
porlalivre.com, 113
pornography, 125–126
Porno Para Ricardo, 74, 99; aesthetics of, 108; "No comas tanta pinga comandante," 89–90, 100, 101, 107–108; "Patria o Muerte por la Vida," 111; "Patria y Vida," 110–112; "Tipo normal," from the album *Rock para las masas . . . cárnicas*, 101
portability, 28–30, 57, 118, 122–123, 125; digital media and, 77, 141, 149; mass commercialization of, 124–125; politics of, 149–150; of the song form, 77. *See also* "portable postsocialisms"
"portable postsocialisms": aesthetics of, 114, 115–127; memes and, 192
Portantiero, Juan Carlos, 212
Portela, Ena Lucía, 15, 33, 35
postcolonial identities, 128
postcommunist media transitions, 126
"postmodern condition," 223n5
post-neoliberalism, 215, 216
Postone, Moishe, 44, 46, 214–215
postsocialism, 219, 223n5; Asian, 28; cultural studies of, 126; definition of, 211–213; end of history and, 197–198; music and, 69–112; new cultural map of, 98–99; *pachanga* and, 77–90; portability of, 28–29, 57, 139–140; postsocialist end-times, 211–221; researching, 2–3; and transitional socialism, 213
postsocialismos de bolsillo, 28–29, 139–140
postsocialist condition, 223–224n7: Cuban postsocialism and, 217; Cuban socialism and, 219–220; definition of, 1–30
postsocialist critical theory, 1, 221. *See also* critical theory
postsocialist imaginaries, 4, 29, 139, 146, 202, 215
postsocialist media theory, 125, 126–127
postsocialist solidarity, 178
postsocialist soundscape, 89–90
postsocialist survivalism, 92, 115, 116
postsocialist transitions, "civil society" and, 169
"post-Soviet condition," 167, 215, 223n2
Prague, Soviet invasion of, 177
Prensa Latina, 138, 184
Price, Rachel, 204–205, 226n35
Prieto, José Manuel, 226n1
Primavera magazine, 123
Primer Encuentro Internacional de la Canción de Protesta, 72
privatization, 28, 153, 161
producibility, 125
Prohibition, 58–59, 82

propaganda, 82, 87–88, 142, 164, 169, 172, 174
protests, 150. *See also specific events*
protest songs, 74, 75, 104–105, 106, 110
"public," meaning of, 152–153
public sphere: access to, 13; Cuban socialism and, 169–170; definition of, 164–165; as regulative utopia, 165–166
Puerto Rico, 98
punk, 27, 77, 99–109
Pussy Riot, 100, 103
Putin, Vladimir, 57, 216

¿Qué pasa USA?, 122
quinceañeras, 119, 122, 123

race, 77, 90, 153; Cuban Revolution and, 61–63; integration, performance of, 86; TV shows and, 145; in United States, 61–63
racism: in Cuba, 62–63, 97; institutional, 62–63
radical politics, 215
radio, 80, 82, 95, 98, 101, 102, 230n18. *See also specific stations and programs*
Radio Caracol, 147
Radio Habana Cuba, 80, 82
Radio-Rebelde, 79, 80
Radio Swan, 82, 180
raulista market reforms, 10, 11, 12, 18–19, 47, 63
Reagan, Ronald, 36, 192
Rectification of Errors and Negative Tendencies, 33, 201
reggaeton, 27, 70, 75, 77, 94, 97, 99, 109–112, 157; moral panic over, 90, 97–98, 123; popularity of, 93; rise of, 88; ubiquity of, 91, 96–97; and vulgarity, 90–92, 96–98
reggaetoneros, 109–1110. *See also specific artists*
regulatory environment, 160, 161, 195, 215
remittances, 8, 9, 60, 149, 150
repartos, 95, 231n39; *reparterismo*, 88, 95; *reparto* subcultures, 70
Resolutions 98/2018 and 99/2018 of the Ministry of Communications, 153–154

Revolico, 113–114, 148
Revolución y pachanga, 46–47, 77–90, 111
revolution, rethinking notion of, 220
revolutionary consciousness, 124–125
Revolutionary Offensive, 33, 44, 51, 83
revolutionary soundscape, 71, 77–90, 151
Revueltas, José, 37
rhythmanalysis, 75–76
Rialta magazine, 187
Ricardo, David, 44–45
right-wing conservatism, 216–217
Riofrancos, Thea, 225n30
Rivalta, Gertrudis, *Mujeres Muchacha*, 128
Roa, Raúl, 77
Rocha, Glauber, 39, 142, 163
Rodríguez, Marta María, 177
Rodríguez, Reina María, 115, 127; *The Book of Clients*, 136–137; *Variedades de Galiano*, 137
Rodríguez, Silvio, 72–74, 75; "El necio," 72–73, 75, 92, 230n7; "Ojalá," 110; "Te doy una canción," 108
Rojas, Rafael, 169, 229n56
Romero, Leonardo, arrest of, 177
RT in Spanish, 161
ruinology, 57, 75, 76, 91
Russia, 100, 103, 136, 161; invasion of Ukraine, 177; Russian Duma, 177; Russian postsocialist imperialism, 216
Russian Revolution, 40, 227n7

Saavedra, Lázaro, *Reencarnación*, 88
Salkey, Andrew, 51
Sánchez, Yoani, 96, 183, 187; *Generación Y*, 172
San Cristóbal, 61
Sanders, Bernie, 226n36
@SanMemero, 190
Sartre, Jean-Paul, 36, 39, 41–42, 51, 58
Schafer, R. Murray, 229–230n2
screen politics, Cuban revolutionary, 142–143
screen(s), 27; and collective political identity, 142; mediation of, 141; portable, 141; "screen cultures," 27, 141

"second economy," digitalization of, 114
secondhand clothing, 136–137
Second Life, 132
Segato, Rita, 217–218
self-determination, 177
self-employment, 132, 156; legalization of, 8, 163, 224n12
self-empowerment, 128, 132
self-image, 132, 137, 155
Serbia, 180
sexism, 129–130
sex workers. See *jinteras*
Shakur, Assata, 62
Sherrit International Corp., 22
"shock doctrine," 214
Sierra Madero, Abel, 229n56
single-party state, 17, 211–212
Sino-Soviet split, 42
Siré, Néstor, 118, 161
sneakernets, 117, 118, 120–121, 125–126, 156, 157, 158, 160–161
social conservatism, 216–217
socialism, 17, 22, 123–124; "actually existing socialism," 15–16, 18, 23–24, 28, 35, 79–80, 82, 85, 125, 179, 192, 197; capitalism and, 22, 198; cha-cha-chá and, 78–79; defeat of, 217; definition of, 219; legacy of, 15; rethinking, 229n51; subsidized through capitalism, 22. See also Cuban socialism
socialist bloc (former) 113, 117; fall of, 7, 8, 34, 60, 72, 128, 200–201. See also Eastern and Central Europe
socialist media theory, 124, 125, 126
socialist survival, myth of, 22, 25, 219
social justice, vocabularies of, 210–211, 215, 220, 221
social media, 28, 90, 111, 114, 125, 164, 173–174, 176, 203. See also specific media and platforms
solares, 95
Solís, Denis, 239n20
#SomosContinuidad, 10
#SomosCuba, 10
son, 69, 76, 90
Sontag, Susan, 36, 39, 41, 83–84
Sony, 70
Soplillar, Ciénaga de Zapata, Cuba, 163

Souls, 62
sound(s), city spaces and, 75–76; of Cuban socialism, 67–112;
soundscape, 71, 229–230n2
South Africa, apartheid regime in, 62
Soviet socialist realism, rejected by Guevara, 84
Soviet Union, 7, 34–35, 42, 66, 82; 1987 law on joint ventures with foreign capital, 21–22; constitution of 1936, 209; Cuba and, 177; Cuban exceptionalism and, 217; fall of, 22, 34, 115, 116, 200–201; Guevara's critique of, 45–46, 213; Hungary, intervention, 50; Prague, invasion of, 177; monopoly on "actually existing socialism," 79; old left and, 85; orthodoxy of, 45; revisionism of, 45
soy, 210
Spain, 22, 55, 73–74, 113, 214
Sparks, Colin, 126, 161, 166
Special Period of the 1990s, 7, 22, 62–63, 114, 129, 158, 160, 193–195, 200, 206, 238n12; humor during, 201–202; return of, 202–204, *203*
Spotify, 70, 74
Stalin, Joseph, 45, 231n19
Starbucks, 23
state: apparatus, 17, 70, 71, 86–88, 97, 160, 161, 167, 198, 234n7; capitalism, 16, 67, 141, 158, 220, 224n22; Guevara, image of, 126; revolutionary, 147; shortcomings of, 215; theory of, 211–212
state media, 10, 96, 113–114, 172, 181; state media monopoly, 149; state media policy, 156–157
state policy, 148; cultural, 77, 86–88, 90, 97, 123, 171; media, 156–157
state-sanctioned violence, 110, 218
statization, 85, 156, 161, 209, 212; of communications technology, 160; democracy and, 212–213; of information, 160; rhetorical framework of, 82
stereotypes: colonial tropical, 79; gendered, 79, 129–130
Steyerl, Hito, 66, 121, 122
strategic statism, 176

streetnets (SNETs), 153–154, 160
submarine telegraph cable system, 149
Suchel products, 129
sugar, 22, 23, 209, 210; Ten Million Sugar Harvest, 87–88
surveillance, 148, 150, 153, 155, 160, 164, 172, 219
survivalism, 201–206, *203*, 217, 219, 226n35
Swedish embassy, 180
Sweezy, Paul, 43, 44, 45, 46, 47

Taller de Periodismo de Investigación (Investigative Journalism Workshop), 184
Tanco Armero, Nicolás, 69
Tarea de Ordenamiento, 203
Tata, 153
Teatropello, 64
Telecom Italia, 234n20
telecommunication services, 150
Telecom Venezuela, 149
Telegram, 28, 114, 138, 179, 192
telegraph cable system, 149
telenovelas, 115, 146; Korean *doramas*, 147; *la novela brasileña*, 146; *la novela nacional* (Cuban-made soaps), 146
Telesur, 138, 161
television, 101, 116; expansion of, 143. See also TV shows; *specific channels and programs*
Televisión Serrana (TVS), 235n37
testimonio, 181, 184
Thatcherism, 36, 214
Thiel, Frank, 122
Third Cinema Movement, 39, 66, 142
Third World: emancipation struggles of the 1960s, 78, 79; Marxisms, 214
Third Worldism, 37, 178
Thousand and One Texts: Volume 1, A, 166–168
timba, 70, 88, 90, 95
TINA (there is no alternative) myth, 73
Tizza, La, 187–188
Tlostanova, Madina, 167–168, 170, 174, 180, 216
tolerance, spectacle of, 170
Torres, Raúl, 111
totalitarianism, democracy and, 198
tourism, 22, 34–35, 55–56, 88, 89, 130, 228–229n47; COVID-19 and, 204; Cuba as new global destination, 34; history of, 58–59; Prohibition and, 58–59; reactivation of US in December 2014, 226n2; sexual tourism, 133; state dependence on, 149; "tourists of the revolution," 124; US citizens in Cuba, 58–59
TP-Link, 150
trade agreements, 19, 22, 34, 92–93, 113, 204
"transition," meaning of, 214
transnational capital, 13, 17, 23, 149, 156
transportation, 94, 151; *almendrones* and, 92–93; informal, 93; photography of, 76; urban spaces and, 94–95
Trápaga, Luis, *Mass media*, 143–144, *143*
travel, 120; archive, 37; family, 150; literature 35–37, 40, 50–51, 67; new patterns of, 13; restrictions, 9, 28; travel to socialism as genre, 34–40;
Tremenda Nota, 186
tribu: Retratos de Cuba, La, 56
Tribuna de la Habana, 63
Trinchera, La, 186
troll farms, 181
Trotsky, Leon, 39, 209
trova movement, 104–106, 110, 111
Trump, Donald, 103, 111, 204
Turati, Marcela, 184
Tutek, Hrvoje, 199
TV shows, 122–123, 144–145, 156–157; British consumption of US, 160; foreign, 157, 160; Korean *doramas*, 147; *la novela brasileña*, 146; *la novela nacional* (Cuban-made soaps), 146; pirated, 119; state, 176–177; telenovelas, 115, 146, 147. See also *specific shows*
Twitter, 138–139, 142, *175*, 176, 177, 178, 179

Ukraine, Russian invasion of, 177
Underguater, 204–205
underwater fiber optic system, 149
@unguajirocubano, 176

Unilever, 129
Unión Patriótica de Cuba, 175
United States, 19, 42–43, 88–89; changing policy in, 9–10, 204, 226n2; civil rights movement, 63; companies and internet connectivity, 150; Cuban Revolution and, 61; diplomatic rapprochement with, 8, 31, 60–66, 152, 156, 226n2; dissident groups and, 180; embargo by, 21–22, 31, 63, 81, 129, 148, 150, 152, 155, 174, 178, 180; institutional racism in, 61–63; investments in Cuba regime change projects, 180–181; isolation of Cuba by, 81–82; policy toward Cuba, 8, 9–10, 21–22, 31, 60–66, 63, 81–82, 129, 148, 150, 152, 155, 174, 178, 180–181, 204, 217, 226n2; political crises of 1960s, 57; pornography from, 125–126; propaganda race and, 82; Trump administration, 204; "wet foot, dry foot" policy, 64. *See also specific locations*
University of Information Science (UCI), 8
"Urban Latin" label, 95–96
urban spaces, 93; sound and, 75–76; transportation and, 94–95
Uruguay, 24, 214
US Central Intelligence Agency (CIA), 14, 48; "Castro and His Critics," 48–49
US Department of the Treasury, 150, 180, 190
US Guantánamo Bay Naval Base, 200

Valdés, Elpidio, 174, *175*
Vale tudo, 115, 146
Van den Berg, Laura: *The Third Hotel*, 218–219
Varadero, Cuba, 59, 72
Varda, Agnes, *Salut les Cubains*, 78–79
Varela, Carlos, 105
Vargas Llosa, Mario, 37
Vasallo, Carlos, 147
Venezuela, 19, 64, 66, 149, 161; 2019 street protests in, 73; economic crisis in, 202–203; oil trade agreements with, 34, 202; Revolución Bolivariana, 8; trade agreements with, 92–93, 202
Verdery, Katherine, 2, 3, 198
Vice, 118
videotapes, 158
Vietnam, 22, 113, 200
Vietnam War, 57
Vikings, 122
Villaverde, Cirilo: *Cecilia Valdés*, 132
Voces cubanas, 172
Vox (Spain), 74
Vox Media, 118
VPN networks, 148
vulgarity, 89, 90–99

Walsh, Rodolfo, 184
water: contamination of, 22; shortages, 22
Watt, Ian, 238n10
WBLS-FM, 95
Weiss, Julia, 118
welfare state, dismantling of, 215
WhatsApp, 28, 114, 138, 174, 179, 192, 193
Whitfield, Esther, 184
wi-fi: cards, 148; networks, 117; signals, *154*; spots, 151–152
Wikileaks, 180
Williams, Raymond, 3, 16, 160
Wittel, Andreas, 29
womanhood, 122, 128, 133
woman of fashion, 115–127, 118–119, 127, 128, 137–138, 139–140
women, 218; consumer imaginaries and, 127–140; consumption and, 128; economic crisis of the 1990s and, 127–140; fashion and, 113–140; media images of, 127–140; postcolonial identities and, 128; representation of, 129; rights of, 187. *See also* womanhood; woman of fashion
Wynwood district, Miami, 153

Xerox 914 photocopier machine, 124, 142–143

Yohandry's Blog, 172, 187
Yomil y Dany, 134

@YoSíTeCreo, 176
Yotuel, 110; "Ojalá pase," 110
@YoUsoMiNasobuco, 190
youth culture, 72, 75, 83
YouTube, 61, 64, 72, 73, 75, 90, 110, 111, 175, 179, 185, 229n56, 236n55
Yúdice, George, 94, 119

Zapya, 148
Žižek, Slavoj, 72, 80, 81, 82, 199, 231n19
zombie genre, 206–211; capitalism and, 208–209; consumerism and, 208–209
ZTE, 150
Zunzuneo, 180